W9-API-473

THE GEOGRAPHY OF TOURISM AND RECREATION

The Geography of Tourism and Recreation presents a comprehensive introduction to tourism, leisure *and* recreation and to the relationships between them. Illustrated throughout, this accessible text includes a wealth of international case studies spanning Europe, North America, Australasia and Asia. Each chapter highlights the methods of analysis used by geographers to analyse recreation and tourism, and highlights the similarities and differences between the way recreation and tourism is analysed. Recent perspectives developed in human geography are introduced (e.g. gender studies and post-modernism) and a range of chapters examine:

- the demand of recreation and tourism
- the supply of recreation and tourism
- the impacts of recreation and tourism
- tourism and recreation in urban and rural environments
- tourism and recreation in wilderness areas and other peripheral regions
- tourism and recreation planning and policy
- the future for tourism and recreation

Spanning the spectrum of recreation and tourism, this book introduces both landmark studies and the most recent contributions to the field to present the first detailed evaluation of how recreation and tourism are separate and yet integrated aspects of the wider leisure phenomenon.

Colin Michael Hall is based at the Centre for Tourism, University of Otago, New Zealand. **Stephen John Page** is Associate Professor at the Centre for Tourism Research, Massey University at Albany, New Zealand.

THE GEOGRAPHY OF TOURISM AND RECREATION

Environment, Place and Space

C.M. Hall and S.J. Page

London and New York

First published 1999 by Routledge
11 New Fetter Lane, London EC4P 4EE

Simultaneously published in the USA and Canada
by Routledge
29 West 35th Street, New York, NY 10001

© 1999 Colin Michael Hall and Stephen John Page

The rights of C. M. Hall and S. J. Page to be identified as the Authors of this work have been
asserted by them in accordance with the Copyright, Designs and Patents Act 1988.

Typeset in Sabon by Keystroke, Jacaranda Lodge, Wolverhampton
Printed and bound in Great Britain by Bath Press Ltd

All rights reserved. No part of this book may be reprinted or reproduced or utilised in any
form or by any electronic, mechanical, or other means, now known or hereafter invented,
including photocopying and recording, or in any information storage or retrieval system,
without permission in writing from the publishers.

British Library Cataloguing in Publication Data
A catalogue record for this book is available from the British Library

Library of Congress Cataloging in Publication Data
Hall, Colin Michael, 1961–
The geography of tourism and recreation: environment, place, and
space / Colin Michael Hall & Stephen John Page.
Includes bibliographical references and index.
1. Tourist trade. 2. Recreation areas. I. Page, Stephen John,
1961– . II. Title.
G155.A1H343   1999
338.4'791–dc21   98-29662
CIP

ISBN 0–415–16003–0 (hbk)
ISBN 0–415–16004–9 (pbk)

CONTENTS

PLATES

FIGURES

TABLES

ACKNOWLEDGEMENTS

The purpose of this book is to provide an account of the growth, development and changes that are occurring within the geography of tourism and recreation. A purpose made all the more interesting because it is written by two geographers who, at the time was manuscript was completed, did not work in geography departments. While the book covers a lot of material, the authors acknowledge that there are a number of significant areas which have not been fully covered, and could not be unless the book was almost twice its size.

To a great extent this book concentrates on the developed world. However, it is not a discussion solely of Anglo–North American Geography, as this would neglect the substantial contribution of geographers from Australia, New Zealand and the South Pacific; rather it deals with the literature on the geography of tourism and recreation in English. This is not to deny the substantial research base that European geographers have in tourism and recreation. But, with a small number of significant exceptions, such as Doug Pearce in New Zealand who has introduced much of the European literature to North America and Australasia (e.g. Pearce 1989), the majority of English-speaking geographers have developed most of their work in tourism and recreation in isolation from the European experience.

This book therefore serves to identify many of the major concerns and interests of geographers in the fields of tourism and recreation. There is clearly a substantial body of work in the sub-discipline. However, as the book also notes, the field is not seen as seriously as perhaps it could be. A conclusion with substantial implications not only for the further development of the sub-discipline but also for the growth of Tourism Studies as a separate field of academic endeavour. Indeed, the book observes that we are in a time of transformation and change in terms of a better positioning of tourism and recreation issues within the contemporary concerns of social theory and human geography, while simultaneously also having increased demands to be more 'applied' with respect to industry and tourism education. It is within this context that this book is written.

Stephen Page would like to acknowledge the financial assistance provided by Massey University in 1996 through the auspices of its University Research Award to provide the time to undertake the literature review for the research reported in this book. A period of sabbatical leave from Massey University in 1996 and 1998 also provided the much needed time to complete sections of the book.

In particular, the support and advice from Professor Paul Spoonley was gratefully received. Other forms of university support, including the typing assistance provided by Lynn Tunna and the academic support of Dr John Monin and other colleagues is also acknowledged. A number of people also made this book possible, including: Massey University's library staff and the enormous number of journal articles and books they supplied; together with the continued interest of colleagues in what may have seemed an esoteric activity being based in a Department of Management. One should also acknowledge the obstacles overcome during the writing of the book. Hiding away at home was a welcome escape from a particular issue. Writing this book has taught me a lot: one has to face up to the problems in front of us and not to seek solace in writing a book.

A number of people have also contributed ideas and the time to discuss themes and offer hospitality including: Martin Oppermann, Simon Milne, Charles Johnston, Pip Forer, Doug Pearce, Tom Hinch, Roy Wood, Graham and Frances Busby and the staff at Seale Hayne campus at the University of Plymouth, Jayne Hoose, Thea Sinclair, Stephen Witt, David Airey, Paul Fidgeon and Rosemary for letting me drag her around all those tourist and recreational sites in 1996 and 1998. She always knew geographers were odd! Lastly, Sue for all the emails and her usual support and encouragement.

Also, thanks to Stephen Williams, Staffordshire University for engendering my early interest in the geography of leisure and recreation and for permission to reproduce material from his *Recreation and the Urban Environment* text.

Other people who have had a very formative effect for both authors are Professor Tony Vitalis, Robin Smith and the Department of Management Systems at Massey University at Palmerston North; and the Faculty of Commerce and Administration at Victoria University of Wellington.

Michael would like to thank Bill Bramwell, Dick Butler, Cate Clark, Dave Crag, Jenny Craik, Ross Dowling, Ian Dutton, Bill Faulkner, Thor Floggenfeldt, Sandra Haywood, James Higham, Tom Hinch, John Jenkins, Geoff Kearsley, Linda Kell, Bernard Lane, Neil Leiper, Alan Lew, Niki Macionis, Steve Mark, Simon McArthur, Alison McIntosh, Peter Murphy, Vanessa O'Sullivan, Doug Pearce, John Pigram, Maurice Roche, Chris Ryan, Isabelle Sebastian, John Selwood, Robin Shaw, Kirsten Short, Valene Smith, John Swarbrooke, Lesley Tipping, Geoff Wall, Jim Walmesley, Bernie Walsh, Josette Wells, and Heather Zeppel, who have all contributed in various ways to some of the ideas contained within, although the interpretation of their thoughts is, of course, my own.

Gavin Bryars, Bruce Cockburn, Elvis Costello, Stephen Cummings, Lilith Fair, *The Sundays*, Ed Kuepper, Neil and Tim Finn, and Sarah McLachlan also helped ensure that the book was completed. Ingrid Van Aalst, Angela Elvey, Chris Daly, Helen Gladstones, John Jenkins, Linda Kell, Simon McArthur, Jacqui Pinkava, Kirsten Short and Josette Wells provided much appreciated moral support which, as usual, will be repaid with food, wine and services rendered. Finally, he would like to thank friends for coping with yet another book and having yet more tourism experiences damaged by analysis.

Lastly, the authors would like to express their appreciation to Routledge for their continued interest in the project. Sarah's continued phone calls and emails to chase progress were a great encouragement for speedy completion.

C. Michael Hall   Stephen Page
City Rise   Albany

PERMISSIONS

A number of organisations and bodies have provided the authors with permission to reproduce material in the book. The former London Docklands Development Corporation provided permission for Plates 3.1, 3.2, and 3.3. HMSO kindly granted permission for the use of Figure 2.3, Tables 2.3, 2.4, 2.5, 2.6, 2.7, 2.8 and 2.9 which was greatly appreciated. *The Geographical Association* provided permission to redraw Figure 2.6 (although it is a pity they feel the need to charge such high copyright fees when much of the work of the GA relies on goodwill and contributions from geographers who receive no payment); Routledge kindly agreed to allow Stephen Page to reproduce material from his *Urban Tourism* book in this publication, particularly the Figures he provided for the former publication. Likewise, the authors are grateful to Routledge for permission to reproduce other material from their publications.

The Planner kindly agreed to the use of Figure 2.7; Addison Wesley Longman for permission to reproduce material from numerous sources, including Figure 2.12, 3.1, 3.2 and 3.3. *The Journal of Leisure Research* for Table 2.1; John Wiley and Sons for Table 2.2 and Figure 3.5; Butterworth Heinemann for Figure 3.9; David Fulton Publishers for Figure 5.5; International Thomson Business Publishing for Figure 6.3; Travel and Tourism Intelligence for the use of Tables and Figures which are duly acknowledged. E and FN Spon for Table 2.3; The John Hopkins Press for the use of Table 3.3. Lastly, to Dr Stephen Williams and Routledge to reproduce material from his publication on urban recreation.

If any unintentional use of copyright material has been made in this book, the authors would be grateful if copyright owners could contact them via the publishers. Every effort has been made to trace the owners of copyright material.

1

INTRODUCTION
Tourism Matters!

Tourism is widely recognised as the world's largest industry. The figures on the size and significance of tourism are staggering. For example, according to the World Tourism Organization (WTO) (1996) in 1995

- World tourist arrivals reached 567 million, 3.8 per cent over 1994 figures.
- More than 360 million passengers were carried on international air services, an increase of 5 per cent over the preceding year.
- International tourism receipts (excluding international transport) increased by 7.2 per cent between 1994 and 1995 to US$372 billion. International fare receipts in 1995 were estimated at US$60 billion.
- Tourism receipts represented more than 8 per cent of the world merchandise exports and one-third of world trade in services.

However, tourism, tourists, and their impacts, are clearly not evenly distributed. Substantial differentiation occurs at a variety of international, regional and local scales. For example, to continue the snapshot from 1995:

- The Middle East was the fastest growing region (11.8 per cent for arrivals and 29.7 per cent for tourism receipts), followed by South Asia and East Asia and the Pacific.
- The Americas showed a substantial growth of tourist arrivals in 1995 of 4.4 per cent, while international tourism receipts for the whole

continent stagnated at 0.2 per cent above the 1994 level.
- Africa witnessed a slight improvement in the growth rate of tourist arrivals, while tourism receipts rose by almost 6 per cent.
- Europe continued to be the most visited region of the world in 1995 with close to two-thirds of international tourist arrivals.
- East Asia and the Pacific lost its position as the fastest growing region with an 8.6 per cent growth in arrivals and a nearly 12 per cent increase in tourism receipts. The region generated close to 90 million trips, of which 70 per cent were intraregional. In 1995, the number of Japanese travelling abroad reached 15 million (+10 per cent over 1994 figures).
- International tourism grew faster in developing countries both for arrivals and receipts, reflecting a wider redistribution of tourism revenues in favour of the traditional and new emerging tourism destinations in the third world.
- Europe outbound travel was up by almost 2 per cent. The long-haul market from Europe has grown faster than intra-European travel.

Yet tourism is also highly dynamic and is strongly influenced by economic, political, social, environmental and technological change. For example, following the dramatic downturn in a number of South-East Asian economies in the second half of 1997 and early 1998, the WTO revised its outbound figures for intraregional travel in the East Asia Pacific (EAP) region from a previous estimate for 1998 of 8 per cent growth to a revised estimate of there being no growth, while in terms of travel from EAP countries to outside the region the change was from an original estimate of 6.3 per cent growth to a fall of 2 per cent. In addition, of great significance in terms of outbound tourism and the overall competitiveness of some international tourism destinations is the extent to which the devaluation of some Asian currencies will serve to attract tourists. The WTO estimated that travel from Europe to EAP will now grow some 15 per cent in 1998 (compared to an original forecast of 7.2 per cent), while travel from the Americas will increase to an annual rate of growth of 12.5 per cent, up from the original forecast of 5.3 per cent (WTO 1998).

The immediate economic significance of such figures is to be seen not only in tourist destination and tourist generating areas but also in those destinations from which tourists switch their travel in order to take advantage of cheap prices. However, changes in the international tourism market will also be related to domestic holiday travel, as consumers can switch their travel plans not only between international destinations but also between domestic and international destinations. Tourism, as with other forms of economic activity, therefore reflects the increasing interconnectedness of the international economy. Indeed, by its very nature in terms of connections between generating areas, destinations and travel routes or paths, tourism is perhaps a phenomenon which depends more than most not only on transport, service and trading networks but also on social, political and environmental relationships between the consumers and producers of the tourist experience. Such issues are clearly of interest to geographers. For example, according to Mitchell (1979: 237), in his discussion of the contributions that geography can make to the investigation of tourism:

> The geographer's point-of-view is a trilogy of biases pertaining to place, environment and relationships ... In a conceptual vein the geographer has traditionally claimed the spatial and chorographic

aspects as his realm ... The geographer, therefore, is concerned about earth space in general and about place and places in particular. The description, appreciation, and understanding of places is paramount to his thinking although two other perspectives (i.e. environment and relationships) modify and extend the primary bias of place.

Yet despite the global significance of tourism and the potential contribution that geography can make to the analysis and understanding of tourism, the position of tourism and recreation studies within geography is not strong. However, within the fields of tourism and recreation studies outside mainstream academic geography, geographers have made enormous contributions to the understanding of tourism and recreation phenomena. It is therefore within this somewhat paradoxical situation that this book is being written, while the contribution of geography and geographers is widely acknowledged and represented in tourism and recreation departments and journals, relatively little recognition is given to the significance of tourism and recreation in geography departments, journals, non-tourism and recreation specific geography texts, and within other geography sub-disciplines. This book therefore seeks to explain how this situation has developed, indicate the breadth and depth of geographical research on tourism and recreation, and suggest ways in which the overall standing of research and scholarship by geographers on tourism and recreation may be improved.

This first chapter is divided into several sections. First, it examines the relationship between tourism and recreation. Second, it provides an overview of the development of various approaches to the study of tourism and recreation within geography. Finally, it outlines the approach of this book towards the geography of tourism and recreation.

THE RELATIONSHIP BETWEEN TOURISM AND RECREATION

Tourism, recreation and leisure are generally seen as a set of interrelated and overlapping concepts.

While there are many important concepts, definitions of leisure, recreation and tourism remain contested, in terms of how, where, when and why they are used. In a review of the meaning of leisure, Stockdale (1985) identified three main ways in which the concept of leisure is used:

- as a period of time, activity or state of mind in which choice is the dominant feature; in this sense leisure is a form of 'free time' for an individual;
- an objective view in which leisure is perceived as the opposite of work and is defined as non-work or residual time; and
- a subjective view which emphasises leisure as a qualitative concept in which leisure activities takes on a meaning only within the context of individual perceptions and belief systems and can therefore occur at any time in any setting.

According to Herbert (1988) leisure is therefore best seen as time over which an individual exercises choice and undertakes activities in a free, voluntary way.

Leisure activities are of considerable interest to geographers (e.g. Lavery 1975, Coppock 1982; Herbert 1987). Traditional approaches to the study of leisure by geographers focused on leisure in terms of activities. In contrast, Glyptis (1981a) argued for the adoption of the concept of leisure lifestyles which emphasised the importance of individual perceptions of leisure. 'This allows the totality of an individual's leisure experiences to be considered and is a subjective approach which shifts the emphasis from activity to people, from aggregate to individual and from expressed activities to the functions which these fulfill for the participant and the social and locational circumstances in which he or she undertakes them' (Herbert 1988: 243). Such an experiential approach towards leisure has been extremely influential. For example, Featherstone (1987: 115) argued that, 'The significance and meaning of a particular set of leisure choices . . . can only be made intelligible by inscribing them on a map of the class-defined social field of leisure and lifestyle practices in which their meaning and significance is relationally defined with reference to structured oppositions and differences'. Similarly, such an experiential definition of leisure was used by Shaw and Williams (1994) in their critical examination of tourism from a geographical perspective.

However, while such a phenomenological approach to defining leisure, and therefore tourism and recreation, is valuable in highlighting the social context in which leisure is both defined and occurs, such an approach will clearly be at odds with 'objective', technical approaches towards definitions which can be applied in a variety of situations and circumstances (see chapter 2). Yet it should be emphasised that such definitions are being used for different purposes. A universally accepted definition of leisure, tourism and recreation is an impossibility. Definitions will change according to their purpose and context. They are setting the 'rules of the game' or 'engagement' for discussion, argument and research. By defining terms we give meaning to what we are doing.

Even given the subjective nature of leisure, however, at a larger scale it may still be possible to aggregate individual perceptions and activities to provide a collective or commonly held impression of the relationship between leisure, tourism and recreation. In this sense, tourism and recreation are generally regarded as subsets of the wider concept of leisure (Coppock 1982; Murphy 1985; Herbert 1988).

Figure 1.1 illustrates the relationship between leisure, recreation and tourism. Broken lines are used to illustrate that the boundaries between the concepts are 'soft'. Work is differentiated from leisure with there being two main realms of overlap: first, business travel, which is seen as a work oriented form of tourism in order to differentiate it from leisure based travel; second, serious leisure, which refers to the breakdown between leisure and work pursuits and the development of leisure career paths with respect to their hobbies and interests (Stebbins 1979). As Stebbins (1982: 253) observed:

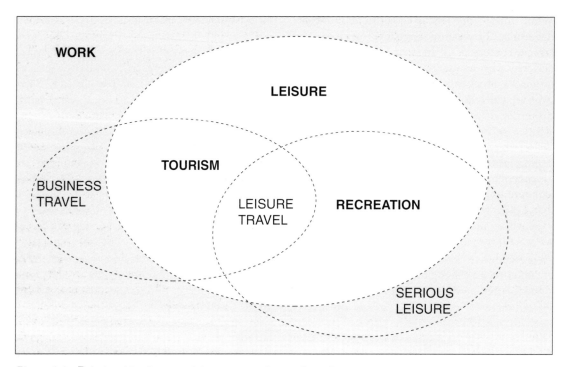

Figure 1.1: Relationships between leisure, recreation and tourism

leisure in postindustrial society is no longer seen as chiefly a means of recuperating from the travail of the job . . . If leisure is to become, for many, an improvement over work as a way of finding personal fulfillment, identity enhancement, self-expression, and the like, then people must be careful to adopt those forms with the greatest payoff. The theme here is that we reach this goal through engaging in serious rather than casual or unserious leisure

Figure 1.1 also indicates the considerable overlap that exists between recreation and tourism. For example, Bodewes (1981) saw tourism as a phenomenon of recreation. Similarly, Pearce (1987a, p.1) observed the 'growing recognition that tourism constitutes one end of a broad leisure spectrum'.

Historically, research in outdoor recreation developed independently of tourism research. As Crompton and Richardson (1986, p.38) noted: 'Traditionally, tourism has been regarded as a commercial economic phenomenon rooted in the private domain. In contrast, recreation and parks has been viewed as a social and resource concern rooted in the public domain'. Outdoor recreation studies have focused on public-sector (i.e. community and land management agencies) concerns, such as wilderness management, social carrying capacity, and non-market valuation of recreation experiences. In contrast, tourism has tended to have a more 'applied orientation' which concentrates on traditional private-sector (i.e. tourism industry) concerns, such as the economic impacts of travel expenditures, travel patterns and tourist demands, and advertising and marketing (Harris, McLaughlin and Ham 1987).

Although the division between public and private activities may have held relatively true from the end of the post-war period through to the early 1980s, in recent years the division between public and private sector activities has been substantially eroded in western countries

(Hall and Jenkins 1995). The distinction between tourism and recreation may therefore be regarded as one of degree. Tourism primarily relates to leisure and business travel activities which centre around visitors to a particular destination, which will typically involve an infusion of new money from the visitor into the regional economy (Hall 1995). According to Helber (1988: 20) 'In this sense, tourism can be viewed as a primary industry which, through visitor spending, increases job opportunities and tax revenues, and enhances the community's overall economic base'. On the other hand, recreation generally refers to leisure activities which are undertaken by the residents of an immediate region, while their spending patterns will involve 'a recycling of money within the community associated with day, overnight and extended-stay recreation trips' (Helber 1988: 20–21).

Natural settings and outdoor recreation opportunities are clearly a major component of tourism, perhaps especially so since the development of interest in nature-based and ecotourism activities (e.g. Valentine 1984, 1992; Weiler and Hall 1992; Lindberg and McKercher 1997). Indeed, outdoor recreation and tourist resources should be seen as complimentary contexts and resources for leisure experiences (Fedler 1987). Nevertheless, while authors such as Pigram (1985: 184) take the view that 'tourism is carried on within an essentially recreational framework', others such as Murphy (1985) have expressed an opposing view, conceptualising recreation as one component of tourism. However, this argument smacks of something of the 'glass is half-full or half-empty' argument. The reality is that as tourism and recreation studies have grown and borrowed concepts from each other (Ryan 1991) and as society has changed, particularly with respect to the role of government, so the demarcation line between recreation and tourism has rapidly become 'fuzzy and overlap is now the norm' (Crompton and Richardson 1986: 38). As Pigram (1985: 184) argued:

> Little success has been afforded to those attempting to differentiate between recreation and tourism and such distinctions appear founded on the assumption that outdoor recreation appeals to the rugged, self-reliant element in the population, whereas tourism caters more overtly for those seeking diversion without too much discomfort.

Similarly, in a wider context, Jansen-Verbeke and Dietvorst (1987: 263) argued that 'in the perception of the individual at least, the distinction between recreation and tourism is becoming irrelevant'. As with Shaw and Williams (1994), we would argue that this is not completely the case, particularly with respect to how individuals define their own activities. However, it is readily apparent that there is increasing convergence between the two concepts in terms of theory, activities and impacts, particularly as recreation becomes increasingly commercialised and the boundaries between public and private responsibilities in recreation and leisure change substantially. Indeed, it is interesting to note the inclusion of a same-day travel, 'excursionist' category in official international guidelines for the collection and definition of tourism statistics, thereby making the division between recreation and tourism even more arbitrary (United Nations 1994).

Tourism may therefore be interpreted as but one of a range of choices or styles of recreation expressed either through travel or a temporary short-term change of residence. Technical definitions of tourism are examined in more detail in chapter 2.

THE DEVELOPMENT OF THE GEOGRAPHY OF TOURISM AND RECREATION

Tourism and recreation have been the subject of research and scholarship in Anglo-American geography since the 1930s (McMurray 1930; Jones 1933; Selke 1936; Carlson 1938). Brown (1935: 471) offered what he termed 'an invitation to geographers' in the following terms: 'From the geographical point of view the study of tourism offers inviting possibilities for the development of new and ingenious techniques for research, for the discovery of facts of value in their social implications in what is virtually a virgin field'. However, as Campbell (1966: 85) wryly commented, 'it would appear that this invitation was declined'. As Deasy (1949: 240) observed: 'because of the inadequate attention to the tourist industry by geographers, there exists a concommitant dearth of techniques, adaptable to the collection, analysis, interpretation and cartographic representation of geographical data of the subject'. Yet the period from 1945 to the late 1960s is perhaps not as barren as Campbell would have us believe.

Building on the initial research on tourism and recreation in American economic geography in the 1930s, research was primarily undertaken in the post-war period in the United States on the economic impact of tourism in both a regional destination setting (e.g. Crisler and Hunt 1949; Deasy and Griess 1966) and on travel routes (Eiselen 1945). Although Cooper's (1947) discussion of issues of seasonality and travel motivations foreshadowed some of the geographical research of 1980s and 1990s, interest in this area of study lay dormant for many years. Nevertheless, the geography of recreation and tourism was at least of a sufficient profile in the discipline to warrant a chapter in an overview text on the state of geography in the United States in the 1950s (McMurray 1954).

In Britain significant research was undertaken by Gilbert (1939, 1949) on the development of British seaside resorts. However, little further direct research was undertaken on tourism and recreation in the United Kingdom until the 1960s. In Canada over the same period substantive geographical research on tourism was primarily focused on one geographer, Roy Wolfe (1964), whose early work on cottaging in Ontario (1951, 1952), laid the foundation for later research on the geography of second home development (e.g. Coppock 1977a).

While significant work was undertaken on tourism and recreation from the 1930s to the 1950s it was not really until the 1960s that

research started to accelerate with a blossoming of publications on tourism and recreation in the 1970s. During the 1960s several influential reviews were undertaken of the geography of tourism and recreation (Murphy 1963; Winsberg 1966; Wolfe 1967; Mitchell 1969a and b; Mercer 1970), while a substantive contribution to the development of the area also came from regional sciences (e.g. Guthrie 1961; Christaller 1963; Piperoglou 1966). Nevertheless, even as late as 1970, Williams and Zelinsky (1970: 549) were able to comment that 'virtually all the scholarship in the domain of tourism has been confined to intra-national description and analysis'. Indeed, in commenting on the field of tourism research as a whole they observed:

> In view of its great and increasing economic import, the probable significance of tourism in diffusing information and attitudes, and its even greater future potential for modifying patterns of migration, balance of payments, land use, and general socio-economic structure with the introduction of third-generation jet transport and other innovations in travel, it is startling to discover how little attention the circulation of tourists has been accorded by geographers, demographers, and other social scientists.
> (Williams and Zelinsky 1970: 549)

Similarly, Mercer (1970: 261) commented: 'Until recently geographers have had surprisingly little to say about the implications of growing leisure time in the affluent countries of the world. Even now, lesiure still remains a sadly neglected area of study in geography.'

During the 1970s and early 1980s, a number of influential texts and monographs appeared in the geography literature (e.g. Cosgrove and Jackson 1972; Lavery 1971; Coppock and Duffield 1975; Matley 1976; Robinson 1976; Coppock 1977a; Pearce 1981, 1987a; Mathieson and Wall 1982; Patmore 1983; Pigram 1983; Smith 1983a), giving the appearance of a healthy area of research. However, despite the growth in publications by geographers on tourism and recreation, concerns were being expressed about the geography of tourism. In the introduction to a special issue of *Annals of Tourism Research* on the geography of tourism, Mitchell (1979: 235) observed that 'the geography of tourism is limited by a dearth of published research in geographical journals, the relatively few individuals who actively participate in the sub-discipline, and the lack of prestige the subject matter specialty has in geography'. In the same issue, Pearce (1979: 246), in an excellent historical review of the field, commented, 'even after half a century, it is difficult to speak of the geography of tourism as a subject with any co-herence within the wider discipline of geography or in the general field of tourism studies'. More recently, Pearce (1995a: 3) argued that 'the geography of tourism continues to lack a strong conceptual and theoretical base' even so, models such as Butler's (1980) cycle of evolution and those reviewed in Pearce (1987a) have assisted to a limited degree in developing a conceptual under-standing, while Mitchell (1991: 10) also expressed concern that 'there is no widely accepted para-digm or frame-of-reference that serves as a guide to tourism research'. These comments therefore raise questions about the current status of the geography of tourism and recreation, and it is to these concerns that we will now turn.

THE STATUS OF THE GEOGRAPHY OF TOURISM AND RECREATION

The study of the geography of tourism and recreation does not occur in isolation from wider trends in geography and academic discourse nor of the society of which we are a part. Tourism and recreation geographers are 'a society within a society', academic life 'is not a closed system but rather is open to the influences and commands of the wider society which encompasses it' (Johnston 1991: 1). The study of the development and history of a discipline 'is not simply a chronology of its successes. It is an investigation of the sociology of a community, of its debates, deliberations and deci-sions as well as its findings' (Johnston 1991: 11).

Tourist geographers are a subcommunity of the geographic community within the wider community of academics, scientists, and intellectuals which is itself a subset of wider society, that society has a culture, including a scientific subculture within which the content of geography and tourism is defined. Action is predicated on the structure of society and its knowledge base: research praxis is part of that programme of action, and includes tourism research. The community of tourism academics is therefore an 'institutionalizing social group' (Grano 1981: 26), a context within which individual tourism academics are socialised and which defines the internal goals of their sub-discipline in the context of the external structures within which they operate (after Johnston 1991). The content of the sub-discipline must be linked to its milieu, 'so that disciplinary changes (revo-lutionary or not) should be associated with significant events in the milieu' (Johnston 1991: 277). Similarly, Stoddart (1981: 1) in his review of the history of geography stated, 'both the ideas and the structure of the subject have developed in response to complex social, economic, ideological and intellectual stimuli'.

'The contents of a discipline at any one time and place reflects the response of the individuals involved to external circumstances and influences, within the context of their intellectual social-ization' (Johnston 1983a: 4). Grano (1981) developed a model of external influences and internal change in geography that provides a valuable framework within which to examine the geography of tourism and recreation (Figure 1.2). The figure is divided into three interrelated areas:

- *knowledge* – the content of the geography of tourism and recreation studies
- *action* – tourism and recreation research within the context of research praxis; and
- *culture* – academics and students within the context of the research community and the wider society.

Table 1.1: Categorisation of main approaches to the geography of tourism and recreation

Pearce (1979)	Smith and Mitchell (1990)	Mitchell and Murphy (1991)	Pearce (1995a)	Hall and Lew (1998)
spatial patterns of supply	spatial patterns	environmental considerations	tourism models	environmental considerations
spatial patterns of demand	Third world tourism	regional considerations	demand for tourist travel	regional considerations
geography of resorts	evolution of tourism	spatial considerations	international tourism patterns	spatial considerations
tourist movements and flows	impacts of tourism	evolutionary considerations	intra-national travel patterns	evolutionary considerations
impact of tourism	tourism research methods		domestic tourist flows	tourism planning
models of tourist space	planning and development		spatial variations in tourism	urban tourism
	coastal tourism		national and regional structures of tourism	modernisation and development
	tourism accommodation		spatial structure of tourism on islands	gender and identity
	resort cycles		coastal resorts	place marketing and promotion
	tourism concepts		urban areas	globalisation and economic and cultural change
	tourism destinations			sustainable development

KNOWLEDGE   ACTION   CULTURE

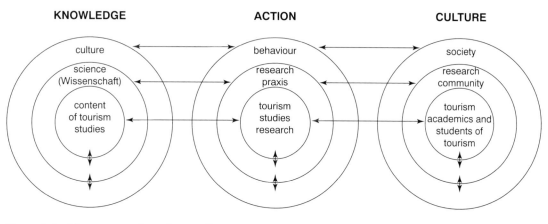

Figure 1.2: The context of tourism studies
Source: After Grano 1981

KNOWLEDGE

The Dictionary of Human Geography (Johnston *et al.* 1986) defines geography as 'The study of the earth's surface as the space within which the human population lives' (Haggett 1986: 175). Such a concise definition is deceptively simple and conceals the changing and contested nature of academic geography and, consequently, the geography of tourism and recreation. The development of geography as an academic discipline and its ability to provide specialist educational can be dated to the 1870s when geography departments were established in Germany (Taylor 1985). Similar developments were closely followed in the UK and the USA, although the main growth of the discipline came in the twentieth century. James (1972) argued that the establishment of specialised programmes of training marked the evolution of geography from the classical age as it entered the contemporary period. Freeman's (1961) *Hundred Years of Geography* identified six principal trends within geography. These were:

1 *The encyclopedic trend* where new information about the World was collated for the rulers, mercantile classes and residents of western Europe and North America.

2 *The educational trend* where an academic discipline began to establish its need to generate knowledge, determine relevance and ensure its own reproduction to derive its future. The development of geographical work in schools, colleges and universities characterised this trend.

3 *The colonial tradition* with the early decades of the twentieth century characterised by a concern with the environment. In the UK, the focus on Empire, and its spatial and political organisation from a metropolitan hub made extensive use of geographical skills.

4 *The generalising trend* describes the use to which data generated through the encyclopedic and colonial tradition. The methods used to interpret this data formed the basis of the early paradigms of the discipline's development.

5 *The political trend* was indicative of the way in which contemporary uses of geographical expertise were used for political purposes (e.g. the re-drawing of the map of Europe after World War 1).

6 *The specialisation trend* was the natural corollary of the expansion of knowledge in geography and the inability of one person to be an expert in every field. The expansion of more rigorous research training required geographers to specialise.

Following on from these trends, Johnston (1991: 38) argued that 'some of these trends represent philosophies, some methodologies, and some ideologies with regard to the purpose of academic geography'. However, Johnston regarded three particular paradigms as being especially important in the development of human geography: exploration, environmental determinism and possibilism, and regional studies.

Exploration

Exploration refers to the situation where unknown areas of the world (to those who live outside of them) are explored to collect and classify information. Many of these activities were financed by geographical societies as well as by philanthropists. The Royal Geographical Society of London (RGS) was one such example and even today the RGS is a major sponsor of expeditions which are reported in its publication – *The Geographical Journal*. The theme of exploration remains significant in tourism geography particularly as the images of places conveyed by explorers in the metropolitan regions has served to create destination images that remain to the present day. For example, the 'discovery' of the Pacific by Europeans was the crucial point for the imaging of the Pacific as a Romantic Paradise (Douglas and Douglas 1996).

Environmental Determinism and Possibilism

Environmental determinism and possibilism were two competing approaches which, according to Johnston (1991), were early attempts at generalisation in the modern period. These approaches sought explanations rather than just descriptions of patterns of human occupation on the earth. The underlying assumption was that human activity was controlled by the elements in the physical environment within which it was located. Environmental determinism can be dated

to the research by Darwin and the *On the Origin of Species* (published in 1859), where ideas on evolution were used by an American geographer William Morris Davies to develop the model of land form development. The nineteenth century also saw a number of geographers become protagonists of environmental determinism, especially the German geographer Ratzel, and the American geographer Ellen Churchill Semple, whose book *Influences of Geographic Environment* (1891) stated that 'man is the product of the earth's surface'.

The response to determinism was the counter-thesis possibilism. French geographers presented arguments to show that people perceive a range of alternative uses to which the environment could be put. This was, in part, determined by their own cultural traditions and predispositions. The debate on possibilism and determinism continued into the 1960s and has had some influence on tourism geography because of the extent to which concepts such as place, cultural landscape and heritage underly much debate about tourism's impacts.

The Region

Ideas of the region and regional geography dominated British and American geography up until the 1950s, based on the principle that generalisations and explanations were best derived from an areal approach. Johnston (1991) points to the role of Herbertson (1905) in dividing the earth into natural regions and the attempt to examine areas at a smaller scale to identify particular characteristics. In North America, the influence of Hartshorne's ongoing research established the focus of geography as a concern for areal differentiation so that the principal purpose of geographical scholarship is *synthesis*, an integration of relevant characteristics to provide a total description of a place – a region – which is identifiable by its peculiar combination of those characteristics (Johnston 1991: 43). This established regional geography as a powerful focus for the discipline which remains a feature of many school, college and university programmes even in the 1990s. The development of regional synthesis required topical specialisms in geography to contribute to the regional paradigm.

Regional concepts continue to play a major role in the geography of tourism and recreation and underly four main areas of research and scholarship:

- *regional tourism geographies* a number of collections of regional material has been developed by geographers in recent years, in part influenced by the development of regional economic and political blocs, which serve as frameworks for the development of baseline studies of contemporary tourism processes. Major regional reviews of tourism have been undertaken by geographers on western Europe (Williams and Shaw 1988), Canada (Wall 1989), eastern Europe (Hall, D.R., 1991), Europe (Montanari and Williams 1995), polar regions (Hall and Johnston 1995), Australia (Hall 1995), China (Lew and Wu 1995), the South Pacific (Hall and Page 1996), the Pacific Rim (Hall 1997), and South and South-East Asia (Hall and Page 1999);
- *destination regions* given the importance of the destination as an analytical concept in tourism significant effort has been given to the ways in which destination regions can be identified, managed, and marketed (see Smith and Brown 1981; Mitchell 1984; Smith 1983a, 1987, 1995; Heath and Wall 1992);
- *regional planning and development* the delineation of political and administrative regions provide a focus for administrative and planning research as well as a focus for the encouragement of development efforts through tourism and recreation. There is a significant body of research in this area, particularly with reference to Europe and the overall focus by government on tourism as a tool for economic development (e.g. see Pearce 1988a, 1992a, 1995a, b; Williams and Shaw 1988; Hall, D.R., 1991; Heath and Wall 1992; Hall *et al.* 1997; Hall 1999); and

- *synthesis and integration* the importance of synthesis and integration within regions has proven to be an important component in the development of approaches to integrated resource management within a regional context (e.g. see Lang 1988; Wight 1993, 1995; Pearce 1995b; Hall 1999).

Johnston (1991) also charts the development of geography as a discipline, focusing on a number of other trends which provided a direction for development. These are:

- the growth of *systematic studies* and adoption of a scientific method, where methods of investigation developed;
- the development of a new focus around the *spatial variable* and the analysis of spatial systems in the 1960s and 1970s where spatial analytical techniques were developed and systems theory was introduced;
- the development of *behavioural geography* as a response to the spatial science approaches, recognising that human behaviour could not easily be explained using logical positivist models. Behavioural geography focuses on the processes which underlie human decision-making and spatial behaviour rather than the outcomes which are the focus of much conventional spatial analysis (Gold 1980);
- the rise of *humanistic geography* with its emphasis on the individual as a decision-maker. The behavioural approach tended to view people as responses to stimuli to show how individuals respond to build models to predict possible outcomes. In contrast, humanistic geography treats the individual as someone constantly interacting with the environment which changes both self and milieu (Johnston 1991). It does not use any scientifically-defined model of behaviour, with each paradigm recognising appropriate contexts where the respective approaches are valid;
- *applied geography*, which refers to 'the application of geographical knowledge and skills to

Table 1.2: Approaches to geography and their relationship to the study of tourism and recreation

Approach	Key concepts	Exemplar studies
Spatial analysis	positivism, locational analysis, maps, systems, networks, morphology	• spatial structure: Fesenmaier and Lieber 1987 • spatial analysis: Smith 1983b; Wall et al. 1985; Hinch 1990 • tourist flows and travel patterns: Williams and Zelinsky 1970; Corsi and Harvey 1979; Forer and Pearce 1984; Pearce 1987a, 1990a, 1993b, 1995a; Murphy and Keller 1990; Oppermann 1992 • gravity models: Malamud 1973; Bell 1977 • morphology: Pigram 1977 • regional analysis: Smith 1987
Behavioural geography	behaviouralism, behaviourism, environmental perception, diffusion, mental maps, decision-making, action spaces, spatial preference	• mental maps: Walmsley and Jenkins 1992; Jenkins and Walmsley 1993 • environmental cognition: Aldskogius 1977 • tourist spatial behaviour: Carlson 1978; Cooper 1981; Debbage 1991 • tourist behaviour: Murphy and Rosenblood 1974; Pearce 1988a • environmental perception: Wolfe 1970
Humanistic geography	human agency, subjectivity of analysis, hermeneutics, place, landscape, existentialism, phenomenology, ethnography, lifeworld	• placelessness of tourism: Relph 1976 • historical geography: Wall and Marsh 1982; Marsh 1985; Towner 1996
Applied geography	planning, remote sensing, Geographic Information Systems (GIS), public policy, cartography, regional development	• planning: Murphy 1985; Getz 1986a; Dowling 1993, 1997; Hall et al. 1997; Hall 1999 • regional development: Coppock 1977a, b; Pearce 1988b, 1990a, 1992a • tourism development: Pearce 1981, 1989; Cooke 1982; Lew 1985; Murphy 1985 • indigenous peoples: Mercer 1994; Butler and Hinch 1996; Lew and van Otten 1997 • rural tourism and recreation: Coppock and Duffield 1975; Getz 1981; Glyptis 1991; Page and Getz 1997; Butler, Hall and Jenkins 1998 • urban tourism and recreation: Ashworth 1989, 1992b; Law 1992, 1993, 1996; Page 1995a; Hinch 1996; Murphy 1997 • health: Clift and Page 1996

- destination marketing: Dilley 1986; Heath and Wall 1992
- place marketing: Ashworth and Voogd 1988; Madsden 1992; Fretter 1993
- public policy and administration: Cooper 1987; Pearce 1992b; Jenkins 1993; Hall 1994; Hall and Jenkins 1995
- tourism impacts: Pigram 1980; Mathieson and Wall 1982
- destination life cycle: Butler 1980; Cooper and Jackson 1989; Debbage 1990
- attractions: Lew 1987
- GIS: Kliskey and Kearsley 1993
- national parks: Nelson 1973; Olwig and Olwig 1979; Marsh 1983; Calais and Kirkpatrick 1986; Cole et al. 1987; Davies 1987; Hall 1992a; McKercher 1993c
- heritage management: Gale and Jacobs 1987; Lew 1989; Ashworth and Tunbridge 1990; Hall and McArthur 1996
- sustainable development: Butler 1990, 1991, 1992, 1998; Pigram 1990; Ashworth 1992b; Cater 1993; Dearden 1993; McKercher 1993a, 1993b; Cater and Lowman 1994; Ding and Pigram 1995; Murphy 1994; Mowforth and Munt 1997; Hall and Lew 1998

Radical approaches

neo-Marxist analysis, role of the state, gender, globalisation, localisation, identity, postcolonialism, postmodernism role of space

- political economy: Britton 1982; Ley and Olds 1988
- social theory: Britton 1991; Shaw and Williams 1994
- semiotic analysis: Waitt 1997
- place promotion and commodification: Ashworth and Voogd 1990a, 1990b, 1994; Kearns and Philo 1993; Waitt and McGuirk 1996; Chang et al. 1996; Tunbridge and Ashworth 1996
- cultural identity: Squire 1994
- gender: Kinnaird and Hall 1994

the solution of economic and social problems' (Johnston 1986: 17); and

- *radical approaches* to geography, often with a neo-Marxist base (Peet 1977), but which have broadened in the 1980s and 1990s to consider issues of gender, globalisation, localisation, identity, postcolonialism, postmodernism and the role of space in critical social theory (e.g. Harvey 1987, 1988, 1989a, 1989b, 1990, 1993; Soja 1989; Benko and Strohmmayer 1997).

All of the above approaches to geography have relevance to the study of tourism and recreation. However, their application has been highly variable with the greatest degree of research being conducted in the areas of spatial analysis and applied geography (Table 1.2). It is useful to note that two of the most influential books on the geography of tourism and recreation: Pearce (1987a, 1995a) on tourism and Smith (1983a) on recreation primarily approach their subjects from a spatial perspective although both give an acknowledgement to the role of behavioural research. In contrast, the text on geographical perspectives on tourism by Shaw and Williams (1994) provides a far more critical approach to the study of tourism with acknowledgement of the crucial role that political economy, production, consumption, globalisation and commodification play in the changing nature of tourism. In one sense, Pearce (1995a) *Tourism Today: A Geographical Analysis* and Shaw and Williams (1994) *Critical Issues in Tourism: A Geographical Perspective* represent the two most significant strands in present day tourism and recreation geography. The former, dominant approach, represents a more 'traditional' form of spatial analysis and 'applied' geography (in the sense that it may be immediately useful to some public sector and commercial interests). The latter, emerging approach, represents more discursive and reflexive forms of analysis with a broader perspective on what the appropriate focus for the study of tourism and recreation should be. Indeed, in many

ways Shaw and Williams (1994) represents an explicit response to Britton's (1991) call for a theorisation of geography of tourism and leisure

> that explicitly recognises, and unveils, tourism as a predominantly capitalistically organised activity driven by the inherent and defining social dynamics of that system, with its attendant production, social, and ideological relations. An analysis of how the tourism production system markets and packages people is a lesson in the political economy of the social construction of 'reality' and social construction of place, whether from the point of view of visitors and host communities, tourism capital (and the 'culture industry'), or the state – with its diverse involvement in the system.
>
> (Britton 1991: 475)

To many students of the geography of tourism and recreation such a call would not seem appropriate as it would be seen to be taking geography too far from its spatial core interpreting the mapping of decision-making outcomes in space. This should be no surprise though, as the sub-discipline reflects the wider turmoil in the discipline as a whole in terms of competition between various frameworks of analysis. Nevertheless, while conventional spatial science can yield useful information, it does little to promote an understanding of the processes by which outcomes at given points of time are actually reached, nor does it do much to connect the geography of tourism and recreation to wider debates and issues in the social sciences.

One of the great stresses in the geography of tourism and recreation is the extent to which it connects with other components of the discipline. While it is quite easy to agree with Matley's (1976:5) observation that 'There is scarcely an aspect of tourism which does not have some geographical implications and there are few branches of geography which do not have some contribution to make to the study of the phenomenon of tourism', (also see Mercer 1970) one must also note that the relative influence of these branches has proven to be highly variable over the past 70 years.

One of the great difficulties has been that while tourism and recreation geographers have seen the significance of relationships to other geographical sub-disciplines and, indeed, other disciplines, such relationships are not reciprocal. For example, while Mercer (1970) recognised the significance of recreation, tourism and leisure for social geography (also see Williams 1979), textbooks, such as that of Jackson and Smith (1984), do not examine such concepts. Similarly, a text such as Whitehead (1993) on the *Making of the Urban Landscape* failed to note the role of tourism and recreation activities in urban environments. Perhaps the most significant indicator of the way the geography of tourism and recreation is seen by the wider discipline can be found in Johnston's (1991) standard work on postwar Anglo-American geography. Here the terms leisure, recreation and tourism are absent from the index, while the only comment on the subject is three lines in the environmentalism section of the chapter on applied geography: 'A topic of special interest was the study of leisure, of the growing demand for recreation activities on the environment' followed by reference to the work of Patmore (1970, 1983) and Owens (1984) (two of which have the wrong publication dates in the text!). This is not to denigrate Johnston's magnificent work of scholarship. It is probably an appropriate comment on the perception of the standing of tourism and recreation geography in Anglo-American geography, that the only area where tourism and recreation is considered significant is in rural areas where, perhaps, tourists and recreationists are seen as a nuisance! The reasons for this situation are manifold but perhaps lie in the cultural and action dimensions of geographical research.

ACTION: THE DEVELOPMENT OF AN APPLIED GEOGRAPHY OF TOURISM AND RECREATION

Within the literature on geographical research, there was a growing concern for relevance in the 1950s (see Johnson 1991). Part of that concern may have been a function of trying to improve the marketability of the discipline. At the same time, this call for relevance was accompanied by the growth of scientific methods in geography which highlighted the growing systematic focus and concern with applying geographical principles and concepts to real world problems. One possible interpretation of the post–1945 concern with relevancy and more belatedly, an applied focus, may be related to the expansion of undergraduate student enrolments in geography departments and the need to secure employment opportunities beyond teaching. The 1960s also saw the development of notable studies (e.g. Stamp 1960) extolling the virtues of the geographer's art and tools in relation to their contribution to society. Yet recreation and tourism received only a passing mention in that seminal study, as geography remained preoccupied with the move towards 'scientific method', 'logical positivism', quantification and a move away from regional description to more systematic forms of spatial analysis. Such developments were crucial since they provided the training and foundations for the next generation of geographers who were to begin to nurture the recreation–tourism continuum as a legitimate research focus. But one consequence of geography's development in the 1950s and 1960s and the rise of a more 'applied' focus was the increasing move towards narrow specialisation which appears to have reached its natural peak in the 1990s. Johnston (1991) outlines an increasing tension within geography in the 1960s and 1970s over the focus of the discipline, which in part transcended the debate over radical approaches (see Harvey 1974). The basic tension related to how geographers should contribute their skills to the solution of societal problems. This questioned the philosophical basis of geography – who should the geographer benefit with an applied focus?

Both British and American geography conferences in the 1970s saw an increasing debate and awareness of the value of geographers contributing to public policy. Coppock (1974) felt that policy makers were unaware of the contribution geographers could make to policy making. But critics questioned the value of advising governments which were the paymasters and already constrained in what geographers could undertake research. Harvey (1974) raised the vital issue of 'what kind of geography for what kind of public policy?', arguing that individuals involved in policy making were motivated by

> personal ambition, disciplinary imperialism, social necessity and moral obligation at the level of the whole discipline, on the other hand, geography had been co-opted, through the Universities, by the growing corporate state, and geographers had been given some illusion of power within a decision-making process designed to maintain the status quo.
> (Johnston 1991: 198)

However, Johnston (1991) also points to a liberal contribution to an applied geography which can be dated to Stamp's land use survey of Britain in the 1930s and his involvement in post-war land use planning (Stamp 1948). While much of this early 'applied geography' was set in an empiricalist tradition, Sant's (1982) survey of applied geography traces the use of the term back to the late nineteenth century with the early conferences of the International Geographical Union (IGU). While the title lapsed until the 1960s, the principal interest in applied geography has been promulgated by that organisation and a number of publications have resulted (i.e. Ackerman 1963). Sant's (1982) study concurs with Johnston's (1991) analysis, in that geographers' interest in applied geography in the 1930s – 1950s was based on:

- administrative regionalisation (Gilbert 1951);
- land use surveys (Stamp 1948);
- terrain analysis and air-photointerpretation (Taylor 1951); and
- urban and regional planning.

Stamp's (1960) influential book on *Applied Geography* documents his own research activities in geography and the spirit of the book highlights how a spatial focus could offer so many potential areas for study. Sant (1982: 8) assesses Stamp's contribution as follows:

> there is a deceptive innocence about Stamp's book which stems not from naivety but from confidence in his own judgement and experience. He had achieved much and his credentials commanded attention. Today we live in a less confident age. Perhaps this is because we have a greater propensity to invent complexities . . . At any rate, the scope and methods of applied geography are more elaborate than they were a generation ago.

Sant (1982) argued that applied geography was not a sub-discipline but had a dependent relationship with academic geography. It has a different *modus operandi*. It is intended to offer prescription, has to engage in dialogue with 'outsiders' not familiar with the discipline, its traditions, problems and internal conservatism and ability to overtly criticise developments which are not central to the prevailing paradigm. While the discipline has published a range of journals with an applied focus (e.g. *Applied Geography*) and offers a number of applied courses in Universities, the term is used loosely. As Sant (1982: 136) argued, 'the crux of applied geography is (at the risk of tautology) fundamentally that it is about geography. That is, it deals with human and physical landscapes.' What is interesting to note in Sant's (1982) text is the inclusion of recreation and the contribution of geographers to this area of applied geography, a feature reiterated in the study edited by Kenzer (1989) and the brief mention by Johnston (1991) noted above.

Some commentators, however, feel that the rise of an 'applied focus' has meant the discipline has lost touch with its roots, and thereby compromised the ability of 'explicating the relationship between people, places, cultures and the global/regional mix of each' (Kenzer 1989: 2). One indication of this, according to critics is the greater emphasis on techniques and their application to geographical concerns among human geographers and a subsequent decline in real-world, fieldwork-oriented studies. For example, the application of Geographical Information Systems (GIS) in research has meant a move away from traditional fieldwork and more laboratory-based analysis, which is distant from the real world. The natural corollary of this development, as critics suggest, is the potential loss of the 'core' in human geography if applied studies become dominant and traditional concepts and the roots of the discipline are no longer taught. It is ironic, therefore, that in many undergraduate geography degrees where the development of geographical thought is taught, the broader context of applied geography often receives a limited or poor treatment in contrast to the emphasis now placed on quantification, computer-based analysis and skills-based training.

In contrast, supporters of a more applied focus have argued that despite the apparent splintering and fragmentation of geography in the late 1980s and 1990s as a function specialisation, it has made a valid contribution to society. Many able geographers have recognised the need to move away from academia in order to make their skills, knowledge and perspective of use to society through a range of contributions while still being capable of reflexive analysis of their actions.

In the case of recreation and tourism, many geographers involved in these areas may no longer be based in geography departments in universities. But they maintain and extend the value of a geographical analysis and understanding for the training and research in the wider field of recreation and tourism studies. The discipline of geography, in the UK at least, paid very little attention to the growing role of geographers in the educational and research environment of tourism. Only in the 1990s have organisations such as the Institute of British Geographers acknowledged the significance of recreation and tourism as a serious area of academic study. In contrast, the Association of American Geographers and the Canadian Association of Geographers have been much more active with their study groups being established since the 1970s. International

organisations such as the International Geographical Union Study Group on the Geography of Sustainable Tourism (lifespan: 1994–2000) (formerly the Commission on Tourism and Leisure, 1984–1992) provided another forum for research developments and interaction by geographers and non-geographers with similar research interests. Nevertheless, despite such initiatives, the relationship of the geography of tourism and recreation to the broader discipline of geography has suffered two major problems:

- the rise of applied geography within the discipline, and tourism and recreation geography within it, has seen critics view it as rather ephemeral and lacking in substance and rigour; and
- in some countries (e.g. the UK), national geographical organisations and geography departments have often failed to recognise the significance of recreation and tourism as a legitimate research area capable of strengthening and supporting the discipline.

One consequence is that many geographers who have developed recreational and tourism research interests in the 1980s and 1990s, have left the inherent conservatism and ongoing criticism of their research activity to move to fresh pastures where autonomous tourism research centres or departments have eventuated. This does not, however, denigrate the excellent contribution that leading geographers such as Patmore, Coppock, Glyptis and Pearce have made to establishing recreation and tourism as serious areas of academic study within the discipline. Nevertheless, a significant number of geographers are now based in Business Schools or tourism, recreation or lesiure departments where their research interests are aligned within a multidisciplinary environment that can cross-fertilise their research and support an applied focus. Indeed, in some respects, history is perhaps repeating itself all over again, where planning emerged as a discipline and split from some of its geographical roots and where the development of environmental studies departments has also lead to a departure of geographers to such centres.

In the 1980s and 1990s, many geographers unwilling to have the progress of their careers impeded by views held by peers who did not see tourism and recreation as mainstream spatial research have similarly split from the discipline. For example, in New Zealand, with the exception of one or two notable researchers, all the geographers with a tourism or recreation focus are now located in Business Schools, Departments of Tourism and Recreation or other non-geographical bases. This situation is not dramatically different to the situation in Australia where educational expansion in this area has made extensive use of professional geographers to develop and lead such developments (Weiler and Hall 1991). As Janniskee and Mitchell (1989: 159) concluded

> this is certainly an interesting and exciting time to be a recreation geographer. After a slow start, the sub-discipline has achieved a critical mass and seems destined to enjoy a bright future ... There is no question that the application of recreation geography knowledge and expertise to problem solving contexts outside academia offers potential rewards of considerable worth to the sub-discipline: more jobs for recreation geographers, a stimulus to academic research with implications for problem solving, a more clearly defined sense of purpose or social worth, and greater visibility, both within and outside academic circles.

It is interesting to note that Janiskee and Mitchell (1989: 159) also perceive that

> since there is no clear distinction between 'basic' and 'applied' research, nor any appreciable threat to quality scholarship, there is no simmering argument on the issue of whether applied research is good for recreation geography. Rather, the real question is whether recreation geographers will have the resources and the zeal to move into the problem solving domain on a much more widespread and consistent basis.

Whilst this may be true in a North American context, it is certainly not the case in the UK, and a number of other countries where applied geographical research in recreation and tourism has been viewed as dissipating the value and skills of the geographer for pecuniary reward, or without contributing to the development of the discipline. Ironically, however, the proliferation of 'dabblers' (i.e. people who do not consider themselves recreation geographers, but contribute papers to journals using simplistic notions of tourism and recreation) has grown and still abound in the geography, and to a lesser extent, in the recreation and tourism journals. Indeed, tourism and recreation have been 'discovered' by geographers and other social scientists in the late 1980s and 1990s as tourism is utilised by government to respond to the effects of global economic restructuring and increasing concerns over conserving the environment (Hall and Lew 1998). Such contributions, according to Janniskee and Mitchell (1989: 157) 'although welcome, are not a satisfactory substitute for output of a substantial number of specialists doing scientific – theoretical – nomothetic research which is needed for the area to progress'. Calls for a 'heightened awareness and appreciation of problem solving needs and opportunities outside the traditional bounds of scholarly research' (Janiskee and Mitchell 1989: 159) are vital if academics are to connect with the broad range of stakeholders and interests that impinge upon geography and academia. Geographers with knowledge and skills in the area of tourism and recreation research need to develop a distinctive niche by undertaking basic and applied research to address public and private sector problems, which illustrates the usefulness of a spatial, synthesising and holistic education. For this reason, it is worth considering the skills and techniques the geographers can harness in tourism and recreation research.

CULTURE

The cultural dimensions of the geography of tourism and recreation – the sociology of knowledge of the sub-discipline – as with that of tourism and recreation studies as a whole, have been little studied. This is extremely unfortunate as it means there is a very incomplete comprehension of where the sub-discipline has been, which must also clearly affect our understanding of where it might go. As Barnes (1982: 102–3) commented:

> Social, technical and economic determinants routinely affect the rate and direction of scientific growth . . . It is true that much scientific change occurs despite, rather than because of, external direction or financial control . . . Progress in the disinterested study [of certain] . . . areas has probably occurred just that bit more rapidly because of their relevance to other matters.

Similarly, Johnston (1991: 24–5) observed:

> the study of a discipline must be set in its societal context. It must not necessarily be assumed, however, that members of academic communities fully accept the social context and the directives and impulses that it issues. They may wish to counter it, and use their academic base as a focus for their discontent. But the (potential) limits to that discontent are substantial. Most academic communities are located in universities, many of which are dependent for their existence on public funds disbursed by governments which may use their financial power to influence, if not direct, what is taught and researched. And some universities are dependent on private sources of finance, so they must convince their sponsors that their work is relevant to current societal concerns.

As noted above, research into the geographical dimensions of tourism has received relatively little attention in the wider fields of academic geography. Several related factors can be recognised as accounting for this situation:

* there is only a narrow set of official interest in conducting research into the geography of tourism;
* tourism is not regarded as a serious scholarly subject;
* not only are there substantial unresolved theoretical issues in conducting geographical studies of tourism and recreation but much theorisation is also relatively weak;

* tourism and recreation geographers have had little success in promoting their sub-discipine in the broader geographical context; and
* many tourism and recreation geographers are now operating in non-geography departments or in the private sector.

Unlike some areas of tourism research, such as politics and public policy for example (Hall 1994; Hall and Jenkins 1995), there is some government support for research and consulting on the geography of tourism and recreation. However, such research support tends to be given to the analysis of spatial patterns of tourist flows and issues of infrastructure location rather than areas of applied geographical research in gender and social impacts which may produce unwanted political results. Indeed, even support for research on the environmental impacts on tourism has the potential to produce politically contestable results, particularly if the results are not seen as supportive of industry interests. Therefore, funding for tourism and recreation research will tend to reinforce the more conservative spatial science aspects of the geography of tourism and recreation at the expense of more fundamental analysis which would have a greater capacity to extend the theoretical contributions of the sub-discipline. Despite the apparent lack of interest in studies of the broader dimensions of tourism by government and industry, and the community conflicts that occur in relation to tourism development, it is important to recognise that such research may be of an extremely practical nature. The results of such research may help facilitate and improve tourism planning through an increased understanding of decision-making processes (e.g. Murphy 1985), and help maintain the long-term viability of tourist destinations.

Despite the extensive growth of research on tourism and recreation in the 1980s and 1990s, many people still do not regard tourism as a serious subject of study, often equating it with booking a holiday at a travel agency or learning how to pour a beer. Indeed, research on tourism is often seen as frivolous. The observation of Matthews (1983: 304) that 'at a typical American university, a political scientist with a scholarly interest in tourism might be looked upon as dabbling in frivolity – not as a serious scholar but as an opportunist looking for a tax-deductible holiday', holds almost universal applicability. Similar to Smith's (1977: 1) observations on the anthropology of tourism in the 1970s, it is a topic that still appears to be thought by many in the discipline as unworthy of consideration by the serious geography scholar. Indeed, Mitchell (1997), a noted scholar within tourism and recreation geography, in a personal communication following a discussion on RTSnet (the interest newsgroup of the recreation, tourism and sport speciality group of the Association of American Geographers) regarding the position of recreation and tourism in American geography, argued that

> Recreation geography, has never been a valued member of the establishment, because, it is believed, it is impossible to be serious about individuals and groups having fun. Note the subtitle of the feminist oriented tourism conference being held in California this month ('Tourism is not about having fun'). In spite of the fact that tourism is the number one economic activity in the world, that recreation (especially passive recreation) takes up a large portion of the population's time, and that sport is almost a religion for many in this country, geographers who study these phenomena are not highly regarded.

There are also substantial methodological, theoretical and geographical problems in conducting geographical research. Problems have arisen because of the multiplicity of potential frameworks for analysis as well as relatively weak theorisation in some quarters. As Iaonnides (1996: 221) notes, 'Although tourism geography has long been an established specialization, the weak theoretical grounding associated with this research area relegates it to the discipline's periphery'.

The lack of a clearly articulated or agreed upon methodological or philosophical approach to geography *per se*, let alone the geography of tourism and recreation, may create an intellectual and perceptual minefield for the researcher, particularly as the value position of the author will have an enormous bearing on the results of any research. Burton (1982: 323–4), for example, argued that leisure and tourism research is plagued by problems of 'lack of intellectual co-ordination and insufficient cross-fertilization of ideas among researchers; an inadequacy of research methodologies and techniques; and a lack of any generally agreed concepts and codes in the field'. However, in contrast, Hall (1994: 7) argued that 'In fact, the debate which marks such concepts should probably be seen as a sign of health and youthful vigour in an emerging area of serious academic study and should be welcomed and encouraged rather than be regarded as a source of embarrassment'.

Another factor which may have influenced the standing of the geography of tourism and recreation is the extent to which the sub-discipline is being promoted to the discipline as a whole. For example, in the American context, Mitchell (1997) argued:

> There is no one individual super star in the US who has popularized the subject matter through publications and/or personality. From my perspective a lot of good geographic research has been published and the research frontier has been advanced, however, little of this research has appeared in the geographic literature; rather it tends to be found in specialty or multi-disciplinary journals ... Lots of publications are produced but they do not engender the kind of interest or reputation that leads to widespread recognition.

In the British context, the publication of *Critical Issues in Tourism* by Shaw and Williams (1994) as part of the Institute of British Geography Studies in Geography Series has helped raise the profile of the area. Nevertheless, the situation remains that the key academic audience of the majority of research and publications by tourism and recreation geographers are people within tourism and recreation departments rather than geography. However, there are some signs that this situation may be changing. First, there is the publication of a new journal *Tourism Geographies* in 1999 (edited by Alan Lew and published by Routledge) which seeks to promote the sub-discipline both within its immediate audience and beyond. To some extent the emergence of this specialised journal may be regarded as a sign of maturity of the field akin to other specialist geography journals (e.g. *Applied Geography, Journal of Transport Geography*). Second, there are activities of the IGU Study Group on the Geography of Sustainable Tourism which is co-hosting a number of conferences and special sessions with other IGU Commissions, such as Sustainable Rural Systems, and with national associations, such as the Association of American Geographers, in 1999 and 2000. Third, the increased significance of tourism and recreation in urban and rural environments in contemporary society has led to a greater appreciation of the potential significance of the field. In other words, tourism is now such a significant activity in the cultural landscape, it would be pretty hard for other geographies to ignore it much longer! Finally, tourism and recreation geographies are now arguing that they have something to contribute to the wider discipline, particularly in such areas as understanding the service economy, industrialisation, and regional development (e.g. Iaonnides 1995, 1996; d'Hauteserre 1996), as well as more traditional resource management concerns and sustainability (e.g. Zurick 1992; Hall and Lew 1998).

The final factor influencing the standing of the sub-discipline is the extent to which geographers in the field are increasingly undertaking employment outside geography departments and in tourism, recreation and leisure studies departments, business schools, and environmental studies and planning departments. Across most of the Western world tourism has become recognised as a major employer which, in turn has placed demands on educational institutions to produce graduates with qualifications relevant to the area. Therefore, there has been a substantial growth in the number of universities and colleges which offer undergraduate and graduate qualifications in tourism, recreation and hospitality which provide potential employment for tourism and recreation geographers. The opportunity to develop a career path in tourism and recreation departments which are undergoing substantial student growth or in a new department, will clearly be attractive to individuals whose career path may be slower within long established geography departments and who carry the burden of being interested in a sub-discipline on the outer edge of mainstream geographic endeavour. As Johnston (1991: 281) recognised 'this reaction to environmental shifts is undertaken by individual scholars, who are seeking not only to defend and promote their own status and careers within it'.

The massive growth of tourism and recreation studies outside geography also means that increasingly many geographers publish in tourism and recreation journals rather than geography journals. Such publications may be extremely significant for tourism studies but may carry little weight within geography beyond the sub-discipline, e.g. Butler's (1980) hugely influential paper on the destination life cycle. This has therefore meant the geographers who work in non-geography departments may find themselves being drawn into inter-disciplinary studies with only weak linkages to geography. The question that of course arises is does this really matter? Disciplines change over time, areas of specialisation come and go depending on intrinsic and extrinsic factors. As Johnston (1991: 9) observes:

> The continuing goal of an academic discipline is the advancement of knowledge. Each discipline pursues that goal with regard to particular areas of study. Its individual members contribute by conducting research and reporting their findings, by integrating material into the disciplinary corpus, and by pedagogical activities aimed at informing about, promoting and reproducing the discipline: in addition, they may argue the discipline's 'relevance' to society at large. But there is no fixed set of disciplines, nor any one correct division of academic according to subject matter. Those disciplines currently in existence are

contained within boundaries established by earlier communities of scholars. The boundaries are porous so that disciplines interact. Occasionally the boundaries are changed, usually through the establishment of a new discipline that occupies an enclave within the pre-existing division of academic space.

However, to borrow the title of a leading geography textbook of the 1980s, *Geography Matters!* (Massey and Allen 1984), it matters because concepts at the heart of geography such as spatiality, place, landscape and region are critical, not only to the geography of tourism and recreation but to tourism and recreation studies as a whole.

In commenting on work undertaken by geographers in the tourism field, Britton (1991: 451) noted that they have 'been reluctant to recognise explicitly the capitalistic nature of the phenomenon they are researching . . . This problem is of fundamental importance as it has meant an absence of an adequate theoretical foundation for our understanding of the dynamics of the industry and the social activities it involves.' However, such a criticism can be made of tourism and recreation studies overall (Hall 1994).

TRANSFORMING THE GEOGRAPHY OF TOURISM AND RECREATION

The situation described in this chapter is that of an area of academic endeavour which is at a critical point in its evolution. Tourism and recreation geography is an applied area of study which is at the periphery of its own discipline but with strong connections to academic research and scholarship outside the area. Dominated by systematic spatial analysis it has a relatively weak theoretical base which has exacerbated its inability to influence wider disciplinary endeavours. Nevertheless, in recent years there appear to be signs of a transformation in its character and fortunes. First, there has been a major growth in the number and quality of publications by tourism and recreation geographers which, although not influencing

geography outside the sub-discipline, has had a major impact on the direction of tourism and recreation studies. Second, there is clearly a conscious attempt to provide a stronger theoretical base to tourism and recreation geography which would both be informed by and contribute to contemporary social theory, particularly with respect to such issues as globalisation, localisation, commodification, restructuring and sustainability (e.g. Britton 1991; Hall 1994; Shaw and Williams 1994; Hall and Jenkins 1995; Ioannides 1995, 1996; Montanari and Williams 1995; Hall and Lew 1998). Finally, tourism and recreation geographers are seeking to promote their work more actively in academic and non-academic spheres.

This book reinforces several of the above themes. At one level it seeks to highlight the scope, nature and contribution of geography and geographers to the study of tourism and recreation. However, at another it also aims to provide some insights into the nature of the theoretical transformations which are occuring in the field.

This book does not, however, address the issue of coastal regions in relation to recreation and tourism. A great deal of research has already considered the potential, impacts and management issues in the coastal environment and a number of studies (e.g. Patmore 1983; Fabbri 1990; Goodhead and Johnson 1996) adequately document this area. In terms of tourism, the coastal environment has been the traditional focus of both the historian (e.g. Walton 1983) and the historical geographer (e.g. Gilbert 1939, 1949 and Towner 1996). In fact contemporary patterns of holidaymaking in the coastal environment have also been the focus of numerous studies of tourism from a spatial perspective as mass tourism attracted interest from geographers since the 1960s (Naylon 1967). In fact, one can also argue that this has been the focus of many dabblers who have visited areas and written short statistical overviews of tourism patterns and activities in mass tourism regions, reflected in the vast number of studies published by the *This Changing World* section of the journal *Geography*. In a methodological context, many of these studies have contributed nothing more than factual evidence to the growing body of knowledge on tourism. Such descriptive analyses have simply perpetuated the criticisms from within the discipline that have continued to marginalise the research activities of geographers in tourism. Mass tourist destinations in countries such as Spain have been well documented in the publication of Williams and Shaw's (1988, 1991) 'Tourism and Economic Development in Western Europe'. This notable study provides many examples of the geographer's interest in tourism and coastal regions as do many other lesser known studies (e.g. Pompl and Lavery 1993; Barke *et al.* 1996). Thus given the lack of space and need for selectivity as well as an international perspective, the coastal recreation and tourism focus is not discussed explicitly in this book in any detail due to the wide range of studies elsewhere and the useful introductory synthesis in texts such as Pearce (1987a). However, a range of examples derived from the coastal environment are discussed throughout the book, particularly in relation to the impacts of tourism and recreation.

The following two chapters examine the demand and supply elements of tourism and recreation. Chapter 2 examines how the demand for tourism and recreation is conceptualised and analysed, the concepts developed to derive a focus for research and the implications for a geographical analysis. In chapter 3, the main techniques and methods of evaluating tourist and recreational resources are discussed as a basis for the next chapter that looks at the interactions of demand and supply variables in relation to the impacts of tourism and recreation. The role of the state and government policy as a determinant of tourist and recreational opportunities is examined, as are issues of access to public and private space for tourists and recreationists.

Chapter 4 examines the differing types of impacts generated by tourist and recreational activities and the way in which different methodologies have been devised to analyse the environmental, socio-cultural and economic impacts. The following chapters (5 to 7) then consider the distinctive nature of tourist and recreational activities in a variety of contexts (urban, rural and wilderness areas) emphasising their role in shaping and influencing people's tourist and recreational opportunities, and the effects of such activities on the places in which they occur.

One of the strongest contributions of geography in the tourism and recreation field is in terms of the development of planning and policy analysis. Chapter 8 reviews the need for developing a planning and policy framework at different geographical scales with particular concern for the different traditions of tourism planning which exist. Chapter 9, the final chapter, examines the future prospects of the field and the potential contributions geography and geographers may make to understanding tourism and recreation phenomenon.

Tourism and recreation have been the direct subject of geographical analysis for over 70 years and have developed into a significant area of applied geography. In that time methodologies and philosophies have changed as has the subject matter. Tourism is now regarded as the world's largest industry. Tourism and recreation are complex phenomena with substantial economic, socio-cultural, environmental and political impacts at scales from the global through to the individual. It is now time for geographers not only to develop a deeper understanding of the processes which lead to the spatial outcomes of tourism and recreation, but also to convey this understanding to other geographers, students of tourism and recreation, the public and private sectors and the wider community which is affected by these phenomena.

2

THE DEMAND FOR RECREATION AND TOURISM

INTRODUCTION

Understanding why human beings engage in recreational and tourism activities is an increasingly important and complex area of research for social scientists. Historically, geographers have only played a limited part in developing the literature on the behavioural aspects of recreational and tourists' use of free time, tending to have a predisposition towards the analysis of aggregate patterns of demand using quantitative measures and statistical sources. This almost rigid demarcation of research activity has, with a few exceptions (e.g. Goodall 1990; Mansfeld 1992), meant that behavioural research in recreation and tourism has only recently made any impact on the wider research community (e.g. see Walmesley and Lewis 1993 on the geographer's approach to behavioural research), with notable studies (e.g. Walmesley and Jenkins 1992; Jenkins and Walmesley 1993) applying spatial principles to the analysis of recreational and tourism behaviour. For this reason, this chapter discusses some of the key behavioural issues associated with recreation and tourism demand followed by an analysis of the major data sources which researchers use, emphasising how the geographer has used and manipulated them to identify the patterns, processes and implications of such activity.

Within the literature on recreation and tourism, there is a growing unease over the physical separation of the theoretical and conceptual research that isolates behavioural processes and spatial outcomes and fails to derive generalisations applicable to understanding tourism in totality (see chapter 1). According to Moore et al. (1995: 74) there are common strands in the 'relationships between the various motivating factors applicable to both leisure and tourism; and as Leiper (1990) argued, tourism represents a valued category of leisure, where there is a degree of commonality between the factors motivating both tourist and recreational activities and many of the needs, such as relaxation or being with friends can equally be fulfilled in a recreational or tourism context. Although there is some merit in Leiper's (1990) approach, grouping leisure into one amorphous category assumes that there are no undifferentiated attributes which distinguish tourism from leisure. It is interesting to note that Leiper's (1990) approach, has a great deal of validity if one recognises that some tourism motivations may in fact differentiate tourism from leisure experiences just as the reverse may be true and that ultimately the particular range of motives associated with a tourism or recreational activity will be unique in each case despite a range of similarities. For this reason, the following discussion examines recreational demand emphasising many of the explanations commonly advanced in the recreational literature followed by a discussion of the tourism context and the issues raised, bearing in mind the need to compare and contrast each literature base in the light of the arguments advanced by Moore et al. (1995) and Leiper (1990).

RECREATIONAL DEMAND

Human activity related to recreation and tourism is a function of an individual's or group's willingness or desire to engage in such pursuits. Yet understanding this dimension in recreation and tourism requires a conceptual approach which can rationalise the complex interaction between the desire to undertake leisure activities, however defined, and the opportunities to partake of them. As Coppock and Duffield (1975: 2) argued:

> the success of any study of outdoor recreation depends on the synthesis of two contrasting elements: the sociological phenomenon of leisure or . . . that part of leisure time which an individual spends on outdoor recreation [and tourism] and . . . the physical resources that are necessary for the particular recreational activities.

In other words, Coppock and Duffield (1975) acknowledged the need to recognise the interrelationship between human demand as participation or a desire to engage in recreation and tourism, and the supply of resources, facilities and opportunities which enable such demand to be fulfilled. The concepts of demand and supply have largely been developed and applied to conventional market economies, where the individual has a choice related to the consumption of recreation and tourism (see Shaw 1979 for a discussion of these issues in the former Soviet Union). According to Smith (1989: 45)

> Recreation geographers use the work [demand] in at least four different ways. The most traditional sense is a neoclassical definition: demand is a schedule of the quantities of some commodity that will be consumed at various prices . . . A second definition of demand is that of current consumption . . . [which] . . . is of limited utility to recreation planners because it tells nothing about trends in participation or about current levels of unmet need. Demand is also used to refer to unmet need. This is sometimes referred to as latent demand . . . Finally, demand is used to describe the desire for a psychological experience.

In contrast, Patmore (1983: 54) acknowledges, 'leisure is far more easily recognised than objectively analysed . . . the difficulties are only in part

conceptual: equally important are the nature and limitations of available data', which this section will seek to explain in a recreation context.

According to Pigram (1983) there is a general lack of clarity in the use of the term demand in the recreational literature. One can distinguish between demand at a generic level, where it refers to an 'individual's preferences or desires, whether or not the individual has the economic or other resources necessary for their satisfaction' (Pigram 1983: 16) reflecting behavioural traits and preference for certain activities. At another level, there are the specific activities or participation in activities often expressed as visitation rates and measured to reflect the actual observed behaviour. One factor which prevents observed demand equating with participation, is the concept of latent demand (the element which is unsatisfied due to a lack of recreational opportunities). Knetsch (1969) identified the mismatch and confusion between participation and demand, arguing that you cannot simply look at what people do and associate it with what people want to do, so ideally any analysis of demand should also consider why people do not participate and examine ways of overcoming such obstacles by the provision of new resources as well as understanding social and cultural barriers.

Most research has examined effective demand which is actual participation rather than latent demand and the geographers' contribution has largely been related to the spatial and temporal expression of demand in relation to supply (i.e. demand at specific sites). This is very much resource specific and dates back to the geographical tradition of resource identification, use and analysis which can be traced to at least the 1930s. However, Coppock and Duffield (1975) also distinguish between passive recreation and active recreation, thereby beginning to differentiate between different forms of demand. While passive recreation is by far the most important type numerically, it is difficult to study due to its diffuse and often unorganised nature. Coppock and Duffield (1975: 40) argued that active recreation in the countryside differs from passive recreation in a number of ways. Not only are participants a minority of those visiting the countryside for outdoor recreation, but they are generally younger and differ in respect of a number of socio-economic characteristics: they often depend on particular (and sometimes scarce) recreational resources in the countryside ... yet as with passive recreation, information about such activities is scanty.

This illustrates the necessity of trying to measure recreational demand together with gauging the types of factors which can facilitate and constrain recreational demand. But what motivates people to engage in recreational activities?

Argyle (1996) argues that part of the reason why people undertake leisure and recreational activities can be found in the process of socialisation and personality traits, where childhood influences such as parents and peers are forms of social influence and learning that affect future activity choice. In fact, nearly half of adult leisure interests are acquired after childhood, and personality factors influence preferences towards specific forms of recreation. However, understanding the broader psychological factors which motivate individuals to undertake forms of recreation is largely the remit of psychologists, being an intrinsic form of motivation (i.e. something one is not paid to undertake).

A simplistic approach to recreational motivation is to ask recreationalists what actually motivates them. Crandall (1980) outlined 17 factors from leisure motivation research (Table 2.1), derived from a synthesis of previous studies in this field, while Kabanoff (1982) identified a similar list of factors (Table 2.2). From Tables 2.1 and 2.2 it is apparent that relaxation, the need for excitement and self satisfaction are apparent though Argyle (1996) argues that specific motivations are evident in particular forms of recreation. Torkildsen (1992: 79), however, posits that homeostasis is a fundamental concept associated with human motivation where people have an underlying desire to maintain a state of internal stability. Human needs, which are 'any lack or deficit within the individual either acquired or physiological' (Morgan and King 1966: 776), disturb the state of homeostasis. At a basic level, human needs have to be met where physiological theory maintained that all human behaviour is motivated. This leads to one of the most commonly cited studies in relation to recreation and tourism motivation – Maslow's hierarchy of human needs.

Maslow's Hierarchy Model of Human Needs and Recreational and Tourist Motivation

Within the social psychology literature on recreation and tourism, Maslow's (1954) needs hierarchy remains one of the most commonly cited theories of motivation. It is based on the principle of a ranking or hierarchy of individual needs (Figure 2.1), based on the premise that self-actualisation is a level to which people should aspire. Maslow argued that if the lower needs in the hierarchy were not fulfilled then these would dominate human behaviour. Once these were satisfied, the individual would be motivated by the needs of the next level of the hierarchy. In the motivation sequence, Maslow identified 'deficiency or tension-reducing motives' and 'inductive or arousal-seeking motives' (Cooper et al. 1993: 21), arguing that the model could be applied to work and non-work contexts. Despite Maslow's research shaping much of the recreation and tourism demand work, how and why he selected five basic needs remains unclear, though its universal application in recreation and tourism appears to have a relevance in relation to understanding how human action is related to understandable and predictable aspects of action compared to research which argues that human behaviour is essentially irrational and unpredictable.

While Maslow's model is not necessarily ideal, since needs are not hierarchical in reality because some needs may occur simultaneously, it does emphasise the development needs of humans, with individuals striving towards personal growth. Therefore, Maslow assists in a recreational (and

Table 2.1: Crandall's list of motivations

1	**ENJOYING NATURE, ESCAPING FROM CIVILISATION** To get away from civilisation for a while To be close to nature	**10**	**RECOGNITION, STATUS** To show others I could do it So others would think highly of me for doing it
2	**ESCAPE FROM ROUTINE AND RESPONSIBILITY** Change from my daily routine To get away from the responsibilities of my everyday life	**11**	**SOCIAL POWER** To have control over others To be in a position of authority
3	**PHYSICAL EXERCISE** For the exercise To keep in shape	**12**	**ALTRUISM** To help others
4	**CREATIVITY** To be creative	**13**	**STIMULUS SEEKING** For the excitement Because of the risks involved
5	**RELAXATION** To relax physically So my mind can slow down for a while	**14**	**SELF-ACTUALISATION (FEEDBACK, SELF-IMPROVEMENT, ABILITY UTILISATION)** Seeing the results of your efforts Using a variety of skills and talents
6	**SOCIAL CONTACT** So I could do things with my companions To get away from other people	**15**	**ACHIEVEMENT, CHALLENGE, COMPETITION** To develop my skills and ability Because of the competition To learn what I am capable of
7	**MEETING NEW PEOPLE** To talk to new and varied people To build friendships with new people	**16**	**KILLING TIME, AVOIDING BOREDOM** To keep busy To avoid boredom
8	**HETEROSEXUAL CONTACT** To be with people of the opposite sex To meet people of the opposite sex	**17**	**INTELLECTUAL AESTHETICISM** To use my mind To think about my personal values
9	**FAMILY CONTACT** To be away from the family for a while To help bring the family together more		

Source: Crandall (1980)

Table 2.2: Kabanoff's list of leisure needs

	Leisure needs scale	Items comprising scales	Item means
1	Autonomy	Organise own projects and activities	2.78
		Do things you find personally meaningful	3.39
2	Relaxation	Relax and take it easy	3.20
		Give mind and body a rest	2.94
3	Family activity	Bring family closer together	2.81
		Enjoy family life	3.30
4	Escape from routine	Get away from responsibilities of everyday life	2.85
		Have a change from daily routine	3.12
5	Interaction	Make new friends	2.35
		Enjoy people's company	2.55
6	Stimulation	To have new and different experiences	2.66
		For excitement and stimulation	2.89
7	Skill utilisation	Use skills and abilities	2.89
		Develop new skills and abilities	2.61
8	Health	Keep physically fit	2.47
		For health reasons	2.46
9	Esteem	Gain respect or admiration of others	2.11
		Show others what you're capable of	2.15
10	Challenge/competition	Be involved in a competition	1.87
		Test yourself in difficult or demanding situations	2.31
11	Leadership/social power	Organise activities of teams, groups, organisations	1.79
		To gain positions of leadership	1.48

Source: Kabanoff (1982)

tourism context) in identifying and classifying the types of needs people have. Tillman (1974) summarised some of the broader leisure needs of individuals within which recreational needs occur and these may include the pursuit of:

- new experiences (i.e. adventure);
- relaxation, escape and fantasy;
- recognition and identity;
- security (freedom from thirst, hunger or pain);
- dominance (to control one's environment);
- response and social interaction (relating and interacting with others);
- mental activity (to perceive and understand);
- creativity;
- a need to be needed; and
- physical activity and fitness.

A different perspective is offered by Bradshaw (1972) who argued that social need is a powerful force, explaining need by classifying it as normative, felt, expressed and comparative need. Mercer (1973), McAlvoy (1977) and Godbey (1976) extended Bradshaw's argument, within a recreational context modifying the four categories of need by adding created, changing and false needs. Normative needs are based on value judgements, often made by professionals who establish that what they feel is appropriate to the wider population. Felt needs, which individuals may have but not necessarily express are based on what someone wants to do and is a perceived need. Expressed needs relate to those needs and preferences for existing recreational activities which are often measured but can only be a partial

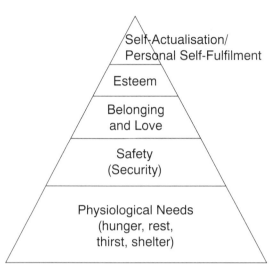

Maslow's hierarchy of needs

Figure 2.1: Maslow's hierarchy of needs

view of demand, since new recreational opportunities may release latest demand. Comparative needs are apparent where existing provision for the general population are compared with special groups (e.g. the elderly, ethnic minorities or disabled) to establish if existing provision is not fulfilling the needs of the special group. Created needs may result from policy-makers and planners introducing new services or activities which are then taken up by the population. A false need is one that may be created by individuals or society and which is not essential and may be marginal to wider recreational needs. Changing needs, however, are a recognition of the dynamic nature of human needs which change through time as individuals develop and their position in the life-cycle changes. Thus, what is important at one point in the life cycle may change through time as an individual passes through four key stages (Ken and Rapoport 1975):

- youth (school years);
- young adulthood;

- establishment (extended middle-age); and
- final phase (between the end of work and of life).

Other researchers (e.g. Neulinger 1981 and Iso-Ahola 1980) prefer to emphasise the importance of perceived freedom from constraints as a major source of motivation. Argyle (1996) synthesises such studies to argue that intrinsic motivation in leisure relates to three underlying principles:

- social motivation;
- basic bodily pleasures (e.g. eating, drinking, sex and sport); and
- social learning (how past learning explains a predisposition towards certain activities).

One useful concept which Csikszentmihaly (1975) introduced to the explanation of motivation was that of flow. Individuals tend to find a sense of intense absorption in recreational activities, when self-awareness declines, and it is their peak experience – a sense of flow – which is the main internal motivation. The flow is explained as a balance resulting from being challenged and skill which can occur in four combinations:

- where challenge and skill are high and flow results;
- where the challenge is too great, anxiety results;
- if the challenge is too easy, boredom may occur; and
- where the challenge and skill level is too low, apathy may result.

But this does not mean that everyone always seeks recreational activities which provide forms of high arousal. Some recreational activities may just fulfil a need to relax, being undemanding and of low arousal. As Ewert and Hollenhurst (1989) reported, those who engaged in outdoor recreational sports with a high risk factor (i.e. white-water rafting) viewed the sport as providing a flow experience, and the study predicted that as their skill level improved they would increase the level of participation and risk. Yet even though this occurred the internal motivation of the group remained unchanged, where low and high arousal seem to be juxtaposed. Thus, levels of arousal vary from time to time, a factor which can be used by adventure tourism operators to manage the adventure experience and increase the level of satisfaction of participants (Hall and McArthur 1994).

Recreation may also lead to an enhanced self-image, where the identity becomes a basis for motivation because recreational activities can lead to a sense of belonging to a particular and iden-tifiable group. Some activities may also require the development of special skills and enhanced self-esteem. Where recreational activities require a degree of competency, Bandura (1977) proposed that perception of one's ability to perform the skill is a motivator and may result in self-efficacy, a form of self-confidence and judgement of one's ability.

In spite of the significance of motivation, it is apparent that no single theory or even a clear con-sensus exists in relation to recreation. Instead, 'in theories of motivation need is seen as a force within the individual to gain satisfactions and completeness. There appear to be many levels and types of need, including the important needs of self-actualisation and psychological growth' (Torkildsen 1992: 86). An understanding of needs and intrinsic motivation and some of the ideas implicit in studies of recreational motivation may offer a range of insights into why people engage in recreational activities. But not only is it necessary to understand why people engage in recreation, but also what factors or barriers may inhibit them from participating. Torkildsen (1992) outlines the influences on leisure participation in terms of three categories: personal, social and circumstantial and opportunity factors. These influences (Table 2.3) are also of value in understanding some of the constraints on recreation.

Table 2.3: Influences on leisure participation

Personal	Social and circumstantial	Opportunity factors
Age	Occupation	Resources available
Stage in life-cycle	Income	Facilities – type and quality
Gender	Disposable income	Awareness
Marital status	Material wealth and goods	Perception of opportunities
Dependants and ages	Car ownership and mobility	Recreation services
Will and purpose in life	Time available	Distribution of facilities
Personal obligations	Duties and obligations	Access and location
Resourcefulness	Home and social environment	Choice of activities
Leisure perceptions	Friends and peer groups	Transport
Attitudes and motivation	Social roles and contacts	Costs: before, during, after
Interests and preoccupations	Environment factors	Management: policy and support
		Marketing
Skill and ability – physical, social and intellectual	Mass leisure factors	
Personality and confidence	Education and attainment	Programming
Culture born into	Population factors	Organisation and leadership
Upbringing and background	Cultural factors	Social accessibility
		Political policies

Source: Torkildsen (1992)

BARRIERS TO RECREATION

Kay and Jackson's (1991) notable study of 366 British adults' recreational constraints identified:

- 53 per cent who cited money as the main constraint;
- 36 per cent who felt lack of time was the main limitation; and
- conflicts with family or work, transportation problems and health concerns as other contributory factors.

A study in Alberta which surveyed 1891 people asked respondents to rate 15 possible barriers to a desired activity and the results highlighted social isolation, accessibility, personal reasons (lack of confidence or skill), costs, time and facilities as the main constraints. It has been proposed that such constraints have a specific ordering in terms of importance with the most significant constraints being interpersonal ones, followed by structural ones (e.g. lack of time or money). Yet such arguments have been queried by Shaw *et al.* (1991) who found that in a survey of 14,674 Canadians, of 11 constraints, only lack of energy and ill-health were associated with a lower rate of participation. Therefore, barriers may be negotiable or solvable as Kay and Jackson (1991) suggest. Patmore (1983) summarises the main physical barriers to recreation in terms of:

- seasonality;
- biological and social constraints;
- money and mobility; and
- resources and fashions;

with the availability of time also being a major constraint.

Coppock and Duffield (1975: 8) recognised the principal variations which exist in terms of demand due to variable uses of leisure time-budgets by individuals and groups in relation to the day, week and year. Both Coppock and Duffield (1975) and Patmore (1983) use similar data sources (e.g. the UK's Pilot National Recreation Survey (British Travel Association and Univeristy of Keele 1967 and 1969) and sociological studies of family behaviour in the pioneering study by Young and Wilmott 1973) to examine time-budgets, variations in demand and constraining factors. One of the most important distinctions to make is that 'the weekend thus represents a large increase in the time that can be committed to leisure pursuits, which in turn affects the weekend time budget' (Coppock and Duffield 1975: 14). Yet when one looks beyond the day and week to the individuals and groups concerned, a wider range of influences emerge which are important in explaining recreation patterns.

Argyle (1996) highlights the fact that one of the main reasons for examining constraining and facilitating factors is to understand how many people engage in different kinds of leisure, how much time they spend on it, and how this varies between men and women, young and old, and other groups' (Argyle 1996: 33). This is because some groups such as 'women, the elderly and unemployed face particular constraints which may affect their ability to engage in leisure and recreational activities which people do because they want to, for their own sake, for fun, entertainment or self-improvement, or for goals of their own choosing, but not for material gain' (Argyle 1996: 33).

SEASONALITY

Patmore (1983: 70) argued that 'one of the most unyielding of constraints is that imposed by climate, most obviously where outdoor activities are concerned. The rhythms of the seasons affect both the hours of daylight available and the extent to which temperatures are conducive to participant comport outdoors.' This is reflected in the seasonality of recreational activity which inevitably leads to peaks in popular seasons and a lull in less favourable conditions. Patmore (1983) identified a continuum in recreational activities from those which exhibit a high degree of seasonality to those with a limited degree of variation in participation by season. The first type, which are the most seasonal include outdoor activities, often of an informal nature which are weather dependent. The second, an intermediate group is transitional in the sense that temperature is not necessarily a deterrent since a degree of discomfort can be experienced by the more hardened participants (e.g. when walking and playing sport). The last group is indoor activities which can be formal or informal, and have virtually no seasonality. In addition, the physical constraints of season, climate and weather inhibit demand by curtailing the periods of time over which a particular resource can be used for the activity concerned (Patmore 1983: 72) although resource substitution (e.g. using a man-made ski slope instead of a snow-clad one) may assist in some contexts but often the man-made resource cannot offer the same degree of excitement or enjoyment.

FINANCIAL RESOURCES AND ACCESS TO RECREATIONAL OPPORTUNITY

Argyle (1996) observed that while many studies emphasised lack of money as a barrier to engaging in recreational activities, Coalter (1993) found that it had little impact on participation in sports. In fact, Kay and Jackson (1991) also acknowledged that money or disposable income was a barrier to undertaking activities which were major consumers of money (drinking and eating socially) whereas it had little impact on sport which was comparatively cheap. Income, occupation and access to a car combined have a significant impact on participation, and as Patmore (1983: 78) succinctly summarised, 'those with more skilled and responsive occupations, with higher incomes, with ready access to private transport and with a longer period spent in full-time education tend to lead a more active and varied leisure

life, with less emphasis on passive recreations both within and beyond the home'. It is the car which has provided the greatest degree of personal mobility and access to a wider range of recreational opportunities in time and space since the 1960s in many developed countries (and earlier in some cases like the USA and Canada). For example, most car-owning households in UK studies have twice the propensity to participate in sport and recreation than non-car owning households (Hillman and Whalley 1977). Even so, Martin and Mason (1979: 62) observe that: 'one of the paradoxes of leisure is that while time and money are complementary in the production of leisure activities, they are competitive in terms of the resources available to the individual. Some leisure time and some money to buy leisure goods and services are both needed before most leisure activities can be pursued.'

GENDER AND SOCIAL CONSTRAINTS

The influence of gender on recreation remains a powerful factor influencing participation, a feature consistently emphasised in national surveys of recreational demand. As Argyle (1996: 44) argues

there is an influential theory about this topic, due to a number of feminist writers, that women have very little or no leisure, because of the demands of domestic work and the barriers due to husbands who want them at home . . . [and] . . . that leisure is a concept which applies to men, if it is regarded as a reaction to or contrast with paid work. (see Deem 1986)

Thus, women with children appear to have less time for recreation, while those in full and part time employment have less time available than male counterparts (see Argyle 1996 for more discussion of this topic). These general statements find a high degree of support within the recreational literature, with gender differences in part explained by the male free time occurring in larger blocks and in prime time (e.g. evenings and weekends) (Pigram

1983). Even so, studies by Talbot (1979) explore this theme in more detail. Rodgers (1977) documents the wide discrepancy in male:female participation in sport as a form of recreation within a European context where for every 100 females engaging in sport, there were 188 male participants in Britain, 176 in Spain, 159 in France, 127 in Belgian Flanders, 127 in Norway, 116 in The Netherlands and 111 in former West Germany. While definitions and the variations in data sources may in part explain the variability, the presence of a gender gap is prominent.

Age also exerts a strong influence on participation in recreation, with Hendry *et al.* (1993) describing adolescence as the peak time of leisure needs. Therein lies two key explanations of participation and constraints. Stage in the life cycle presents a useful concept to explain why women with young children appear to have fewer opportunities for recreation than adolescents. Likewise, physical vigour and social energy are traditionally explained in terms of a decline in the later stages of adulthood resulting in a decline in active recreation throughout later life. The Greater London Recreation Survey of 1972 (Greater London Council 1976) identified some of these traits in that:

- activities exist where participation markedly declined by age (e.g. energetic sports like football);
- activities occur with sustained participation through the life-cycle (e.g. tennis and indoor swimming); and
- some activities exist where participation increased as a person got older (e.g. golf and walking).

In fact these results not only illustrate the importance of age (and to a degree gender), but also the need to consider the significance of the life-cycle in relation to changes or 'triggers' (Patmore 1983). One such trigger is retirement and while it is sometimes interpreted as a stressful life event, Long (1987) found that for 58 per cent of male retirees, there was no change in their leisure

activities, while 8 per cent undertook education, 3 per cent developed an interest in photography and 3 per cent partook of sport. What Argyle (1996: 63) emphasises from studies of retirement are that 'people carry on with the same leisure as before, though they are more passive and more house-bound, and do not take up much new leisure'.

RESOURCES AND FASHIONS

While models of participation and obstacles to recreation have attempted to predict the probability of people participating in activities, using variables such as age, sex, marital status, and social variables (e.g. housing tenure, income and car ownership), predictions decline in accuracy when attempting to identify individual activities (e.g. golf). What such recreational models often fail to acknowledge is the role of choice and preference given a range of options. In this respect, geographical proximity to recreational resources and access to them is a major determinant. This is demonstrated by Burton (1971), who found that in Britain, people were three times as likely to use a recreational resource if they lived between half and three-quarters of a mile away, a feature emphasised by Patmore (1983) and Page *et al.* (1994) in research on urban parks. Veal (1987) expressed this using classic distance–decay theory reproduced in Figure 2.2. This shows that the proximity to a recreational resource increased the propensity for use at a swimming pool, yet for leisure centres where attendees used cars to visit them, the distance–decay function had a less rapid decline in attendance in relation to distance. Outside urban areas, the occurrence of recreational resources are more varied in their spatial distribution, and recreational opportunities need to be closely examined in relation to demand and supply. To provide a number of detailed insights into the patterns of recreation in different countries, and how demand is influenced and constrained, a number of national recreational

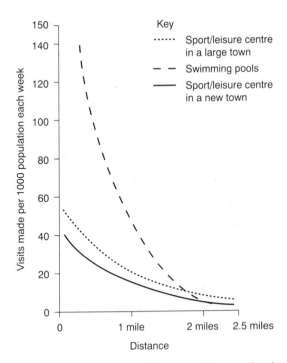

Figure 2.2: The impact of distance and geographical catchment areas on the provision of leisure facilities
Source: based on Veal (1987)

patterns are examined followed by a case study of regional demand.

MEASURING RECREATIONAL DEMAND

Most geographers acknowledge the continued lack of suitable data on recreational demand, as Patmore (1983: 55) explains:

> prior to the 1960s sources were scattered and fragmentary, and lacked any coherent basis. The studies undertaken for the American Outdoor Recreation Resources Review Commission and published in 1962 gave the impetus for work in Britain. Two wide-ranging national surveys were carried out later in the latter part of that decade: the Pilot National Recreation Survey ... and the Government social survey's Planning for Leisure ... These surveys remain unique at national level.

Although such surveys also have a number of limitations: they were 'one-off' studies, the methods of data collection did not allow comparability of the data for each survey, and the results are often dated on publication due to the time required to analyse the results, they were a starting point for analysing demand. Yet since 1972 no major survey specifically focused on leisure has been undertaken in the UK, although the General Household Survey (GHS) has included a number of questions on leisure.

PROBLEMS AND METHODS OF MEASURING RECREATIONAL DEMAND

When seeking to understand individuals' recreational habits, asking individuals questions about their recreational habits using social survey techniques remains the most widely used approach. Even so, researchers recognise that precision is needed to identify participation, non-participation and the frequency of each. For this reason, questions on surveys need to follow the type of format used on the GHS, to provide both a temporal and quantitative measure of demand. Patmore (1983: 57) cites the GHS which begins by asking respondents: 'What ... things have you done in your leisure time ... in the four weeks ending last Sunday?'

Survey data rarely record all the information a researcher seeks (e.g. respondents' recall ability may not accurately record the full pattern), or respondents have a different understanding of a term to that intended by the researcher. As a result, a variety of survey techniques are necessary to derive a range of complementary and yet unique insights into recreation demand.

Within the recreation literature, three techniques have primarily been used:

- a continuous record of recreation activities of a sample population for a given time period which involves respondents keeping a diary of activities (the time-budget approach);

- questionnaire surveys which require respondents to recall activities either in the form of an individual case study, which are detailed and sometimes contain both qualitative and quantitative questions and which are inevitably small-scale due to the time involved in in-depth qualitative interviews; and
- questionnaire surveys which are large scale, enabling sub-samples to be drawn which are statistically significant. Such surveys can be derived using simple and unambiguous questions which focus on a specific recreation activity or one that covers the entire spectrum of leisure activities (e.g. the GHS which surveyed 17,574 people in 1993 in Great Britain aged 16 and over). To illustrate how these techniques have been used and the way such data has been analysed, the time-budget approach and national surveys of recreational activities are now examined.

TIME-BUDGET SURVEY TECHNIQUES

According to Coppock and Duffield (1975: 5) 'recreation takes place in that portion of people's lives in which they are free (within constraints) to choose their activities, that is, their leisure time, [and] how they spend their time (time-budgets) is of paramount importance in any attempt to establish recreational demand, since it determines where recreational activities are possible'. Therefore time-budget analysis is a vital tool in analysing demand. This method has not been widely used due to the difficulty for individuals of accurately keeping records, though in 1966 and 1974 to 1975 the British Broadcasting Corporation used its Audience Research Department to recruit people to keep a diary for a full week with half hour entries. Yet even in such a short time span, diarist willingness to record information accurately declined towards the end of the week (Patmore 1983). However, pioneering research by Glyptis (1981a) used a diary technique which examined a sample of 595 visitors to the countryside. Respondents kept a diary record

spanning three days and five evenings, recording the dominant pursuit in half hour periods. While respondents identified up to 129 different leisure activities, each cited an average of 11. The value of the study was that through the use of cluster analysis to statistically analyse the sample and to group the population (see Smith 1989 for more detail of this technique), it identified the leisure life-styles of respondents with distinct groupings, where people of different social classes engaged in similar activities. The value of such research is in the identification of factors beyond simplistic analogies of demand determined by biological, social and economic factors.

NATIONAL EVALUATIONS OF RECREATIONAL DEMAND: INTERNATIONAL PERSPECTIVES

The United Kingdom

Since the publication of Patmore's (1983) detailed review of data sources for analysing leisure and recreation patterns in the UK, Veal (1992) updated the situation pointing to the GHS and the role of the Australian Commonwealth government in commissioning the first National Recreation Participation Survey in Australia 1985/86. This section examines demand at the national level in a number of countries to provide comparisons. Table 2.4 outlines the results from the GHS as a national survey of leisure and recreation habits, with the range of activities included and variations through time. However the most up to date and accessible source which documents these issues in the UK is the Office of Population and Censuses (OPCS) *Social Trends*. The 1996 edition compiles data from a wide variety of sources and examines:

- use of time for leisure and other activities showing that men in full-time employment had around two more hours of free time than women in full-time employment;

Table 2.4: Trends in leisure participation in Great Britain 1977–86

| | Participating in 4 weeks prior to interview annual average rate – persons aged 16 and over (percentage) | | | |
	1977	1980	1983	1986
Amateur drama/music	3	3	3	4
Athletics (including jogging)	1	1	2	3
Badminton	2	2	2	2
Bowls	1	1	1	1
Bowls/tenpin	1	1	1	2
Camping/caravaning	1	1	1	1
Cinema/film clubs	10	10	7	8
Cricket	1	1	1	1
Cycling	1	1	2	2
Dancing	15	14	11	11
Darts	9	7	7	6
DIY	35	37	36	39
Exhibitions/shows	2	2	2	3
Fairs/arcades/fetes/carnivals	4	4	2	4
Fishing	2	2	2	2
Football	3	3	3	3
Gardening	42	43	44	43
Going out for a drink	64	54	54	55
Going out for a meal	1	40	40	47
Golf	2	2	2	3
Gymnastics/athletics	–*	1	1	1
Historic buildings/sites/towns	8	9	8	9
Horse riding	1	1	1	1
Keep fit/yoga	1	2	3	3
Listening to records/tapes	62	64	63	67
Museums/art galleries	4	3	3	4
Outings by car/motorbike/boat	2	2	1	4
Reading books	54	57	56	59
Sewing/knitting	29	28	27	27
Snooker/billiards/pool	6	7	8	9
Squash	2	2	3	2
Swimming (indoor pool)	5	6	7	9
Swimming (sea, outdoor pool)	2	2	4	2
Table tennis	2	2	1	1
Tennis	1	2	1	1
Theatre/ballet/opera	5	5	4	5
Visits to countryside	5	4	3	3
Visits to parks	4	4	4	4
Visits to seaside	7	7	7	7
Walking (2 miles or more)	17	19	19	19
Zoos	1	2	1	1
SAMPLE SIZE	**23,171**	**22,594**	**19,050**	**12,209**

Note: *Less than 0.5 per cent
Source: General Household Surveys/OPCS cited Veal in (1992)

Table 2.5: Participation in home-based leisure activities in Great Britain by gender and age 1993–94 (%)

Males	16–19	20–24	25–29	30–44	45–59	60–69	70+	16+
Watching TV	99	100	99	99	99	99	97	99
Visiting/entertaining friends or relations	96	97	97	97	94	94	91	95
Listening to radio	93	95	95	94	91	86	83	91
Listening to records/tapes	96	96	93	86	76	66	50	79
Reading books	55	589	54	60	61	59	58	59
Gardening	24	22	37	52	62	65	55	51
DIY	34	44	61	68	65	58	35	57
Dressmaking/needlework/knitting	2	3	3	3	3	3	4	3
Females								
Watching TV	99	99	99	99	99	99	99	99
Visiting/entertaining friends or relations	98	98	99	98	96	95	94	96
Listening to radio	97	95	92	91	88	84	77	88
Listening to records/tapes	97	96	92	88	75	62	42	75
Reading books	75	70	70	71	71	74	67	71
Gardening	11	23	34	51	57	54	39	45
DIY	16	35	39	40	34	23	10	30
Dressmaking/needlework/knitting	19	30	30	37	44	48	38	38

Source: General Household Survey, Office of Population Censuses and Surveys, HMSO (1996)

- participation in home-based leisure activities in 1993–94 indicated that watching television is the most important pastime, while other activities vary by age and sex (i.e. gardening is more popular among men aged 25 years or more) (see Table 2.5);
- using data from the Henley Centre for Forecasting, Table 2.6 shows that the most commonly undertaken free time activity outside the home amongst adults in 1994–95 was a visit to a public house, with the greatest difference in participation occurring between men and women's attendance at spectator sports. Variations by social class indicate that non-manual workers engage in leisure activities more regularly than manual workers while age affects the type of activities people choose to undertake;
- in terms of sporting activities, men are consistently more likely than women to

Table 2.6: Participation in leisure activities away from home in Great Britain by gender 1994–95

	Males	*Females*	*All persons*
Visit a public house	70	68	64
Meal in a restaurant (not fast food)	60	64	62
Drive for pleasure	47	47	47
Meal in a fast food restaurant	45	40	42
Library	36	43	40
Cinema	35	32	34
Short break holiday	32	28	30
Disco or night club	29	22	25
Historic building	27	24	25
Spectator sports event	31	13	22
Theatre	19	22	21

Source: The Henley Centre for Forecasting cited in HMSO (1996)

participate in sport, with 72 per cent of men and 57 per cent of women undertaking at least one activity in the four weeks prior to being interviewed for the GHS (Table 2.7);

- participation by socio-economic group (Table 2.8) illustrates that 82 per cent of those in professional occupations compared with 48 per cent in the unskilled manual group had undertaken a physical activity in the four weeks prior to the GHS. Non-manual groups were more likely to participate in swimming or running/jogging whereas those in manual groups were more likely to participate in darts and cue sports (snooker, pool or billiards);

- in terms of tourism, the proportion of British adults taking at least one holiday a year has remained at about 60 per cent for the last 20 years, though the proportion taking two or more holidays a year has almost quadrupled since 1966 (Figure 2.3). Those in non-manual classes were most likely to have two or more holidays a year. In 1994, the British population took 58 million holidays abroad of which 32 million were spent in Britain, which is broadly similar to the volume of domestic British holidays taken in 1966.

- the most popular period for holiday taking is August followed by July, though the destinations

for domestic holiday are dominated by the West Country, where almost a quarter of holidays were spent in 1994. This is followed by Scotland and Wales. Travel by car remains the preferred mode of transport and self-catering is more widely used (51 per cent) than serviced accommodation (30 per cent). The average cost of a domestic holiday in 1994 was £146 per person; and

- in terms of overseas holidays (Table 2.9), Spain regained its position as the popular British destination in 1994 though its dominance has waned since 1971. France remains a popular holiday and day trip destination. Since the relaxation of customs regulations on duty paid goods, approximately 80 per cent of all British overseas holidays were spent in Europe in 1994, with the USA being the most popular non-European destination.

Poland

According to Olszewska (1989) the Polish Central Statistical Office time-budget analysis of the Polish population aged 18 or over in 1984 examined 45,087 respondents in 5,400 households. The relationship between work and non-work was identified and using a 24 hour mean time budget

Table 2.7: Participation in the most popular sports, games and physical activities in the UK by gender and age 1993–94 (%)

	16–19	20–24	25–29	20–44	45–59	60–69	70+	16+
Males								
Walking	45	46	48	48	47	45	33	45
Snooker/pool/billiards	56	47	34	23	14	8	3	21
Swimming	23	19	19	21	12	8	3	15
Cycling	37	19	21	16	11	6	5	14
Soccer	44	27	19	9	2	0	0	9
Females								
Walking	40	41	41	41	42	36	20	37
Keep fit/yoga	29	28	26	22	14	8	6	17
Swimming	26	25	22	24	14	8	3	16
Cycling	14	12	8	9	7	4	2	7
Snooker/pool/billiards	26	17	6	4	2	1	0	5
Tenpin bowls/skittles	9	9	5	4	2	1	0	3

Source: General Household Survey, Office of Population Censuses and Surveys: Continuous Household Survey, Department of Finance and Personnel, Northern Ireland, HMSO (1996)

Table 2.8: Participation in the most popular sports, games and physical activities in Great Britain by socio-economic group 1993–94 (%)

	Professional	Employers and managers	Intermediate and junior non-manual	Skilled manual and non-professional	Semi-skilled manual and personal service	Unskilled manual	All socio-economic groups
Walking	57	46	42	39	36	31	41
Swimming	27	19	18	10	11	8	15
Snooker/pool/billiards	11	12	8	17	10	9	12
Keep fit/yoga	13	12	18	6	9	8	12
Cycling	14	9	9	10	8	9	10
Darts	6	5	4	8	6	6	6
Weightlifting	7	5	5	6	4	3	5
Golf	9	10	5	6	2	2	5
Running/jogging	11	6	4	3	2	2	5
Soccer	6	3	3	6	3	3	4

Source: General Household Survey, Office of Population Censuses and Surveys, HMSO (1996)

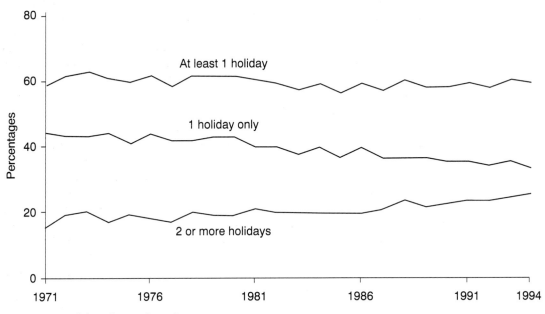

Figure 2.3: Holidays: by number taken per year
Source: Redrawn from British National Travel Survey, British Tourist Authority HMSO (1996)

Table 2.9: Destinations of British holidays taken abroad (%)

	1971	1981	1991	1994
Spain	34.3	21.7	21.3	26.4
France	15.9	27.2	25.8	22.2
Greece	4.5	6.7	7.6	7.6
United States	1.0	5.5	6.8	5.7
Portugal	2.6	2.8	4.8	3.9
Italy	9.2	5.8	3.5	3.9
Cyprus	1.0	0.7	2.4	3.3
Irish Republic	–	3.6	3.0	2.7
Netherlands	3.6	2.4	3.5	2.6
Turkey	–	0.1	0.7	2.4
Germany	3.4	2.6	2.7	2.0
Austria	5.5	2.5	2.4	1.8
Other countries	19.0	18.4	15.6	15.4
All destinations (thousands)	4,201	13.341	20,788	27,336

Source: International Passenger Survey, Central Statistical Office, HMSO (1996)

saw leisure consuming four and a half hours a day compared to physiological needs at ten and a quarter hours a day. The striking feature of the results is that leisure time outstripped work for the first time, due to the introduction of Saturdays as a non-work day, a decrease in the number of economically active in the population and the new law in 1982–83 allowing a two year paid child-care leave allowance. While 54.3 per cent of respondents undertook paid work, which lasted an average of 7 hours 12 minutes a day, 95.6 per cent enjoyed leisure time on average of 4 hours 42 minutes per day which was spent:

- watching television (80.3 per cent);
- as passive rest (38 per cent);
- reading newspapers and magazines (32.5 per cent); and
- in casual social interaction (24.1 per cent).

In an average day, respondents spent 18.8 per cent of leisure time on religious practices, 15.4 per cent of time going for walks and 12.4 reading books. Key factors 'associated with the different uses of leisure were age, sex, education, family, status, occupation, income and place of residence' (Olszewska 1989: 27).

Hungary

Fukaz (1989) examines the Csepel project undertaken in Hungary, which in 1969 sampled 400 blue-collar workers in one of the country's largest metal factories. Further in-depth interviews were undertaken in the period 1969–72, 1975–79 and 1979–82, to collect time-budget data as well as in-depth case studies. The longitudinal nature of the survey up to 1982 allows changes to be charted through time and a simulation sample in 1985 (not using the original 1969 workers) provided a further in-depth case study. While the Csepel project is not representative of the Hungarian population, macroeconomic changes in Hungarian society are reflected in the lifestyles of the population and these are reflected in the Csepel sample.

Over the period 1969–85, hours of work in Hungary were reduced from 48 to 40 hours a week, which is often argued by researchers as a precondition for the expansion of leisure. But in Hungary the reduction in official hours of work was accompanied by increases in overtime working and the growth of second jobs. Fukaz (1989: 41) argued that 'as Hungary's economy developed, the prestige of leisure appears to have grown . . . Only 6.4 per cent in 1976 and 3.9 per cent in 1979 preferred work to leisure on Saturdays'. Yet the evidence from the Csepel study indicates that 'the main obstacles to a growth and enrichment of leisure in Hungary are not rooted in inadequate leisure education, or in a weakening or absence of leisure values. Rather, the barriers have been erected by objective material and financial conditions. The latter have discouraged individuals from using reductions in official work time to enhance their leisure' (Fukaz 1989: 42) preferring to use the time in some cases for pecuniary reward.

In terms of leisure activities undertaken by the Csepel workers, these were largely related to passive forms of recreation. The most popular activities were watching television and just relaxing though seasonal variations exist, with winter leisure being home-based but urban work patterns tend to dominate leisure in present day Hungary. The growth of second home ownership (Dingsdale 1986) has also characterised weekend and vacation leisure time for those families with access to such resources.

These three examples of recreational demand show that the patterns of leisure activities for each population exhibit a common range of characteristics, in terms of the predominance of passive activities, the constraints of urban living which largely structure the time-budgets of those in employment due to weekday work commitments. In other words, the patterns of demand highlighted in the three national surveys point to the existence of factors which facilitate and constrain recreational activities in each particular context. However, so far the discussion of demand has focused

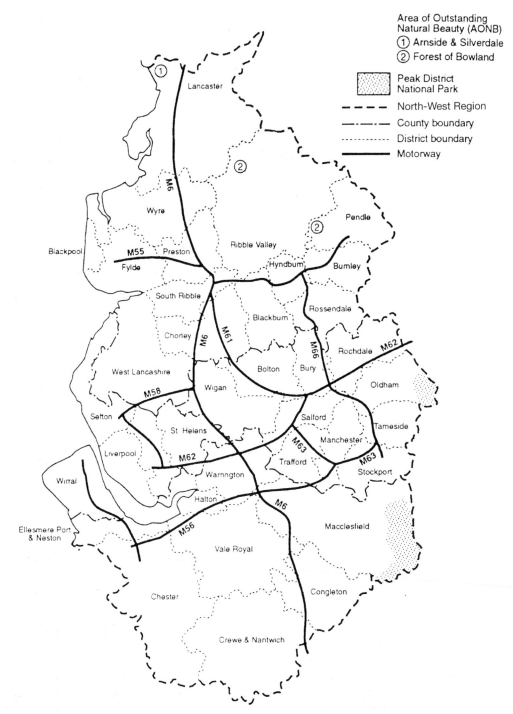

Figure 2.4: North-West England

on national patterns, and therefore attention now turns to the regional level to examine the contribution the geographer can make to the analysis of demand within a regional geographic framework.

THE REGIONAL DEMAND FOR LEISURE AND RECREATION IN NORTH-WEST ENGLAND

Within the studies of national recreational demand reviewed in the previous section, it is clear that the analysis of geographical patterns of demand were relatively scant, given the tendency for national studies to lack a regional dimension. It is the spatial variations in demand which are of interest to the geographer and a number of studies have been undertaken which utilise the geographer's spatial analytical approach to examine demand patterns. The North-West of England is one such area which has seen a significant contribution made to understanding the scale and nature of regional recreational demand including evidence in Rodgers (1969) insights from the Pilot National Recreation Survey, Rodgers (1977)

Table 2.10: Comparative demographic, economic and household data: North-West England (NW) and the United Kingdom (UK)

Population profile (thousands)		1961	1971	1981	1991	1994
NW: resident population	Male	3,099	3,193.2	3,124.0	3,109.7	3,131.3
	Female	3,308	3,441.0	3,335.2	3,286.5	3,280.7
	All persons	6,407	6,634.2	6,459.2	6,396.2	6,422.0
UK population – all persons		52,807	55,928	56,352.2	57,807.9	58,394.5

Employment structure (thousands)		1978	1981	1986	1991	1995
NW: Employees in employment		2,671	2,452	2,308	2,373	2,297
UK: Employees in employment		22,931	21,816	21,426	22,118	21,928
NW: Self-employed		222	231	288	326	290
UK: Self-employed		2,023	2,284	2,864	3,362	3,330
NW: Claimants of unemployment benefit		225	428	456	304	249
UK: Claimants of unemployment benefit		1,518	2,999	3,333	2,451	2,292
NW: Work related government supported training		–	–	40	45	30
UK: Work related government supported training		–	–	285	338	235
NW: Total civilian work-force		3,118	3,112	3,093	3,048	2,865
NW: Civilian work-force	Male	1,877	1,860	1,791	1,718	1,598
	Female	1,240	1,252	1,301	1,330	1,267
UK: Total civilian work-force		26,472	27,099	27,909	28,269	27,785
UK: Civilian work-force	Male	16,143	16,418	16,331	16,052	15,493
	Female	10,329	10,681	11,578	12,217	12,292

Table 2.11: Weekly earnings for employees in 1995: average gross weekly earnings

	£ Total	£ O/Time	£170	£220	£300	£400	Average weekly hours	Over time hours
All full-time employees (thousands)								
NW	354.2	27.6	8.1	21.6	46.6	70.3	42	3.4
UK	373.4	26.7	7.7	20.1	43.8	67.7	41.9	3.3
Manual male full-time employees								
NW	290.4	43.3	10.9	28.9	61.4	85.3	44.9	5.6
UK	290.2	43.7	11.0	28.9	60.9	85	45.2	5.7
Non-manual male full-time employees								
NW	414.4	12.8	5.5	14.7	32.5	56.2	39.1	1.3
UK	442.4	12.5	5.0	12.8	29.7	53.1	39.0	1.2
All female full-time employees								
NW	254.1	6.6	23.1	48.7	72.8	88.8	37.5	0.9
UK	269.3	6.5	21.4	43.7	68.6	86.2	37.6	0.8
Female manual full-time employees								
NW	187.5	12.3	49.6	74.5	92.5	98.2	40.2	2.0
UK	182.0	11.6	51.8	76.5	93.7	99.1	39.8	1.9
Female non-manual full-time employees								
NW	270.6	5.4	16.5	42.4	68.0	86.4	37.0	0.7
UK	287.7	5.1	15.1	36.7	63.2	83.4	37.0	0.6

Dwelling stock (thousands)	1981	1986	1991	1994
NW	2,466	2,526	2,593	2,637
UK	21,586	22,601	23,712	24,248

contribution to leisure in the North-West and Rodgers and Patmore (1972) Leisure in the North-West.

The North-West of England (see Figure 2.4) is an interesting region with a variety of socio-economic contrasts ranging from the urban decline apparent in inner-city areas through to a range of country districts with high levels of prosperity akin to South-East England (see Tables 2.10, 2.11 and 2.12 for a comparison of key socio-economic indicators for North-West England with the situation in the United Kingdom). What Rodgers (1993) explored was the changing political climate for leisure provision at national level, namely the rolling back of the frontiers of the state and changing social philosophy

that active and creative leisure pursuits deserved to be promoted as widely as possible, with the support of public funding and subsidy, to an increasing emphasis on the concept that the provision of recreation is simply another service industry best left to the operation of the market for most efficient delivery at least cost.

(Rodgers 1993: 118)

Table 2.12: Household income by source 1980–81 and 1994–95

Percentage of average gross weekly household income		NW	UK
Wages and salaries	1980–81	72.8	72.9
	1994–95	64.6	64.4
Self-employment	1980–81	6.0	6.1
	1994–95	7.1	9.5
Investments	1980–81	3.1	3.6
	1994–95	4.6	4.4
Annuities and pensions	1980–81	2.7	3.0
	1994–95	6.7	6.4
Social Security benefits*	1980–81	14.4	13.2
	1994–95	15.7	13.5
Other income	1980–81	1.0	1.2
	1994–95	1.2	1.8
Average gross weekly household income (£)	1980–81	148	150.5
	1994–95	340.9	369.3

Note: (*) These figures cannot directly be compared due to rebates and allowances related to rent/rates/council tax/housing benefit being excluded from gross income calculations after 1994

Source: Regional trends, HMSO (1996)

This marks a shift in political ideology: that leisure is no longer a significant welfare service to be delivered to all sectors of the population at free or subsidised prices due to the contribution it makes to enhanced quality of life. Thus the move to a market-driven approach (Bennington and White 1988) requires local authorities as the principal planners of community-based leisure provision to recognise the existence of leisure markets which comprise different forms of recreational demand in time and space. Local leisure markets are diverse, where a multitude of factors may affect their composition. For example those where unemployment, social stress due to the environmental factors and low rates of population growth exist may offer little commercial opportunity for the private sector despite real leisure needs. Yet if left to the market such needs may not be served adequately due to the apparent lack of prosperity or ability of individuals to pay for a resource that poor people view as a luxury item when they cannot always command the financial resources to meet basic needs. Thus, at a regional level, a detailed district by district assessment of the market is necessary to show which areas and markets may still require local authority support to avoid gross inequalities in access and provision from developing any further.

Rodgers (1993) used two principles to underpin an analysis of leisure markets:

- a significant proportion of demand is age related and changes through time will affect future needs; and
- socio-economic well-being is a powerful determinant of the volume and pattern of demand in the present and the future.

By combining these factors in an overall assessment, Rodgers (1993) was able to develop a typology of districts and their ability to support a market-based approach to leisure provision. In terms of age-related markets, Rodgers (1993: 119–20) identified four groups:

- the teenage–young adult, who is active and a major generator of recreational demand, especially active pursuits. Within the North-West, this group exhibits an almost universal decline;
- the family phase (aged 25–44 years), with a distinctive set of leisure interests;
- a post-family phase (aged 45–60 years), where active recreational interests are in decline but an interest in general leisure activities are strong; and
- the elderly, with a significant range of passive leisure interests.

By analysing forecast population growth in each of these groups, Rodgers (1993: 125) concluded that for planning future leisure provision the following characteristics needed to be incorporated into any geographical assessment of demand:

- A common feature of districts in the region is the absence of growth, except in the family phase. Rates of growth of 4 per cent above the national average are apparent, in the age group 25–44 years for 1981–91. The opportunities for market driven provision include: fitness training, outdoor pursuits in the countryside, water-sports and ten-pin bowling.
- In the post-family phase, growth rates are less than the national average, with a degree of localised growth in the industrial towns of Greater Manchester, West Lancashire and districts of North Cheshire through not in Merseyside. The most prominent activities are: bowls, fishing, dance, keep fit and walking which are likely to have little appeal for private sector operators.
- The youth market exhibits a clear decline, except for areas where planned growth exists (e.g. new towns), with rates above the national average for Merseyside and parts of inner Manchester. In the period 1981–91, a decline of 13 to 17 per cent exists in most districts, with the exception of Cheshire and West Lancashire.

- Among the elderly, trends are complex but no patterns of growth are evident in traditional retirement areas.
- A number of extremes exist in sub-regional patterns of demand, with weaknesses in Merseyside which stretches beyond the inner city districts. In East Cheshire (e.g. Congleton, Crewe and Nantwich) a profile of demand akin to the affluent South-East of England exists with different sub-groupings of demand in other areas.

One of the most significant contributory factors to the size and nature of demand is clearly related to socio-economic contrasts. Social well-being (see D.M. Smith 1977 for a discussion of the concept of social well-being and welfare geography) is, according to Rodgers (1993: 126), 'a strong influence on both the volume and structure of leisure demand and on the relative roles of public and commercial provision in meeting it'.

Using the Department of Environment (DOE) Social Deprivation Index (see Townsend 1979 and Page 1988 for a discussion of deprivation indices), which derives negative indices based on unemployment, overcrowding, single-parent and pension households, housing quality and ethnic origin, Rodgers (1993) ranked the districts in the North-West on this composite measure of social stress and also included levels of car ownership. The results were used to identify a range of geographically-based leisure markets which were strong or weak in terms of demand, particularly in relation to their capacity to pay for recreational activities in a market-driven local leisure economy. By combining the rankings of social well-being and car ownership data with the age-related changes in the leisure market, Rodgers (1993) produced Figure 2.5.

Figure 2.5 is a unique assessment of a regional recreational demand because it classifies demand into four main groups:

- Approximately 12 districts are in the top left quadrant of Figure 2.5, which represent areas of prosperity with comparatively little unemployment, high levels of car ownership and income generation and low levels of social stress. These districts exhibit some strength in demand despite a drop in numbers of people aged 13–24 years, while growth in the family and post-family sectors exists. These districts have the most appeal to commercial providers. Rodgers (1993: 127) suggests that

for large sections of the community and for many recreations a blend of private-sector and voluntary body provision, with local authorities acting largely with a market philosophy, might offer an effective formula. The case for massive direct subsidy is relatively weak, against the stronger conflicting claims of less fortunate areas

in the allocation of scarce public sector resources for recreation. Even so, pockets of target groups exist (e.g. housewives, the young and active elderly) who would benefit from some subsidy of their activities. In the north-west of the region, problems of access to recreational resources also exist in largely rural districts.

- A grouping which occupies the bottom right corner of Figure 2.5 scores low on prosperity while the age-related markets show a major decline. This reflects the limited growth in a single age category and districts of population loss (e.g. Merseyside and some of the textile towns). Both the absolute numbers and spending power of the population are declining, where the case of recreational provision for social reasons is essential due to the concentration of disadvantaged groups (e.g. the unemployed, the poor, single-parent families, the elderly and ethnic minorities). Dependence upon state benefits underpins the case for public subsidy for provision due to the multiple deprivation existing in such areas.
- A further six districts such as Hyndburn and Rochdale score high on low prosperity indices, with selective growth in family and post-family groups with a strong ethnic dimension.

The welfare case for provision is also apparent in this category.
- The remaining districts exhibit relatively prosperous populations with limited growth potential, with limited justification for public funding of their recreational services.

Whilst Rodgers (1993) admits the allocation of scarce public resources raises controversial decision-making choices it does illustrate the value of a spatial analytical approach to recreation, if a wide range of data and factors are taken into account. In other words, this case study illustrates the geographer's ability to synthesise a wide range of complex data sources and concepts to derive a series of spatially-contingent generalisations and groupings of the population for a region as diverse as North-West England. Using concepts from social geography (e.g. social well-being and deprivation) and combining demographic data from districts across the region, the geographer is able to highlight the challenge for regional and local planners in the allocation of declining absolute public sector resources for recreational provision. Regional analysis epitomises the geographer's interest in places and differences and similarities in both time and space. The greatest contribution geographical research has made is to the site-specific studies of demand, most notably site surveys. For this reason, the remaining focus of this section on recreation examines recreation site surveys.

THE SPATIAL ANALYSIS OF DEMAND AT THE MICRO LEVEL: SITE SURVEYS

Within the growing literature on geographical studies of recreation in the 1960s and 1970s, site surveys have become the most documented (a feature reiterated in Chapter 6). As Glyptis (1981b: 277) indicated 'numerous site surveys – mostly set in the format devised by Burton (1966) . . . established the characteristics of visitors and

Figure 2.5: A typology of leisure markets in North-West England
Source: Redrawn from Rodgers (1993)

their trips. Social profiles, trip distances, modes of transport and the duration, purpose and frequency of visits are well documented, (Elson 1977). Glyptis (1981b) also noted that the 1980s were a time ripe for behavioural analysis which had been neglected in relation to site surveys. While reviews of site surveys are too numerous to list (see Harrison 1991), novel research methods which examine the behaviour rather than the socio-economic characteristics of recreationalists have remained less common in the published literature, although some reports have probed this area (e.g. Locke 1985). Glyptis' (1981b) analysis of one 242 ha site – Westwood Common, Beverley near Hull (UK) is one such example. By employing participant observation methods to examine an undulating grassland area of common pasture land, 13 km from the urban area of Hull, the spatial distribution of site use by recreationalists was observed and analysed. The main recreational activities observed at the site were sitting, sunbathing, walking, picnicking, informal games and staying inside one's car. On a busy Sunday in summer, up to 2,000 visitors came to the site. Using dispersion maps, observational mapping permitted the visitor distributions to be located in time and space while length of stay (using car

registration data) and maps of use for different days and time complemented traditional social survey methods to analyse visitor behaviour. Both the site features, access points, availability of parking and location of landscape features and facilities permit a more detailed understanding of site use. Glyptis (1981b) used observations on five days in August and September during 11 am to 6 pm to collate data. Visitor arrivals at the site during the weekend occurred between 12 and 2 pm, and peak use occurred at 4.30 pm, with the majority of visitors spending one to two hours on site. The gradual increase in intensity of use by time of day, varied by activity with informal games and picnicking declining after Sunday lunch and walking increased throughout the afternoon. Local users also displayed a preference to use the site at off-peak times, with increased patterns of dispersion and clumping through time (Figure 2.6). This reflects access roads, with visitors parking near to (within 15 yards) the site they visited. Visitors were also recorded going to landmarks and facilities (e.g. viewpoints) as well as buying refreshments (e.g. from mobile vans) with the density of use increasing through the day rather than the distribution.

Glyptis (1981c) devised a simple model to

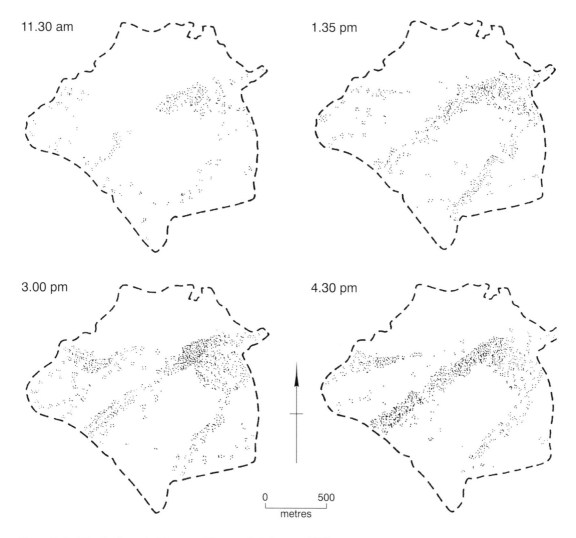

Figure 2.6: Distribution of visitors at Westwood, 3 August 1975
Source: Glyptis (1981b)

explain the dynamics of visitor dispersion (Figure 2.7). Figure 2.7 shows that initial visitors to a site choose a favoured location, linked to parking areas with further inflows of visitors during the early afternoon marking an 'invasion phase' which extends the initial cluster. Thereafter, as the pace of arrivals slows, a degree of infilling and consolidation occurs. Then as people depart, dispersion occurs, with a more irregular pattern of distribution arising although it can be affected by new arrivals in the afternoon who intensify the pattern. What Glyptis (1991: 119) recognised was that even though 'sites clearly experience an increase in visitor density, visitor dispersion in a spatial sense remains fairly constant, even with space to spare and no restrictions on public

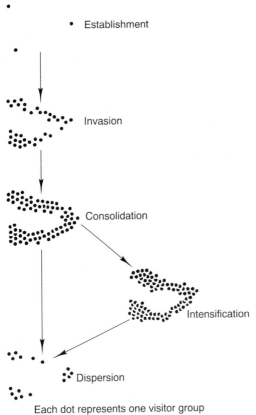

- Establishment

Invasion

Consolidation

Intensification

Dispersion

Each dot represents one visitor group

Figure 2.7: Glyptis's model of visitor dispersion at an informal recreation site
Source: Redrawn from Glyptis (1981c)

access'. Using nearest neighbour analysis, Glyptis (1981c) was able to measure the distances between groups of visitors, and that comfortable levels of tolerance exist for visitors in terms of proximity to other people, although the amount of personal space recreationalists require may vary between different cultures. In fact, Glyptis (1991: 119) remarked that 'as levels of use increase on a given day, the percentage occupancy of space actually decreases: visitors only ever use about a fifth of the space available to them, and at times of heaviest use they choose to occupy even less. In other words, site carrying capacity changes

continually'. This study also highlighted the significance of recreation sites with multiple-uses, where a variety of recreational needs are capable of being met and as Burton's (1974) survey of Cannock Chase, Staffordshire (UK) found, individual sites cannot be viewed in isolation: there are relationships between them and understanding them is vital to site management. Glyptis (1981c) highlighted a certain degree of consistency in visitor use of a site, explaining the patterns as a function of the resource base, visitor use and behavioural factors. It may be possible to accommodate or reduce capacity through simple modifications as 'the geographer is well placed to examine fundamental aspects of . . . recreation, to diagnose issues in site management, and to propose solutions (Glyptis 1981b: 285). Therefore, having outlined many of the factors and dimensions of recreational demand at a variety of spatial scales from the national, regional and local level, the discussion now turns to tourism demand.

TOURISM DEMAND

One of the fundamental questions tourism researchers consistently seek to answer is: why do tourists travel? This seemingly simple proposition remains one of the principal challenges for tourism research. D.G. Pearce (1995a: 18) expands this proposition by asking 'What induces them to leave their home area to visit other areas? What factors condition their travel behaviour, influencing their choice of destination, itineraries followed and activities undertaken?' Such questions underpin not only issues of spatial interaction, but also lead the geographer to question:

- why tourists seek to travel;
- where they go; and
- when they go and how they get there.

These basic issues have spatial implications in terms of the patterns of tourism, where tourism impacts will occur and the nature of management challenges for destinations which may attract a 'mass market' or be seeking to develop tourism from a low base. In other words, an understanding of tourism demand is a starting point for the analysis of why tourism develops, who patronises specific destinations and what appeals to the client market. However, geographers are at a comparative disadvantage in answering some of the principal questions associated with tourism demand since 'geographers have not been at the forefront of this research which has been led by psychologists, sociologists, marketers and economists. Some of these researchers have touched on such issues as the potential significance of variations in motivation on destination choice' (D.G. Pearce 1995a: 18). However tourist behaviour and the analysis of motivation has not traditionally been the logical positivist and empirical approach of traditional forms of spatial analysis on tourism with some exceptions (e.g. Walmesley and Jenkins 1992). The area of tourist behaviour has a more developed literature within the field of social psychology than geography and the emphasis in this section is on the way such approaches assist in understanding how tourist behaviour may result in the spatial implications for tourism.

WHAT IS TOURISM DEMAND?

The precise approach one adopts to the analysis of tourism demand is largely dependent upon the disciplinary perspective of the researcher. Geographers view demand in a uniquely spatial manner as 'the total number of persons who travel, or wish to travel, to use tourist facilities and services at places away from their places of work and residence' (Mathieson and Wall 1982: 1), whereas in this context demand 'is seen in terms of the relationship between individuals' motivation [to travel] and their ability to do so' (D.G. Pearce 1995a: 18) with an attendant emphasis on the implications for the spatial

impact on the development of domestic and international tourism. In comparison, the economist emphasises 'the schedule of the amount of any product or service which people are willing and able to buy at each specific price in a set of possible prices during a specified period of time. Psychologists view demand from the perspective of motivation and behaviour' (Cooper *et al.* 1993: 15).

In conceptual terms, there are three principal elements to tourism demand:

- *Effective or actual demand* comprises the number of people participating in tourism, commonly expressed as the number of travellers. This is most commonly measured by tourism statistics which means that most official sources of data are measures of effective demand.
- *Suppressed demand* is the population who are unable to travel because of circumstances (e.g. lack of purchasing power or limited holiday entitlement) which is called *potential demand*. Potential demand can be converted to effective demand if the circumstances change. There is also *deferred demand* where constraints (e.g. lack of tourism supply such as a shortage of bedspaces) can also be converted to effective demand if a destination or locality can accommodate the demand.
- *No demand* is a distinct category for the population who have no desire to travel.

According to Cooper *et al.* (1993: 16) the demand for tourism may be viewed in other ways using a number of other concepts:

- *substitution of demand* where the demand for a specific activity is substituted by another activity; and
- *redirection of demand* where the geographical distribution of tourism is altered due to pricing policies of competing destinations, special events or changing trends and tastes.

Therefore, it is apparent that the analysis of

tourism demand as an abstract concept remains firmly within the remit of tourism economics (Bull 1991; Witt and Witt 1989). However, the factors which shape the tourist decision-making process to select and participate in specific forms of tourism is largely within the field of consumer behaviour and motivation.

TOURIST MOTIVATION

According to Mountinho (1987: 16) motivation is 'a state of need, a condition that exerts a push on the individual towards certain types of action that are seen as likely to bring satisfaction'. In this respect Cooper *et al.* (1993: 20) rightly acknowledge that 'demand for tourists at the individual level can be treated as a consumption process which is influenced by a number of factors. These may be a combination of needs and desires, availability of time and money, or images, perceptions and attitudes'. Not surprisingly, this is an incredibly complex area of research and it is impossible within a chapter such as this to overview the area in depth. Nevertheless, P. Pearce's (1993) influential work in this field outlined a 'blueprint for tourist motivation', arguing that in an attempt to theorise tourist motivation one must consider the following issues:

- the conceptual place of tourism motivation;
- its task in the specialism of tourism;
- its ownership and users;
- its ease of communication;
- pragmatic measurement concerns;
- adopting a dynamic approach;
- the development of multi-motive perspectives;
- resolving and clarifying intrinsic and extrinsic motivation approaches.

(After P. Pearce 1993)

To date no all-embracing theory of tourist motivation has been developed which has been adapted and legitimised by researchers in other contexts. This is largely due to the multidisci-plinary nature of the research issues identified above and the problem of simplifying complex psychological factors and behaviour into a set of constructs and ultimately a universally acceptable theory that can be tested and proved in various tourism contexts. As a result, Cooper *et al.* (1993: 20) prefer to view the individual as a central component of tourism demand to understand what motivates the tourist to travel. Their research rightly acknowledges that:

> no two individuals are alike, and differences in attitudes, perceptions and motivation have an important influence on travel decisions [where] attitudes depend on an individual's perception of the world. Perceptions are mental impressions of . . . a place or travel company and are determined by many factors which include childhood, family and work experiences. However, attitudes and perceptions in themselves do not explain why people want to travel. The inner urges which initiate travel demand are called travel motivators.
>
> (Cooper *et al.* 1993: 20)

If one views the tourist as a consumer, then tourism demand is formulated through a consumer decision-making process, and therefore one can discern four elements which initiate demand:

- *energisers of demand* (i.e. factors that promote an individual to decide on a holiday);
- *filterers of demand* which means that even though motivation may exist, constraints on demand may exist in economic, sociological or psychological terms;
- *affecters* which are factors that may heighten or suppress the energisers that promote consumer interest or choice in tourism; and
- *roles* where the family member involved in the purchase of holiday products and the arbiter of group decision-making on choice of destination, product and the where, when and how of consumption.

These factors underpin the tourist's process of travel decision-making although it does not explain why people choose to travel.

MASLOW'S HIERARCHY MODEL AND TOURIST MOTIVATION

Within the social psychology of tourism there is a growing literature which has built upon Maslow's work (discussed earlier in relation to recreation) to identify specific motivations beyond the concept of needing 'to get away from it all' pioneered by Grinstein (1955), while push factors motivating individuals to seek a holiday exist and pull factors (e.g. promotion by tourist resorts and tour operators) encourage as attractors. Ryan's (1991: 25–9) analysis of tourist travel motivators (excluding business travel) identifies the following reasons commonly cited to explain why people travel to tourist destinations for holidays, which include:

- a desire to escape from a mundane environment;
- the pursuit of relaxation and recuperation functions;
- an opportunity for play;
- the strengthening of family bonds;
- prestige, since different destinations can enable one to gain social enhancement among peers;
- social interaction;
- educational opportunities;
- wish fulfilment; and
- shopping.

From this list, it is evident that while

all leisure involves a temporary escape of some kind . . . tourism is unique in that it involves real physical escape reflected in travelling to one or more destination regions where the leisure experience transpires . . . [thus] a holiday trip allows changes that are multi-dimensional: place, pace, faces, lifestyle, behaviour, attitude. It allows a person temporary withdrawal from many of the environments affecting day to day existence.
(Leiper 1984 cited in D.G. Pearce 1995: 19)

Within most studies of tourist motivations these factors emerge in one form or another, while researchers such as Crompton (1979) emphasise that socio-psychological motives can be located along a continuum, Iso-Ahola (1980) theorised tourist motivation in terms of an escape element complemented by a search component, where the tourist is seeking something. However, probably Dann's (1981) conceptualisation is one of the most useful attempts to simplify the principal elements of tourist motivation into:

- travel as a response to what is lacking yet desired;
- destination pull in response to motivational push;
- motivation as fancy;
- motivation as classified purpose;
- motivation typologies;
- motivation and tourist experiences;
- motivation as definition and meaning.

This was simplified a stage further by McIntosh and Goeldner (1990) into:

- physical motivators;
- cultural motivators;
- interpersonal motivators; and
- status and prestige motivators.

On the basis of motivation and using the type of experiences tourists seek, Cohen (1972) distinguished between four types of travellers:

- *The organised mass tourist*, on a package holiday, who is highly organised. Their contact with the host community in a destination is minimal.
- *The individual mass tourist*, who uses similar facilities to the organised mass tourist but also desires to visit other sights not covered on organised tours in the destination.
- *The explorers*, who arrange their travel independently and who wish to experience the social and cultural lifestyle of the destination.
- *The drifter*, who does not seek any contact with other tourists or their accommodation, seeking to live with the host community (see V.L. Smith 1992).

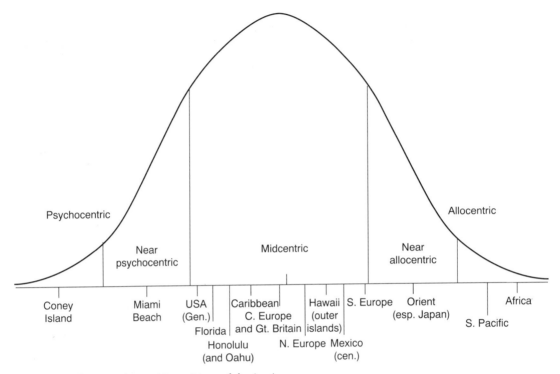

Figure 2.8: Plog's psychographic positions of destinations
Source: Redrawan from Plog (1977)

Clearly, such a classification is fraught with problems, since it does not take into account the increasing diversity of holidays undertaken and inconsistencies in tourist behaviour (Pearce 1982). Other researchers suggest that one way of overcoming this difficulty is to consider the different destinations tourists choose to visit, and then establish a sliding scale similar to Cohen's (1972) typology, but which does not have such an absolute classification.

In contrast, Plog (1974) devised a classification of the US population into psychographic types, with travellers distributed along a continuum (see Figure 2.8) from psychocentrism to allocentrism. The psychocentrics are the anxious, inhibited and less adventurous travellers while at the other extreme the allocentrics are adventurous, outgoing, seeking out new experiences due to their inquisitive personalities and interest in travel and adventure. D.G. Pearce (1995) highlights the spatial implications of such conceptualisations, that each tourist type will seek different destinations which will change through time. However, criticisms by P. Pearce (1993) indicate that Plog's model is difficult to use because it fails to distinguish between extrinsic and intrinsic motivations without incorporating a dynamic element to encompass the changing nature of individual tourists. P. Pearce (1993) discounts such models, suggesting that individuals have a 'career' in their travel behaviour where people: 'start at different levels, they are likely to change levels during their life-cycle and they can be prevented from moving by money, health and other people. They may also retire from their travel career or not take holidays at all and therefore not be part of the system' (P. Pearce 1993: 125).

Figure 2.9 outlines Pearce's model based on a

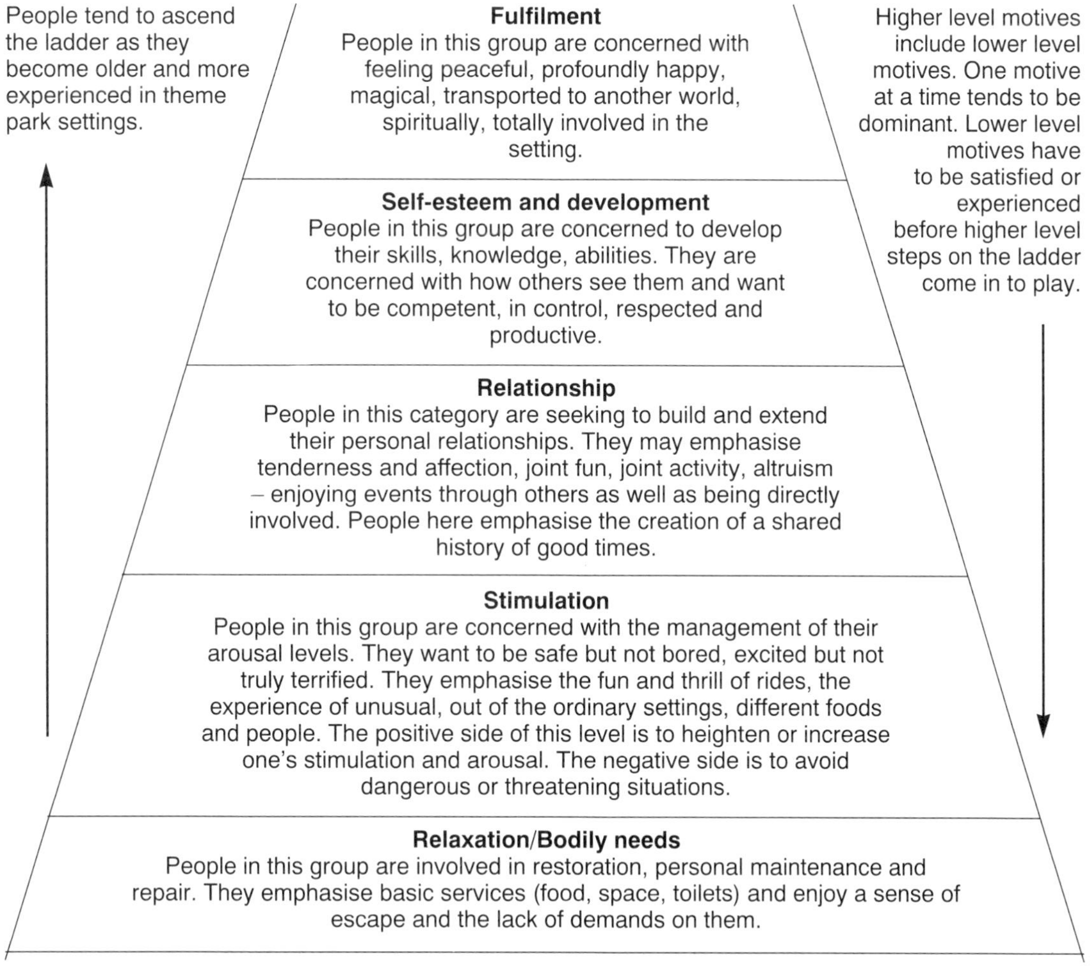

People tend to ascend the ladder as they become older and more experienced in theme park settings.

Fulfilment
People in this group are concerned with feeling peaceful, profoundly happy, magical, transported to another world, spiritually, totally involved in the setting.

Self-esteem and development
People in this group are concerned to develop their skills, knowledge, abilities. They are concerned with how others see them and want to be competent, in control, respected and productive.

Relationship
People in this category are seeking to build and extend their personal relationships. They may emphasise tenderness and affection, joint fun, joint activity, altruism – enjoying events through others as well as being directly involved. People here emphasise the creation of a shared history of good times.

Stimulation
People in this group are concerned with the management of their arousal levels. They want to be safe but not bored, excited but not truly terrified. They emphasise the fun and thrill of rides, the experience of unusual, out of the ordinary settings, different foods and people. The positive side of this level is to heighten or increase one's stimulation and arousal. The negative side is to avoid dangerous or threatening situations.

Relaxation/Bodily needs
People in this group are involved in restoration, personal maintenance and repair. They emphasise basic services (food, space, toilets) and enjoy a sense of escape and the lack of demands on them.

Higher level motives include lower level motives. One motive at a time tends to be dominant. Lower level motives have to be satisfied or experienced before higher level steps on the ladder come in to play.

Figure 2.9: The leisure ladder for theme park settings (domestic visitors)
Source: P. Pearce (1993)

leisure ladder, which builds on Maslow's hierarchical system where there are five motivational levels which are:

- a concern with biological needs;
- safety and security needs;
- relationship development and extension needs;
- special interest and self development needs; and
- fulfilment or self-actualisation needs.

Cooper *et al.* (1993: 23) argue that 'the literature on tourism motivation is still in an immature phase of development, it has been shown that motivation is an essential concept behind the different patterns of tourism demand.' From the existing literature on tourist motivation, the problems of determining tourist motivation can be summarised as follows:

- Tourism is not one specific product, it is a combination of products and experiences which meet a diverse range of needs.
- Tourists are not always conscious of their deep psychological needs and ideas. Even when they do know what they are, they may not reveal them.
- Tourism motives may be multiple and contradictory (push and pull factors).
- Motives may change over time and be inextricably linked together (e.g. perception, learning, personality and culture are often separated out but they are all bound up together) and dynamic conceptualisations such as P. Pearce's (1993) leisure ladder are crucial to advancing knowledge and understanding in this area.

Having examined some of the issues associated with what motivates tourists to travel, attention now turns to the process of measurement and recording tourist demand using statistical measures.

THE MEASUREMENT OF TOURISM DEMAND: TOURISM STATISTICS

Ritchie (1975, cited in Latham 1989: 55) argued that 'an important part of the maturing process for any science is the development or adaptation of consistent and well-tested measurement techniques and methodologies which are well-suited to the types of problems encountered in practice'. In this context, the measurement of tourists, tourism activity and the effects on the economy and society in different environments is crucial to the development of tourism as an established area of study within the confines of social science. Burkart and Medlik (1981) provide a useful insight into the development of measurements of tourism phenomenon by governments during the 1960s and their subsequent development through to the late 1970s. While it is readily acknowl-

edged by most tourism researchers that statistics are a necessary feature to provide data to enable researchers, managers, planners, decision-makers and public and private sector bodies to gauge the significance and impact of tourism on destination areas, Burkart and Medlik (1981: 74) identify three principal reasons for statistical measurement in tourism:

- to evaluate the magnitude and significance of tourism to a destination area or region;
- to quantify the contribution to the economy or society, especially the effect on the balance of payments;
- to assist in the planning and development of tourism infrastructure and the effect of different volumes of tourists with specific needs; and
- to assist in the evaluation and implementation of marketing and promotion activities where the tourism marketer requires information on the actual and potential markets and their characteristics.

Consequently, tourism statistics are essential to the measurement of the volume, scale, impact and value of tourism at different geographical scales from the global to the country level down to the individual destination. Yet an information gap exists between the types of statistics provided by organisations for users and the needs of users. The compilation of tourism statistics provided by organisations associated with the measurement of tourism have established methods and processes to collect, collate and analyse tourism statistics (World Tourism Organisation (WTO) 1996), yet these have only been understood by a small number of researchers and practitioners. Thus, this section attempts to demystify the apparent sophistication and complexity associated with the presentation of statistical indicators of tourism and their value to spatial analysis, since geographers have a strong quantified methods tradition (Johnston 1991), which is reflected in the use and reliance upon such indicators to understand spatial variations and patterns of tourism activity. All too often, undergraduate and many postgraduate texts assume a prior knowledge of tourism statistics and they are only dealt with in a limited way by most tourism texts, and where such issues are raised they are usually discussed in over technical texts aimed at a limited audience (e.g. Frechtling 1996).

A commonly misunderstood feature which is associated with tourism statistics is that they are a complete, and authoritative source of information (i.e. they answer all the questions posed by the researcher). Other associated problems are that statistics are recent and relate to the previous year or season implying that there is no time lag in their generation, analysis, presentation and dissemination to interested parties. In fact, most tourism statistics are 'typically measurements of arrivals, trips, tourist nights and expenditure, and these often appear in total or split into categories such as business or leisure travel' (Latham 1981: 55). Furthermore, the majority of published tourism statistics are derived from sample surveys with the results being weighted or statistically manipulated to derive a measure which is supposedly representative of the real world situation. In reality, this often means that tourism statistics are subject to significant errors depending on the size of the sample.

The statistical measurement of tourists is far from straightforward and Latham (1989) identifies a number of distinctive and peculiar problems associated with the tourist population:

- Tourists are a transient and highly mobile population making statistical sampling procedures difficult when trying to ensure statistical accuracy and rigour in methodological terms.
- Interviewing mobile populations such as tourists is often undertaken in a strange environment, typically at ports or points of departure or arrival where there is background noise which may influence responses.
- Other variables, such as the weather may affect the responses.

Even where sampling and survey-related problems can be minimised, one has to treat tourism statistics with a degree of caution because of additional methodological issues that can affect the results. For example, tourism research typically comprises:

- Pre-travel studies of tourists' intended travel habits and likely choice of destination (*intentional studies*);
- Studies of tourists in-transit to provide information on their actual behaviour and plans for the remainder of their holiday or journey (*actual and intended studies*);
- Studies of tourists at the destination or at specific tourist attractions and sites, to provide information on their actual behaviour, levels of satisfaction, impacts and future intentions (*actual and intended studies*); and
- Post-travel studies of tourists on their return journey from their destination or on-site experience or once they have returned to their place of residence (*post-travel measures*).

In an ideal world, where resource constraints are not a limiting factor on the generation of statistics, each of the aforementioned approaches should be used to provide a broad spectrum of research information on tourism. In reality, organisations and government agencies select a form of research which meets their own particular needs. In practice, most tourism statistics are generated with practical uses in mind and they usually, though not exclusively, can be categorised as follows:

- Measurement of tourist volume, enumerating arrivals, departures and the number of visits and stays;
- Expenditure-based surveys which quantify the value of tourist spending at the destination and during the journey; and
- The characteristics and features of tourists to construct a profile of the different markets and segments visiting a destination.

But before any tourism statistics can be derived, it is important to deal with the complex and thorny issue of defining the population – the tourist. Therefore, how does one define and differentiate between the terms tourism and tourist?

DEFINING TOURISM

The terms travel and tourism are often interchanged within the published literature on tourism, though they are normally meant to encompass 'the field of research on human and business activities associated with one or more aspects of the temporary movement of persons away from their immediate home communities and daily work environments for business, pleasure and personal reasons' (Chadwick 1994: 65). These two terms tend to be used in differing contexts to mean similar things, although there is a tendency for the United States to continue to use the term 'travel' when in fact they mean tourism. Despite this inherent problem that may be little more than an exercise in semantics, it is widely acknowledged that the two terms are used in isolation or in unison to 'describe' three concepts:

- the movement of people;
- a sector of the economy or an industry;
- a broad system of interacting relationships of people, their needs [sic] to travel outside their communities and services that attempt to respond to these needs by supplying products.

(after Chadwick 1994: 65)

From this initial starting point, one can begin to explore some of the complex issues in arriving at a working definition of the terms 'tourism' and 'tourist'.

In a historical context, Burkart and Medlik (1981: 41) identify the historical development of the term 'tourism', noting the distinction between the endeavours of researchers to differentiate between the concept and technical definitions of tourism. The concept of tourism refers to the 'broad notional framework, which identifies the essential characteristics, and which distinguishes tourism from the similar, often related, but different phenomena'. In contrast, technical definitions have evolved through time as researchers modify and develop appropriate measures for statistical, legislative and operational reasons implying that there may be various technical definitions to meet particular purposes. However, the concept of tourism, and its identification for research purposes is an important consideration in this instance for tourism statistics so that users are familiar with the context of their derivation.

While most tourism books, articles and monographs now assume either a standard definition or interpretation of the concept of tourism, which is usually influenced by the social scientists perspective (i.e. a geographical, economic, political, sociological approach or other disciplines) Burkart and Medlik's (1981) approach to the concept of tourism continues to offer a valid assessment of the situation where five main characteristics are associated with the concept.

- Tourism arises from the movement of people to, and their stay in, various destinations.
- There are two elements in all tourism: the journey to the destination and the stay including activities at the destination.
- The journey and the stay take place outside the normal place of residence and work, so that tourism gives rise to activities which are distinct from those of the resident and working populations of the places, through which tourists travel and in which they stay.
- The movement to tourist destinations is of a temporary, short-term character, with the intention of returning home within a few days, weeks or months.
- Destinations are visited for purposes other than taking up permanent residence or employment remunerated from within the places visited.

(Burkart and Medlik 1981: 42)

Furthermore, Burkart and Medlik's (1981) definition of tourism as a concept is invaluable because is rightly recognises that much tourism is a leisure activity, which involves a discretionary use of time and money, and recreation is often the main purpose for participation in tourism. But this is no reason for restricting the total concept in this way and the essential characteristics of tourism can best be interpreted to embrace a wider concept. All tourism includes some travel but not all travel is tourism, while the temporary and short term nature of most tourist trips distinguish it from migration. Therefore, from the broad interpretation of tourism, it is possible to consider the technical definitions of tourism (also see Leiper 1990, for a further discussion together with Medlik 1993 and Hall 1995 for a concise set of definitions).

TECHNICAL DEFINITIONS OF TOURISM

Technical definitions of tourism are commonly used by organisations seeking to define the population to be measured and there are three principal features which normally have to be defined (see BarOn 1984 for a detailed discussion):

- Purpose of travel (e.g. the type of traveller, be it business travel, holiday makers, visits to friends and relatives or for other reasons);
- The time dimension involved in the tourism visit, which requires a minimum and a maximum period of time spent away from the home area and the time spent at the destination. In most cases, this would involve a minimum stay of more than 24 hours away from home and less than a year as a maximum; and
- Those situations where tourists may or may not be included as tourists, such as cruise passengers, those tourists in-transit at a particular point of embarkation/departure and excursionists who stay less than 24 hours at a destination (e.g. the European duty free cross-channel day trip market).

Among the most recent attempts to recommend appropriate definitions of tourism was the World

Tourism Organisation (hereafter WTO) International Conference of Travel and Tourism in Ottawa in 1991 which reviewed, expanded and developed technical definitions where: tourism comprises 'the activities of a person travelling outside his or her usual environment for less than a specified period of time and whose main purpose of travel is other than exercise of an activity remunerated from the place visited', where 'usual environment' is intended to exclude trips within the areas of usual residence and also frequent and regular trips between the domicile and the workplace and other community trips of a routine character where 'less than a specified period of time' is intended to exclude long-term migration, and 'exercise of an activity remunerated from the place visited' is intended to exclude only migration for temporary work. The following definitions were developed by the WTO:

- *International tourism:* consists of inbound tourism.
- Visits to a country by non-residents and outbound tourism residents of a country visiting another country.
- *Internal tourism:* residents of a country visiting their own country.
- *Domestic tourism:* internal tourism plus inbound tourism (the tourism market of accommodation facilities and attractions within a country).
- *National tourism:* internal tourism plus outbound tourism (the resident tourism market for travel agents and airlines).

(WTO cited in Chadwick 1994: 66)

In order to improve statistical collection and improve understanding of tourism, the United Nations (UN) (1994) and the WTO (1991) also recommended differentiating between visitors, tourists and excursionists. The WTO (1991) recommended that an international tourist be defined as: 'a visitor who travels to a country other than that in which he/she has his/her usual residence for at least one night but not more than

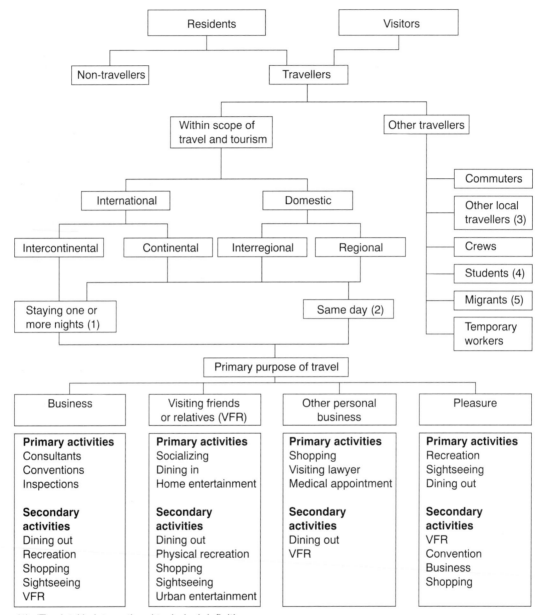

(1) 'Tourists' in international technical definitions
(2) 'Excursionists' in international technical definitions
(3) Travellers whose trips are shorter than those which qualify for travel and tourism, e.g. under 50 miles (80km) from home
(4) Students travelling between home and school only – other travel of students is within scope of travel and tourism
(5) All persons moving to a new place of residence including all one-way travellers such as emigrants, immigrants, refugees, domestic migrants and nomads

Figure 2.10: A classification of travellers
Source: Chadwick (1987)

one year, and whose main purpose of visit is other than the exercise of an activity remunerated from within the country visited'; and that an international excursionist, e.g. cruise ship visitors, be defined as 'a visitor residing in a country who travels the same day to a country other than which he/she has his/her usual environment for less than 24 hours without spending the night in the country visited and whose main purpose of visit is other than the exercise of an activity remunerated from within the country visited'. Similar definitions were also developed for domestic tourists, with domestic tourists having a time limit of 'not more than six months' (WTO 1991; UN 1994).

Interestingly, the inclusion of a same-day travel, 'excursionist' category in UN/WTO technical definitions of tourism, makes the division between recreation and tourism even more arbitrary, and there is increasing international agreement that 'tourism' refers to all activities of visitors, including both overnight and same-day visitors (UN 1994: 5). Given improvements in transport technology, same-day travel is becoming increasingly important to some countries, with the UN (1994: 9) observing, 'day visits are important to consumers and to many providers, especially tourist attractions, transport operators and caterers'.

Chadwick (1994) moves the definition of tourists a stage further by offering a typology of travellers (tourists) which highlights the distinction between tourist (travellers) and non-travellers (non-tourists) which is summarised in Figure 2.10. Figure 2.10 is distinctive because it highlights all sections of society which are involved in travel of some kind but also looks at the motivation to travel. It is also useful because it illustrates where technical problems may occur in deciding which groups to include in tourism and those to exclude.

From this classification of travellers, the distinction between international and domestic tourism needs to be made. Domestic tourism normally refers to tourist travel from their normal domicile to other areas within a country. In contrast, international tourism normally involves a tourist leaving their country of origin, to cross into another country which involves documentation, administrative formalities and movement to a foreign environment.

DOMESTIC TOURISM STATISTICS

D.G. Pearce (1995) acknowledges that the scale and volume of domestic tourism world-wide exceeds that of international tourism, though it is often viewed as the poorer partner in the compilation of statistics. For example, most domestic tourism statistics tend to underestimate the scale and volume of flows since certain aspects of domestic tourist movements are sometimes ignored in official sources. The 'visits to friends and relatives, the use of forms of accommodation other than hotels (for example, second homes, camp and caravan sites) and travel by large segments of a population from towns to the countryside are not for the most part included' (Latham 1989: 65). This is supported by the WTO who argue that 'there are relatively few countries that collect domestic travel and tourism statistics. Moreover some countries rely exclusively on the traditional hotel sector, thereby leaving out of account the many travellers staying in supplementary accommodation establishments or with friends and relatives' (WTO 1984, cited in Latham 1989: 65). Therefore the collection of domestic tourism statistics requires the use of different data sources aside from the more traditional sources such as hotel records which identify the origin and duration of a visitor's stay.

To assist in the identification of who to include as a domestic tourist, WTO (1983) suggests that the following working definition: 'any person, regardless of nationality, resident in a country and who travels to a place in the same country for not more than one year and whose main purpose of visit is other than following an occupation remunerated from within the place visited'.

Such a definition includes domestic tourists

where an overnight stay is involved and domestic excursionists who visit an area for less than 24 hours and do not stay overnight. In fact, Latham (1989: 66) points to the variety of definitions which exist aside from those formulated by WTO and the following issues complicate matters:

- *Purpose of visit* all countries using this concept define a domestic tourist as one who travels for a purpose other than to perform a remunerated activity.
- *The length of trip and/or distance travelled* certain definitions state that travellers should, for example, be involved in an overnight stay and/or travel a prescribed minimum distance.
- *Type of accommodation* for practical reasons, some countries restrict the concept of domestic tourism to cover only those persons using commercial accommodation facilities.

(After Latham 1989: 66)

Problems in applying WTO definitions may also reflect an individual country's reasons for generating such statistics, which may not necessarily be to contribute to a better understanding of statistics *per se*. For example, WTO (1981) identified four uses of domestic tourism statistics:

- To calculate the contribution of tourism to the country's economy, whereby estimates of tourism's value to the Gross Domestic Product is estimated due to the complexity of identifying the scope of tourism's contribution;
- To assist in the marketing and promotion of tourism, where government-sponsored tourism organisations seek to encourage its population to take domestic holidays rather than to travel overseas (see Hall 1997 for a discussion of this activity among Pacific Rim countries);
- To aid with the regional development policies of governments which harness tourism as a tool for area development where domestic tourists in congested environments are encouraged to travel to less developed areas and to improve the quality of tourism in different environments; and

- To achieve social objectives, where socially-oriented tourism policies may be developed for the underprivileged which requires a detailed understanding of the holiday-taking habits of a country's nationals.

Regional and local tourist organisations also make use of such data to develop and market destinations and different businesses within the tourism sector. But how is domestic tourism measured?

Burkart and Medlik (1981) argue that two principal features need to be measured: first, the volume, value and characteristics of tourism among the population of the country, second, the same data relating to individual destinations within the country.

WTO (1981 cited in Latham 1989) considers the minimum data requirements for the collection of domestic tourism statistics in terms of arrivals and tourist nights in accommodation classified by:

- month;
- type of grade of accommodation establishment; and
- location of the accommodation establishment and overall expenditure on domestic tourism.

Latham (1989) argues that it is possible to generate additional data from such variables including length of stay, occupancy rate and average expenditure. Many countries also collate supplementary information beyond the minimum standards identified by WTO, where the socio-economic characteristics of tourists are identified, together with their use of tourist-transport, and purpose of visit, though the cost of such data collection does mean that the statistical basis of domestic tourism in many less developed countries remains poor.

The methods used to generate domestic tourism statistics are normally based on the estimates of volume, value and scale derived from sample surveys due to the cost of undertaking large scale surveys of tourist activities. The immediate problem facing the user of such material is the type of errors and degree of accuracy which can be attached to such data. For example Latham (1989) identifies the following sample surveys which are now used to supplement data derived from hotel records:

- *Household surveys*, where the residents of a country are interviewed in their own home to ascertain information of tourist trips for the purpose of pleasure. A useful example of a pan-European study is the EC Omnibus study. Even so, little progress has been made internationally to collate common data on household surveys since OECD's attempt in 1967 to outline the types of data which national travel surveys should collect.
- *Destination surveys*, where high levels of tourist activity occur in a region or resort. Such studies frequently compile statistics on accommodation usage, sample surveys of visitors and may be linked to existing knowledge derived from household surveys.
- *En route surveys*, where tourists are surveyed en route to examine the characteristics and features of tourists. Although it is a convenient way to interview a captive audience depending upon the mode of transport used (see Page 1994a,b), the results may not necessarily be as representative without a complete knowledge of the transport flows for mode of tourist-transport being surveyed.

The problem of incomplete questionnaires or non-response may occur where such surveys require a respondent to post the form back to the surveyor (see Hurst 1994 for a review on the use of this survey type).

INTERNATIONAL TOURISM STATISTICS

The two principal organisations which collate data on international tourism are the World Tourism Organisation (WTO) and the Organisation for Economic Cooperation and Development (OECD). In addition, international regional tourism organisations such as the Pacific Asia Travel Association and the ASEAN Tourism Working Group also collect international tourism statistics (Hall 1997).

Page (1994b) reviews the major publications of the first two organisations in relation to international tourism, noting the detailed contents of each. In the case of WTO, the main source is the *Yearbook of Tourism Statistics*, which contains a summary of the most salient tourism statistics for almost 150 countries and territories. In the case of OECD, their *Tourism Policy and International Tourism*, referred to as the 'Blue Book' is less comprehensive, covering only 25 countries but this does contain most of the main generating and receiving areas. While the main thrust of the publication is government policy and the obstacles to international tourism, it does expand on certain areas not covered in the WTO publication (for a more detailed discussion of data sources see Withyman 1985).

In contrast to domestic tourism, statistics on international tourism are normally collected to assess the impact of tourism on a country's balance of payments. Though as Withyman (1985: 69) argued:

> Outward visitors seem to attract less attention from the pollsters and the enumerators. Of course, one country's outward visitor is another country's (perhaps several countries) inward visitor, and a much more welcome sort of visitor, too, being both a source of revenue and an emblem of the destination country's appeal in the international market. This has meant that governments have tended to be generally more keen to measure inward than outward tourism, or at any rate, having done so, to publish the results.

This statement indicates that governments are more concerned with the direct effect of tourism on their balance of payments. Yet such statistics are also utilised by marketing arms of National Tourism Organisations to base their decisions on who to target in international campaigns. The wider tourism industry also makes use of such data as part of their strategic planning and for more immediate purposes where niche markets exist. Even so, Shackleford (1980) argued that the collection of tourism statistics should be a responsibility of the state to meet international standards for data collection (WTO 1996). However, it is increasingly the case that only when the economic benefits of data collection can be justified will national governments continue to compile tourism statistics. Where resource constraints exist, the collection and compilation of tourism statistics may be impeded. This also raises important methodological issues related to what exactly is being measured. As Withyman (1985: 61) argued: 'In the jungle of international travel and tourism statistics, it behoves the explorer to step warily; on all sides there is luxuriant growth. Not all data sources are what they appear to be – after close scrutiny some show themselves to be inconsistent and often unsuitable for the industry researcher and planner'. The key point Withyman (1985) recognises is the lack of comparability in tourism data in relation to what is measured (e.g. is it visitor days or visitor nights?) and the procedures and methodology used to measure international tourism.

Frechtling (1976) concluded that the approaches taken by national and international agencies associated with international tourism statistics was converging towards common definitions of trip, travel and traveller (see Chadwick 1994 for a fuller discussion). Yet the principal difficulty which continues to be associated with this is whether business travel should be considered as a discrete activity in relation to tourism. Chadwick (1994: 75) notes that 'the consensus of North American opinion seems to be that, despite certain arguments to the contrary ... business travel should be considered part of travel and tourism'. While BarOn (1984) examines the standard definitions and terminology of international tourism as used by the UN and WTO, research by Ngoh (1985) is useful in that it considers the practical problems posed by such definitions when

attempting to measure international tourism and find solutions for the difficulties.

Latham (1989) suggests that the main types of international tourism statistics collated relate to:

- volume of tourists;
- expenditure by tourists; and
- the profile of the tourist and their trip characteristics.

As is true of domestic tourism, estimates form the basis for most statistics on international tourism since the method of data collection does not generate exact data. For example, volume statistics are often generated from counts of tourists at entry/exit points (i.e. gateways such as airports and ports) or at accommodation. But such data relates to numbers of trips rather than individual tourists since one tourist may make more than one trip a year and each trip is counted separately. In the case of expenditure statistics, tourist expenditure normally refers to tourist spending within a country and excludes payments to tourist-transport operators. Yet deriving such statistics is often an indirect measure based on foreign currency estimates derived from bank records, from data provided by tourism service providers or more commonly from social surveys undertaken directly with tourists. Research by White and Walker (1982) and Baretje (1982) directly questions the validity and accuracy of such methods of data collection, examining the main causes of bias and error in such studies.

According to Edwards (1991: 68–9), 'expenditure and receipts data apart, tourist statistics are usually collected in one of the five following ways':

- *Counts of all individuals entering or leaving the country* at all recognised frontier crossings, often using arrival/departure cards where high volume arrivals/departures are the norm. Where particularly large volumes of tourist traffic exist, a 10 per cent sampling framework is normally used (i.e. every tenth arrival/departure card). Countries such as New Zealand actually match the arrival/departure cards, or a sample, to examine the length of stay.

- *Interviews* carried out at frontiers with a sample of arriving and/or departing passengers to obtain a more detailed profile of visitors and their activities within the country. This will often require a careful sample design to gain a sufficiently large enough sample with the detail required from visitors on a wide range of tourism data including places visited, expenditure, accommodation usage and related items.

- *Selecting a sample of arrivals* and providing them with a self-completion questionnaire to be handed in or posted. This method is used in Canada but it fails to incorporate those visitors travelling via the United States by road.

- *Sample surveys of the entire population of a country* including travellers and non-travellers, though the cost of obtaining a representative sample is often prohibitive.

- *Accommodation arrivals and nights spent* are recorded by hoteliers and owners of the accommodation types covered. The difficulty with this type of data collection is that accommodation owners have no incentive to record accurate details, particularly where the tax regime is based on the turnover of bed-nights (see Page 1989 for a discussion of this problem in the context of London).

The last area of data collection is *profile statistics*, which examine the characteristics and travel habits of visitors. For example, the UK's International Passenger Survey (IPS) is one survey that incorporates volume, expenditure and profile data on international tourism.

The United Kingdom's International Passenger Survey

As a government-sponsored survey, which began in 1961, the International Passenger Survey now covers all ports of entry/exit to the UK. It is based on a stratified random sample of tourists arriving and departing from the UK by air and sea (see Griffith and Elliot 1988 for further details on the sample design features of IPS). According to Latham (1989: 64), IPS' four principal aims are:

1 To collect data for the travel account (which acts to compare expenditure by overseas visitors to the UK with expenditure overseas by visitors from the UK) of the balance of payments;
2 To provide detailed information on foreign visitors to the UK, and on outgoing visitors travelling overseas;
3 To provide data on international migration; and
4 To provide information on routes used by passengers as an aid to aviation and shipping authorities.

METHODOLOGICAL ISSUES

Latham (1989) reviews the major types of questionnaire/social survey type of data collection used for tourism statistics. He reports that among state-sponsored tourism research in the United States, conversion studies are a popular method to examine and evaluate advertising campaigns and visitor surveys, to assess a sample of visitors to individual states. The use of other methods of data collection are also discussed (e.g. diary questionnaires, participant observation and personal interviews – see Perdue 1985b, and Mullins and Heywood 1984). Yet few studies consider the issue of sampling, sample design and the sources of error which may arise from such surveys (Aaker and Day 1986; Cannon 1987). In fact the lack of research on the reliability of the estimate from a sample survey (the standard error) is rarely discussed in most tourism surveys (see Latham 1989: 71–2 for a more technical discussion of this point). In many cases, large tourism surveys focus on the logistics of drawing the sample and the bias which may be reflected in the results. Therefore, any tourism survey will need to pay careful attention to the statistical and mathematical accuracy of the survey, especially the survey design and effect it may have on the results, a feature which is discussed in great detail by Ryan (1995).

Ryan (1995) provides an excellent review of survey design, questionnaire design, sampling and also provides an insight into the statistical techniques to use for different forms of tourism data. As a result it serves as an important reference point for issues of methodology and the technical issues associated with the statistical analysis of tourism data. Without reiterating the excellent features of Ryan's findings, it is appropriate to consider some of the main accuracy problems associated with the collection of domestic and international tourism statistics.

PROBLEMS OF ACCURACY

Ryan (1995) argues that errors in data collection can lead to errors in data analysis. Among the most frequently cited problems associated with domestic and international tourism statistics are:

- the methods by which the data are collected, which are influenced by administrative, bureaucratic and legislative factors in each country;
- sample sizes which are too small and lead to unacceptable sampling errors and in some instances where the sample design is flawed; and
- the procedures for collecting tourism statistics are not adhered to by the agency collecting the data.

In addition, Edwards (1991: 68) argues that a 'fourth potential reason – arithmetic mistakes and data processing errors – only occasionally produce significant errors'. In fact, Edwards (1991: 68) supports the cause of 'tourist statisticians

[who] are both knowledgeable and conscientious, but are having to work with tools which they know could produce inaccurate or misleading data', concluding that for any set of tourist data, potential sources of error obviously depend on the method of collection employed. This, in turn, tends to be largely determined by the legislative and administrative framework and by the financial and manpower resources available.

In the case of tourist expenditure and receipts data, organisations such as the International Monetary Fund (IMF) issue guidelines for the compilation of balance of payments statistics. But errors may occur where leakage results from tourist services paid for in overseas bank accounts and in extreme cases, where a black market exists in currency exchange. Edwards (1991) suggests that a regular programme of interviews with departing tourists and returning residents may assist in estimating levels of expenditure.

Despite the apparent problems which may exist with tourism statistics, Edwards (1991: 72) argues that data on arrivals and nights spent for most destinations outside of Europe appear reasonably reliable.

> Within Europe, data for both inbound and outbound travel are fairly satisfactory for the UK. Greece, Portugal, Spain and [the former] Yugoslavia all appear to have usable frontier arrivals data. The most serious problems are in core continental European countries such as France, Germany, Italy and the Netherlands for which there are no adequate volumetric measures of travel in either direction.
>
> Accommodation arrivals and nights data are clearly gross understatements for many European countries . . . often expenditure and receipts data appear better indicators. Outside Europe, the major problems are also in relation to high volume land flows, as between Canada and the USA (in both directions), from the USA to Mexico and from Hong Kong to China.

Therefore, in view of these potential constraints, Edwards (1991) advocates that researchers should compile a range of data from different sources which will not only highlight the deficiencies in various sources, but also extend the existing base-line data. Although Edwards (1991) provides guidelines for comparative tourism research using a range of data for different countries (also see Dann 1993 for the limitations of using different tourism indicators such as nationality), trends in tourism data remain one of the main requirements for travel industry organisations. Edwards (1991: 73) lists key issues to consider in examining tourism trends (i.e. Have arrivals or accommodation data been changed in coverage or definition? Have provisional data for earlier years been subsequently revised? Has the reliability of the data changed and how are changing tastes in travel products affecting the statistics?). Even so, the analysis of trends remains the fundamental starting point for most research studies in tourism. Having considered the issues associated with how tourism statistics are generated, attention now turns to the ways in which geographers analyse such statistics, and variations in tourism activity at different scales.

PATTERNS OF TOURISM: INTERNATIONAL PERSPECTIVES

D.G. Pearce's (1995) seminal study on the geographer's analysis of tourism patterns offers an excellent synthesis reflecting his international contribution to the methodological development of spatial analysis of tourism. By using geographical methodologies and concepts, D.G. Pearce (1995) uses statistical sources and primary data on tourist activity patterns to analyse the processes and patterns associated with the dynamics of domestic and international tourist activity. This section can only provide a limited evaluation of the geographer's approach to analysis of the presentation of spatially oriented insights on modern day tourism demand (for more detail consult D.G. Pearce 1995).

GLOBAL PATTERNS OF TOURISM

WTO provides the main source of data for international tourism, collated from a survey of major government agencies responsible for data collection. While most international tourists are expressed as 'frontier arrivals' (i.e. arrivals determined by means of a frontier check), the use of arrival/departure cards (where used) offers additional detail to the profile of international tourists, and where they are not used periodic tourism surveys are often used. WTO statistics are mainly confined to all categories of travellers, and in some cases geographical disaggregation of the data may be limited by the collecting agency's use of descriptions and categories for aid of simplicity (e.g. rest of the world) rather than listing all categories of arrivals.

In terms of the growth of international travel, Table 2.13 documents the expansion of outbound travel with constant growth in the 1960s in an age of discovery of outbound travel for many developed nations. The late 1960s saw international travel expanded by new technology in air travel (e.g. the introduction of the Boeing 747 jumbo jet and the 737 as well as the DC10) which led to rapid growth until the oil crisis in the early 1970s. Growth rates have varied in the 1980s, with 'shock waves' to the upward trend being caused by events such as the Gulf Crisis, but international travel has maintained strong growth rates, often in excess of 5 per cent per annum. In contrast, international receipts from travel have outperformed arrivals, with consistent rates of growth (with the exception of the oil crisis and Gulf Crisis) of 10–20 per cent which is indicative of the powerful economic effect of tourism for countries. Table 2.14 outlines the top tourism destinations for 1980 and 1994, where the ranking of France has remained prominent throughout the fourteen year period with certain developing nations such as China recording major growth and with the exception of the USA and China, Europe still dominates the pattern of arrivals by country with comparatively little change in the

Table 2.13: International tourist arrivals and tourist receipts 1950–95

Years	Arrivals of tourists from abroad (day visitors excluded)		Receipts from international tourism (international transport excluded)	
	Total (Thousands)	% change over previous year	Total (US$Million)	% change over previous year
1950	25,282	–	2,100	–
1960	69,320	10.61	6,867	12.58
1961	75,323	8.66	7,284	6.07
1962	81,381	8.04	8,029	10.23
1963	90,071	10.68	8,887	19.65
1964	104,601	16.13	10,073	13.35
1965	112,863	7.90	11,604	15.20
1966	119,980	6.31	13,340	14.96
1967	129,782	8.17	14,458	8.38
1968	131,201	1.09	14,990	3.68
1969	143,511	9.38	16,800	12.07
1970	165,787	15.52	17,900	6.55
1971	178,853	7.88	20,850	16.48
1972	189,129	5.75	24,621	18.09
1973	198,906	5.17	31,054	26.13
1974	205,667	3.40	33,822	8.91
1975	222,290	8.08	40,702	20.34
1976	228,873	2.96	44,436	9.17
1977	249,264	8.91	55,637	25.21
1978	267,076	7.15	68,845	23.74
1979	283,089	6.00	83,340	21.05
1980	286,249	1.12	105,198	26.23
1981	288,616	0.83	107,432	2.12
1982	288,586	–0.01	100,873	–6.11
1983	291,854	1.13	102,448	1.56
1984	319,052	9.32	112,467	9.78
1985	329,538	3.29	117,374	4.36
1986	340,549	3.34	142,067	21.04
1987	366,858	7.73	174,232	22.64
1988	401,710	9.50	201,540	15.67
1989	430,933	7.27	218,369	8.35
1990	459,212	6.56	264,714	21.22
1991	465,844	1.44	271,880	2.71
1992	503,258	8.03	308,745	13.56
1993	517,607	2.85	314,249	1.78
1994	545,878	5.46	345,540	9.96
1995	561,027	2.78	380,693	10.17

Source: World Tourism Organisation (WTO) (1996)

Table 2.14: The world's top twenty tourism destinations in 1980 and 1994

Country	Tourist arrivals (thousands) 1980	Rank 1980	Tourist arrivals (thousands) 1994	Rank 1994	Average annual growth Rate (%) 1980/94	% share of arrivals worldwide 1980	1994
France	30,100	1	61,312	1	5.21	10.52	11.23
United States	22,500	3	45,504	2	5.16	7.86	8.34
Spain	23,403	2	43,232	3	4.48	8.18	7.92
Italy	22,087	4	27,480	4	1.57	7.72	5.03
Hungary	9,413	10	21,425	5	6.05	3.29	
China	3,500	19	21,070	6	13.68	1.22	3.86
United Kingdom	12,420	7	21,034	7	3.83	4.34	3.85
Poland	5,664	13	18,800	8	8.95	1.98	3.44
Austria	13,879	5	17,984	9	1.83	4.85	3.28
Mexico	11,945	8	17,182	10	2.63	4.17	3.15
Czech Republic	–	–	17,000	11	–	–	3.11
Canada	12,876	6	15,971	12	1.55	4.50	2.93
Germany	11,122	9	14,494	13	1.91	3.89	2.66
Switzerland	8,873	11	12,200	14	2.30	3.10	2.23
Greece	4,796	17	10,713	15	5.91	1.68	1.96
Hong Kong	1,748	27	9,331	16	12.71	0.61	1.71
Portugal	2,730	22	9,132	17	9.01	0.74	1.32
Malaysia	2,105	25	7,197	18	9.18	0.74	1.32
Singapore	2,562	23	6,268	19	6.60	0.90	1.15
Netherlands	2,784	21	6,178	20	5.86	0.97	1.13

Source: World Tourism Organisation (1996)

ranking of the first seven destinations. However, China is the notable success story in terms of growth in receipts while a number of European destinations (e.g. Netherlands and Belgium) have retained the volume of arrivals but their ranking of expenditure has dropped.

As the world's largest tourism markets by expenditure, the USA and Germany have retained their prominence in the top two rankings for 1980 and 1994 whereas Japan has increased its importance as an outbound high spending market as had a number of other Pacific Rim nations such as Taiwan, Singapore and South Korea. As a result of the growth of major outbound growth and travel within the Pacific Rim region, a case study of the outbound South Korean market is now examined.

CASE STUDY: Tourism demand in East Asia Pacific – the case of the South Korean outbound market and activity patterns in New Zealand (Kyung-Sik Woo and Stephen Page)

Prior to the Asian financial crisis, Korea represented one of the major outbound markets in the Asia-Pacific region (McGahey 1996; Hall 1997). Outbound travel grew from 484,000 in 1985 to 752,000 in 1988 to 3.1 million in 1994, which quadrupled in a six year period up to 1994 (Table 2.15). By 1995, outbound travel reached 3.8 million, representing 9 per cent of the national population of 45 million. Within New Zealand, inbound Korean arrivals increased consistently between 1989 and 1995 as the fastest growing market and remained the focus of industry attention until the Asian financial crisis (New Zealand Tourism Board 1995), despite any substantive and detailed research to consider the needs, aspirations and impact of this market in New Zealand.

Holiday travel has remained a major reason to visit, while females outnumbered males in holiday travel by 54.4 per cent:45.66 per cent in 1994 and VFR by 63.5 per cent:36.5 per cent, housewives comprising the majority of outbound female visitors. Male visitors dominated in the purpose of visiting in relation to business travel (91 per cent), to attend a convention (87.7 per cent) and official travel (91.3 per cent). The age profile of the most common outbound Korean tourist was the 31–40 age group followed by the 21–30 age group, with a significant proportion of 'honeymooners' and unmarried women office workers. According to the 1994 National Overseas Travel Survey (McGahey 1996), shopping was a major leisure activity for Korean tourists, with an average spend of US$413 per person on purchases such as cosmetics, alcoholic beverages, electronic goods, clothing and toys. McGahey (1996) observed that 40 per cent of these purchases were as gifts.

The Korean inbound market in New Zealand

According to New Zealand's International Visitor Survey (New Zealand Tourism Board 1995), the Korean market was estimated to have generated NZ$225 million of spending at 1995 prices. This equated to an average spend per person of approximately NZ$345 a day, the highest amount for any inbound market. In the 12 months ended March 1996, Koreans comprised 8 per cent of New Zealand's international visitor market, increasing from 2,018 in 1987 to 4,184 visitors in 1990 to 5,830 in 1994. The significance of this market was reflected in the New Zealand Tourism Board's (1995) optimistic forecasts for a further doubling of visitor arrivals over the next five years and a target of 114,000 arrivals. However, the size of the impact of the Asian financial crisis on Korea can be illustrated by the 78 per cent drop in Korean visitors to New Zealand in December 1997 compared with the previous year, with there being an expected 75 per cent drop in arrivals from South Korea in 1998 over the previous year (Coventry 1998).

In contrast to the age profile of the entire Korean tourist outbound market, the main age group of visitors to New Zealand was dominated by the visitors aged 45–64 years, predominantly those aged 55–64 (New Zealand Tourism Board 1995). Yet among those visitors aged under 24 years, females outnumber males as unmarried women office workers or female tertiary level students who are more likely to travel than their male counterparts, since the former enjoy relatively more leisure time.

Since group travel tends to predominate among the inbound Korean market the length of stay in New Zealand was conditioned by two key factors. First, it is a medium long-haul

T

y purpose of trip, 1985–94

1987	*1988*	*1989*	*1990*	*1991*	*1992*	*1993*	*1994*
510.5	752.2	1,213.1	1,563.9	1,856.0	2,043.3	2,419.9	3,154.3
2.5	18.5	37.0	37.8	35.1	35.4	35.0	41.0
32.3	31.2	25.9	25.7	26.3	25.7	26.4	24.9
9.1	8.6	10.2	13.0	17.2	18.3	16.0	13.6
1.2	1.1	1.0	0.8	0.9	0.9	0.7	0.8
2.1	1.9	1.2	1.1	1.1	1.2	1.0	0.9
52.8	38.7	24.8	21.6	19.4	18.6	20.8	19.0

.orean holiday entitle-
ment ... ss than 10 paid days a year and is not available in one block. Therefore, the maximum length of stay for most outbound Korean tourists is less than one week. According to research (New Zealand Tourism Board 1995), Korean tourists perceived the main appeal of visiting New Zealand as its unspoiled natural phenomena such as the hot springs in Rotorua and volcanic areas like Mount Tongariro (Figure 2.10). This reflects the limited spatial activity patterns which most inbound Korean tourists were likely to experience, typically including arrival and departure through Auckland International Airport, with time spent in Auckland, Rotorua, Waitomo Caves, Taupo and returning to Auckland (Figure 2.10). The following results report the findings of a survey (Kyung-Sik Woo 1996) to understand the inter-relationship between the time constraints of Korean inbound travel and the spatial distribution of such visitors beyond the limited knowledge base derived from the 442 Korean tourists included in the New Zealand International Visitor Survey 1995/1996.

KOREAN TOURISTS' ACTIVITY PATTERNS IN NEW ZEALAND IN 1996

Methodological issues

Using a time-budget methodology, a survey in July 1996 was used to produce a systematic record of a person's use of time over a given period to hereby understand the sequence, timing and duration of the tourists' activities in relation to the location of the activities. The technique provides a systematic record of a person's use of time over a given period, typically for a short period ranging from a single day to a week (Pearce 1988a; Debbage 1991). One of the fundamental assumptions in using this research method is that tourist behaviour and activities are the result of choices, a point illustrated by Floor (1990). Pearce (1988a) argues that there has been a comparative neglect of tourist activities by tourism researchers, compounded by the lack of available data. Where questionnaire surveys have addressed such issues, the results have often failed to provide a comprehensive assessment of tourist activities, both formal/informal and the relative importance of each.

Thrift (1977) provides an assessment of three principal constraints on tourists' daily activity patterns which are:

- *comparability constraints* (e.g. the biologically based need for food and sleep);
- *coupling constraints* (e.g. people need to interact and undertake activities with other people);
- *authority constraints* (e.g. where activities are controlled, not allowed or permitted at a certain time).

Thus both Chapin (1974) and Thrift (1977) identify choices and constraints which will influence the specific activities and context of tourist daily activities. The use of time-budgets via diaries to record tourists' activity patterns has been used in a number of contexts as research by Gaviria (1975), Cooper (1981), P. Pearce (1981), Pearce (1986) and Debbage (1991) indicates (also see the section in this chapter on its use in recreational research). Methodological issues raised by these studies highlight the problem of selecting appropriate temporal measures to record tourists' activities. P. Pearce (1981) used three main time periods (morning, afternoon and evening) with Gaviria (1975) selecting quarter-hour periods and Cooper (1981) using five time sequences. While the recording of activities by time is a demanding activity for tourists, Pearce (1986) argues that the main methodological concerns for such surveys are: the type of technique to be used; the period to be covered; and the type of sample selected. In addition, Chapin (1974) argues that such studies can choose to use three main survey techniques which are:

- *a check list technique*, where respondents select the list of activities they engage in from a pre-categorised list;
- *the yesterday technique*, where subjects are asked to list things they did the previous day, where and when they did them; and
- *the tomorrow technique*, where the participant keeps a diary on what they will do, where and when they will undertake them.

Although time-budget studies may still be viewed as experimental in tourism research, they do offer great potential to gain a detailed insight into tourist activity patterns.

The survey

During three weeks in July 1996, a time-budget survey was developed using the 'yesterday technique' and the time sequencing technique advocated by P. Pearce (1981) as part of a more detailed survey of inbound Korean tourists. The complete survey was designed to be completed by Korean tourists during their tour of the North Island of New Zealand and four sites were selected as distribution points for the surveys during the tourists' initial familiarisation point of their tour in Auckland and Rotorua. Two major hotels and two Korean restaurants were selected to provide a degree of close contract with Korean tourists in a familiar environment. Due to the highly organised nature of the Korean itineraries, a one-page diary was distributed at the key sites over a three week period. One immediate problem facing the use of the budget approach, was in soliciting responses. While a Korean researcher approached the respondents on a random basis, it was essential to keep the survey to one A4 page to encourage participation. As a result, only time-budgeted questions could be included and key demographic data was omitted. (A separate survey by the authors was undertaken examining demand issues among Korean tourists which did consider the profile of visitors.) However, from participant observation conducted during the data collection, it is apparent that the sample of 78 tourists who were prepared to participate in the time-budget exercise were typical of the Korean tourist then visiting New Zealand, being largely aged 31–50, being of middle class status, earning between

NZ$40,000 and $60,000 a year and undertaking a multi-destination tour.

Activity patterns of Korean tourists in Auckland and Rotorua

According to D.G. Pearce (1995a) few data are collected to examine circuit tourism, which this market is following, since it follows a predetermined circuit pattern. Data exist in a New Zealand context (e.g. Oppermann 1993, 1994) on the touring patterns of international tourists which builds on Forer and Pearce's (1984) innovative study of coach tours by nights spent at key nodes and inter-regional flows. Forer and Pearce (1984) established the Auckland to Rotorua and Taupo axis by examining tour group itineraries for package tours. While it is apparent that a great deal of continuity and similarity exists in terms of the Korean tour group itineraries which follow a series of linear routes, activity patterns of the tour groups and their specific time-budgets remain largely unresearched.

One immediate feature which emerges from the 78 completed schedules is that the activity patterns of the visitors closely follow the tour itineraries. The respondents were undertaking three commonly used itineraries developed by tour companies which comprised (see Figure 2.11):

- Itinerary 1: Auckland to Rotorua and return to Rotorua (12 tourists);
- Itinerary 2: Auckland to Rotorua and Waitomo Caves and return to Auckland (39 tourists); and
- Itinerary 3: Auckland to Rotorua and Waitomo Caves to Taupo and return to Auckland (27 tourists).

Both itinerary 1 and 2 record only a limited amount of free time, being the shortest tour schedules among inbound visitors to New Zealand. The typical itinerary commences at 0700 and finishes at 1800–1900 hours, with sightseeing comprising the major activity (30 per cent), undertaken over two nights and three days. During the 53–59 hour period, respondents spent their time:

- sleeping (33 per cent)
- touring (30 per cent)
- free time (14 per cent)
- transfers (12 per cent)
- eating/meals (11 per cent).

On the basis of these results, three types of Korean tourists could be identified based on time-budget research by Ashworth and Dietvorst (1995):

- *Organised sightseeing oriented visitors*, who comprise the large majority of visitors, with a city tour in a chartered coach during the day, interspersed with shopping before or after meals and a limited amount of free time spent walking around attractions and taking photographs. Evenings were spent at the accommodation base to rest after the day's activities.
- *Shopping and conviviality oriented tourists*, where shopping activities were conducted near to the accommodation base in the morning. The age profile of this group was younger (typically under 40 years of age), in search of specialist markets, tourist attractions and not venturing far from the accommodation base. In the evening, this group spent their leisure time at a wide variety of fun-related facilities (e.g. at a pub, gambling at the Casino in Auckland or at a nightclub). In Rotorua, this group spent most of their free time at Korean pubs in the central tourist district.
- *Health and sports oriented tourists*, comprising the majority of the senior group (aged 50 plus years) and a number of business travellers who pursued largely 'private leisure' activities. Whilst no 'typical' activity patterns could be discerned during the day,

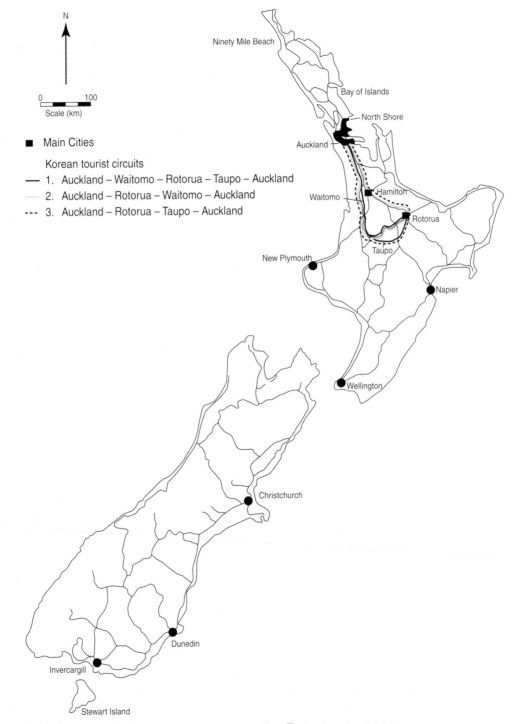

Figure 2.11: Korean tourists' urban activity patterns in New Zealand as circuit tours

with some preferring walking or going shopping, the time spent on these activities was much less than the two former groups. In the afternoon, sports activities dominated (e.g. golf and fishing) and in the early evening they frequented health facilities followed by relaxation for the remaining part of the evening.

Whilst the results from the Korean case study indicate that removal of travel restrictions in 1989 have significantly increased outbound travel, there were significant 'pull' factors promoting Korean travel to New Zealand (e.g. immigration policy, no-visas agreement, new air services and 15,000 Korean residents living in Auckland promoting VFR traffic) which can be related to the motivational literature and the unique attractions available in New Zealand. The analysis of tourist activity patterns shows that in urban areas, Korean visitors do not venture far from their accommodation base. This limits the flow and distribution of visitors, with a tendency for bunching and concentration at key nodes around Auckland, Rotorua and Taupo. Concerns over a saturation of tourists at key attraction sites accentuates the problem of managing the geographical patterns of this short and concentrated experience of New Zealand tourism. Many attractions are unable to cope with the arrival of large numbers of tour groups simultaneously, as this highly organised and almost regimented form of tourism is posing significant strains on the visiting infrastructure. In this respect, a spatial analysis of activity patterns and time-budgets illustrates not only the shape of existing demand, determined by tour operators and group leaders, but also the geographical interaction and time constraints under which these tourists visit New Zealand. This has clear implications for the type of tourism experience they require.

PATTERNS OF DOMESTIC TOURISM

According to WTO, domestic tourism is estimated to be up to ten times greater in volume than international tourism and yet comparatively little research has been undertaken on this neglected area of tourism activity. D.G. Pearce (1995: 67) argues that this may be attributed 'to the less visible nature of much domestic tourism, which is often more informal and less structured than international tourism, and a consequent tendency by many government agencies, researchers and others to regard it as less significant'. This problem of neglect is compounded by a paucity of data, since it is not a straightforward matter of recording arrivals and departures. It requires an analysis of tourism patterns and flows at different spatial scales, to consider spatial interaction of tourists between a multitude of possible origin and destination areas within a country as well as a detailed understanding of inter-regional flows.

Where government agencies and other public sector organisations undertake data collection of domestic tourism 'the results are not often directly comparable, limiting the identification of general patterns and trends' (D.G. Pearce 1995: 67). For this reason, the innovative research undertaken by D.G. Pearce (1993b) is worthy of attention here since it comprises one of the few systematic analysis of domestic tourism in a country, which in this case is New Zealand.

As D.G. Pearce (1995: 67) rightly acknowledges 'there are still few examples of comprehensive inter-regional studies where the analysis is based on a complete matrix of both original and destination regions . . . [since] few appropriate and reliable sets of tourism statistics exist which might be used to construct such a matrix'. Nationwide surveys are undertaken which are weighted to reflect the population base. One of the few comprehensive studies which yields an origin–destination matrix is the somewhat dated New Zealand Domestic Travel

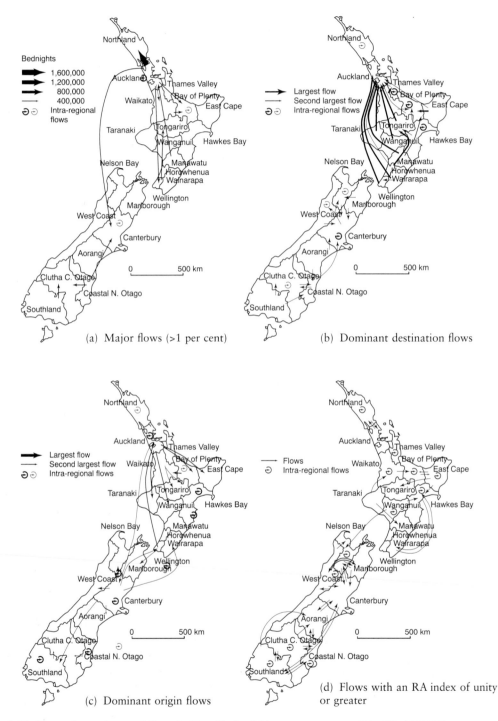

Figure 2.12: Domestic tourist travel flows in New Zealand (three years average 1987/88–1989/90)
Source: Pearce (1995a) and NZTB (1991b)

Survey (NZDTS), established in 1983 (New Zealand Tourism Board 1991a). Although this study is currently being updated to incorporate results of a 1996 survey, the only available statistics are those analysed by Pearce (1993b) which still outline the basic principles and patterns inherent in this national tourism data set, since the NZDTS has not been updated since 1989/90.

THE NEW ZEALAND DOMESTIC TOURISM SURVEY

This is a national omnibus survey, based on a stratified national sample taken over 47 weeks of the year. The survey seeks information on the travel habits of the participants in the four weeks preceding the survey, with a domestic tourist trip defined as 'a journey outside a person's home locality ... which involved a minimum of one night away from home' (NZTB 1991b). In the 1989 survey, some 12,354 people aged 15 years or more were interviewed, of whom 28 per cent had completed a trip prior to the interview. The data are weighted to reflect the total domestic population, with results presented at a regional level.

By calculating net flows from the origin–destination matrix for each region, it is possible to calculate those regions with significant destinations where the number of nights spent in the region exceed those spent by that region's residents elsewhere (net positive flow). In contrast, where a net flow occurs, those regions may be viewed as major generating regions. As Figure 2.12(a) indicates, using domestic bednights spent in each region, the net balance (positive or negative) identifies a number of key characteristics:

- The five leading regions (Auckland, Wellington, Canterbury, Bay of Plenty and Waikato) accounted for 53 per cent of bednights.
- Auckland generated 8.5 million bednights, almost 20 per cent of the total.
- The five regions with the least bednights accounted for only 6.5 per cent of the total.

The patterns of demand in part reflect the population base (i.e. Auckland contained 27.3 per cent of the country's population) although Auckland only generated 19.8 per cent of bednights, and received only 14 per cent of bednights. In terms of net flows, some 11 regions have positive balances (i.e. are destinations) though this varies by region. Figure 2.12(b) also shows that a north to north-east pattern of destinations exists on the North Island (Northland to East Cape), with the central North Island area (Tongariro National Park and Lake Taupo) emerging prominently. On the South Island, Clutha Central Otago (containing Queenstown and Lakes District) has the largest positive balance.

To complement the patterns of demand, D.G. Pearce (1993b) also provided a detailed analysis of the domestic tourism flows based on the origin–destination matrix by region. Figure 2.12(a) examines the twenty largest tourism flows (i.e. flows which account for more than 1 per cent of the national total). In contrast, Figure 2.12(b) identifies the dominant destination flows while Figure 2.12(c) illustrates the dominant origin flows. Some seven of the twenty dominant flows originate from Auckland while three other flows are focused on the Auckland region. Inter-regional flows also appear to be significant in Auckland, Bay of Plenty; Canterbury and Northland reflecting the physical area and distances involved as well as the available resources. The top 20 flows account for 33 per cent of national tourism demand, indicating a major diversity in domestic travel patterns. Figures 2.12(c) and 2.12(d) indicate the extent of travel between neighbouring regions and inter-regional travel and the dominance of the major urban areas as generators of demand although inter-island flows are relatively weak. To examine the magnitude of the flows against a predicted value, D.G. Pearce (1993b) employed the Relative Acceptance (RA) index, to examine the relative success of a region in attracting tourists from a generating region.

Using the formula

$$RA_{ij} = \frac{A_{ij} - E_{ij}}{E_{ij}}$$

Where RA_{ij} is the relative acceptance from origin $_i$ to destination $_j$.

A_{ij} is the actual flow from origin $_i$ to destination $_j$.

E_{ij} is the expected flow from $_i$ and $_j$.

Calculating E_{ij} makes the assumption that origin destination independence or indifference which holds that the flow from $_i$ to $_j$ reflects the total flow to $_j$. It is obtained by the formula:

$$E_{ij} = \frac{N_i \, N_j}{N}$$

Where N_i is the observed number of visitors from region $_i$ in the country as a whole.

N_j is the observed number of visitors in region $_j$.

N is the total number of visitors in the country as a whole.

Source: D.G. Pearce (1993b)

As a result, 'as Auckland received 14 per cent of all domestic bednights, the model predicts that it should receive 14 per cent of the bednights from each of New Zealand's 22 regions . . . [and] this technique has the advantage of eliminating the effects of absolute size and enables the identification of unusually high or low flows. The RA index has a range from −1 to plus infinity, with positive values indicating a greater than expected flow and negative values the reverse' (D.G. Pearce 1995a: 72).

What Figure 2.12(d) shows is that distance rather than population size is a major factor shaping larger than expected flows. With the exception of Auckland, Canterbury and Wellington and some North Island regions adjacent to the major centres, strong intra-regional flows exist. There are also a number of clusters of flows between regions in the upper and lower half of the South Island as well as in the central North Island.

It is evident from the existing research on domestic tourism that patterns may prove complex to disaggregate and a range of innovative methodologies and statistical techniques may need to be applied if the complexities are to be understood. Not only does the NZDTS indicate that the domestic market contains a variety of flows and activity patterns among the population in both time and space, but it also illustrates the geographers' valuable contribution in trying to understand the impact on the national tourism system so that regions and local areas can appreciate what planning and management techniques they may need to employ.

CONCLUSIONS

The analysis of behavioural issues in recreational and tourism research indicates that 'in behavioural terms then, there seems little necessity to insist on a major distinction between tourism and leisure phenomena. Therefore, it should follow that a greater commonality between the research efforts in the two areas would be of advantage' (Moore *et al.* 1995: 75) although different social theoretical approaches exist towards the analysis of recreation and tourism phenomena. As a result, Moore *et al.* (1995: 79) conclude that 'there is little need, if any, to take a dramatically different approach to the behavioural analysis of tourism and leisure'. One needs to view each activity in the context of the everyday life of the people involved to understand how each is conceived. There is a clear distinction within the literature between what motivates recreationalists and tourists, and comparative studies of similar groups of people and the similarities and differences between these motivations has yet to permeate the research literature. While geographers have focused on recreational and tourist behaviour in relation to demand issues, the analysis has largely been quantitative, site specific and has not adapted a comparative methodology to examine the recreation–tourism continuum.

3

THE SUPPLY OF RECREATION AND TOURISM

Within the literature on recreation and tourism, there is a paucity of conceptual and theoretical research on the supply component of these activities (Sinclair and Stabler 1992). The geographer has traditionally approached the supply of recreation and tourism from a somewhat traditional spatial analysis perspective reflecting the tendency to apply concepts and models from economic geography and to a lesser degree from cognate areas of geography where the underlying concern has been with location and the spatial distribution of recreational and tourism resources which shape the activity patterns and spectrum of opportunity for leisure pursuits.

THE SUPPLY FACTOR IN RECREATION

According to Kreutzwiser (1989: 21) 'supply refers to the recreational resources, both natural and man-made, which provide opportunities for recreation. It is a complex concept influenced by numerous factors and subject to changing interpretations. It is also a concept which has prompted much thought in terms of classification and evaluation' particularly among geographers. Yet Coppock and Duffield (1975: 151) pursue this theme a stage further in a spatial context arguing that it is the 'spatial interaction between the homes of recreationalists and the resources they use [which] has emerged as a key factor in the

demand/supply model' arguing for an integrated analysis of such interactions to explain how the activity patterns of recreationalists in terms of their origins and destinations affects the supply variable in terms of where they go, what they do there and how this affects the resource base. For this reason, this section commences with a discussion of the underlying approach used to describe and document the supply of recreational opportunities by geographers which is followed by an analysis of the spatial interaction of demand and supply to illustrate how the two components are inter-related. This is developed in relation to the three characteristics that geographers have synthesised to analyse recreational activities, namely:

- the locational characteristics associated with the supply of different forms of recreational resource;
- the patterns of demand and usage; and
- the spatial interactions which occur between the demand for and supply of the recreational resource, emphasising journey patterns and the patterns of usage of specific resources. This gives rise to concentrated, dispersed and combinations of each pattern at the site of the resources which therefore raises questions as to how to evaluate the capacity of such resources to accommodate users and to reconcile conflicts in use and the identification of management and planning issues.

HOW HAS THE GEOGRAPHER APPROACHED THE ANALYSIS OF RECREATIONAL SUPPLY ISSUES?

The geographer's approach is epitomised in many of the classic recreational texts (e.g. Patmore 1970; Lavery 1971; Simmons 1974; Pigram 1983) where the supply perspective is largely dependent upon the evaluation and assessment of resources for recreation. The concept of a resource can often be taken to include those tangible objects in nature which are of an economic value and used for productive purposes. But when looking at leisure and recreation, natural resources have an important bearing, particularly those such as water bodies, countryside and open space. The fact that resources have a physical form (i.e. coal and iron ore) does not actually mean they constitute a resource. Such elements only become a resource when society's subjective evaluation of their potential leads to their recognition as a resource to satisfy human wants and needs (O'Riordan 1971).

Yet a resource is far from just a passive element – it has to be used creatively to meet certain socially valued goals. Thus recreational resources are 'an element of the natural or man-modified environment which provides an opportunity to satisfy recreational wants. Implicit is a continuum ranging from biophysical resources to man-made facilities' (Kreutzwiser 1989: 22). However, according to Glyptis (1989: 135), to 'couple recreational with resources complicates definitions . . . In a recreational context resources are the natural resources of land, water and landscape, together with man-made resources including sport centres, swimming pools, parks and playing fields' though she also notes that few recreational activities make use of resources solely designed or in existence for recreational purposes.

Recreation in rural contexts (chapter 6) often occurs alongside agriculture, forestry and water supply functions (Goodall and Whittow 1975). In this respect, the identification of recreational resources needs to recognise the management implications of multiple use. While Glyptis (1989) also outlined the needs of many forms of recreation which have few land needs, this analysis is concerned with recreational forms that have a land use component given the geographers interest in how human activities and phenomenon are interrelated and occur on the earth's surface. Yet even Glyptis' (1989) review pays little explicit attention to the resource base – the supply dimension – beyond highlighting Patmore's (1983)

> perspective [which] is specifically geographical, but with full recognition of the interplay of social, economic and political factors, and with a wealth of data . . . The bulk of the text concerns [sic] contemporary patterns of recreational activity and the demands they place on the land and water resources, with myriad references to management issues and solutions.
>
> (Glyptis 1989: 137)

But this still does not illuminate the approaches, concepts and specific skills the geographer brings to the analysis of recreational supply issues.

The wanton absence of such studies within the published literature and the tendency for writers to step sideways and develop simplistic descriptions of recreational resources confirms two of the weaknesses which S. L. Smith (1983a: 184) argued confronted the study of recreation: 'recreational geography is still at the stage of naive phenomenology and induction in the 1980s'. What this statement means is that as researchers discover more recreational phenomena, they classify it and develop specialist areas of study, where external pressures (e.g. government and business funding of research) combine to generate a situation of naive induction. Naive induction is where the use of relatively unsophisticated concepts are used to study the subject, even though complex analytical techniques may be employed (e.g. multiple regression and factor analysis) to understand recreational phenomena. This is particularly the case in terms of the supply function of recreation. A lack of theoretically derived research has meant that the geographer has failed to develop this area beyond the use of simple spatial analytical tools. Thus the underlying theoretical framework remains inadequate despite the limited degree of theoretically informed research (e.g. Perkins 1993) and novel attempts to integrate the leisure and tourism functions within an urban context using constructs related to power and political decision making (Doorne 1998). The assessment by Smith (1983a) remains an important debating point in recreational geography, particularly in relation to supply issues. For this reason, Smith's (1983a) synthesis of the field remains one of the only comprehensive surveys of the research geographers have undertaken on recreation. For this reason, it is worthy of discussion, not necessarily because it is the most up-to-date study of recreational geography but because it illustrates the variety of approaches geographers have developed. Smith (1989: 304) listed the principal research questions geographers pose which outline the particular concerns for supply issues:

- Where are the resources? What is their quality and capacity? What effect will use of those resources have on the resource base and the local environment? What will the effect be on other people who live in the area and on other users?
- How easy is it for people to travel to the resource or facility? What are their travel costs? Are there other constraints, such as problems of physical accessibility, inconvenient scheduling, excessive admission fees, and racial, linguistic, and social barriers?
- What new facilities or resources need to be supplied? What areas have priority for the new supply? Who should pay to support those who play? How many people are expected to use a new facility at a given location?
- What are the regional differences in recreation preferences? Why do these exist? Do they represent differences in tastes, culture, or historical inequalities?

According to Smith (1983a), geographers have approached the analysis of recreational geography in a number of ways, including:

- descriptive research on location;
- descriptive research on travel;
- explanatory research on location;
- explanatory research on travel;
- predictive research on location;
- predictive research on travel;
- normative research on location; and
- normative research on travel.

For this reason, each of the types of research are briefly discussed to emphasise the geographer's contribution to supply research where relevant. Due to the constraints of space, the principal themes discussed here are: descriptive research on location and travel, explanatory research on location and travel and normative research on location. More detail on other aspects of the research developed in this context can be found in Smith (1983a).

DESCRIPTIVE RESEARCH ON LOCATION AND TRAVEL

Smith (1983a: 1) argued that the 'description of location is the study of differences' which can be classified in terms of description of facility of recreational resource location, where the distribution of resources pertinent to the specific activity can be enumerated and mapped. Within this context the inventories of recreational resources has attracted a great deal of attention, which arguably underpins much of the preliminary research undertaken to establish recreational supply features in quantity and quality. Resource inventories (e.g. the Outdoor Recreation Resources Review Commission, Chubb and Chubb 1981; also see chapter 7) typifies this approach, whereby the quantity and number of designated public recreation areas were tabulated and mapped by area along US coastlines. A more complex method is to develop a typology of resource types and uses such as Clawson and Knetsch's (1968) widely cited model of recreational resources which can be classified as: urban and rural resource-based, intermediate and user-orientated. Additional variables which might be added to such classifications include: man-modified and natural resources; formal and informal; intensive and extensive; fragile and resistant; while public and private ownership may also be included (Wall 1989). *The Canada Land Inventory* (Canada, Department of Regional Economic Expansion 1972) is a useful example of one such inventory that set out to provide an overview of 'the quality, quantity, and distribution of natural recreation resources within the settled points of Canada; to indicate comparative levels of recreation capability for non-urban lands based upon present preferences; to indicate the types of recreation and land use. The classification is illustrated in Table 3.1. While there are criticisms of this approach related to the

consistency of data collection and interpretation, it provides a valuable synthesis on the potential of Canadian land resources to support recreational activity. Smith (1983a) also explores more advanced methods used to classify recreational resources, including deglomerative methods (where resources are sub-divided into distinct groups) and agglomerative methods (where resource types are grouped into general categories). An interesting example of a deglomerative study is Filoppovich's (1979) assessment of recreational development around Moscow. In contrast, Dubaniewicz's (1976) examination of the Lodz Voivodiship in Poland explored aggregate patterns of recreational development, having located, mapped and defined biotic and abiotic resources and human resource patterns at a regional level. Deglomerative studies remain more widely used than the latter. Yet such methods of analyses pay less attention to the importance of human (i.e. subjective) evaluations

Table 3.1: The land use classes of the Canada land inventory

Classes		
1	Very high capability	These lands have natural capability to engender very high total annual use of one or more intensive activities. These lands should be able to generate and sustain a level of use comparable to that evident at an outstanding and large bathing beach or a nationally known ski slope.
2	High capability	These lands have natural capability to engender and sustain high total annual use based on one or more intensive activity.
3	Moderately high capability	These lands have a natural ability to engender and sustain moderately high total annual use based on moderate to intensive or intensive activities.
4	Moderate capability	These lands have natural capability to engender and sustain moderate total annual use based on dispersed activities.
5	Moderately low capability	These lands have natural capability to engender and sustain moderately low total annual use based on dispersed activities.
6	Low capability	These lands lack the natural quality and significant features to rate higher, but have the natural capability to engender and sustain low total annual use based on dispersed activities.
7	Very low capability	These lands have practically no capability for any popular type of recreation activity, but there may be some opportunity for very specialised activities with recreation aspects, or they may simply provide open space.

Table 3.2: Linton's landscape evaluation scale

Landforms	Points	Land uses	Points
Mountains	8	Wild landscapes	6
Bold hills	6	Richly varied farming	5
Hill country	5	Varied forest with moors and farms	4
Plateau uplands	3	Moors	3
Low uplands	2	Treeless farms	1
Lowlands	0	Continuous forest	−2
		Urban and industrial land	−5

Source: Linton (1968)

of resources for recreation (e.g. Coppock and Duffield's 1975 assessment of recreational potential in the countryside).

One of the notable debates in resource studies for recreation in the late 1960s and early 1970s related to preferential descriptions of recreational resources, namely aesthetic studies which measure human preferences and how they respond to landscape alterations. Fines (1968) influential study in East Sussex epitomises this approach, where a group of people with a background in design work were asked to assign a value to a series of landscape photographs compared to a reference photograph with an indifferent landscape. Once the landscapes were assessed by individuals, a consensus score was assigned and then the people were asked to rank landscapes viewed around East Sussex. While Linton (1968) disagreed with both the nomenclature and scale used by Fines, he concluded that two key elements existed in the landscape: land use and landforms. These could be mapped and categories established, where a composite score could be devised to reflect the beauty of the landscape (Table 3.2). Linton (1968) developed his study in Scotland and again, controversy was associated with the almost arbitrary use of a points system, where urban areas were seen as low scoring. Yet urban areas remain important for recreation and tourism (chapter 5) and it seems naive to dismiss certain resources in such a generalised manner. While a great deal of debate exists in relation to such approaches to landscape evaluation, it does illustrate the importance of human perception and recognition of what is attractive and valued by different people in relation to recreational time. In terms of descriptive research on travel, it has little immediate relevance to supply unless one is concerned with the impact of demand on the resource base. As a result, the geographer's concern with recreational travel using concepts such as nodes, routes, mode of travel and accessibility of resources for recreationalists has little immediate value.

EXPLANATORY RESEARCH ON LOCATION AND TRAVEL

Moving from purely descriptive to explanatory research illustrates the importance of location as a recreational facility which someone may want to use. Smith (1983a) outlined two concerns regarding the location of such facilities: those factors affecting public and those affecting private location decisions, although the distinction between such issues has blurred where public–private sector involvement, co-operation and management has complicated traditional locational models developed in economic geography, which has separated public and private goods (Hall and Jenkins 1995). For example, Mitchell (1969b) applied central place theory to the location of urban parks as public recreational resources, establishing that a hierarchy existed, but it rather simplified a number of real world issues by substituting assumptions, while also ignoring influential variables such as land prices, availability and political influences (see chapter 5). Other studies (e.g. Mitchell and Lovingwood 1976; Haley 1979) adopted empirical measures to examine correlations between variables which might explain locational patterns, where Haley (1979) observed that present day patterns often reflect the demands of previous generations. Likewise, where new suburban developments did not require developers to provide park facilities, a dearth of parks exist. Likewise, communities in such areas have not sought such provision due to local factors (e.g. private recreation sites and access to the urban fringe). The role of private recreation provision was examined by Mitchell and Lovingwood (1976) and Lovingwood and Mitchell (1978) who mapped 172 public and 112 private recreational facilities, using nearest-neighbour analysis to examine the spatial patterns. They concluded that public facilities had a tendency to cluster while private facilities had a regular pattern of distribution for campgrounds, country clubs and miscellaneous uses, while water based facilities and hunting/fishing clubs tended to cluster. The outcome of their analysis was that:

- public facilities are concentrated in areas of population density to meet the wider good and in accessible locations; having no major resource considerations; and
- private facilities are located on one of two bases: either in or near open space, as in the case of campgrounds and country clubs and are located throughout the region, or conversely, water-based facilities and hunting clubs are closely tied to a land or water location, clustering around the resource.

In contrast, much of the geographical research on private recreational facility development has been based on the approach developed in retail marketing and location studies, where location is seen as the critical success factor, although Bevins *et al.* (1974) observed that this was not necessarily a critical factor for private campgrounds in north-east USA. Within most studies of recreational location, principal concepts related to the threshold population, catchment areas or hinterlands and distance to travel to the facility. As Crompton and Van Doren (1976) observed, tram companies in mid-nineteenth century America built amusement parks at the end of tramlines to attract weekend visitors illustrating the importance of recreational travel as part of the overall experience.

PREDICTIVE RESEARCH ON LOCATION

The geographer's tradition of model building to predict location of characteristics of private enterprise has been applied to recreational geography in terms of the transfer of location theory and site selection methods. Within the research on location theory, transport cost has played a significant role based on Von Thünen's agricultural land use model and Vickerman (1975) simplistically applied the model to predict urban recreation businesses. Yet the use of concepts such as locational interdependence, where the potential buyers are not uniformly distributed in space, means that business may be able to exercise a degree of control over their clients by their location. Such studies based on the early work of economic geographers such as Christaller (1933), Lösch (1944) and Reilly (1931) developed a number of principles which geographers have used to underpin locational modelling recreational research. While subsequent research by Isard (1956) and Greenhut (1956) can be added to the list, S. Smith (1983: 106) summarises the contribution of such studies to the analysis of recreational location choices by business:

1 A firm with relatively low transportation costs and a relatively large market area will have a

greater chance of success than a firm with high transportation costs and a small market area.

2 Some trade-offs are possible between transportation costs, production costs, land rents, and market size.

3 Transportation costs include both the cost of bringing resources to the site of the firm, and the costs of distributing the product to the customer. The relative costs of transporting both resources and products determine, in part, where the firm will locate: high resource transportation costs pull a business close to the resource; high product transportation costs pull a business close to the market.

4 Some types of business seek to locate close to each other; some are indifferent to each other; some are repelled by each other.

5 Different locations will be attractive to different types of businesses. Attractiveness is based on resources; market location; transportation services; availability of capital, labour, and business services; and personal preferences of the decision-maker.

6 Firms in any given industry will tend to divide up the available market by selecting different locations to control different spatial segments of the market.

7 The size of the market and the number and location of competitors tend to limit the size of the potential development.

These need to be examined in relation to the decision making of entrepreneurs and individual firms. In terms of site selection methods, feasibility studies have provided a starting point for geographers seeking to assess the most suitable site from a range of alternatives, with the purpose of maximising profit (or wider social benefits in the public sector) though comparatively little research has been published given the scope of such studies (i.e. sources of capital, management issues, design and development issues, market size, population characteristics, economic profile of the potential market and the suitability of the site) and the tendency for such documents to remain commercially sensitive in both the public and private sector. What is evident from the existing research seeking to predict locational characteristics for recreational activities and facilities is the reliance upon economic geography, particularly retail geography with its concomitant concern for marketing.

NORMATIVE RESEARCH ON LOCATION

Within the public sector, the objectives for locational decision-making are distinctly different (or at least traditionally have been different despite changing political philosophies towards public recreation provision). The characteristics of public sector provision have traditionally been associated with taxes paying for facility provision and its ongoing operation, with a collective use which cannot be withheld, so that access is not knowingly prohibited to anyone. In other words, their contribution to the quality of life and wider social well-being of the population affected underpins public provision which cannot easily be accommodated into conventional locational theory which is market driven. Austin (1974) identifies recreational facilities as 'site preferred' goods, where proximity to their location is often seen as a measure of their use (i.e. its utility function). Thus, maximum distances exist as in the case of urban parks (see chapter 5). The object, therefore, in public facility location for recreation is to balance the 'utility' factor with minimising the distance people have to travel and providing access to as many people as possible; though Cichetti (1971) examined a number of the problems associated with different methods of balancing travel distances, social utility and other approaches to demand maximisation. Smith (1983a) reviews a range of methods of analysis used by geographers to assist in work on public facility. Site selection, namely models, which emphasise: mechanical analogues, comparative needs assessment, demand maximisation, heuristic programming and intuitive modelling (see Smith 1983a: 156–168 for more detail).

SUPPLY AND DEMAND IN RECREATIONAL CONTEXTS: SPATIAL INTERACTIONS

Given the comparative neglect of recreational supply issues by geographers and the overriding emphasis in demand studies and impact assessment (Owens 1984), it is pertinent to acknowledge the geographer's synthesising role in recognising that 'recreationalists and the resources they use are separated in space, [and] the interaction between demand and supply creates patterns of movement, and the distances between origins and destinations influence not only the scale of demand, but also the available supply of resources (Coppock and Duffield 1975: 150). Few studies, with the exception of Coppock and Duffield (1975), acknowledge this essential role the geographer has played in contextualising the real world impact of recreational activities in a spatial framework. While many recreational researchers may view such contributions as passé, they are notable since no other discipline offers such a holistic and integrative assessment of recreation and tourism phenomena. Coppock and Duffield (1975) acknowledge the resource base as a precondition to assessing the 'space needs' of recreationalists in that the amount of land, the activities to be undertaken, length of journey and nature of the resource help to determine the type of interactions which occur. Clawson *et al.*'s (1960) typology (Table 3.3) and its subsequent application to England and Wales (Law 1967) both confirm the importance of distance and the 'zones of influence' of recreational resources according to whether they had a national, regional, sub-regional, intermediate or local zone of influence, using actual distance to classify the resource according to the 'pull' or attraction of each. Law (1967) argued that the majority of day trippers would be drawn from no more than 48 kms away. What Coppock and Duffield (1975) recognised was that it was not individual but groups of resources which attract active recreation.

At a descriptive level, the relationships in Table 3.3 indicate that the Clawson *et al.* (1960) model appears to have an application, where, in a:

- 0–16 km zone, many resource needs for recreation can be met in terms of golf, urban parks and the urban fringe;
- 16–32 km zone, the range of activities is greater, though particular types of resource tend to dominate activity patterns (e.g. horse-riding, hiking and field sports); and
- 32 km or greater, sports and physical pursuits with specific resource requirements (e.g. orienteering, canoeing, skiing and rock-climbing) exist.

Yet despite increased mobility of recreationalists, the majority of popular activities are undertaken relatively near to the home. To expand upon these findings, attention now turns to the supply of recreational resources within the context of the urban fringe.

Recreational Resources and the Urban Fringe

The impact of urbanisation on the development of industrial societies and the effects in terms of recreational resource provision is discussed in detail in chapter 6. Yet the growing consumption of rural land for urban uses has led to increased concerns for the loss of non-urban land. Pigram (1983: 106) observed that 'every year some 1.2 ha of rural land are converted to urban and built-up uses across America' and the greatest competition over the retention of land for recreational uses is in the city-periphery or what is termed the 'urban fringe'. Elson (1993) recognised the considerable potential of the urban fringe as a resource able to accommodate recreation and sport for four reasons:

Table 3.3: A general classification of outdoor recreational uses and resources

Item	User-oriented	Type of recreation area resource-based	Intermediate
General location	Close to users; on whatever resources are available	Where outstanding resources can be found; may be distant from most users	Must not be too remote from users; on best resources available within distance limitation
Major types of activity	Games, such as golf and tennis; swimming, picnicking, walks, horse-riding; zoos, etc.; play by children	Major sightseeing, scientific, historical interest; hiking, mountain climbing, camping, fishing, hunting	Camping, picnicking, hiking, swimming, hunting, fishing
When major use occurs	After hours (school or work)	Vacations	Day outings and weekends
Typical sizes of areas	One to a hundred or at most to a few hundred acres	Usually some thousands of acres, perhaps many thousands	A hundred to several thousand acres
Common types of agency responsibility	City, county, or other local government; private	National parks and national forests primarily; state parks in some cases; private, especially for seashore and major lakes	Federal reservoirs; state parks; private

Source: Clawson, Held and Stoddard 1960: 136

- It comprises an area of recreational supply, accessible with good public transport to large populations (though Fitton (1976) and Ferguson and Munton (1978, 1979) recognised the inaccessibility to the most deprived areas of inner London). As the Countryside Commission (1992) noted, one in five informal recreational day trips to the countryside had a return trip of less than 10 miles;
- They can be an overflow location for recreational and sporting activities displaced from urban areas;
- It can function as an 'interceptor area', reducing pressure on more fragile and vulnerable rural resources;

- It may be an area of opportunity as environmental improvements and landscape regeneration (e.g. the reclamation of former quarry sites or gravel extraction can generate new forms of recreation including fishing, sailing and informal use). As Elson (1993) observes, with active recreation the fastest growing sector of countryside recreation in the UK, the urban fringe has the potential to absorb such uses. Thus by altering supply, it is assumed that demand may be directed to new resources. In this sense, the urban fringe is a useful example in which to examine the nature of spatial interactions between demand and supply.

THE GREEN BELT CONCEPT

Within the UK the urban fringe has been a created landscape. In the 1930s the green belt concept was developed in London, along with many other European cities, based on the influential work of Raymond Unwin and the 1933 Green Belt Act. Unwin helped establish the principle of creating a band of open space on the city's periphery in order to compensate for the lack of open space in the built urban environment. These principles were embodied in post-war planning during the 1950s (Ministry of Housing and Local Government 1955). While such designations were intended to limit urban sprawl, recreational provision was never their intended purpose. Elson (1986) shows that planning authorities in the West Midlands, Manchester and Sheffield identified green belt plans (e.g. green wedges, recreation and amenity areas) in their development plans only to find them downgraded or removed through the ministerial assessment of the plans. In fact, Harrison (1991: 32) argued that

> public authorities adopted a standards approach to provision that was a legacy of the inter-war period with its heavy emphasis on organised sport rather than on a wider range of individual and family pursuits. Moreover, while these standards were based on the number of active members of the population who might be expected to participate . . . even the minimum standard of provision of 2.4 hectares per 1000 head of population could not be met in inner cities.

As a result, the urban fringe and its green belt was seen as the likely location for provision. At a policy level it is interesting to note that in the late 1960s both the Countryside Commission and local authorities used green belts as a mechanism to reduce standards of provision in the inner city (see Harrison 1991 for more discussion of the politics of green belt land and recreational use). Even so, Harrison (1980–81) found that the carrying capacity of many sites could be improved through better resource management, with the Greater London Council (1975) study of London's green belt indicating that organised activities constituted half of the trips to the green belt for recreation.

In spatial terms, approved green belts now comprise 3,824,000 acres or 12 per cent of the land of England and it is expected to continue to grow as more cities use this mechanism for urban containment. For example, Elson (1993) reports that the designation of 12 community forests in the UK of between 8,000–20,000 ha will add environmental improvements and resources for the urban fringe. One notable development which predates much of the early research on the urban fringe is the Countryside Commission's (1974) involvement in the establishment of Country Parks in the urban fringe, following on from a UK government white paper *Leisure and the Countryside* (1966). The Countryside Commission viewed Country Parks as an area of '25 acres in extent, with basic facilities, for the public to enjoy informal open air recreation' (Harrison 1991: 95). While a number of studies account for the evolution of country park policy (Zetter 1971; Slee 1982; Groome and Tarrant 1984), it is clear that the researchers point to the absence of research which indicates whether park provision provides the experiences recreationalists require. Despite growing provision of country parks in the 1970s, disparities existed in their spatial distribution, with large conurbations having only limited provision (Ferguson and Munton 1979).

Thus, spatial inequalities in supply simply reinforced existing patterns of provision though country parks have assisted in retaining land for recreation at a time of pressure for development. Fitton (1979), for example, found that while Country Parks comprised 0.13 per cent of the land surface of England and Wales, they accounted for 4.2 per cent of trips, a finding supported by Elson (1979) whose analyses of 31 sites visited in South-East England found that urban fringe sites with a range of facilities were visited more frequently than other recreational destinations though patterns of use were related to distance–decay functions, distance from individuals' home area, other attractions, individual choice and a range of other factors. As Harrison (1991: 103) suggests, Country Parks 'had not achieved a separate identity but people's experiences of particular sites within [them] . . . contributed to their own separate evaluations of what particular locations offered'. The continual gap between provision and users was evidenced in the Countryside Commission's (1988) study which concluded that while 58 per cent of people had heard of a Country Park, only 26 per cent could name one correctly reflecting a lack of promotion and general awareness of their existence.

At a national level, Country Parks only appear to have a minor role to play in diverting demand from the countryside, with some parks having catchments that are extremely localised. For example, Harrison (1981, 1983) found that 75 per cent of visitors to south London's green belt were car users. Their study discovered that inner city residents never comprised more than 10 per cent of users. Although sites were also accessible to those not having access to a car over short distances, Groome and Tarrant (1984) found public transport to Country Parks effective over a 5–8 km distance (i.e. short distance) for a local population. At an aggregate level, it is clear that Country Parks (and the forerunner – Regional Parks) in the UK play a vital role in locating recreational resources near to demand. The somewhat dated 1981 National Survey of Countryside Recreation found that 40 per cent of destinations were within the urban area or within 1 km (Sidaway and Duffield 1984), with a further 22 per cent in the countryside around urban areas. Only 16 per cent of destinations were located 10 km from the urban areas.

As Figure 3.1 shows, the spatial distribution of visits to South London's green belt were predominantly within or close to the built environment, and given the rapid expansion of urban fringe use, it is not surprising that conflicts arise over its use. The more recent experiments in the urban fringe, including the introduction of Countryside Management to resolve small-scale conflicts (e.g. trespass, vandalism, litter and footpath mainte-

nance) develops a conciliatory approach to problems that fall outside the remit of the planning framework. The example of Havering in Greater London (Figure 3.2) illustrates how the development of a management plan by a project officer acknowledged the problems of multiple use and the legacy of former derelict land.

In the case of Havering, the scale of dereliction and the variety of land agencies involved created problems for the development of recreation provision. While the Countryside Commission (1983) reviewed Havering's scheme and found a legacy of poor public provision in public housing areas and inadequate recognition of Rights of Way, landscaping schemes also remained a neglected feature. Expecting the London Borough of Havering to set a precedent for land owners to follow has taken a long time to reach fruition. Nevertheless, the approach has brought modest success through environmental improvements establishing attractive recreational facilities by effectively tidying up many sites (Harrison 1991). The success of such projects was also followed by a new initiative in 1985 – the Groundwork Trust, based on a scheme in St Helens' urban fringe (Groundwork Foundation 1986).

Variability in the usage of Country Parks reflects public knowledge of their existence and the attraction of individual locations. The precise location of recreation sites in the urban fringe appears to directly influence usage, with those located near to residential areas which permit residents to walk to them, recording highest usage rates. As Harrison (1991: 166) concludes

the recreational role played by sites in the urban fringe will differ depending upon their ease of access to local people who walk or cycle to them and not necessarily on the preferences of a wider constituency served by car . . . [and] the recreational role of countryside areas embedded in the urban area or abutting it is likely to be very different from that of more distant countryside sites.

What is clear is that the supply of recreational resources alone (e.g. Country Parks) is not sufficient in the urban fringe if the needs and recreational

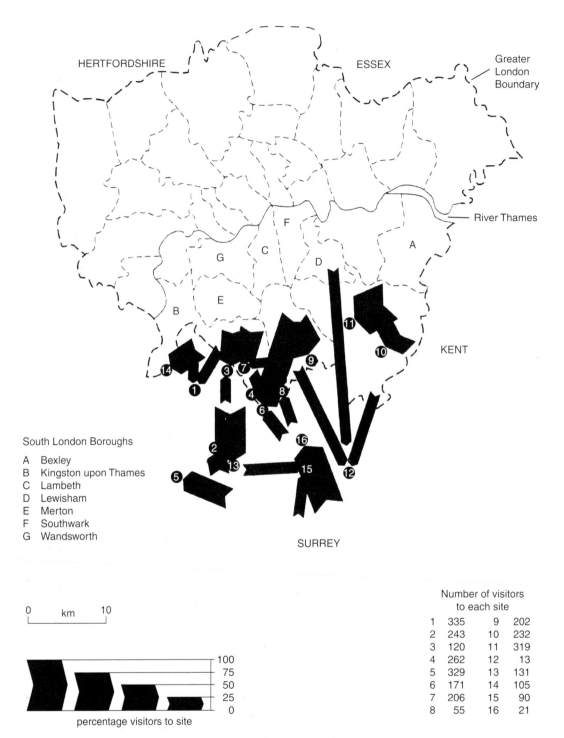

South London Boroughs

A Bexley
B Kingston upon Thames
C Lambeth
D Lewisham
E Merton
F Southwark
G Wandsworth

Number of visitors to each site			
1	335	9	202
2	243	10	232
3	120	11	319
4	262	12	13
5	329	13	131
6	171	14	105
7	206	15	90
8	55	16	21

Figure 3.1: Number and origin of visitors to sites in South London's green belt
Source: modified from Harrison (1981)

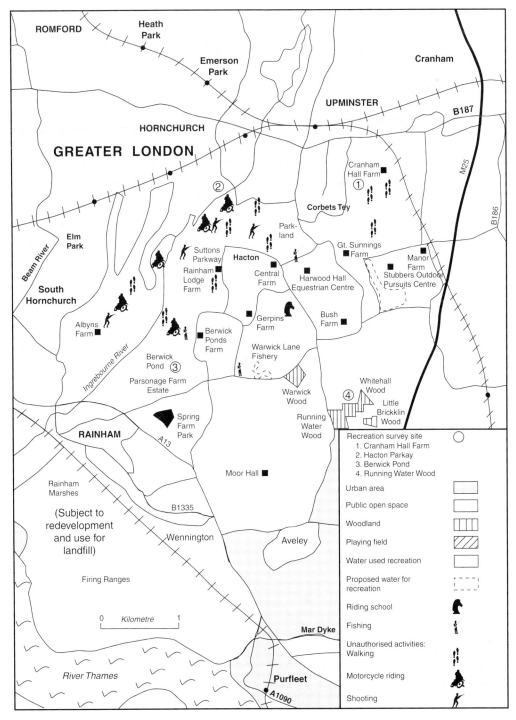

Figure 3.2: The London Borough of Havering's urban fringe countryside management area
Source: Countryside Commission (1982)

preferences of users are not analysed since these factors directly affect recreational behaviour.

THE SUPPLY OF TOURISM

Within most conventional texts on tourism, the issue of supply attracts comparatively little attention. According to Sinclair and Stabler (1992: 2) 'past research on the tourism industry can be classified into three main categories: first, descriptions of the industry and its operation, management and marketing; second, the spatial development and interactions which characterise the industry on a local, national and international scale; and third, the effects which result from the development of the industry'. However, Shaw and Williams (1994) prefer to view the issue in relation to two other concepts: production and consumption. Shaw and Williams (1994: 16) acknowledge that the production and consumption of tourism are important approaches to the analysis of tourism since *production* is the method by which a complex array of businesses and industries are involved in the supply of tourism services and products, and how these are delivered to consumers, and *consumption* is how, where, why and when the tourist actually consumes tourism services and products. Sessa (1993: 59), however, considers 'tourism supply is the result of all those productive activities that involve the provision of goods and services required to meet tourism demand and which are expressed in tourism consumption' which comprises: resources for tourists, infrastructure, receptive facilities, entertainment, sports venues as well as tourism reception services (Table 3.4). While there is a degree of overlap in this conceptualisation of tourism supply with leisure and recreational uses which is inevitable, it highlights the scope of productive activities associated with tourism supply.

The feature which makes many of these resources of interest to the geographer is what Urry (1990) describes as 'spatial fixity'. In other

Table 3.4: Elements of the tourism industry

Tourism resources
- Natural resources
- Human resources

General and tourism infrastructure
- Means of communication and travel
- Social installations
- Basic installations
- Telecommunications

Receptive facilities
- Hotels, guest houses, towns and villages
- Condominiums
- Complementary residences
- Residences for receptive personnel
- Food and beverage installations

Entertainment and sports facilities
- Recreational and cultural facilities
- Sports facilities

Tourism reception services
- Travel agencies
- Hotel and local promotional offices
- Information offices
- Car hire
- Guides, interpreters

Source: Sessa (1983)

words, tourists are mobile consumers and able to consume at a global level. This contrasts with most forms of supply which are fixed at specific locations. Perhaps the exception here are the transnational corporations that are able to relocate capital at a global level to meet shifts in demand. Underlying the concept of spatial fixity is the nature of tourism entrepreneurs who are largely small scale in their operations and less able to access forms of capital to relocate to new sources of demand. Thus supply is often unable to respond geographically to demand beyond a fixed point and this means that peaks and troughs in demand at particular locations need to be managed through differential forms of pricing (Seaton and Bennett 1996) and the use of seasonal labour (Ball 1989).

Law (1993) expands upon these simple notions arguing that

> in many respects tourism is the geography of consumption outside the home area; it is about how and why people travel to consume ... [On] the production side it is concerned to understand where tourism activities develop and on what scale. It is concerned with the process or processes whereby some cities are able to create tourism resources and a tourism industry.
>
> (Law 1993: 14)

Law emphasises here the way in which scale is a critical concept in understanding supply issues together with the ways in which the tourism industry is organised and geographically distributed through time and space. While production and consumption have been the focus of the more theoretically derived explanations of tourism production (e.g. Mullins 1991), such approaches raise conceptual issues related to how one should view production and consumption in the context of urban tourism. The purpose of this chapter is to address how one can examine the relationship between production and consumption in terms of the supply of products. Both the tourist's consumption (often expressed as the demand – examined in chapter 2) and the products and services produced for their visit (the supply) form important inputs in the overall system of tourism and the wider development of society. However, prior to examining different facets of production, the geographer's contribution to theoretical analysis in this area is examined.

TOWARDS A CRITICAL GEOGRAPHY OF TOURISM PRODUCTION

According to Britton (1991: 451) the geography of tourism has suffered from weakly developed theory since 'geographers working in the field have been reluctant to recognise explicitly the capitalistic nature of the phenomenon they are researching'. While Shaw and Williams (1994) review the concepts of production and consumption, it is pertinent to examine critically Britton's (1991) innovative research in this area since it provides a theoretical framework in which to interpret tourism production. Within the tourism production systems are:

- economic activities designed to produce and sell tourism products;
- social groups, cultural and physical elements included in tourism products as attractions; and
- agencies associated with the regulation of the production system.

In a theoretical context, Britton (1991: 455) argued that the tourism production system was 'simultaneously a mechanism for the accumulation of capital, the private appropriation of wealth, the extraction of surplus value from labour, and the capturing of (often unearned) rents from cultural and physical phenomena (especially public goods) which are deemed to have both a social and scarcity value'. The production system can be viewed as having a division of labour between its various components (transport, accommodation, tour operators, attractions and ancillary services) as well as markets (the demand and supply of tourist products) and regulatory agencies (e.g. industry associations) as well as industry organisations and structures to assist in the production of the final product. Britton (1991: 456) rightly points out that 'the geography texts on tourism offer little more than a cursory and superficial analysis of how the tourism industry is structured and regulated by the classic imperatives and laws governing capitalist accumulation'.

The tourism industry is made up of a range of separate industry suppliers who offer one or more component of the final product which requires intermediaries to coordinate and combine the elements which are sold to the consumer as a

Plate 3.1: Hotels on small islands such as Fiji aimed at the luxury end of the market have to import many of the products and materials adding to the leakage noted by Britton. This picutre shows the Sheraton Hotel, Denaurau Island, Fiji

Plate 3.2: Tour guiding is an important aspect of tourism supply and the management of the visitor experience. Here, a tour guide is taking a group of European tourists around Taman Mini Indonesia, a cultural theme park in Jakarta, Indonesia

discrete package. Both tour operators and travel agents have a vital role to play in this context, when one recognises the existence of a supply chain (Figure 3.3). What this emphasises is the variety of linkages which exist and the physical separation of roles and responsibilities to the supply chain (see Page 1994b). While information technology may assist in improving communication and coordination between different components associated with the production of tourism, other developments (notably horizontal and vertical integration) assist in addressing the fragmentation of elements within the supply system. Strategic alliances also assist in this regard, since suppliers in one part of the system are dependent on those either upstream or downstream. Therefore, there is pressure on suppliers to exert control over other suppliers through transaction arrangements (i.e. through long term contracts, vertical and horizontal integration) as well as through commissions, licensing and franchising. The two most powerful organisations in this respect are national airlines and tour wholesalers (also known as tour operators). Through the financial resources and industry leverage these organisations can wield in the tourism business, they are able to exact advantageous business terms and the introduction of computer reservation systems (CRS), now referred to as Global Distribution Systems (GDS) which provides not only integration of the supply chain, but also a competitive advantage in revenue generation through bookings made through these systems.

Likewise, tour operators are able to use economies of scale and their sheer buying power over suppliers to derive a competitive advantage in the assembly of tour components into packages. The tour operators also have the power and ability to shift the product to match demand and to exercise an extraordinary degree of power over both interindustry transactions and the spatial distribution of tourist flows.

Britton (1991) also indicates that the state has a fundamental role to play in encouraging industry groups to meet, coordinate problem solving such as reducing critical incidents (Bitner *et al.* 1990) in the supply chain. In addition, the state makes a major contribution in terms of funding the marketing of regions and destinations via National and Regional Tourism Organisations (Pearce 1992b) so that place promotion takes place (Ashworth and Voogd 1990; Page 1995a). The state also may offer inducements to underwrite major supply inputs where territorial competition or development may not otherwise occur. Interventions in the market

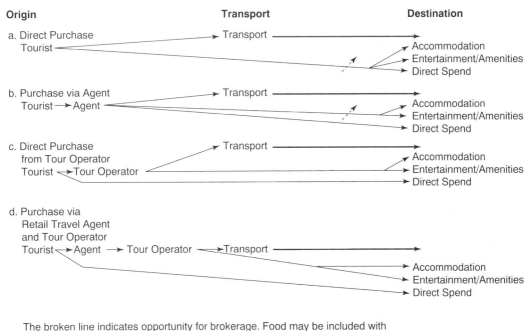

The broken line indicates opportunity for brokerage. Food may be included with
accommodation or be in 'direct spend'.

⟶   Transaction Chain

⟶   Tourist Travel (to a domestic or international destination)

Figure 3.3: Four types of tourism transaction chain
Source: After Witt *et al.* 1991: 81

include the underwriting of national 'flag-carrier'
airlines (see Kissling 1990) and public economic
and welfare goals are emphasised to justify state
intervention.

One of the interesting areas, hitherto rejected in
geographical research on tourism supply is labour
supply and markets (see Shaw and Williams 1994
for a good synthesis of the literature). Since in the
tourism business many workers simultaneously
provide and are part of the consumed product,
service quality assumes a vital role. This is broadened in many research studies to include the
'tourist experience' (Ryan 1996). While Britton
(1991) rightly points to the role of capitalist
social relations in the production of tourist
experiences, such experiences cannot easily be

characterised as tangible elements of tourist
supply. This poses major difficulties for capital,
where quality of service is easily influenced by
personal factors, the behaviour and attitude of
staff, as well as by the perception of the consumer
in relation to their expectations, values and belief
system. One result, is that much of the demand
for labour is not necessarily recognised through
formal qualifications but through personal qualities which leads to an undervaluing of labour.
Add to this the fact that the labour willing to
supply such skills is often casual and female (and
often with a local ethnic component), the tourism
labour market is characterised by ethnic and
gender divisions, with relatively poor employment
conditions existing relative to other sectors (Baum

1994). For example, in the Australian context, the Industry Commission characterised the tourism workforce and its working conditions as follows:

- it is, on average, young;
- it is characterised by female, part-time employment;
- it has more casual and part-time work than other industries, but the majority of hours are nevertheless worked by full-time employees;
- it is lowly unionised;
- it is relatively low skilled work;
- the hours of work are sometimes considered unsociable;
- the pay is relatively low;
- it is a mobile workforce with high turnover rates; and
- the workforce has low levels of formal educational qualifications.

(Industry Commission 1995: 21)

Thus to understand some of these components of the tourism production system the geographer is required to understand concepts related to capital–labour relations, the business environment associated with the competitive strategies of enterprises, economic concepts (e.g. transaction analysis), product differentiation, international business as a mode of operation and global markets, along with basic business and marketing concepts. Within a capitalist mode of production this is essential so that one can understand how each component in the tourism production system operates (i.e. how it develops products, generates profits and competes with other businesses) and how social groups and places are incorporated into the production system, so that the production system and the spatial relationships which exist can be fully understood. To illustrate these ideas, the example of international hotel chains is used to examine relationships between the geography of supply, functions, the industrial structure of the business and the social relations which exist.

INTERNATIONAL HOTEL CHAINS

The hotel industry is arguably a global industry, since it fulfils some of the criteria which distinguish businesses as truly global, whereby it may be one which can create a competitive advantage from its activities on a worldwide basis. Alternatively it may be one in which the strategic positions of competitors in major geographic or national markets are fundamentally affected by their overall global positions (Porter 1980: 175). Much of the debate on the influence of international hotel chains can be dated to the research by Dunning and McQueen (1982) on what constitutes a multinational, international and transnational firm. Dunning and McQueen's (1982) use of an international hotel company, which has direct investments and other types of contractual agreements in more than one country remains a simple but effective definition (also see Shaw and Williams 1994: 120–5).

Gannon and Johnson (1995) provide an interesting and comparatively up-to-date assessment of the principal global hotel company characteristics (recent changes may have changed the precise size of their holdings, but Table 3.5 does illustrate the scale and order of magnitude of global hotels). While Table 3.5 illustrates that Choice Hotels International was the largest group, at the other end of the scale Orient-Express has 12 units yet operates globally, implying that size of operation is not necessarily a precondition to achieving global status. Go and Pine (1995) examine some of the corporate strategies to explain the differences between the companies according to countries they operate in. While in Table 3.5, 'domicile continent' identifies the operating base and likely source of finance, which illustrates that no global companies operate in Africa, Oceania or South America. (See Gannon and Johnson 1995 for more detail on possible explanations for the geographical patterns of operation and strategies for expansion and development by area.)

Britton (1991) analysed the product which hotel chains offered in terms of their competitive strategies.

Table 3.5: Global hotel company characteristics

Number	Name	Domicile continent	Units world-wide	Countries world-wide	FIM (%)
1	Accor	Europe	2,127	73	65.2
2	Choice Hotels International	North America	2,663	25	16.6
3	Forte	Europe	910	33	63.1
4	Hilton International	Europe	151	48	78.1
5	Holiday Inn World-Wide	Europe	1,772	56	98.8
6	Hyatt International	North America	202	35	42.6
7	Inter-Continental	Asia	106	47	98.1
8	ITT Sheraton	North America	472	63	52.5
9	Marriott	North America	749	21	6.4
10	Meridien	Europe	55	33	94.5
11	Orient-Express	Asia	12	8	100
12	Radisson	North America	255	23	60.8
13	Ramada	Asia	158	39	98.7

Source: Gannon and Johnson 1995

a package of on-premises' services which provide a certain experience (ambience, lifestyle) based on kinds and qualities of accommodation, on-site recreation and shopping facilities, and catering; the offering of off-premises' services (airport shuttles, local excursions, booking facilities); and a trademark guarantee which signals to the customer a predictable quality of service.

The competitive strategies which follow from these features are based on an understanding of the customer (i.e. needs and preferences), where the brand name is able to command a premium price in the market place. Britton (1991: 460) explains the commercial advantage of international chains in terms of:

- the firms' location in the customers' home country;
- experience in understanding demand through operating hotels in the domestic markets; and
- managerial expertise and staff training to ensure the elements of the tourists' experience related to the brand name are met through appropriate training and operating manuals.

The key to successful competition is for the hotel company to internalise its form – specific intellectual property (i.e. training methods and manuals), while ensuring profit levels for share-holders. Unfortunately, this is extremely difficult when staff leave and move to competitors since the intellectual property is essentially 'know-how'. Yet this is often the basis for horizontal integration into overseas markets, with management contracts a preferred mechanism for operation rather than outright ownership to control design, operation, pricing and staffing, though the same companies (e.g. Holiday Inns) prefer to use franchising as a mechanism to control managerial, organisational and professional input.

One notable dimension here is the effect of international hotel and tourism development on less developed countries. For example, in Kenya, 60 per cent of hotel beds were accounted for through equity participation schemes with such hotel groups (Rosemary 1987; Sinclair 1991). The implications are that where international involvement occurs, there is a concomitant loss of central control and leakage of foreign earnings, and where there is concentrated development to

enclaves, remote from local population this inevitably leads to little benefit for the host country.
Despite these problems, attitudes towards such
development among a survey of 22 developing
countries (WTO 1985) saw the benefits out-
weighing the cash. This can lead to dependency
relationships as Britton (1980a) indicated in his
innovative study of the distribution of ownership
and commercial control by metropolitan tourist
markets of less developed world destinations.

Britton's model of tourism development (Figure
3.4) illustrates the nature of tourism dependency,
where international tourism organisations (in the
absence of strong government control), develop
and perpetuate a hierarchical element to tourism
development. While dependency theory is useful
in explaining how capitalist production leads to

the resulting patterns of care in tourism demand
and supply, it is evident that this is only a simplification of the wider geographical dimensions of
capital – labour relations in a global context,
where political ceremony perspectives assist in
explaining the processes leading to the spatial patterns of tourism development that occur. The
economic dynamics of the tourism production
system begin to help to develop a more central
perspective of tourism which fits into the broader
conceptualisation of capitalist accumulation, and
the social construction of reality, though marketing and the construction of place may provide new
areas for future geographical research. In fact,
what one realises from a critical analysis of
tourism using political economy perspectives is
that it is a constantly changing phenomenon, with

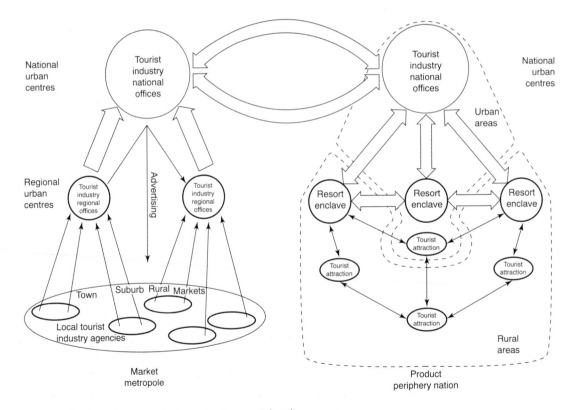

Figure 3.4: An enclave model of tourism in a peripheral economy
Source: Redrawn from Britton (1980a)

an ever changing spatial organisation. The processes affecting the political economy of production and consumption require a critical awareness of the role and activities of entrepreneurs, the flow of capital and its internationalisation, the impact of industrial and regional restructuring, urban development, changes in the service economy and how the production of tourism results in new landscapes of tourism in a contemporary society.

Aside from theoretical analysis, geographers have developed other concepts and methods of analysis and attention now turns to these approaches.

THE LEISURE PRODUCT

Within the context of urban tourism, Jansen-Verbeke (1986) viewed the urban area as a 'leisure product' (Figure 3.5) which comprises *primary*

elements including a variety of facilities that can be grouped into:

- an activity place, thereby defining the overall supply features within the city, particularly the main tourist attractions; and
- a leisure setting, which includes both the physical elements in the built environment and the socio-cultural characteristics which give a city a distinct image and 'sense of place' (see Walmesley and Jenkins 1992 for a discussion of this concept) for visitors;

and *secondary elements* which consist of:

- the *supporting facilities and services* which tourists consume during their visit (e.g. hotel and catering outlets and shopping facilities) which shape the visitor's experience of the services available in the city; and
- *additional elements* which consist of the tourism infrastructure which conditions the

PRIMARY ELEMENTS		SECONDARY ELEMENTS
Activity place	**Leisure setting**	
Cultural facilities • Concert halls • Cinemas • Exhibitions • Museums and art galleries • Theatres	**Physical characteristics** • Ancient monuments and statues • Ecclesiastical buildings • Harbours • Historical street pattern • Interesting buildings • Parks and green areas • Water, canals and river fronts	• Hotels and catering facilities • Markets • Shopping facilities
Sports Facilities • Indoor and outdoor		
Amusement facilities • Bingo halls • Casinos • Festivities • Night clubs • Organised events	**Socio-cultural features** • Folklore • Friendliness • Language • Liveliness and ambience of the place • Local customs and costumes • Security	**ADDITIONAL ELEMENTS** • Accessibility and parking facilities • Tourist facilities: information offices, signposts, guides, maps and leaflets

Figure 3.5: The elements of tourism
Source: Modified from Jansen-Verbeke (1986)

visit, such as the availability of car parking, tourist-transport provision and accessibility and tourist-specific services (e.g. Visitor Information Centres and tourist signposting).

Shaw and Williams (1994: 202) rightly argue that 'while such an approach allows a systematic consideration of the supply side of urban tourism, it is not without its difficulties. For example, in many cities, the so-called secondary elements of shops and restaurants may well be the main attractions for certain groups of visitors'. Nevertheless, the supply-side variables within the context of the urban tourism system help to understand the inter-relationships between supply and demand and the interaction between the consumers and the products. In this respect, it is also useful to identify what aspect of the 'leisure product' tourists consume; some may consume only one product (e.g. a visit to an art gallery) while others may consume what Jansen-Verbeke (1988) terms a 'bundle of products' (i.e. several products during their visit or stay such as a visit to a theatre, museum and a meal in a restaurant).

Jansen-Verbeke (1986) examined this concept within the inner city tourism system to identify the nature of tourists visiting the inner city and the organisations responsible for the promotion of the inner city as an area for tourists to visit. The role of organisations promoting urban areas for tourism is discussed in more detail in chapter 6, but to explain Jansen-Verbeke's (1986) analysis it is useful to consider the relationship which she believes exists between the product, the tourist and the promoter. Promoters affect the relationship in two ways:

- they build an image of the inner city and its tourists' resources to attract potential tourists, investors and employers; and
- the promotion of the inner city may also lead to direct product improvement.

Consequently, the model Jansen-Verbeke (1986) constructs (Figure 3.5), illustrates how dif-

ferent elements of the inner city tourism system are interrelated and the significance of the inner city as a leisure product. However, the public and private sector have distinct roles to play in this context.

THE ROLE OF THE PUBLIC AND PRIVATE SECTOR IN TOURISM SUPPLY

Pearce (1989: 32) observed that the

provision of services and facilities characteristically involves a wide range of agents of development. Some of these will be involved indirectly and primarily with meeting the needs of tourists, a role that has fallen predominantly to the private sector in most countries . . . Other agents will facilitate, control or limit development . . . through the provision of basic infrastructure, planning or regulation. Such activities have commonly been the responsibility of the public sector with the government at various levels being charged with looking after the public's interest and providing goods and services whose cost cannot be attributed directly to groups or individuals.

Pearce's comments illustrates the essential distinction between the role of the private and public sector in the provision of services and facilities for tourists that has existed for much of this century. However, the tendency to privatise and commercialise functions that were once performed by government has been almost universal in Western nations since the late 1970s and has affected the nature of many national government's involvement in the tourism industry (Hall 1994). According to Hall and Jenkins (1995) three principal reasons for this trend can be identified. Governments are interested in

- reducing the dependency of public enterprises on public budgets;
- reducing public debt by selling state assets; and
- raising technical efficiencies by commercialisation.

This has meant that there has been a much

greater blurring in the roles of the public and private sectors with the development of enterprise boards, development corporations and similar organisations.

The private sector

As Britton (1991) observed earlier, the private sector's involvement in tourism is most likely to be motivated by profit, as tourism entrepreneurs (Shaw and Williams 1994) invest in business opportunities. This gives rise to a complex array of large organisations and operators involved in tourism (e.g. multinational chain hotels – Forte and the Holiday Inn) and an array of smaller

businesses and operators, often employing less than 10 people or working on a self-employed basis (Page *et al.* 1999). If left unchecked, this sector is likely to give rise to conflicts in the operation of tourism where the state takes a *laissez faire* role in tourism planning and management.

The public sector

In contrast to the private sector, the public sector involves government at a variety of geographical scales and may become involved in tourism for various economic, political, social and environmental reasons (Table 3.6). The International

Table 3.6: Some reasons for government involvement in tourism

Economic Reasons
- to improve the balance of payments in a country;
- to attract foreign exchange;
- to aid regional (or local) economic development;
- to diversify the economy;
- to increase income levels;
- to increase state revenue from taxes; and
- to generate new employment opportunities.

Social and Cultural Reasons:
- to achieve social objectives related to 'social tourism' to ensure the well-being and health of families and individuals;
- to protect cultural mores, traditions, resources and heritage;
- to promote a greater cultural awareness of an area and its people; and
- to promote international understanding.

Environmental Reasons:
- to undertake the stewardship of the environment and tourism resources to ensure that the agents of development do not destroy the future basis for sustainable tourism development; and
- to create a natural resource which will serve to attract tourists.

Political Reasons:
- to further political objectives by promoting the development of tourism in order to broaden the political acceptance of a government among visitors;
- to control the development process associated with tourism;
- to protect the public interest and the interests of minorities; and
- to further political ideology.

Sources: Jenkins and Henry (1982); Pearce (1989); Hall (1994); Hall and Jenkins (1995).

Union of Tourist Organisations, the forerunner to the WTO, in their discussion of the role of the state in tourism (1974) identified five areas of public sector involvement in tourism: co-ordination, planning, legislation and regulation, entrepreneur stimulation. To this may be added two other functions, a social tourism role, which is very significant in European tourism (Murphy 1985), and a broader role of interest protection (Hall 1994).

Much intervention in tourism is related to market failure, market imperfection and social need. The market method of deciding who gets what and how is not always adequate, and there-fore government often changes the distribution of income and wealth by measures that work within the price system. Across the globe almost every industry has been supported at various times by subsidies, the imposition of tariff regulations, taxation concessions, direct grants and other forms of government intervention, all of which serve to affect the price of goods and services and therefore influence the distribution of income, production and wealth. The size or economic importance of the tourism industry, so commonly emphasised by the public and private sectors, is no justification in itself for government intervention; within market-driven economies justification must lie in some aspect of: (i) market failure; (ii) market imperfection; or (iii) public/social concerns about market outcomes. Therefore, implicit in each justification for intervention is the view that government offers a corrective alternative to the market (Hall and Jenkins 1998).

The role of the state as entrepreneur in tourist development is closely related to the concept of the 'devalorisation of capital' (Damette 1980). The 'devalorisation of capital' is the process by which the state subsidises part of the cost of production, for instance by assisting in the provi-sion of infrastructure or by investing in a tourism project where private venture capital is otherwise unavailable. In this process what would have been private costs are transformed into public or social costs. The provision of infrastructure, particularly

transport networks, is regarded as crucial to the development of tourist destinations (Page 1999). There are numerous formal and informal means for government at all levels to assist in minimising the costs of production for tourism developers. Indeed, the offer of government assistance for development is often used to encourage private investment in a particular region or tourist project. For instance, through the provision of cheap land or government backed low-interest loans.

As well as acting as entrepreneurs governments can also stimulate tourism in several ways: first, financial incentives such as low-interest loans or a depreciation allowance on tourist accommodation or infrastructure, although 'their introduction often reflected both the scarcity of domestic investment funds and widespread ambition to undertake economic development programmes' (Bodlender and Davies 1985, in Pearce 1992b: 11); second, sponsoring research for the benefit of the tourism industry rather than for specific individual organ-isations and associations; third, marketing and promotion, generally aimed at generating tourism demand, although it can also take the form of investment promotion aimed at encouraging capi-tal investment for tourism attractions and facilities (Hall 1995).

One of the more unusual features of tourism promotion by government tourism organisations is that they have only limited control over the prod-uct they are marketing, with very few actually owning the goods, facilities and services that make up the tourism product (Pearce 1992b). This lack of control is perhaps testimony to the power of the public good argument used by industry to justify continued maintenance of government funding for destination promotion. However, it may also indicate the political power of the tourism lobby, such as industry organisations to influence government tourism policies (Hall and Jenkins 1995).

Throughout most of the 1980s and the early 1990s, 'Thatcherism' (named after Conservative Prime Minister Margaret Thatcher) in the United

Kingdom and 'Reaganism' (named after Republican President Ronald Reagan) in the United States, saw a period of retreat by central government from active intervention. At the national level, policies of deregulation, privatisation, free-trade, the elimination of tax incentives, and a move away from discretionary forms of macro-economic intervention, were and have been the hallmarks of a push towards 'smaller' government and lower levels of government intervention. Given such demand for smaller government in Western society in recent years, there have been increasing demands from government and economic rationalists for greater industry self-sufficiency in tourism marketing and promotion. The political implications of such an approach for the tourism industry are substantial. As Hughes (1984: 14) noted, 'The advocates of a free enterprise economy would look to consumer freedom of choice and not to governments to promote firms; the consumer ought to be sovereign in decisions relating to the allocation of the nation's resources.' Such an approach means that lobbyists in the tourism industry may be better shifting their focus on the necessity of government intervention to issues of externalities, public goods, and merit wants rather than employment and the balance of payments (Hall 1994). 'Such criteria for government intervention have a sounder economic base and are more consistent with a free-enterprise philosophy than employment and balance of payments effects' (Hughes 1984: 18). Nevertheless, as Pearce (1992b: 8) recognised, 'general destination promotion tends to benefit all sectors of the tourist industry in the place concerned; it becomes a 'public good' . . . The question of 'freeloaders' thus arises, for they too will benefit along with those who may have contributed directly to the promotional campaign.'

In many cases, the state's involvement is to ensure a policy of intervention so that political objectives associated with employment generation and planning are achieved, although this varies from one country to another and from city to city according to the political persuasion of the

organisation involved. Pearce (1989: 44) rightly acknowledges, however, that

> the public sector then is by no means a single entity with clear cut responsibilities and well-defined policies for tourist development. Rather, the public sector becomes involved in tourism for a wide range of reasons in a variety of ways at different levels and through many agencies and institutions . . . [and] there is often a lack of coordination, unnecessary competition, duplication of effort in some areas and neglect in others.

SPATIAL ANALYTICAL APPROACHES TO THE SUPPLY OF TOURISM FACILITIES

Much of the research on tourism supply in relation to facilities and services is descriptive in content, based on inventories and lists of the facilities and where they are located. In view of the wide range of literature that discusses the distribution of specific facilities or services, it is more useful to consider only two specific examples of how such approaches and concepts can be used to derive generalisations of patterns of tourism activity.

The Tourism Business District

Within the literature on the supply of urban tourism, Ashworth (1989) reviews the 'facility approach' which offers researchers the opportunity to map the location of specific facilities, undertaking inventories of facilities on a city-wide basis. The difficulty with such an approach is that the users of urban services and facilities are not just tourists, as workers and residents as well as recreationalists may use the same facility. Therefore, any inventory will only be a partial view of the full range of facilities and potential services tourists could use. One useful approach is to identify the areas in which the majority of tourist activities occur and to use it as the focus for the analysis of the supply of tourism services in such a multifunctional city which meets a wide range of uses for a wide range of users (see chapter 5). This avoids the individual assessments of the location and use of specific aspects of tourism services such as accommodation (Page and Sinclair 1989), entertainment facilities such as restaurants (S. Smith 1983b, 1989) and night-life entertainment facilities (Ashworth *et al.* 1988) and other attractions. This approach embraces the *ecological approaches* developed in human geography to identify regions within cities as a basis to identify the processes shaping the patterns.

The ecological approach toward the analysis of urban tourism dates back to Gilbert's (1949) assessment of the development of resorts, which was further refined by Barrett (1958). The outcome is a resort model where accommodation, entertainment and commercial zones exist and the central location of tourism facilities were dominant elements. The significance of such research is that it identifies some of the features and relationships which were subsequently developed in urban geography and applied to tourism and recreation. The most notable study is Stansfield and Rickert's (1970) development of the Recreational Business District (RBD). This study rightly identifies the multifunctional land use of the central areas of cities in relation to the central area for business (Central Business District (CBD)). Meyer-Arendt (1990) also expands this notion in the context of the Gulf of Mexico coastal resorts, while Pearce (1989) offers a useful critique of these studies. The essential ideas in the RBD have subsequently been extended to urban and resort tourism to try to explain where the location and distribution of the range of visitor-oriented functions occur in space.

Burtenshaw *et al.*'s (1991) seminal study of tourism and recreation in European cities deals with the concept of the Central Tourist District (CTD) where tourism activities in cities are concentrated in certain areas. This has been termed the TBD by Getz (1993a) who argues that it is the

> concentration of visitor-oriented attractions and services located in conjunction with urban central

businesses (CBD) functions. In older cities, especially in Europe, the TBD and CBD often coincide with heritage areas. Owing to their high visibility and economic importance, TBDs can be subjected to intense planning by municipal authorities . . . The form and evolution of TBDs reveals much about the nature of urban tourism and its impacts, while the analysis of the planning systems influencing TBDs can contribute to concepts and methods for better planning of tourism in urban areas.
>
> (Getz 1993a: 583–584)

Therefore, TBDs are a useful framework in which to understand the supply components of urban tourism and how they fit together. Figure 3.6, based on Getz's (1993a) analysis of the TBD, is a schematic model in which the functions rather than geographical patterns of activities are considered. This model illustrates the difficulty of separating visitor-oriented services from the CBD and use of services and facilities by residents and workers. Yet as Jansen-Verbeke and Ashworth (1990) argue, while tourism and recreational activities are integrated within the physical, social and economic context of the city, no analytical framework exists to determine the functional or behavioural interactions in these activities. They argue that more research is needed to assess the extent to which the clustering of tourism and recreational activities can occur in cities without leading to incompatible and conflicting uses from such facilities. While the TBD may offer a distinctive blend of activities and attractions for tourist and non-tourist alike, it is important to recognise these issues where tourism clusters in areas such as the TBD. Even so, the use of street entertainment and special events and festivals (Getz 1997) may also add to the ambience and sense of place for the city worker and visitor. By having a concentration of tourism and non-tourism resources and services in one accessible area within a city, it is possible to encourage visitors to stay there, making it a place tourists will want to visit as is the case in the West End of London (Page and Sinclair 1989). However, the attractions in urban areas are an important component in the appeal to potential visitors.

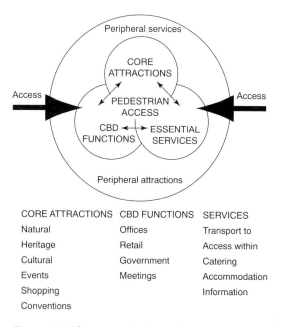

CORE ATTRACTIONS	CBD FUNCTIONS	SERVICES
Natural	Offices	Transport to
Heritage	Retail	Access within
Cultural	Government	Catering
Events	Meetings	Accommodation
Shopping		Information
Conventions	

Figure 3.6: The tourism business district
Source: Based on Getz (1993a)

Tourism attractions

Attractions are an integral feature of urban tourism, which offer visitors passive and more active occupations on which to spend their time during a visit. They also comprise a key component of Jansen-Verbeke's (1986) 'primary element' (Figure 3.5). Recent studies have adapted descriptive analyses of specific types of attractions (e.g. Law 1993) rather than exploring their relationship with urban tourists. Lew (1987 : 54) acknowledges that 'although the importance of tourist attractions is readily recognised, tourism researchers and theorists have yet to fully come to terms with the nature of attractions as phenomena both in the environment and the mind'. As a result, Lew's (1987) study and Leiper's (1990) synthesis and conceptual framework of 'Tourist Attraction Systems' remain among the most theoretically-informed literature published to date. Lew (1987) identifies three perspectives used to understand the nature of tourist attractions. These are:

- the *ideographic perspective*, where the general characteristics of a place, site, climate, culture and customs are used to develop typologies of tourism attractions, involving inventories or general descriptions. For example, the use of Standard Industrial Classification codes (SICs) are one approach used to group attractions (see S. Smith 1989). These approaches are the ones most commonly used to examine tourist attractions in the general tourism literature.
- the *organisational perspective*, in contrast, tends to emphasise the geographical, capacity and temporal aspects (the time dimension) of attractions rather than the 'managerial notions of organisation' (Leiper 1990 : 175). This approach examines scales ranging from the individual attraction, to larger areas and their attractions.
- the *cognitive perspective*, is based on 'studies of tourist perceptions and experiences of attractions' (Lew 1987: 560). P. Pearce (1982: 98) recognises that any tourist place (or attraction) is one capable of fostering the feeling of being a tourist. Therefore, the cognitive perspective is interested in understanding the tourists' feelings and views of the place or attraction.

The significance of Lew's (1987) framework is that it acknowledges the importance of attractions as a research focus, although Leiper (1990) questions the definition of attractions used by many researchers. He pursues the ideas developed by MacCannell (1976: 41), that an attraction incorporates 'an empirical relationship between a tourist, a sight and a marker, a piece of information about a sight'. A 'marker' is an item of information about any phenomenon which could be used to highlight the tourist's awareness of the potential existence of a tourist attraction. This implies that an attraction has a number of components, while conventional definitions only consider the sight (Leiper 1990: 177). In this respect, 'the tourist attraction is a system comprising three elements: a tourist, a sight and a marker' (Leiper 1990 : 178). Although sightseeing is a common tourist activity, the idea of a sight really refers to the nucleus or central component of the attraction (Gunn 1972). In this context a situation could include a sight where sightseeing occurs, but it may also be an object, person or event. Based on this argument, Leiper (1990: 178) introduces the following definition of a tourist attraction as 'a system comprising three elements: a tourist or human element, a nucleus or central element, and a marker or informative element. A tourist attraction comes into existence when the three elements are interconnected'. On the basis of this alternative approach to attractions, Leiper (1990) identifies the type of information which is likely to give meaning to the tourist experience of urban destinations in relation to their attractions.

These ideas were developed further in Leiper's model of a tourist attraction system (Figure 3.7), breaking the established view that tourists are not simply 'attracted' or 'pulled' to areas on the basis of their attractions. Instead, visitors are motivated to experience a nucleus and its markers in a situation where the marker reacts positively with their needs and wants. Figure 3.7 identifies the linkages within the model and how tourist motivation is influenced by the information available and the individual's perception of their needs. Thus, an attraction system can develop only when the following have become connected together:

- a person with tourist needs;
- a nucleus (a feature or attribute of a place that tourists seek to visit); and
- a marker (information about the nucleus).

This theoretical framework has a great deal of value in relation to understanding the supply of urban tourism resources for visitors. First, it views an attraction system as a sub-system of the larger tourism system in an urban area. Second, it acknowledges the integral role for the tourist as consumer – without the tourist (or day tripper) the system would not exist. Third, the systems approach offers a convenient social science frame-

work in which to understand how urban destinations attract visitors, with different markers and nuclei to attract specific groups of visitors. Attention now turns to the development of theme parks in Japan as an example of the geographical and tourist characteristics associated with this form of attraction.

THEME PARKS IN JAPAN

The first theme park was opened in Japan in 1965 near Nagoya. This is a heritage centre which reconstructs a Meiji Village. The next development opened in 1975 and prior to the construction of Tokyo Disneyland, the majority of sites were small scale (see Table 3.7). However, in the period 1988–92, 21 major developments occurred and Table 3.8 outlines the growth and location, with their costs ranging from ¥7 to ¥800 million. Table 3.8 outlines the characteristics of these sites for the production of tourism experiences. Locational factors include access to large centres of population. For example, Tokyo Disneyland receives 70 per cent of its visitors from the Tokyo, Osaka–Kyoto area while other developments have attracted a less national visitor profile, with a greater regional catchment (e.g. Reoma World, Kagawa and Noboribetsu, Hokkaido). The management of theme parks emphasise high quality visitor service, cleanliness, marketing with an impressionable brand and operational efficiency in the back office operations. Tokyo Disneyland acted as a blueprint for many of the theme parks, although continuous improvement and development of the product and experience at Tokyo Disneyland is a feature being endorsed by more recent developers.

As Jones (1994: 115) argues 'political, entrepreneurial and financial factors may literally be considered as the raison d'être of theme parks in Japan'. Following the 1987 Resort Law, local government was positively encouraged to invest in resort area development which could be pump-primed by the Japan Development Bank through

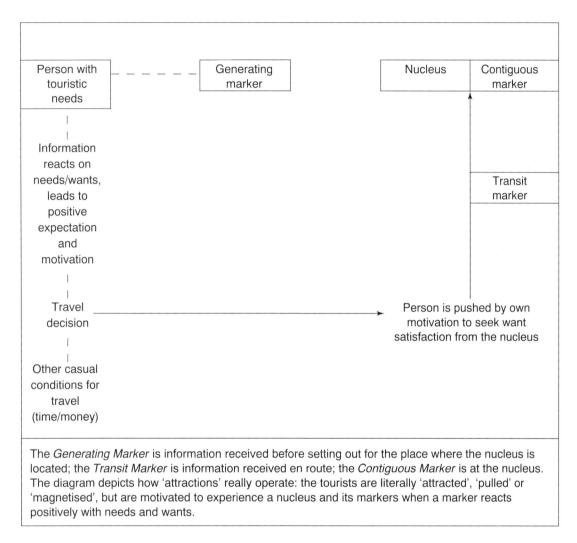

The *Generating Marker* is information received before setting out for the place where the nucleus is located; the *Transit Marker* is information received en route; the *Contiguous Marker* is at the nucleus. The diagram depicts how 'attractions' really operate: the tourists are literally 'attracted', 'pulled' or 'magnetised', but are motivated to experience a nucleus and its markers when a marker reacts positively with needs and wants.

Figure 3.7: A model of a tourism attraction system
Source: Based on Leiper (1990)

the use of preferential interest rates which has helped to galvanise strong public sector support from the initial design through to the provision of financial support (Hall 1997). Domestic tourist and leisure visits have resulted from rising disposable incomes, increased life expectancy, the use of technology (simulations of virtual reality) and the growth of the leisure industry in Japan.

Since 1993, the cost of technology and development has led theme park planners to reassess the significance of continuing a vigorous supply-led pattern of development. In fact in mid-1992, a large number of projects had either been cancelled or delayed due to cost. This is evident from the development cost of Tokyo Disneyland at $863 million (1983 prices) for the first phase. In

Table 3.7: Theme parks in Japan before 1988

Opening date	Location city/prefecture	Stated name	Stated theme
March 1965	Inuyama – City/Aichi	Meiji Museum Village	Meiji era
October 1975	Kyoto-City/Kyoto	Toei Usumasa Film village	Film making
March 1983	Inuyama-City Aichi	Little World	Foreign village
April 1983	Urayasu-City/Chiba	Tokyo Disneyland	Disney animation fantasy
July 1983	Nishisonogi Town/Nagasaki	Nagasaki Holland Village	17th century Holland
April 1986	Fujiwara-Town/Tochigi	Nikko Edo Village	Edo period

Source: Jones (1994: 113)

addition, Reoma World, partly based on Tokyo Disneyland cost $542 million (1991 prices). What the situation in the mid-1990s suggested was that a greater awareness of the market to sustain these developments is required, particularly the entertainment value – are they a passing phase in the tourism and leisure industry, or likely to be the norm for mass entertainment?

Having examined the significance of different approaches towards the analysis of tourism supply in urban areas, attention turns to the significance of different components of Jansen-Verbeke's leisure product and tourism destinations.

TOURIST FACILITIES

Among the 'secondary elements' of the leisure product in urban areas, three components emerge as central to servicing tourist needs. These are:

- accommodation;
- catering;
- shopping; and
- conditional elements.

Accommodation

Tourist accommodation performs an important function in cities: it provides the opportunity for visitors to stay for a length of time to enjoy the locality and its attractions, while their spending can contribute to the local economy. Accommodation forms a base for the tourists' exploration of the urban (and non-urban) environment. The tendency for establishments to locate in urban areas is illustrated in Figure 3.8, which is based on the typical patterns of urban hotel location in West European cities (Ashworth 1989; also see the seminal paper by Arbel and Pizam 1977 on urban hotel location). Figure 3.8 highlights the importance of infrastructure and accessibility when hotels are built to serve specific markets, i.e. the exhibition and conference market will need hotels adjacent to a major conference and exhibition centre as Law (1996) emphasised.

The accommodation sector within cities can be divided into serviced and non-serviced sectors (Figure 3.9). Each sector has developed in response to the needs of different markets, and a wide variety of organisational structures have emerged among private sector operators to develop this area of economic activity. As Pearce (1989) notes, many large chains and corporations now dominate the accommodation sector, using vertical and horizontal forms of integration to develop a greater degree of control over their business activities (see McVey 1986 for a more detailed discussion). (A useful set of studies which focus on the issue of tourist accommodation can be found in Goodall 1989.)

Table 3.8: Theme parks in Japan from 1988

Opening date	Location city/prefecture	Stated name	Stated theme[1]
April 1988	Mise-Village/Saga	Donguri-Village	Pasture in Southern France
August 1988	Manno-Town/Kagawa	Shikoku New Zealand Village	Farm village in New Zealand
November 1988	Kushikino-City Kagoshima	Kushikino Gold Park	Gold
March 1989	Tamano-City/Okayama	Oji Fancy Land	Fantasy characters
June 1989	Matsusaka-City/Mie	Mie Children's Castle	Science for children
July 1989	Koromogawa-Village/Iwate	Tohoku New Zealand Village	Pasture in New Zealand
July 1989	Yamagata-City/Yamagata	Tamadera Fuga Country	History of Mutsu
July 1989	Obihiro-City/Hokkaido	Gluck Kingdom	German town in the middle ages
January 1990	Ureshino-Town/Saga	Hizen Dream Road	Edo Era
April 1990	Mano-Town Niigata	Sado Nishi Mikawa Gold Park	Alluvial gold mining
April 1990	Shuzenji-Town/Shizuoka	Shuzenji Rainbow Village	Foreign village
April 1990	Kitakyushu-City/Fukuoka	Space World	Space and the universe
April 1990	Saikai-Town/Nagasaki	Nagasaki Saikai Paradise	Buddhism
July 1990	Ashibetsu-City/Hokkaido	Canadian World	19th century Canada
July 1990	Noboribetsu-City/Hokkaido	Noboribetsu Marine Park 'Nikusu'	Nordic town and an aquarium
July 1990	Osaka-City/Osaka	Osaka Tenpozan Harbour Village	Ocean/ aquarium
July 1990	Takamiya-Town/Hiroshima	Hiroshima New Zealand Village	Farm village in New Zealand
October 1990	Itsukaichi-Town/Tokyo	Tokyo Sesame Place	Television programme *Sesame Street*
December 1990	Tama-City/Tokyo	Sanrio Pyuro Land	Communication of parents and children
April 1991	Ayauta-Town/Kagawa	Reoma World	Green space and water
April 1991	Hinode-Town/Oita	Harmony Land	Character and village specialities

Source: Based on Jones (1994)

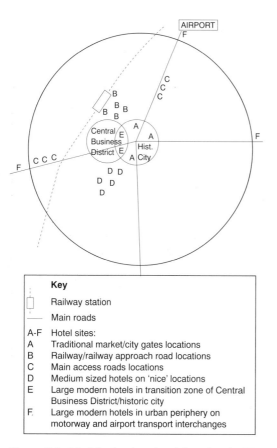

Key

	Railway station
—	Main roads
A-F	Hotel sites:
A	Traditional market/city gates locations
B	Railway/railway approach road locations
C	Main access roads locations
D	Medium sized hotels on 'nice' locations
E	Large modern hotels in transition zone of Central Business District/historic city
F	Large modern hotels in urban periphery on motorway and airport transport interchanges

Figure 3.8: Model of urban hotel location in West European cities
Source: After Ashworth (1989)

Catering facilities

Ashworth and Tunbridge (1990) note that catering facilities are among the most frequently used tourism services after accommodation. For example, of the £15 billion of overseas and domestic tourist spending in the UK in 1990, nearly £2 billion is estimated to be on eating and drinking (Marketpower 1991). What is meant by catering facilities? Bull and Church (1994) suggest that one way of grouping this sector is to use the Standard Industrial Classification which comprises:

- restaurants;
- eating places;

- public houses;
- bars, clubs, canteens and messes; and
- hotels and other forms of tourist accommodation.

Using the products which this sector produces, they further sub-divide the groups into the provision of accommodation and the provision of food for immediate consumption. Whilst there is considerable overlap between the two sectors, there are organisational links between each sector as integration within larger hospitality organisations (e.g. the Forte Group) with their subsidiaries offering various products. One of the immediate difficulties is in identifying specific outlets for tourist use, as many such facilities are also used by residents. Therefore, tourist spending at such facilities also has to be viewed against total consumer spending in this sector. In 1989, Marketpower (1991) found that total consumer spending in the UK on alcoholic drinks and meals outside the home totalled £15 billion. Extracting tourism and leisure spending from this amount can only be an estimate. Bull and Church (1994) provide an indication of the scale of change in the catering and hotel industry in relation to employment and the response of businesses to market demands. The current dominance of transnational corporations in the fast food business worldwide (e.g. MacDonalds and Kentucky Fried Chicken) are notable for their use of franchise methods to acquire market share in other countries in a sector of the market associated with rapid consumer growth. For example, a recent comparison of consumption of fast food in New Zealand found that while consumer spending on fast food rose from 19 per cent of total food spending in 1992 to 23 per cent in 1996, it was significantly behind both Australia and the USA. In Australia, the situation in 1994 was 33 per cent of expenditure of the total food budget and 48 per cent in the USA. Even so, New Zealand like many other developed countries recorded above average rates of growth in the fast food and take away industry at almost double the rate of retail activities in the last five years (Restaurant Brands 1997).

Sector Market segment	Serviced sector		Non-serviced sector (self-catering)	
	Destination	Routes	Destination	Routes
Business and other non-leisure	City/town hotels (Monday–Friday) Resort hotels for conferences, exhibitions Educational establishments	Motels Inns Airport hotels	Apartments	Not applicable
Leisure and holiday	Resort hotels Guest house/ pensions Farm houses City/town hotels (Friday–Sunday) Some educational establishments	Motels Bed and breakfast Inns	Hotels Condominia Holiday villages Holiday centres/ camps Caravan/chalet parks Gîtes Cottages Villas Apartments/flats Some motels	Touring pitches for caravans, tents, recreation vehicles YHA Some hotels

Figure 3.9: Types of tourism accommodation
Source: After Middleton (1988)

Tourist use of catering facilities varies according to the specific service on offer, and on their being located throughout cities, often in association with other facilities (Smith 1983b). Many catering establishments in cities reflect local community needs and tourism complements the existing pattern of use. Nevertheless, Ashworth and Tunbridge (1990: 65) do acknowledge that

restaurants and establishments combining food and drink with other entertainments, whether nightclubs, discos, casinos and the like, have two important locational characteristics that render them useful in this context: they have a distinct tendency to cluster together into particular streets or districts, what might be termed the 'Latin-quarter effect', and they tend to be associated spatially with other tourism elements including hotels, which probably themselves offer public restaurant facilities.

Furthermore, a British Tourist Authority report (1993) recognises that while the quality of food and service in Britain has improved in recent years, food can be a persuasive ingredient in Britain's overall tourist appeal, particularly in urban areas. Nevertheless, the report supports the reform of Britain's Sunday trading laws and licensing hours, as well as the investment in upgrading the language skills of tourism and hospitality workers, in pursuit of improvements to customer service. As the report suggests, food may have improved, but tourist perceptions still lag behind the reality of provision in many urban areas, illustrating the significance of this element is the 'tourist experience' of urban areas. Catering facilities also have a predisposition to cluster within areas where shopping is also a dominant activity, particularly in mall developments where food courts have become a popular concept in the USA and Australasia while cosmopolitan cities have also developed a distinctive café culture aimed at the segment of the resident and visiting market who seek a café ambience.

Tourist shopping

The English Historic Town Forum's (1992) study on retailing and tourism highlights many of the relationships between 'tourism and retail activity [which] are inextricably linked to historic towns with three-quarters of tourists combining shopping with visiting attractions . . . The expenditure is not only on refreshments and souvenirs, as might be expected, but also on clothing and footwear, stationery and books' (English Towns Forum 1992: 3). The study also emphasises the overall significance of the environmental quality in towns which is vital to the success of urban tourism and retailing. In fact the report argues that, 'for towns wishing to maintain or increase leisure visitor levels, the study reveals a number of guide lines. For example, cleanliness, attractive shop fronts and provision of street entertainment are all important to tourists' (English Historic Towns Forum 1992: 3).

Unfortunately, identifying tourist-shopping as a concept in the context of urban tourism is

Table 3.9: Criteria to be considered in distinguishing between intentional shopping and intentional leisure and tourism

Behaviour pattern of visitors
- trip length – short, possibly longer;
- length of stay – limited or rather unplanned;
- time of stay – a few hours during the day, an evening, a full day;
- kinds of activity – window shopping, intentional buying, drinking, eating, various leisure activities, cultural activities, sightseeing;
- expenditure – goods, possibly some souvenirs, drinks, meals, entrance fees to leisure facilities.

Functional characteristics of the environment
- wide range of retail shops, department stores, catering, leisure and other facilities, tourist attractions, spatial clustering of facilities;
- parking space and easy access;
- street retailing, pedestrian priority in open spaces.

Quality of the environment
- image of the place, leisure setting, display of goods on the street, street musicians and artists;
- accessibility during leisure time, including weekends and evenings;
- aesthetic value, image of maintenance and safety;
- architectural design of buildings, streets, shops, windows, sign boards, lighting;
- social effective value, liveliness of the open space;
- animation, entertainment, amusement and surprise.

Hospitableness of the environment
- social, visual, physical;
- orientation, information, symbolism, identification.

Source: Jansen-Verbeke (1991: 9–10)

difficult, since it is also an activity undertaken by other users such as residents). The most relevant research undertaken in this field, by Jansen-Verbeke (1990, 1991), considers the motives of tourists and their activities in a range of Dutch towns. She makes a number of interesting observations on this concept. However, the range of motives associated with tourism and leisure shopping are complex: people visit areas due to their appeal and shopping may be a spontaneous as well as a planned activity. Even so, the quality and range of retail facilities may be a useful determinant of the likely demand for tourism and leisure shopping: the longer the visitor is enticed to stay in a destination, the greater the likely spending in retail outlets.

One important factor which affects the ability of cities to attract tourism and leisure shoppers is the retail mix – namely the variety of goods, shops and presence of specific retailers. For example, the English Historic Towns Forum (1992) notes that over 80 per cent of visitors consider the retailing mix and general environment of the town the most important attraction of the destination. Although the priorities of different tourist market segments vary slightly, catering, accessibility (e.g. availability of car parking, location of car parks and public transport), tourist attractions and the availability of visitor information shape the decision to engage in tourism and leisure shopping. The constant search for the unique shopping experience, especially in conjunction with day trips in border areas and neighbouring countries (e.g. the UK cross-channel tax-free shopping trips from Dover to Calais) are well established forms of tourism and leisure shopping.

The global standardisation of consumer products has meant that the search for the unique shopping experience continues to remain important. The growth of the North American shopping malls and tourist specific projects (Lew 1985, 1989; Getz 1993b) and the development in the UK of out of town complexes (e.g. the Metro Centre in Gateshead and Lakeside at Thurrock,

adjacent to the M25) have extended this trend. For example, in the case of Edmonton Mall (Canada), Jansen-Verbeke (1991) estimates that 10 per cent of the total floor space is used for leisure facilities with its 800 shops and parking for 27,000 cars. Such developments have been a great concern for many cities as out of town shopping has reduced the potential in-town urban tourism in view of the competition they pose for established destinations. The difficulty with most existing studies of leisure shopping, is that they fail to disentangle the relationships between the actual activity tourists undertake and their perception of the environment. For this reason, Jansen-Verbeke (1991) distinguishes between intentional shopping and intentional leisure shopping in a preliminary attempt to explain how and why tourists engage in this activity; she also suggests that several criteria need to be considered to distinguish between intentional shopping and intentional leisure and tourism (Table 3.9).

For many destinations, finding the right mix between shops, leisure facilities and tourist attractions to appeal to a wide range of visitors and residents involves a process of development and promotion to attract investment in town centres. This also recognises the potential for using shopping as a marketing tool by the tourism industry in towns and cities. The English Historic Towns Forum (1992) emphasised this relationship, as 75 per cent of visitors to the cities surveyed combined tourism and shopping.

Only certain shopping centres have the essential ingredients to be promoted as tourism and day trip destinations. The image and manner in which these places are promoted is assuming growing significance. Historic cities in Europe have many of the key ingredients in terms of the environment, facilities, tourism attractions and the ability to appeal to distinct visitor audiences. Many successful cities in Western Europe have used tourism and leisure shopping to establish their popularity as destinations as a gradual process of evolution. For example, research by Page and Hardyman (1996) examines the concept of Town Centre Management as one attempt to address the impact of out-of-town shopping malls and complexes as a threat to tourism and leisure spending in town centres. Their research found that based on concepts developed in North America, town centres can identify their users more closely and undertake in-town improvements to attract the user as a means of developing leisure shopping. In particular, improvements to town centres by city authorities have acted as catalysts to this process by:

- establishing pedestrian precincts;
- managing parking problems and implementing park and ride schemes to improve access and convenience;
- marketing the destination based around an identifiable theme, often using the historical and cultural attractions of a city;
- investing in new and attractive indoor shopping galleries, improving facades, the layout and design of the built environment and making the environment more attractive. The English Historic Towns Forum (1992: 12) identify the following factors which tourism and leisure shoppers deemed important:
  - the cleanliness of the town
  - pedestrian areas/pavements which are well maintained
  - natural features such as rivers and parks
  - the architecture and facades/shopfronts
  - street furniture (seating and floral displays)
  - town centre activities (e.g. outdoor markets and live entertainment).

One illustration of the effect of specific factors which tourists may view as important is evident from the Tidy Britain Group's qualitative study of the cleanliness of capital cities in Europe and the conditions at major tourist sites. The survey examined litter levels and environmental problems, awarding points for cleanliness. While the results of such surveys may be highly variable, due to the sampling methodology used, London featured as the overall winner in relation to the

criteria used. Although Berne's 'the Bear Pit' emerges as the most clean tourist site among those locations surveyed (while Athens' Syntagma Square came bottom of the league), the environment around other facilities visited and used by tourists (e.g. shopping streets, railway stations and parliament buildings) provide additional insights into the environmental quality of those areas which tourists also visit. Although it is difficult to place a great deal of store by *ad hoc* and random surveys such as the Tidy Britain Group, it does illustrate the point that cleanliness, litter and the perceived quality of the local environment may influence tourist views, particularly those seeking to visit shopping streets in major capital cities such as Oxford Street (London), Puerto del Sol (Madrid), Rue de Neuve (Brussels), Kalverstraat (Amsterdam), Bahnhof Platz (Berne), Ermou (Athens), Boulevard Haussman (Paris), Kurfustendamm (Berlin) and Via del Corso (Rome). The impressions which shoppers form of the environmental quality of urban areas may also influence other potential visitors as word of mouth communication is a powerful force in personal recommendation of shopping areas.

Changes which alter the character of the town, where it becomes more tourist orientated, are sometimes characterised by the development of speciality and gift/souvenir shops and catering facilities in certain areas. However, as Owen (1990) argues, many traditional urban shopping areas are in need of major refurbishment and tourism may provide the necessary stimulus for regeneration. Recent developments such as theme shopping (Jones Lang Wooten 1989) and festival marketplaces (Sawicki 1989) are specialised examples of how this regeneration has proceeded in the UK and North America.

The next decade, therefore, would seem to be set for tourism and leisure shopping development to further segment markets by seeking new niches and products. Jansen-Verbeke (1991) describes the 'total experience' as the future way forward for this activity – retailers will need to attract tourism and leisure spending using newly built, simulated or refurbished retailing environments with a variety of shopping experiences. Keown's (1989) experience is that the opportunity to undertake a diverse range of retail activities in a locality increases the tourist's propensity to spend. However, the growing saturation of retailing provision in many industrialised countries may pose problems for further growth in tourism and leisure shopping due to the intense competition for such spending. Urban tourism destinations are likely to have to compete more aggressively for such spending in the new millennium.

The conditional elements

The last feature which Jansen-Verbeke (1986) views as central to the city's 'leisure product' is the conditional elements, such as transport, physical infrastructure and the provision of signposting. To illustrate the significance of these elements in the context of tourist activities, a case study of London Docklands follows. The case study describes how the expectations of developers to create a new focus for tourism and leisure shopping failed to materialise due to the inadequate infrastructure provision and the reluctance of tourists to divert from established patterns of visitor activity.

CASE STUDY: Tourism in London Docklands – supply-side issues

The London Docklands development covers an area of 20km², with 180ha of redundant docks and 88.5km of redundant waterfront which stretches from the Tower of London in the West to Becton in the East (Figure 3.10). The decline and subsequent redevelopment of London Docklands has been extensively documented (Page 1995a,b; Page and Sinclair 1989) and it has followed a similar pattern to other waterfront schemes (Hoyle and Pinder 1992). London Docklands represents one of the world's largest waterfront revitalisation programmes, stimulated and directed by a central government funded quango – the London Docklands Development Corporation (LDDC), with Canary Wharf as its focal point (Plate 3.3). It has caused a great deal of controversy in relation to its accountability and impact on the local planning process. LDDC proceeded to redevelop the land, improve the region's infrastructure and pursue a policy of image promotion (Plate 3.4). By 1990, LDDC claimed that some £8,057 million of investment by the private sector had been committed to redevelopment compared to government funding of £803 million, providing

a private to public leverage ratio of 10:1 for investment in the area.

Central to the redevelopment was the development of the Dockland's Light Railway (DLR) at a cost of £77 million in the 1980s, prior to the planned extension of the Jubilee Underground Line to the area in the late 1990s. Transport is a critical factor in relation to

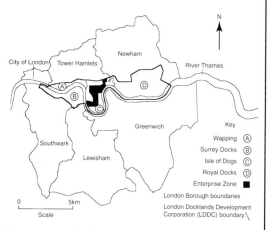

Figure 3.10: The location of London Docklands
Source: Page (1995b)

Plate 3.3: Marketing image of London Docklands (Courtesy LDDC)

Plate 3.4: Marketing image of London Docklands (Courtesy LDDC)

regenerating new centres for tourism and leisure shopping (e.g. Tobacco Dock) as the discussion will show and for this reason it is useful to consider the significance of transport for tourism in Docklands.

Transport for tourism in London Docklands

Transport and tourism is vital to the mobility of visitors to travel at their destination (see Page 1994b). Church (1990: 5) argues that the LDDC's transport policy reflects the ideological goals of central government, which emphasises: limiting public transport expenditure; allowing the market to set priorities and resolve problems; limiting state intervention; promoting private ownership of transport; meeting the demands of road users; promoting wealth creation and the enterprise culture. The absence of strategic transport planning by the LDDC has also meant that the region's transport network has failed to meet accessibility targets emphasised in the LDDC's brief from central government. Its preference for investment in environmentally-damaging road projects (e.g. the 12km Docklands Highway) exemplifies the LDDC ideology on transportation and a certain degree of synergy with central

government transport objectives. What does this mean for tourism in the region?

In the context of London Docklands, awareness of the potential relationship between tourism and urban regeneration was reflected in the LDDC's commissioning of the *Tourist Development in Docklands* report (Llewelyn-Davies 1987). Before 1987, tourism was not a key priority for the LDDC as capital investment in outdoor recreation projects consumed the majority of leisure budgets. Yet the tourism potential of Docklands had been recognised in the mid-1980s by Horwath and Horwath (1986: 149) who argued that it was necessary to raise 'the ambience and image of part or parts of Dockland to establish Docklands as a prime tourist destination in its own right which tourists would seek as a desirable location for their London stay'. Furthermore, the London Tourist Board (1987) estimated that between 1986 and 1996, up to half of London's new tourism developments could be located in Docklands, highlighting its potential role as a new tourism destination. To understand how tourism could be used to stimulate economic development in Docklands, it is pertinent to examine the LDDC's tourism development strategy embodied in the Llewelyn-Davies

(1987) report and the effect of demand-led planning on the region's tourism potential.

Tourism planning and development in Docklands

The LDDC *Tourism Strategy for Docklands* identified the main direction which tourism accommodation and attraction development should follow in Docklands, examining the underlying principles of tourism development in Docklands which sought to maximise the geographical distribution of visitors using three concepts to guide tourist development. Firstly, a riverside corridor bordering Dockland was to be the main focus for visitors. Within this corridor a series of 'visitor destinations' were to be to developed at major docks (Figure 3.11). Each

'destination' should be capable of attracting at least 2 million visitors per annum spread throughout the year. Public transport (DLR) and river boat access was essential to ensure that these focal points were accessible, offering a wide range of attractions including shops, restaurants, nightlife and hotels. LDDC identified five areas which were suitable as 'visitor destinations': Tower Bridge, Wapping, West India Dock, Greenwich (which is outside the LDDC boundary, although it has been incorporated in view of its significance in a London-wide context) and Royal Victoria Dock.

Secondly, a series of 'visitor places' were to be developed near the main corridor of Docklands which comprised single attractions or groups of small attractions capable of attracting up to 1 million visitors per annum, although their visitor

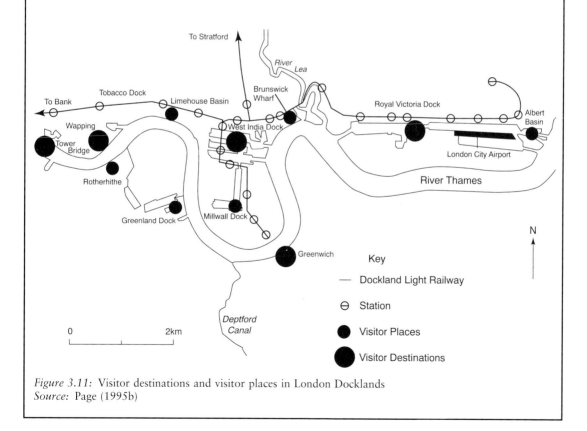

Figure 3.11: Visitor destinations and visitor places in London Docklands
Source: Page (1995b)

markets were likely to be seasonal. Like the 'visitor destinations', they were aimed at visitor leisure activities. Lastly, a number of small scale, isolated and less well known 'visitor features' were to be promoted. These were to be at least one kilometre from the main tourist attractions and capable of attracting up to 100,000 visitors per annum. Therefore, as Figure 3.11 suggests, tourist development in Docklands emphasises the principle of concentrated activity at accessible waterside locations.

To complement the planned development of tourism, in 1990 the LDDC introduced an 'Arts Action Plan for Docklands' which would be an essential part of the quality of life of Docklands providing a creative use of leisure time and enhancing the built environment for workers although the underlying rationale of LDDC's approach to tourism and urban redevelopment is to stimulate 'the supply side of the economy by rolling back the frontiers of the state – decreasing the degree of regulation and intervention by government' (Page and Sinclair 1989: 135). In Docklands, the result has been that private investment has gravitated towards existing areas of tourism development which reveal market potential. In cases where private sector investment in tourism has been pump-primed by LDDC grants (e.g. Tobacco Dock), the LDDC's prioritisation of investment in infrastructure has failed to make destinations accessible.

The case in point is Tobacco Dock. This project cost £50 million and is situated in a restored Grade 1 listed building providing specialist shops and tourist attractions. It was hoped that such developments would resemble the highly successful Covent Garden scheme in central London. Tobacco Dock was expected to create 800 new job vacancies, of which 75 per cent may be filled by local labour in an area of high unemployment. However, due to a recession in the 1990s, the development of tourism

Plate 3.5: Docklands Light Railway (Courtesy LDDC)

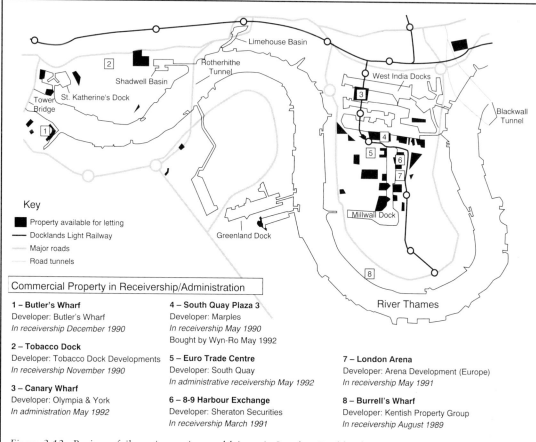

Figure 3.12: Business failures in tourism and leisure in London Docklands, 1992
Source: Modified from *Financial Times* 30/31 May 1992

Key

■ Property available for letting
— Docklands Light Railway
Major roads
Road tunnels

Commercial Property in Receivership/Administration

1 – Butler's Wharf
Developer: Butler's Wharf
In receivership December 1990

2 – Tobacco Dock
Developer: Tobacco Dock Developments
In receivership November 1990

3 – Canary Wharf
Developer: Olympia & York
In administration May 1992

4 – South Quay Plaza 3
Developer: Marples
In receivership May 1990
Bought by Wyn-Ro May 1992

5 – Euro Trade Centre
Developer: South Quay
In administrative receivership May 1992

6 – 8-9 Harbour Exchange
Developer: Sheraton Securities
In receivership March 1991

7 – London Arena
Developer: Arena Development (Europe)
In receivership May 1991

8 – Burrell's Wharf
Developer: Kentish Property Group
In receivership August 1989

at Tobacco Dock has been limited; many shops have closed down, the visitors have not materialised since it is inaccessible and not on tourist itineraries (Plate 3.5). Thus, its potential as a speciality shopping centre for tourism and leisure visitors has not been realised. One important consideration is the effect of the recent recession on new projects such as Tobacco Dock (see Figure 3.12 for an assessment of business failures in Docklands). Even where urban programme grants have been directed towards tourism projects in Docklands, these have not enjoyed the high rates of employment of Liverpool Docks (Department of the Environment 1990).

As the Department of the Environment (1990: 69) acknowledges: 'tourism projects appear to have greater impacts when they are grouped with other tourism projects in a relatively small geographical area. This clustered approach gives a higher profile, enables links to be developed between projects, facilitates joint marketing'.

In Docklands, the spirit of the free market economy has meant that cooperative ventures and partnership schemes have been limited, particularly since few destinations within the region have sufficient attractions to enjoy benefits of clustered development. While the effects of market-led planning and its impact on the landscape of Docklands has placed the region on the tourist map of London, the emphasis on encouraging private sector investment to realise development opportunities in tourism and leisure facilities has been notoriously difficult in a climate of commercial uncertainty. Without adequate investment in public transport infrastructure in Docklands, tourism is unlikely to reach its full potential, remaining a day trip destination, with visitors concentrated at those locations which are easily accessible.

CONCLUSION

This chapter has examined a range of issues and concepts associated with the analysis of recreation and tourism supply issues. One interesting comparison which appears to hold true is Smith's (1983a) criticisms of recreational research being applicable to tourism due to the simplistic conceptualisation of the subject matter. In fact, Britton's (1980a, 1991) innovative and theoretically derived analyses offer a fresh and welcomed attempt to re-think the geography of tourism, particularly the production side which has been notoriously descriptive and somewhat naive in its borrowing of geographical concepts while making no contribution to theory. This chapter has achieved two purposes: the first is to show how the geographer approaches the spatial complexity of supply issues in both recreation and tourism, while introducing some of the concepts, methods and ways of thinking about supply. Second, it has detailed the importance of developing a more meaningful assessment of tourism and the production system by situating the supply of tourism and recreation within the contexts of concepts of core and periphery, consumption and production, and tourism as a capitalist activity.

4

THE IMPACTS OF TOURISM
AND RECREATION

The growth of international and domestic tourism has been matched by a corresponding increase in the numbers of those who study tourism and its impacts. Indeed, it may even be said that tourism research is one of the academic growth industries of the late twentieth century (Hall 1995). The literature on tourism has expanded enormously with the result that research has become, 'highly fragmented, with researchers following separate and often divergent paths' (Mathieson and Wall 1982: 2). Nevertheless, one of the major areas of interest for geographers, as well as other tourism researchers, is on the impacts of tourism and recreation.

Tourism and recreation cannot be studied in isolation from the complex economic, environmental, political, and social milieux in which they occur (Runyan and Wu 1979). If geographers are to make a valid contribution to the study of tourism and recreation and their impacts it is vital that they are aware of the widest possible implications of such events for host communities, particularly as concerns over the sustainability of tourism and recreation grow (Butler 1990, 1991; Hall and Lew 1998). This has therefore meant that there has been substantial interchange of ideas, frameworks and methodologies between geographers and non-geographers in analysing the impacts of tourism and recreation.

There are a number of ways of categorising the impacts of tourism. One of the most common is that used by Mathieson and Wall (1982), which divided impacts into economic, social and physical (environmental categories). A more detailed breakdown of the impacts of tourism has been used by Getz (1977), Ritchie (1984) and Hall (1992b). An overview of these categories is provided in Table 4.1 where they are categorised in terms of their positive or negative nature for a destination community. However, it should be noted that such a division is not absolute as whether something is seen as positive or negative will depend on the goals and value position of an individual with respect to different types of tourism development. The following chapter will provide a broad overview of the impacts of tourism and some of the main issues which arise out of such an analysis.

ECONOMIC ANALYSIS

Within tourism research, 'until recently, attention has concentrated on the more obvious economic impacts with comparatively little consideration being given to the environmental and social consequences of tourism' (Mathieson and Wall 1982: 3–4). However, considerable debate has arisen over methodological problems in the economic analysis of such events, particularly in the use of economic multipliers and cost-benefit analysis (Archer 1976, 1977a, 1977b, 1984; Murphy 1985; Pearce 1989), the evaluation of opportunity cost (Vaughan 1977), and the relationship of tourism and recreation to regional development and employment (Royer, McCool

Table 4.1: Positive and negative dimensions of the impacts of tourism on host communities

Type of impact	Positive	Negative
Economic Dimensions Economic	• Increased expenditures • Creation of employment • Increase in labour supply • Increase in standard of living • Increase in investment	• Localised inflation • Real estate speculation • Failure to attract tourists • Better alternative investments • Capital outflows • Inadequate estimation of costs of tourism development • Undesirable opportunity costs including transfer of funds from health and education
Tourism/Commercial	• Increased awareness of the region as a travel/tourism destination • Increased knowledge concerning the potential for investment and commercial activity in the region • Creation of new facilities, attractions and infrastructure • Increase in accessibility	• Acquisition of a poor reputation as a result of inadequate facilities, improper practices or inflated prices • Negative reactions from existing enterprises due to the possibility of new competition for local manpower and government assistance.
Socio-cultural impacts Social/Cultural	• Increase in permanent level of local interest and participation in types of activity associated with event • Strengthening of regional values and traditions	• Commercialisation of activities which may be of a personal or private nature • Modification of nature of event or activity to accommodate tourism • Potential increase in crime • Changes in community structure • Social dislocation
Psychological	• Increased local pride and community spirit • Increased awareness of non-local perceptions	• Tendency toward defensive attitudes concerning host regions • High possibility of misunderstandings leading to varying degrees of host/visitor hostility.
Political/Administrative	• Enhanced international recognition of region and values • Development of skills among planners	• Economic exploitation of local population to satisfy ambitions of political elite • Distortion of true nature of event to reflect values of political system • Failure to cope • Inability to achieve aims • Increase in administrative costs • Use of tourism to legitimatise unpopular decisions • Legitimation of ideology of local elite
Environmental impacts Physical/Environmental	• Development of new facilities • Improvement of local infrastructure • Conservation of heritage • Visitor management strategies	• Environmental damage • Changes in natural processes • Architectural pollution • Destruction of heritage • Overcrowding • Changed feeding and breeding habits of wildlife

Source: After Getz (1977); Mathieson and Wall (1982); Ritchie (1984); Hall (1992)

and Hunt 1974; Doering 1976; Frechtling 1977; Hudman 1978; Ellerbrook and Hite 1980; Williams and Shaw 1988).

Many economic impact studies focus on what is known as the 'multiplier effect'. This effect is concerned with 'the way in which expenditure on tourism filters throughout the economy, stimulating other sectors as it does so' (Pearce 1989: 205). Several different types of multiplier are in use, each with their own emphasis (Archer 1977, 1982). However, the multiplier may best be regarded as 'a coefficient which expresses the amount of income generated in an area by an additional unit of tourist spending' (Archer 1982: 236). It is the ratio of direct and secondary changes within an economic region to the direct initial change itself. In this context, geographers have not played a major role although multiplier analysis is not devoid of a spatial component with its linkage to regional science and its spatial concerns for quantitative analysis of areas and locations. In some cases, geographers have not pursued the regional analytical approaches of the economists in measuring and analysing tourist activity in a spatial context due to the prevailing geographical paradigms in human geography in the 1960s and 1970s. Although economic geography has overlapped with economics in some cases, tourism and recreation is not an area where this occurred on a wide scale. Likewise, collaborative research between geographers and economists has not emerged as a theme in research until comparatively recently. This is often because each subject area has its own concepts, language, approach and few obvious intersections in the research field because tourism and recreation remained a fringe area for research in the 1960s and 1970s for both geographers and economists.

The economic impacts of tourism and recreation are usually classified as being either primary or secondary in nature (Archer 1982). Primary or direct impacts are those economic impacts which are a direct consequence of visitor spending, e.g. the purchase of food and beverages by a tourist in a hotel. Secondary impacts may be described as

being either indirect or induced. Indirect impacts are those arising from the responding of money in the form of local business transactions, e.g. the new investment of hotel owners in equipment and supplies. Induced impacts are those arising from the additional income generated by further consumer spending, e.g. the purchase of goods and services by hotel employees. For each round of spending per unit of initial visitor expenditure leakage will occur from the regional economy until little or no further re-spending is possible. Therefore, the recreation or tourism multiplier is a measure of the total effects (direct plus secondary effects) which result from the additional tourist or recreational expenditure. However, despite their extensive use, it should be noted that 'multipliers are difficult to calculate precisely under the best circumstances. They require substantial amounts of very detailed data. The methods used are also difficult and require a high degree level of statistical and/or macro-economic expertise' (Smith 1995: 16; see also Saeter 1998).

The size of the visitor multiplier will vary from region to region and will depend on a number of factors including:

- the size of area of analysis;
- the proportion of goods and services imported into the region for consumption by visitors;
- the rate of circulation;
- the nature of visitor spending;
- the availability of suitable local products and services; and
- the patterns of economic behaviour for visitor and local alike.

As a measure of economic benefit from recreation and tourism, the multiplier technique has been increasingly subject to question, particularly as its use has often produced exaggerated results (Archer 1977, 1982; Cooper and Pigram 1984; Frechtling 1987; Pearce 1989). Nevertheless, despite doubts about the accuracy of the multiplier technique, substantial attention is still paid to the results of economic impact studies by government and the private sector as a measure of the success of tourism development or as a way of estimating the potential contribution of a proposed development in order to justify policy or planning decisions. As Smith (1995: 16) noted: 'Regrettably, the abuses of multipliers often seem to be as frequent as legitimate uses – thus contributing further to the industry's lack of credibility.'

The size of the tourist multiplier is regarded as a significant measure of the economic benefit of visitor expenditure because it will be a reflection of the circulation of the visitor dollar through an economic system. In general, the larger the size of the tourist multiplier the greater the self-sufficiency of that economy in the provision of tourist facilities and services. Therefore, a tourist multiplier will generally be larger at a national level than at a regional level, because at a regional level leakage will occur in the form of taxes to the national government and importation of goods and services from regions. Similarly, at the local level, multipliers will reflect the high importation level of small communities and tax payments to regional and national governments (Hall 1995).

According to Murphy (1985: 95), 'for practical purposes it is crucial to appreciate that local multiplier studies are just case studies of local gains and no more' and several questions remain unanswered about the real costs and benefits of tourism on local and regional development. Indeed, a major question should be who are the winners and losers in tourism development? As Coppock (1977b: 1.1) argued in relation to the use of tourism as a tool for economic development: 'Not only is it inevitable that the residents of an area will gain unequally from tourism (if indeed they gain at all) and probable that the interests of some will actually be harmed, but it may well be that a substantial proportion does not wish to see any development of tourism.'

An area which has seen considerable attention by geographers (e.g. Shaw 1985; Getz 1991a, 1991b; Hall 1992b; Hall and Hodges 1996), is the impact of hosting staged, short-term attractions, usually referred to as hallmark, special or mega events (Ritchie 1984; Ritchie and Yangzhou 1987; Hall 1989). The hallmark event is different in its appeal from the attractions normally promoted by the tourist industry as it is not a continuous or seasonal phenomenon. Indeed, in many cases the hallmark event is a strategic response to the problems that seasonal variations in demand pose for the tourist industry (Ritchie and Beliveau 1974). Although, the ability of an event 'to achieve this objective depends on the uniqueness of the event, the status of the event, and the extent to which it is successfully marketed within tourism generated regions' (Ritchie 1984: 2). As with other areas of research on the economic impacts of tourism, the analysis of hallmark events has been characterised by overstated large benefit-cost ratios (Hall 1989, 1992b; Getz 1991b). Several reasons can be cited for this:

- there has been a failure to account for the economic impact that would have occurred anyway but has switched from one industry to another;
- there has been an 'unfortunately common mistake' of attributing all the benefits received from the event to government expenditure, instead of establishing the marginal impact of that contribution' (Burns and Mules 1986: 8, 10);
- the taxation benefits of expenditure generation has been counted as additional to the multiplier 'flow-ons' when they have already been included;
- 'output' rather than 'value-added' multipliers, which can result in major over-estimates of the economic impact of events, are frequently uncritically used; and
- there has been a general failure to delimit the size of the regional economy that is to be studied. The smaller the area to be analysed, the greater will be the number of 'visitors' and hence the greater would be the estimate of economic impact.

One of the primary justifications used by government in the encouragement of tourism development is that of tourism's potential employment benefits (Pearce 1992a; Hall 1994; Jenkins *et al.* 1998). However, as Hudson and Townsend (1992: 64) observed:

[There is] a growing involvement of local authorities in policies to sustain existing tourist developments and encourage new ones, although often the actual impacts of tourism on local employment and the economy are imperfectly understood. The direction of causality between growing employment and increasing policy involvement is often obscure and in any case variable.

One of the ironies of the perceived employment benefits of tourism and recreation is that areas which have tourism as a mainstay of the local economy tend to have high levels of unemployment. For example, two of Australia's major destination areas, the Gold Coast and the Sunshine Coast in Queensland, have had unemployment rates significantly above the national average (Mullins 1984, 1990). Often such a situation is regarded by local politicians as an 'imported problem', by which 'the unemployed flock into these cities for the "good life". Yet data . . . on interstate transferees on unemployment benefits shows that the net number remaining in the Gold Coast and Sunshine Coast over any 12 month period barely makes 1 per cent of these cities unemployed' (Mullins 1990: 39). Instead of 'dole-bludger' (an Australian term which refers to people who deliberately seek unemployment benefits rather than paid employment) and surfer migration, the answer to the unemployment situation rests on the nature of the two region's economies. The economies of both areas are founded on two unstable industries: tourism, which is seasonal, and construction, which is cyclical and is itself related to actual or predicted tourist flows. Therefore, as Mullins (1990: 39) reported, 'high rates of unemployment seem inevitable', although as the economic base of the regions diversifies, unemployment levels should fall.

Another major consideration in the potential contribution of tourism to the national economy is the organisation and spatial allocation of capital

and, in particular, the penetration of foreign or international capital. The distribution and organisation of capital and tourists is also spread unevenly between and within regions, indeed, tourism is often seen as a mechanism for redistributing wealth between regions (Pearce 1990a, 1992a). Geographers have long noted the manner in which tourism tends to distribute development away from urban areas towards those regions in a country which have not been developed (e.g. Christaller 1963), with the core–periphery nature of tourism being an important component of political-economy approaches towards tourism (Britton 1980a, 1980b, 1982), particularly with respect to tourism in the island microstates of the Pacific (Connell 1988; Lea 1988).

More recently, geographers have begun to analyse critically tourism with reference to issues of economic restructuring, processes of globalisation and the development of post-fordist modes of production (e.g. Britton 1991; Hall 1994; Debbage and Iaonnides 1998; Milne 1998; Williams and Shaw 1998). Tourism is a significant component of these shifts which may be described as 'post-industrial' or 'post-Fordist', which refers to the shift from an industrial to an information technology/service base. In addition, tourism is part of the globalisation of the international economy, in which economic production is transnational, interdependent, and multi-polar with less and less dependence on the nation-state as the primary unit of international economic organisation. As Williams and Shaw (1998: 59) recognise:

The essence of tourism is the way in which the global interacts with the local. For example, mass tourism emphasises a global scan for destinations for global (or at least macro-regional) markets, while some forms of new tourism seek to exploit the individuality of places. These global–local relationships are not static but are subject to a variety of restructuring processes.

The notion of the 'globalisation' of tourism implies its increasing commodification. The tourist production system simultaneously 'sells' places in order to attract tourists, the means to the end (travel and accommodation) and the end itself (the tourist experience). Therefore, tourism finds itself at the forefront of an important recent dynamic within capitalist accumulation in terms of the creation and marketing of experiences. Tourists 'are purchasing the intangible qualities of restoration, status, life-style signifier, release from the constraints of everyday life, or conveniently packaged novelty' (Britton 1991: 465). Within this setting, place is therefore commodified and reduced to an experience and images for consumption. However, while place promotion is recognised as increasingly important for tourism and recreation (see chapter 5), there have been insufficient attempts, with the exception of some of the authors noted above, to locate such issues within the context of mainstream tourism studies or tourism geography.

Related to the economic analysis of tourism has been the study of the forecasting of visitor demand and the marketing of the tourist product. Several studies of hallmark events, for example, have attempted to deal with the problem of forecasting visitor demand (see Ritchie and Aitken 1984; Hall 1992b). Nevertheless, substantial methodological problems still remain; and, 'although relatively sophisticated statistical measures have been used, forecasts of tourism demand can produce only approximations' (Uysal and Crompton 1985: 13). As Mathieson and Wall (1982: 133) observed:

> Most of the early studies of the effects of tourism were restricted to economic analyses and enumerated the financial and employment benefits which accrued to destination areas as a result of the benefits of tourism. In recent years a number of studies have emerged that examine the socio-cultural impacts of tourism. In contrast to the economic effects, such impacts are usually portrayed in the literature in a negative light.

THE ANALYSIS OF TOURISM'S SOCIAL IMPACTS

The social impact of tourism refers to the manner in which tourism and travel effects changes in col-

lective and individual value systems, behaviour patterns, community structures, lifestyle and the quality of life (Hall 1995). The major focus of research on the social impacts of tourism is on the population of the tourist destination, rather than the tourist generating area and the tourists themselves, although significant work is also done in this area particularly with respect to outdoor recreationists. The variables which contribute to resident perceptions of tourism may be categorised as either extrinsic or intrinsic (Faulkner and Tideswell 1996). Extrinsic variables refer to factors which affect a community at a macro level, e.g. stage of tourism development, the ratio between tourists and residents, cultural differences between tourists and residents, and seasonality. Intrinsic variables are those factors which may vary in association with variations in the characteristics of individuals in a given population, e.g. demographic characteristics, involvement in tourism and proximity to tourist activity (Hall 1998).

Researchers from a number of disciplinary backgrounds have conducted work on the social impacts of tourism. For example, interest in tourism marketing strategies and increased concern for the social consequences of tourism led to the social psychology of tourism becoming a major area of research (e.g. P. Pearce 1982; Stringer 1984; Stringer and P. Pearce 1984). Research has focused on aspects of the tourist experience as diverse as tourism and culture shock (Furnham 1984), and tourist–guide interaction (P. Pearce 1984). Research in the marketing of the tourist product sees attention being paid to the demand, motivations and preferences of the potential tourist (e.g. Jenkins 1978; Van Raaij and Francken 1984; Kent et al. 1987; Pearce 1989; Smith 1995), the evaluation of the tourist product and potential tourist resources (e.g. Ferrario 1979a, 1979b; Gartner 1986; Smith 1995), the intended and unintended use of tourist brochures (e.g. Dilley 1986), the utility of market segmentation for specific targeting of potential consumers (e.g. Murphy and Staples 1979; Smith 1995), and tourist and recreationist satisfaction. In the latter area, geographers have done a substantial amount of work in the outdoor recreation and ˉback-country use field, particularly with respect to the effects of crowding on visitor satisfaction (e.g. Shelby *et al.* 1989; see also chapter 7).

Marketing research acts as a link between economic and psychological analysis of tourism (Van Raaij 1986) and gives notice of the need for a wider understanding of the social impact of tourism on visitor and host populations. Research on the social-psychology of tourism has run parallel with the research of behavioural geographers in the area, with there being increased interchange between the two fields in recent years (e.g. Jenkins and Walmesley 1993; see also Walmesley and Lewis 1993).

Interestingly, the development of a more radical critique of behaviour in geography also has parallels in the social psychology of tourism as well. For example, the research of Uzzell (1984) on the psychology of tourism marketing from a structuralist perspective offered a major departure from traditional social psychology. Uzzell's (1984) alternative formulation of the role of social psychology in the study of tourism has been reflected in much of the research conducted in anthropological, geographical (e.g. Britton 1991) and sociological approaches to the social impacts of tourism (e.g. Urry 1990, 1991).

The early work of Forster (1964), Cohen (1972, 1974, 1979a, 1979b), Smith and Turner (1973), and MacCannell (1973, 1976), along with the more recent contribution by Urry (1990) has provided the basis for formulating a sociology of tourism, while Smith (1977) and Graburn (1983) have provided a useful overview of anthropology's contributions to the study of tourism. The research of geographers such as Young (1973), Butler (1974, 1975, 1980), D.G. Pearce (1979, 1981), Mathieson and Wall (1982) and Murphy (1985) has also yielded significant early insights into tourism's social impacts.

Many studies of the social impacts of tourism have focused on the impact of tourism on the third world (UNESCO 1976). This research is no doubt necessary, yet caution must be used in applying research findings from one culture to another. Nevertheless, problems of cultural change and anxiety, social stress in the host community, and social dislocation resulting from changes to the pattern of economic production, may be identified in a wide number of studies undertaken in a variety of cultures and social settings (e.g. Farrell 1978; Mathieson and Wall 1982; Clary 1984; Oglethorpe 1984; Meleghy *et al.* 1985; Lea 1988; Getz 1993c; Shaw and Williams 1994; Hall and Page 1996; Weaver 1998).

The social costs of tourism on the host community will vary according to the characteristics of both visitor and host (Pizam 1978). However, tourism does undoubtedly cause changes in the social character of the destination (Long 1984). These changes may be related to the seasonality of tourism (Hartmann 1984), the nature of the tourist (Harmston 1980), the influence of a foreign culture (Mathieson and Wall 1982), and/ or to the disruption of community leisure space (O'Leary 1976). An appreciation by planners of the social costs of tourism is essential for both financial and social reasons. Rejection of visitors by segments of the host community may well result in a decline of the attractiveness of the tourist destination, in addition to the creation of disharmony within the host community (Murphy 1985; Getz 1994b; Page and Lawton 1997a).

Tourism development may initiate changes in government and private organisations (Baldridge and Burnham 1975) in order to cater for the impact of tourism. For instance, additional law enforcement officers may be required (Rothman *et al.* 1979), while special measures may be needed to restrict dislocation created by increased rents and land values (Cowie 1985). Geographers have long emphasised the importance of meaningful community participation in the decision-making process that surrounds the formulation of tourism policy and development (e.g. Butler 1974, 1975; Brougham and Butler 1981; Pearce 1981; Getz 1984; Murphy 1985). Furthermore, studies, such as those of Keller (1984) and Shaw (1985, 1986), indicate that the social impacts of tourism are complex and need to be examined within the context of the various economic, environmental, political and social factors that contribute to tourism development in a destination (Mings 1978; Runyan and Wu 1979; Wu 1982; D.G. Pearce 1989).

Community attitudes towards tourism invariably simultaneously reveal both positive and negative attitudes towards tourism (Butler 1975). For example, various positive and negative attitudes towards tourism were indicated in several studies of resident attitudes towards tourism in northern New South Wales, Australia, in the 1980s (Hall 1990). Pigram (1987) utilised Doxey's (1975) irridex scale of euphoria, apathy, annoyance, and antagonism to investigate resident attitudes in the resort town of Coffs Harbour (Table 4.2). According to Pigram 'the overwhelming majority felt that the economic and otherwise benefits of tourism outweighed the disadvantages' (1987: 67). Despite the overall favourable or apathetic response of residents, several negative reactions towards tourism did emerge from the study. According to Pigram (1987), the greatest impact of tourism on the local community was the perceived increase in the cost of goods and services because of the presence of tourists. The respondents also indicated that they believed that petty crime was also worse during the tourist season, an observation supported by Walmesley *et al.*'s (1981, 1983) study of crime in the region during the late 1970s. Furthermore, the natural environment of the Coffs Harbour area was perceived as slightly worse as a result of tourism with the greatest impact being on the beaches. However, opportunities for public recreation were perceived as the attribute of community life registering the most significant improvement as a result of tourism (Pigram 1987).

Resident attitudes are undoubtedly a key component in the identification, measurement and analysis of tourism impacts. However, investigation of community attitudes towards tourism is not just an academic exercise. Such attitudes are also

Table 4.2: Resident reaction to tourists in Coffs Harbour

Irridex Scale	Survey scale	(% response)
Euphoria	Friendly	29
Apathy	No worry	58
Annoyance	Nuisance	10
Antagonism	Rude/unbearable	3

Source: Pigram (1987: 68)

important in terms of the determination of local policy, planning and management responses to tourism development and in establishing the extent to which public support exists for tourism (Pearce 1980; Page and Lawton 1997a). For example, Getz (1994b) argued that resident perceptions of tourism may be one factor in shaping the attractiveness of a destination, where negative attitudes may be one indicator of an area's ability to absorb tourism. Although Getz suggests that 'identification of causal mechanisms is a major theoretical challenge, and residents can provide the local knowledge necessary to link developments with their consequences' (1994b: 247), it assumes that residents are sufficiently aware, perceptive and able to articulate such views to decision-makers and planners. Nevertheless, negative resident perceptions may lead to adverse reactions towards tourism and create substantial difficulties for the development of further facilities and infrastructure (Page and Lawton 1997a). For example, although communities with a history of exposure to tourism may adapt and change to accommodate its effects (Rothman 1978), active or passive support or opposition may exist at any given time, as interest groups take political action to achieve specific objectives in relation to tourism (Murphy 1985; Hall and Jenkins 1995).

In locations where the original community is 'swamped' by large scale tourism development in a relatively short space of time, disruption to the community values of the original inhabitants is more likely to occur (Hudson 1990a, 1990b). Table 4.3 details the costs and benefits of such tourism development in Broome, Western Australia. However, it must be emphasised that resident attitudes to tourism development will be influenced by where they fit into the existing social and economic order, their personal gains from the development process, and/or their response to the changing environment in light of their preexisting values and attitudes (Hudson 1990b). In addition, it should be noted that while individuals may perceive there to be negative tourism impacts, they may still be favourable towards tourism's overall benefits to the community. Faulkner and Tideswell (1996) referred to this phenomenon as the 'altruistic surplus' and suggested that this could be the result of a mature stage of tourism development in a destination region, whereby residents have adapted to tourism through experience and migration.

In addition to attitudinal studies, a number of other approaches and issues are of interest to the geographer. For example, historical studies of tourism may indicate the role that tourism has in affecting attitudes and values with a destination community (e.g. Wall 1983a; Butler and Wall

1985). Studies of tourism policy may assist in an understanding of the way that governments develop strategies to manage the negative impacts of tourism and in the overall manner that tourism is used in regional development (e.g. Papson 1981; Kosters 1984; Oglethorpe 1984; Hall and Jenkins 1995). Another area of tourism's social impact which has received more attention in recent years is that of health (Clift and Page 1996). Researchers have examined the spatial misinformation provided by travel agents when advising clients of the potential health risks they may face when travelling to Pacific Island destinations (Lawton et al. 1996; Lawton and Page 1997b). What such research shows is the vital role of understanding place, space and the geography of risk in relation to the epidemiology of disease. Whilst geographers have studied disease for many years, making the link between travel and disease is a comparatively new development (Clift and Page 1996). For example, tourism may assist in the spread of disease, while tourists themselves are vulnerable to illness while travelling. Indeed, one of the major focal points for geographer's research on tourist health in recent

Table 4.3: Costs and benefits of tourism development in Broome, Australia

Costs	Benefits
• Marginalisation of the Aboriginal and coloured people • Too much power in vested interests • Destruction of multicultural flavour of the town and the original form of Shinju Matsuri • Increased racism • High accommodation costs/shortage • High local prices • Less friendly/more local conflicts • Environmental impacts (e.g. dune destruction) • Loss of historical character of town and imposition of artificially created atmosphere • More crime/domestic violence	• Expansion of new services, and businesses • More infrastructure and community facilities • More sealed roads and kerbing and guttering • Increased variety of restaurants/entertainment • Restoration of Broome architecture • Better health system • Tidier town

Source: Hudson (1990b: 10)

years has been the spread of AIDS and its association with sex tourism. In fact there is growing evidence that the geographer will continue to develop expertise in this area and a major contribution could be made at a public policy level in the rapid dissemination of disease alerts to GPs and health professionals through the use of GIS technology. Important collaborations have been forged between geographers, tourism and health researchers to ensure this area expands the frontiers of knowledge (Clift and Page 1996).

Prostitution has also been related to tourism in both historical and contemporary settings, with research being focused on tourism in the less developed countries (Jones 1986), issues of gender (Kinnaird and Hall 1994), and sex tourism in particular. Yet prostitution and sex tourism's significant connection to Western tourism should also be noted (Hall *et al.* 1995). For example, tourist promotion may highlight the more licentious attributes of a tourist destination. As Bailie (1980: 19–20) commented:

> Tourism promotion in magazines and newspapers promises would-be vacationers more than sun, sea, and sand; they are also offered the fourth 's' – sex. Resorts are advertized under the labels of 'hedonism', 'ecstacism', and 'edenism' . . . One of the most successful advertizing campaigns actually failed to mention the location of the resort: 'the selling of the holiday experience itself and not the destination was the important factor.

The extent of the relationship between crime and tourism has also been examined by several geographers (e.g. Nichols 1976; Walmesley *et al.* 1981, 1983), with research on Australian hallmark events also examining the relationship between increased visitor numbers and crime rates (Hall *et al.* 1995).

Another area to which geographers have been paying increasing attention is the relationship between tourism and indigenous peoples in both developed and less developed nations. While anthropology has focused considerable attention on the impacts and effects of tourism on indigenous peoples (e.g. V.L. Smith, 1977, 1992),

geographers have assisted greatly in broadening the research agenda to include greater consideration of the way in which indigenous peoples interact with wildlife, the relationship between indigenous peoples and ecotourism and national parks, tourism and land rights, and indigenous business development (e.g. Nelson 1986; Nickels *et al.* 1991; Mercer 1994; Butler and Hinch 1996; Lew and van Otten 1997).

One of the most important concepts in humanistic geography is that of a 'sense of place'. A sense of place arises where people feel a particular attachment or personal relationship to an area in which local knowledge and human contacts are meaningfully maintained. 'People demonstrate their sense of place when they apply their moral or aesthetic discernment to sites and locations' (Tuan 1974: 235). However, people may only consciously notice the unique qualities of their place when they are away from it or when it is being rapidly altered.

The sense of place concept is of significance to tourism development for a number of reasons. The redevelopment and reimaging of communities for tourism purposes (see chapter 5) may force long-term residents to leave and may change the character of the community (Ley and Olds 1988). In these instances, the identification of residents with the physical and social structure of the neighbourhood may be deeply disturbed leading to a condition of 'placelessness' (Relph 1976). Residents of destinations which find themselves faced with rapid tourism development may therefore attempt to preserve components of the townscape including buildings and parks in order to retain elements of their identity.

The conservation of heritage is often a reaction to the rate of physical and social change within a community. Generally, when people feel they are in control of their own destiny they have little call for nostalgia. However, the strength of environment and heritage conservation organisations in developed nations is perhaps a reflection of the desire to retain a sense of continuity with the past (Lowenthal 1975, 1985). In addition, the protec-

Plate 4.1: To what extent does tourism lead to cultural stereotyping and changed perceptions of cultural identity by both locals and tourists? Souvenir shop, Leyden, Holland.

Plate 4.2: Crowding may have substantial impacts not only on the quality of the visitor experience but also on the attraction itself. Entrance to the Cathedral precinct, Canterbury, England.

tion of historic buildings and the establishment of heritage precincts can also have a significant economic return to destinations because of the desire of many visitors to experience what they perceive as authentic forms of tourism (Konrad 1982; Hall and McArthur 1996).

PHYSICAL ENVIRONMENTAL IMPACTS

One of the areas of major interest for geographers is the impacts of tourists and recreationists on the physical environment. The reason for this lies in part in the nature of geography, which has a strong tradition of study of the interactions of humans with their environment (Mitchell and Murphy 1991). Indeed, the impacts of tourism and recreation on the physical environment and the subsequent resource analysis is one area where human and physical geographers find common ground in studying visitor issues (Johnston 1983b). However, another reason is the sheer significance of the physical environment for the recreation and tourism industry. As Mathieson and Wall (1982: 97) commented: 'In the absence of an attractive environment, there would be little tourism. Ranging from the basic attractions of sun, sea and sand to the undoubted appeal of historic sites and structures, the environment is the foundation of the tourist industry.'

The relationship between tourism and the

environment is site and culture dependent and will likely change through time and in relation to broader economic, environmental, and social concerns. As noted in the previous chapter, the recognition of something as a resource is the result of human perception, so it is also with the recognition that there are undesirable impacts on a environmental resource.

Increasing attention has been given to the impacts that tourism and recreation may have on the environmental and physical characteristics of a host community since the early 1970s (Walter 1975; Organisation for Economic Co-operation and Development 1980; Murphy 1985; Smith 1995). Interest in this area of applied geography is partly a response to the growth of tourism and the sheer impact that increased numbers of visitors will have on specific sites. However, concern has also developed because of the activities of environmental interest groups which have often provided an advocacy role for geographers in terms of arguing the results of the research and scholarship in direct involvement in the planning and policy process. The rise of the environmental movement has not only led to improvements in conservation practices but has also encouraged public interest in natural areas. However, 'environmentalism' and 'environmentalist' are often-used terms that are frustratingly vague. According to O'Riordan and Turner (1984: 1):

> Although environmentalists are not the only people who object to much of what they interpret as modern-day values, aspirations and ways of life, it is probably fair to say that one of the two things which unite their disparate perceptions is a wish to alter many of the unjust and foolhardy features they associate with modern capitalism of both a state and private variety. The other common interest is a commitment to cut waste and reduce profligacy by consuming resources more frugally. Environmentalists do not agree, however, about how the transition should be achieved.

Nevertheless, despite confusion about what is meant by an environmentally 'responsible' approach to tourism development, it is apparent that the protection of the natural and cultural resources upon which tourism is based, is essential for the sustainable development of a location (Hall and Lew 1998).

There is no fundamental difference in conducting research on the effects of tourism on the natural environment and research on the environmental impacts of recreation. The footprints of a recreationist are the same as that of the tourist. The majority of research has been undertaken on the effects of tourism and recreation on wildlife and the trampling of vegetation, with relatively little attention being given to impacts on soils and air and water quality (Wall and Wright 1977; Mathieson and Wall 1982; Edington and Edington 1986; Parliamentary Commissioner for the Environment 1997).

The majority of studies have examined the impacts of tourism and recreation on a particular environment or component of the environment rather than over a range of environments. According to Mathieson and Wall (1982: 94): 'there has been little attempt to present an integrated approach to the assessment of the impacts of tourism'. However, there is clearly a need to detect the effects of tourism on all aspects of an ecosystem. For example, the ecology of an area may be dramatically changed through the removal of a key species in the food chain or through the introduction of new species, such as trout, for enhanced benefits for recreational fishermen, or game for hunters (Hall 1995). In addition, it is important to distinguish between perceptions and actual impacts of tourism. For example, many visitors believe an environment is healthy as long as it looks 'clean and green'. The ecological reality may instead be vastly different, an environment can be full of invasive introduced species which, although contributing to a positive aesthetic perception, may have extremely negative ecological implications. For example, while New Zealand promotes its tourism very strongly on the basis of its 'clean, green' image, the reality is quite different with respect to many tourist locations which may have very few indigenous species present and may have very low bio-diversity

(Parliamentary Commissioner for the Environment 1997).

Research on impacts has focused on particular regions or environments which has limited the ability to generalise the findings from one area to another. In addition, research on visitor impacts is comparatively recent and is generally of a reactionary nature to site specific problems. We therefore rarely know what conditions were like before tourists and recreationists arrived. Few longtitudinal studies exist by which the long term impacts of visitation can be assessed. Therefore, there are a number of significant methodological problems which need to be addresssed in undertaking research on the environmental affects of tourism (Mathieson and Wall 1982: 94):

a) the difficulty of distinguishing between changes induced by tourism and those induced by other activities;
b) the lack of information concerning conditions prior to the advent of tourism and, hence, the lack of a baseline against which change can be measured;
c) the paucity of information on the numbers, types and tolerance levels of different species of flora and fauna; and
d) the concentration of researchers upon particular primary resources, such as beaches and mountains, which are ecologically sensitive.

Nevertheless, despite the difficulties that have emerged in studying the relationship between tourism and the natural environment it is apparent that 'a proper understanding of biological, or more specifically, ecological factors can significantly reduce the scale of environmental damage associated with recreational and tourist development' (Edington and Edington 1986: 2).

Tourism and recreation can have an adverse impact on the physical environment in numerous ways, for example the construction of facilities that are aesthetically unsympathetic to the landscape in which they are situated, what D.G. Pearce (1978: 152) has described as 'architectural

pollution', and through the release of air and water-borne pollutants. Tourist or special-event facilities may change the character of the urban setting. Indeed, the location of a facility or attraction may deliberately be exploited in an attempt to rejuvenate an urban area through the construction of new infrastructure as with the 1986 Vancouver Expo and the 1987 America's Cup in Fremantle (Hall 1992b) (see chapter 5). The promotion of tourism without the provision of an adequate infrastructure to cope with increased visitor numbers may well cause a decline in urban environmental quality, for instance, in the impacts of increased traffic flows (Schaer 1978). However, there are a wide range of tourism and recreation impacts on the urban physical environment (Table 4.4) that may have substantial implications for the longer term sustainability of a destination which are only now being addressed in the tourism literature (Page 1995a; Hinch 1996).

Many of the ecological effects of tourist facilities may well take a long time to become apparent because of the nature of the environment, as in the case of the siting of marinas or resorts (Hall and Selwood 1987). The impact of outdoor recreation on the environment has been well documented (Wall and Wright 1977; Mathieson and Wall 1982) and is discussed further in chapter 7. However, research on the physical impacts of tourism on the environment is still at a relatively early stage of development and presents an important area of future research, particularly with respect to sustainable tourism development (Hall and Lew 1998) Where the geographer has employed techniques from environmental science such as Environmental Assessment (EA), the spatial consequences of tourism and recreation activity have not always been fully appreciated. For example, Page (1992) reviewed the impact of the Channel Tunnel project on the natural and built environment and yet the generative effects of new tourist trips had been weakly articulated in the mountains of documents describing the effects to be mitigated, failing to recognise how this might impact on destination areas. Again, planners and

Table 4.4: The impact of tourism on the urban physical environment

1 The urban physical environment
   • land lost through tourism development which may have been used for other purposes
   • changes to urban hydrology

2 Visual impact
   • development of tourism/leisure districts
   • introduction of new architectural styles
   • potential reinforcement of vernacular architectural forms
   • potential contribution to population growth

3 Infrastructure
   • potential overloading of existing urban infrastructure with the following utilities and developments:
     – roads
     – railways
     – car parking
     – electricity and gas
     – sewage and water supply
   • provision of new infrastructure
   • additional environmental management measures to accommodate tourists and adapt areas for tourist use

4 Urban form
   • changes to land use as residential areas are replaced by accommodation developments
   • alterations to the urban fabric from pedestrianisation and traffic management schemes which have been constructed to accommodate visitation

5 Restoration
   • the restoration and conservation of historic sites and buildings
   • reuse of the facades of heritage buildings

Source: After Page (1995: 147)

researchers had failed to recognise how recreational and tourist behaviour cannot easily be incorporated into spatially specific plans for individual infrastructure projects which will have knock on effects for other parts of the tourism system. Page (1999) also reviews the role of geographers in developing more meaningful appraisals of environmental impacts resulting from tourist transport and the need to scrutinise private sector claims of minimising environmental impacts. Nevertheless, tourism's impacts on the natural environment have often been exaggerated. This is because the impacts of tourism have often failed to be distinguished from other forms of development impact or even such factors as overpopulation, poor agricultural practice or poor resource management. This is not to say that tourism has not affected the environment. Yet, what is often at issue are aesthetic or cumulative impacts rather than effects that can be related solely to tourism development. Indeed, to focus on tourism as a form of negative impact on the natural environment is to miss the far greater environmental problems which arise from other forms of economic development such as depletion of fisheries and forest resources and the loss of biodiversity, and the overall lack of monitoring and management of many environments.

Plate 4.3: Footpath erosion on the White Cliffs of Dover: How much is due to recreational versus tourist use?

For example, in the South Pacific, a region threatened by major environmental problems (Hall and Page 1996), there has been no systematic study of the environmental impacts of tourism over the region as a whole. Data and information is highly fragmented (Milne 1990). Base line data, i.e. information regarding the condition of the natural environment prior to tourism development, is invariably lacking. Even in Australia, one of the most economically developed nations in the region, information about the environmental impacts of tourism is relatively poor and, where it does exist, it tends to be available for areas, such as national parks or reserves, which are under government control, rather than for private lands (Hall 1995). In addition, development specific reports, such as environmental impact statements on resort or tourism developments, required by law in many Western countries, are often not required in the countries of the South Pacific

because environmental planning legislation is still being developed (Minerbi 1992; Hall and Page 1996).

Minerbi (1992) recorded a number of environmental and ecological impacts associated with tourism development on Pacific islands (Table 4.5). The range of tourism related impacts is similar to that for many other environments (Mathieson and Wall 1992; Edington and Edington 1986). However, in the case of Pacific islands, tourism impacts may be more problematic because tourism is concentrated on or near the ecologically and geomorphologically dynamic coastal environment. Because of the highly dynamic nature of the coastal environment and the significance of mangroves and the limited coral sand supply for island beaches in particular, any development which interferes with the natural system may have severe consequences for the long term stability of the environment. The impact

Table 4.5 Environmental and ecological impacts of tourism on the Pacific Islands

Environmental degradation and pollution
- Degradation and pollution of the environment due to golf courses
- Pollution by littering

Destruction of habitats and damage to ecosystems
- Poorly managed tourism may result in destruction of high quality natural environments
- Unmanaged human interference of specific species of fauna and flora
- Dynamite blasting and overfishing

Loss of coastal and marine resources
- Interference with inland and coastal natural processes
  - excessive ground water extraction by large resorts induces salt water intrusion and deterioration of water quality and recharge of the aquifer
- Coastal ecosystem damage and destruction through tourism development
- Terrestrial runoff and dredging on coastal areas
  - damage to coral reef and marine resources caused by the construction of tourist infrastructure such as runways, marinas, harbours, parking areas and roads, and use of coral limestone in hotels and resort developments
- Destruction by tourist activities
  - destruction of coral reefs, lagoons, mangroves, saltwater marshes, and wetlands due to excessive visitation and/or unmanaged exploitation of those resources
  - disturbance to near shore aquatic life due to thrill crafts and boat tours
- Introduced exotic species
  - increased sea and air inter-island traffic creates the danger of accidental importation of exotic species, which can be very destructive to indigenous flora and fauna
  - tourism enterprises alter the integrity of the environment and encroach on local lifestyles with imported exotic species for safari hunting
- Damage to sand cay ecosystems
- Damage to mangrove ecosystems
- Damage to coastal rainforest ecosystems
- Loss of sandy beaches and shoreline erosion
  - loss of sandy beaches due to onshore development and construction of seawalls

Coastal pollution
- Waste water discharge and sewage pollution
- Coastal water pollution and siltation due to near shore resort construction and runoff from resort areas results in the destruction of natural habitat, coral and feeding grounds for fish
- Marine and harbour pollution
  - coastal oil pollution due to motorised vehicles and ships

Surface water and ground water diversion
- Diversion of streams and water sources from local use to resort use, with resulting decline in water availability for domestic and other productive uses and farming, particularly taro cultivation

Source: After Minerbi (1992); see also Milne (1990) and Weiler and Hall (1992).

THE IMPACTS OF TOURISM AND RECREATION

of poorly developed tourism projects on the sand cays (coral sand islands) of the Pacific, for example, has been well documented:

- near-shore vegetation clearing exposes the island to sea storm erosion and decreases plant material decomposition on the beach, thereby reducing nutrient availability for flora and fauna;
- manoeuvring by bulldozer (instead of hand clearing) results in scarring and soil disturbance and makes sand deposits loose and vulnerable to erosion;
- excessive tapping of the fresh ground-water lens induces salt water intrusion which then impairs vegetation growth and human water use and renders the cay susceptible to storm damage and further erosion;
- sewage outfall in shallow water and reef flats may led to an excessive build-up of nutrients thereby leading to algal growth which may eventually kill coral;
- seawalls built to trap sand in the short-term impair the natural seasonal distrubtion of sand resulting, in the long run, in a net beach loss and in a reduction of the island land mass; and
- boat channels blasted in the reef act as a sand trap; in time they fill with sand which is no longer circulating around the island; in turn this sand is replaced by other sand eroded from the vegetated edges, changing the size and shape of the island and in time threatening the island's integrity.

(Baines 1987)

Another component of the coastal environment in the Pacific and in other tropical and sub-tropical areas which are substantially affected by tourism is the clearing and dredging of mangroves and estuaries for resorts. Mangroves and estuarine environments are extremely significant nursery areas for a variety of fish species. The loss of natural habitat due to dredging or infilling may therefore have a dramatic impact on fish catches. In addition, there may be substantial impacts on the whole of the estuarine food chain with a subsequent loss of ecological diversity. A further consequence of mangrove loss is reduced protection against erosion of the shoreline thereby increasing vulnerability to storm surge. Therefore, removal of mangroves will not only have an adverse impact on the immediate area of clearance, but will also affect other coastal areas through the transport of greater amounts of marine sediment (Clarke 1991).

In concluding his examination of the impacts of tourism development on Pacific islands, Minerbi (1992: 69) was scathing in his criticism of the environmental impacts of tourism:

Resorts and golf courses increase environmental degradation and pollution. Littering has taken place on beaches and scenic lookouts and parks. Marine sanctuaries have been run over and exploited by too many tourists.

Resorts have interfered with the hydrological cycle by changing groundwater patterns, altering stream life, and engaging in excessive groundwater extraction. Coastal reefs, lagoons, anchialine ponds, wastewater marshes, mangroves, have been destroyed by resort construction and by excessive visitations and activities with the consequent loss of marine life and destruction of ecosystems. Beach walking, snorkeling, recreational fishing, boat tours and anchoring have damaged coral reefs and grasses and have disturbed near shore aquatic life . . .

Tourism has presented itself as a clean and not polluting industry but its claims have not come true.

Such expressions of concern clearly give rise to questions regarding how sustainable tourism can really be and the need to provide limits on the expansion of tourism and corresponding human impact. Indeed, observation of the potential combined pressures of the social and environmental impacts of tourism has long led researchers to speculate as to whether there exists a carrying capacity for tourist destinations (e.g. Hall 1974; McCool 1978; Getz 1983) (see chapters 7 and 8). Yet regardless of the empirical validity of the notion of carrying capacity (Wall 1983b), attention must clearly be paid by planners to the ability of an area to absorb tourism in relation to the possibilities of environmental and social degradation (see chapter 9).

Plate 4.4: The tourist image of paradise often has hidden costs on the environment as this picture of the Sheraton Hotel, Denarau Island, Fiji, suggests when compared with Plate 4.3

Plate 4.5: Coastal erosion measures on Denarau Island, Fiji, to prevent the unstable former mangrove swamp from being denuded

CONCLUSION

The purpose of this chapter has been to give a brief account of some of the potential economic, social and environmental impacts of tourism and recreation. This provides a framework for the discussion of specific forms of tourism and recreation in chapters 5–8 which follow. Tourism and recreation needs to be well managed in order to reduce possible adverse impacts (Murphy 1982). In turn, good management is likely to be related to the level of understanding of tourism and recreation phenomenon. There is clearly a need to go beyond the image of tourism and recreation, and develop rigorous integrated economic, environmental, social and political analysis.

Geographers have contributed much to the understanding of the impacts of tourism and recreation, particularly with respect to the impacts on the physical environment and the spatial fixity of such effects. What the geographer has contributed is a better understanding of the wider consequences of individual impacts and their cumulative effect on the natural environment. However, there has been considerable exchange of approaches and methodologies through the various social sciences which means that the demarcation line between geographical and other approaches is increasingly fuzzy. This is clearly the case when using multi-disciplinary techniques such as EA which has been enhanced by the use of GIS to improve the precision and location of the spatial awareness of impacts. One notable example during the 1980s and 1990s was the planning for the UK's high speed rail link between London and the Channel Tunnel where GIS was used to model the optimum route for a tourist-transport infrastructure project, and where political changes and lobbying directly altered the geographical routing and distribution of its impacts (Goodenough and Page 1994). Nevertheless, no one discipline will have all the answers. Given the complex nature of tourism phenomenon, particularly with respect to 'solving' environmental problems, the development of multi-disciplinary approaches towards recreation and tourism may provide an appropriate starting point for the development of more sustainable forms of tourism.

5

URBAN RECREATION
AND TOURISM

Urbanisation is a major force contributing to the development of towns and cities, where people live, work and shop (see Johnston *et al.* 1994 for a definition of the term urbanisation). Towns and cities function as places where the population concentrates in a defined area, and economic activities locate in the same area or nearby, to provide the opportunity for the production and consumption of goods and services in capitalist societies. Consequently, towns and cities provide the context for a diverse range of social, cultural and economic activities which the population engage in, and where tourism, leisure and entertainment form major service activities. These environments also function as meeting places, major tourist gateways, accommodation and transportation hubs, and as central places to service the needs of visitors. Most tourist trips will contain some experience of an urban area; for example, when an urban dweller departs from a major gateway in a city, arrives at a gateway in another city-region and stays in accommodation in an urban area. Within cities, however, the line between tourism and recreation blurs to the extent that at times one is indistinguishable from the other, with tourists and recreationalists using the same facilities, resources and environments although some notable differences exist. Therefore, many tourists and recreationalists will intermingle in many urban contexts. While most tourists will experience urban tourism in some form during their holiday, visit to friends and relatives, business trip or visit for other reasons (e.g. a pilgrimage to a religious shrine such as Lourdes in an urban area), recreationalists will not use the accommodation but frequent many similar places as tourists. This chapter seeks to examine some of the ways geographers conceptualise, analyse and research urban recreation and tourism, emphasising their contribution in understanding the wider context in which such activities take place. One key feature of the chapter is the emphasis on five specific aspects of geographical enquiry:

- description;
- classification;
- analysis;
- explanation; and
- application of theoretical and conceptual issues to practical problem solving contexts.

According to Coppock (1982), the geographer's principal interest in the geographical analysis of leisure provides a useful starting point in understanding the areas of research which have also been developed in urban recreation and tourism research in that they examine

> the way in which . . . pursuits are linked to the whole complex of human activities and physical features that determine the distinctive characters of places and region, and the interactions between such pursuits and the natural and man-made environments in which they occur . . . [and] the study of the spatial interactions between participants and resources probably represents the most significant contribution the geographer can make.
>
> (Coppock 1982: 2–3)

The focus on the behavioural aspects of recreational and tourism behaviour together with the planning, and more recently, the management implications of such activities in the urban environment have become fruitful areas for geographical research.

GEOGRAPHICAL APPROACHES TO URBAN RECREATION

Despite the growth in geographical research on leisure and recreation (Coppock 1982), the focus on urban issues remained neglected as Patmore (1983: 87) noted in that 'in the past geographers, with their inherently spatial interest, have tended to concentrate on outdoor recreation in rural areas, where spatial demands, and spatial conflicts have been the greatest'. This is a strange paradox according to Patmore (1983) since:

> the greatest changes in recreation habits in the last fifty years have taken place in two opposing directions. High personal mobility has extended opportunities away from the home and brought a growing complexity to the scale and direction of leisure patterns. Conversely, the home has come to provide for a greater range of leisure opportunities, and home-centred leisure has acquired a greater significance. The family has become socially more self-sufficient, its links with the immediate community and with its own extended kinship network weaker. Social independence has been underpinned by greater physical independence of homes in the expanding suburban communities, by the weakening need for communal space that comes with lower housing densities and the command of greater private space.

For the geographer, understanding the spatial implications of such processes and the geographical manifestation of the urban recreational demand for, and the supply of resources requires the use of concepts and methodologies to understand the complexity and simplify the reality of recreational activities to a more meaningful series of concepts and constructs. However, one area which has been largely neglected in reviews of urban recreational

activities is the historical dimension. Although Towner (1996) provides an all-embracing review of tourism and leisure in an historical context, it is important to acknowledge the significance of social, political, economic and geographical factors which shaped the evolution of modern day urban recreation. For this reason, no analysis of urban recreation can commence without an understanding of the historical and geographical processes associated with its development. By focusing on the development of modern day recreation in cities, since their rapid expansion in the early nineteenth century, it is possible to examine many changes to the form, function and format of urban recreation and its spatial occurrence in the nascent urban–industrial cities and conurbations in England and Wales.

THE EVOLUTION OF URBAN RECREATION IN BRITAIN

Within the context of towns and cities, Williams (1995: 8) argues that

> urban populations engage in most of their leisure activities within the same urban area in which they live. The geographical patterns of residence are translated very readily into a pattern of recreation that is focused upon the urban environment, purely by the fact that most people spend the majority of their leisure time in, or close to the home.

This indicates that the patterns of residence and recreation are closely related. The current day patterns of recreation and the ways in which they developed in Britain are fundamental to any understanding of the development of recreational opportunities in urban areas. According to Williams (1995) these passed through three district phases:

Phase I: Foundation

During the nineteenth century public provision for urban recreational activities emerged through legislative provision (e.g. the number of urban parks in Britain increased from 19 between 1820 and 1850, to 111 between 1850 and 1880 (Conway 1991)), while innovations in town planning and urban design led to improved quality of streets and housing areas, expanding the space for recreation. In addition, the nineteenth century saw the social geography of towns and cities in England and Wales (Lawton 1978) develop with social patterns of segregation and suburbanisation fuelled by urban growth. This also affected the expansion of recreational opportunities as cities expanded during the late nineteenth and early twentieth century.

Phase II: Consolidation

The period 1918 to 1939 saw a growth in more specialised forms of urban recreational land uses stimulated by legislation such as the rise of *Small Holdings and Allotments Act* (1908), which expanded the range and type of amenity space in towns and cities, while other gaps in provision (e.g. the National Playing Fields Association formed in 1925) recognised the need for space in urban areas to support the role of sport. Likewise, the 1937 Physical Training and Recreational Act effectively signalled the emergence of public sector aid from central government for local authority provision of playing fields, gymnasia and swimming baths.

Phase III: Expansion

During the post-war period several key trends emerged including 'greater levels and diversity of provision in which traditional resources established in earlier phases have been augmented by new forms of provision designed to reflect the diversity and flexibility of contemporary recreational tastes' (Williams 1995: 20). In fact, one common theme is the recognition of recreation as an element in statutory planning procedures as the range and consumption of land for recreational purposes increased. However, according to Williams (1995: 21)

in the absence of theoretical approaches to describing and explaining the pattern of recreation resources in urban areas, the approach to the task must inevitably become empirical, outlining the typical patterns of provision where older parks and recreation grounds are concentrated towards the core of the settlement [Leicester], whilst a scatter of newer parks and grounds associated with inter-war and post 1945 housing produce further significant zones of provision to the periphery of the city. The outer edges of the built area are important for provision of extensive facilities such as sports grounds and golf courses.

Whilst these conclusions are typical of recreational land use patterns in many towns and cities in England and Wales, one must question the extent to which a purely empirical analysis truly explains the spatial development of recreational resources in Britain's urban areas. For this reason it is valuable to consider both the social, economic and political processes which contributed to the spatial organisation and occurrence of urban recreation in such areas in the period after 1800 because traditional empirical analyses are devoid of the diversity of people and users of such resources. For this reason, a series of historical snapshots taken in 1800, the 1840s, 1880s, 1920s, 1960s and post 1960s help to explain how present day patterns were shaped.

URBAN RECREATION: A SOCIO-GEOGRAPHIC PERSPECTIVE

According to Clarke and Crichter (1985), during the evolution of a capitalist society such as Britain, the analysis of leisure and recreation has traditionally emphasised institutional forms of provision, while each social class has their own histories of organised and informal leisure and recreation. The predominant urban histories are those of male leisure, with female leisure and recreation structured around the family with free time activities associated with the family, the street and neighbourhood in working class society. Within historical analyses of urban recreation during the evolution of mass urban society in Victorian and Edwardian Britain, the emergence of distinctive forms of urban recreation and leisure and their spatial occurrence within different social areas of cities has been associated with a number of concepts, the most notable being 'popular culture' (see Williams 1976 for a discussion of popular culture). As Clarke and Crichter (1985: 55) argue 'the early nineteenth century was to bring a dramatic transformation to the form . . . and context of popular culture, imposing very different parameters of time and space, rhythms and routines, behaviour and attitude, control and commerce'. However, the resulting changes cannot simply be conceptualised as a straightforward linear progression since different influences and cross currents meant that this transformation affected different people and areas at different rates and in varying degrees.

Clarke and Crichter (1985) provide a useful historical analysis of leisure and recreational forms in Britain during the nineteenth and twentieth centuries, with the emphasis on the urban forms and the way in which political factors, forms of social control (Donajgrodski 1978) and the underlying development and functioning of an urban capitalist society; leisure and recreational forms emerged as a civilising and diversionary process to maintain the productive capacity of the working classes as central to the continued development of capitalism. Therefore, the geographical patterns and manifestation of urban recreation and leisure for all social classes in the British city in the nineteenth and twentieth centuries has to be viewed against the background of social, economic and political processes which conditioned the demand and supply of leisure and recreation for each social class. For this reason, it is pertinent to consider the key features of Clarke and Crichter's (1985) historical synthesis of urban leisure and recreation in Britain, since it helps to explain how changes in society shaped the modern day patterns of urban recreation. Clark and Crichter (1985) adopt a cross-section approach to analyse key periods in nineteenth and twentieth century British urban

society to emphasise the nature of the changes and type of urban recreation and leisure pursuits. It also helps to explain how the evolution of urban places and recreational activities emerged.

THE 1800s

As emphasised earlier in the chapter, Britain was in the process of emerging from a pre-industrial state. While cities were not a new phenomenon (Clarke 1981), the movement of the rural population to nascent cities meant that the traditional boundary between work and non-work among the labouring classes was increasingly dictated by the needs of factory or mechanised production. Therefore, pre-industrial flexibility in the work–non-work relationship associated with cottage industries and labouring on the land changed. This led to a clearer distinction between work and non-work time, as time discipline emerged as a portent force during the industrial revolution (Pred 1981). In the pre-industrial, non-urbanised society, leisure and recreational forms were associated with market days, fairs, wakes, holidays, religious and pagan festivals which provided opportunities for sport. While the 1800s are often characterised by brutish behaviour and ribaldry, civilising influences emerged in the form of Puritanism to engender moral sobriety and spatial changes associated with the enclosure movement, which removed many strategic sites of customary activity.

In contrast, the geographical patterns of recreation of the ruling classes:

> eschewed contact with lower orders. Its forms were as yet disparate. Shooting, hunting and horse racing . . . the major flat race classics date from the 1770s onwards . . . For the increasingly influential urban bourgeoisie,[1] the theatre, literature, seaside holidays and music hall denoted more rational forms of leisure which depended for their decorum on the exclusion of the mass of the population.
> (Clarke and Crichter 1985: 55)

[1] In Marxist terminology, the bourgeoisie is the middle classes, or the capitalist ruling class who owned the means of production, through which it exploited the working class.

THE 1840s

In historical analysis, this period is often character-ised as a period of deprivation for the urban working classes. Endemic poverty, associated with rapid urbanisation and inadequate housing, poor living standards and limited infrastructure culminated in high rates of mortality, disease and exploitation of the labouring classes through long hours of work (twelve-hour, six-day weeks) (Page 1988). In terms of urban leisure and recreation, the pre-industrial opportunities for pursuits decreased as did the legal outlets, with many customary pastimes suppressed so that popular culture was conditioned through legislative changes. For example, the *1834 New Poor Law Act* (Rose 1985) aimed to control the movement of 'travel-ling balladeers', 'entertainers' and 'itinerant sales-men' all of whom were deemed as vagabonds and returned to their parish of origin. Similarly, the *1835 Highways Act* was intended to remove street nuisances such as street entertainers and traders while the *1835 Cruelty to Animals Act* sought to surpress working class pastimes involving ani-mals, thereby driving many activities underground and leading to the emergence of a hybrid range of recreational activities including popular theatre, pantomime and circuses. In the late 1840s, railway excursions, pioneered by Thomas Cook also devel-oped. In addition, a range of rational recreation pursuits emerged in purpose-built facilities made possible by Parliamentary Acts including the *Museums Act (1845)*, the *Baths and Wash Houses Act (1846)* and *Libraries Act (1850)*. Social theorists argue that such legislation may have acted as a form of social control (Donajgrodski 1978), to tame a new industrial work force while demarcating recreation and work. Furthermore, the 1840s saw the emergence of the Victorian concept of domesticity and a bourgeois culture, with the use of a gender separation of male and female work.

THE 1880s

Whilst the early Victorian period saw the estab-lishment of urban recreational facilities, improved working conditions and living standards in the mid to late Victorian period were accompanied by greater municipal provision (Briggs 1969). Yet as Clarke and Crichter (1985) argue, four processes were at work in the 1850s and 1860s which led to significant changes in the 1880s:

- a rise of middle class urban recreation which excluded the working classes;
- the expansion of local government's role in leisure and recreational provision;
- an increasing commercialisation and greater capitalisation of urban recreation, relying upon mass audiences and licensing (e.g. the rise of football), which also required large areas of land; and
- attempts by the working classes to organise urban recreation according to their own aspi-rations.

By the 1880s, the pattern of urban conurba-tions had emerged in England which focused on London, the West Midlands, West Yorkshire, Merseyside and Tyneside (Lawton 1978). In addition to these trends in urban recreation, the rise of urban middle class recreational pursuits centred on religion, reading, music and annual holidays reflected a more rational form of recreational activities. Nevertheless, the 1870s saw the growth in public parks and by 1885, nearly 25 per cent of the urban population had access to public libraries. At the same time, informal urban recreation based on the street and neighbourhood based activities largely remains invisible in documentary sources and official records, although limited evidence exists in the form of autobiographies and oral history. For example Roberts (1971, 1976) *'The Classic Slum'* observed that the pub played a major role in informal recreation in Victorian and Edwardian Salford where a community of 3,000 people had

15 beer houses. Through sexual segregation it was possible to observe the rise of male-only urban recreational pursuits in the 1880s. Yet the street life and neighbourhood forms of recreation remained unorganised and informal despite the institutionalisation, segmentation and emergence of a customer–provider relationship in Victorian urban recreational pursuits.

THE 1920s

In Britain, the 1920s are frequently viewed as the era of mass unemployment with social class more spatially defined in the urban environment. While the 1900s saw the rising patronage of the cinema, with 3,000 cinemas operating in Britain by 1926 and audiences of 20 million, with many people visiting the cinemas up to twice a week, this recreational pursuit increasingly met the recreational needs of women as it displaced the Victorian music hall, being more heavily capitalised and more accessible in terms of price and social acceptability. The ideological separation of work and home was firmly enshrined in the 1920s, with a greater physical separation and the rise of annual holidays and day trips using charabancs and the car. Spectator sports also retained large audiences although the social segregation of urban recreation based on social class, mass markets and institutional provision characterised this era.

THE 1960s AND BEYOND

Clarke and Chrichter (1985) identified six distinct trends occurring from the 1960s on:

- rising standards of domestic consumption;
- family centred leisure;
- the decline of public forms of urban leisure and recreation;
- emergence of a youth culture;
- the establishment of ethnic leisure and recreation culture; and

- increased state activity in prescribed spheres of urban recreation and a growing commercial domination of leisure institutions and services;

and it has been well reviewed in the sociological literature (see Pahl 1975).

In terms of urban recreation, various debates exist in relation to the changes induced by a post-industrial society and the implications for urban recreation. Social theorists point to the concomitant changes induced by economic, occupational and technological change, associated with the demise of manufacturing and the rise of the service sector in towns and cities, affecting the pattern of life and recreational activities of urban populations associated with a growing polarisation of wealth and opportunity. Williams (1995: 213) outlines the impact of such changes for post-industrial towns and cities, as older central areas of towns have decayed as they lost their economic rationale. In some cases this has led to the creation of space for recreation, as high density housing and industry has been removed and urban regeneration results.

Williams (1995) also points to the effect of the rise of environmentalism since the 1960s, reflected in the concept of the 'green city' where redundant space is 'greened' to enhance the quality of the city environment while adding recreational opportunities (e.g. greenways, linear parks, green wedges and natural corridors). The greening of cities also has a wider concern with the sustainability of urban life. Williams (1995) also argues that a range of factors militate against the continued well-being of urban recreation provision, many of which are associated with political change outlined in detail by Page et al. (1994). A greater concern with financial costs of publicly provided services and more efficient service delivery and the introduction of Compulsory Competitive Tendering (CCT) (Benington and White 1988; Page et al. 1994) has characterised public and private sector recreational provision in urban areas in the 1980s and 1990s. Henry (1988) argued that the outcome will be determined by the political climate and philosophy prevailing in public sector environments, fluctuating between a limited role for the state characterised by right wing ideology, to one based on principles of social equity and significant levels of public intervention influenced by principles of equality. Having briefly examined the evolution of urban recreational opportunities in Britain since the 1880s, it is pertinent to focus on one example which typifies the development processes in time and space, notably the evolution of parks and open space. This is considered in relation to one particular city in Britain – Leicester.

CASE STUDY: The evolution of parks and open space in Leicester

Open space in towns and cities in Britain traditionally developed through the emergence of commons and walks prior to the nineteenth century, followed by private squares and greens for the wealthy classes. While towns and cities remained small in scale, the populations were able to enjoy recreation in the surrounding rural areas (Clarke 1981). Urban industrial growth in the industrial revolution transformed the spatial form of towns and cities, as open land was consumed for economic and residential development. Two specific legislative changes during Victorian Britain contributed to the development of large parks, namely the *Select Committee on Public Walks (1833)* and the *Health of Towns (1840)*, in a period of concern for the health and social well-being of the labouring classes. As Strachan and Bowler (1976) acknowledged, early park development was prompted by donations from industrialists and landowners, and four pieces of legislation enabled local authorities to purchase land for park development, notably:

- the *Towns Improvement Act (1847)*
- the *Public Health Act (1848)*
- the *Public Parks, Schools and Museums Act (1871)*, and
- the *Public Improvements Act (1860)*.

While Edwardian and subsequent legislation enhanced park development, including the *Housing and Town Planning Act (1909)* and the *Town and Country Planning Acts* of 1932 and 1947, the Victorian era was important in terms of the development of large scale parks and open space.

PARK DEVELOPMENT IN VICTORIAN LEICESTER

Leicester expanded as a Victorian city where its population grew from 18,445 in 1801 to 64,829 in 1851, 174,624 in 1891 and to 211,579 in 1901. While Pritchard (1976) and Page (1988) examine the spatial development of the city (Figure 5.1), and constraints and opportunities for urban development, the city retained a medieval pattern of land development up until the 1800s. The poorly drained River Soar constrained development to the west of the river and also by owners of estates who refused to sell land for development. Most early urban growth in the 1800s occurred to the east and north-east. Prior to 1850, two open spaces existed: St Margaret's Pasture, a 13 acre (5.2 ha) meadow to the north of the urban area and at Southfield's race course established in 1806 (Figure 5.2). In 1838, the city council provided 40 acres (16 ha) of land at Southfield, at Welford to form the first public recreation ground, although only eight acres (3.2 ha) remains today. This was complemented by a series of private gardens and squares laid out from 1785 at the town council's request along New Walk, which today forms the

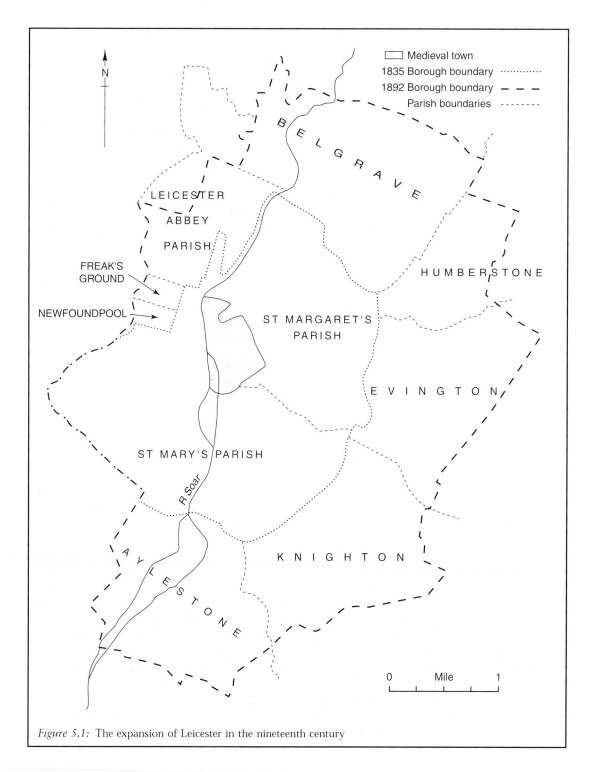

Figure 5.1: The expansion of Leicester in the nineteenth century

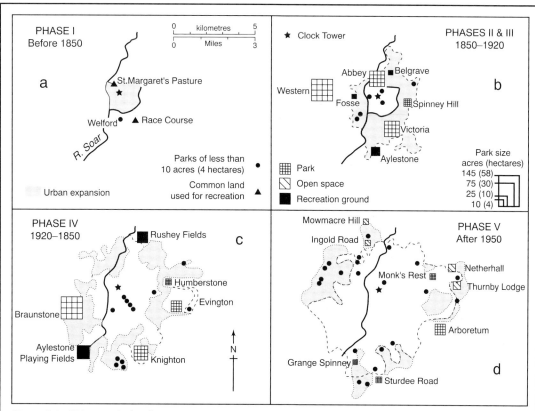

Figure 5.2: Urban park development in Leicester
Source: Redrawn from Strachan and Bowler (1976)

sole surviving urban pedestrian way in England (Strachan and Bowler 1976: 279).

With the growth in population by 1851 urban development occurred to the west of the Soar and the city council developed four parks and recreation grounds (Table 5.1 and Figure 5.2) in the period 1880–1900. Victoria Park (27.6 ha), established in 1882 on city-owned land, was made possible by the relocation of the city's race course from Southfield to Oadby. Abbey Meadows (22.8 ha) purchased in 1877, which fulfilled the purpose of draining a marsh area unsuitable for building, resulted in an ornamental park. The third park, aimed at providing open space access for the fast growing suburb of Highfields, led to the development of

13.6 ha at Spinney hill with a formal park in 1885. The fourth major park, established in the western suburbs, saw the establishment of the new parks estate (71.2 ha) in 1899. Each park developed in the tradition of Victorian formal use with fountains, band-stands, gardens and open stretches of grass. In the case of Abbey Park, boating, river views, greenhouses and formal flower beds attracted users from across the city. To complement formal park provision, recreation grounds were also established in 1892 at Belgrave (4.8 ha) and Fosse Road (4.4 ha) in 1897.

In 1902, the Aylestone site (8 ha) was purchased as a recreation ground which was followed by a lull up until the 1920s. During

Table 5.1: Park development in Leicester

Years	No. of parks established	Area (Hectares)	Average size of new parks
Up to 1850	1	3.2	3.2
1850–1900	7	161.2	23.0
1900–1920	6	18.2	3.0
1920–1950	14	181.7	13.0
1950–	27	97.0	3.6
Total	55	464.5	8.4

Source: Strachan and Bowler (1976)

the period 1900–20, small open spaces in the town centre led to the establishment of three ornamental gardens (Castle, Westcotes and St George's Church), two playgrounds and a small park at Westcotes. After 1920, further urban expansion led to the establishment of six multi-purpose parks with sports facilities, the largest at Braunstone (66.8 ha) in 1925 on the periphery of the city as a focal point of a large inter-war council estate. In contrast, other parks developed in the inter-war period were located in private housing areas such as Humberstone (8 ha) in 1928, Knighton (32.9 ha) in 1937, Evington (17.6 ha) in 1949 in eastern and southern suburbs. To balance the geographical distribution of provision, two large recreation grounds were opened at Rusley Fields (11.4 ha) in 1921 and Aylestone Playing Fields (33.2 ha) in 1946. A number of smaller open spaces were also developed on new council estates at Braunceston Park and Humberstone and a number of amenity open spaces amounting to 40.8 ha.

In the post-war period, attention in Leicester City Council shifted towards provision of small neighbourhood and local facilities as key features of new council estates. Only a limited number of larger open spaces were created on land unsuitable for residential development (e.g. Netherhall's 12.8 ha site in 1958 and Ingeld's 5.6 ha site in 1970). Amenity open space was also incorporated into 13 council estates providing 105.6 ha of open space. A number of small village parks and playgrounds in old villages (e.g. Old Humbestone) contributed to the 27 parks and recreation grounds opened between 1950 and 1975.

As a result Leicester open space is an average of only 2.9 km from the city centre for parks/gardens, 3.6 km for recreation grounds, 3.5 km for playing fields, 3.7 km for sports grounds and 4.6 km for golf courses, illustrating the role of low cost land for such facilities. Thus, as Williams (1995) argues, the level of recreational opportunity in modern day Leicester increases with distance from the city. The result of such patterns of park development and other recreational resources in the case of Leicester is the rationalisation of provision into a geographical planning framework whereby an open space hierarchy results with different parks fulfilling different functions according to their size, characteristics and resource base.

METHODS OF ANALYSING URBAN RECREATION

Within the limited literature on urban recreation, the geographer has developed a number of concepts used within human geography and applied them in a recreational context to understand how the supply of recreational resources fit within the broader recreational context. For example, the use of the concept of a 'hierarchy of facilities' (Patmore 1983), which highlights the catchment relating to the users' willingness, ability and knowledge of the facility or resource (Smith 1983a). What the hierarchy concept does is allow one to ascertain what type of catchment a recreational resource has at different spatial scales, taking into account users' willingness to travel to use them. Constraints of time and distance act as a friction on the potential use of resources. The outcome is an ordered pattern of resources which serve specific catchments depending on their characteristics, whereby the typical levels of provision may include:

- the neighbourhood level (a community centre);
- local areas (e.g. a recreation ground);
- regions within cities; and
- a city-wide level (e.g. an art gallery).

An illustration of such hierarchy for urban open space is illustrated in Table 5.2. The result is an ordered provision, each with their own set of users meeting the needs and aspirations of users which will vary in time and space. Within any urban context the challenge for recreation planning is to match the supply and demand for such resources.

One further technique which Patmore (1983) advocated for urban recreation, is the resource inventory whereby the range of existing resources is surveyed and mapped, in relation to the catchment population. This population can then be compared to existing recommended levels of provision set by organisations for recreational provision. For example, the National Playing

Fields Association in the UK recommends 2.4 ha of space per thousand population, 'excluding school playing fields except where available for general use, woodlands and commons, ornamental gardens, full-length golf courses and open spaces where the playing of games by the general public is either discouraged or not permitted' (Patmore 1983: 118).

Patmore (1983) outlined the range of urban recreational resources and facilities and provides a detailed spatial analysis of their occurrence and level of provision within the UK in terms of:

- capital intensive facilities (those with modest land requirements but a high capital cost – and those with a high capital cost where the land requirement is extensive);
- parks and open spaces; and
- golf courses.

while Williams (1995) adds an interesting array of other contexts including:

- the home;
- the street;
- gardens and allotments;
- playgrounds; and
- other sporting contexts.

To assist in understanding the spatial analysis of these resources and their inter-relationship in an urban context, Williams (1995) developed a typology of urban recreational resources. To achieve this, and to incorporate the perception and use of the resource by urban users, he uses seven variables to construct a simple typology (Table 5.3). However, as Patmore (1983: 98) rightly argues patterns of facility use are not related to location alone: effective access is not synonymous with convenience of location. As a result, barriers to urban recreational use include:

- *physical barriers* based on factors such as age, stage in the family life cycle (e.g. dependent children) and physical access;

Table 5.2: Hierarchical pattern of public open space

Type and main function	Approximate size and distance from home	Characteristics
Regional park Weekend and occasional visits by car or public transport	400 hectares 3.2–8 km	Large areas of natural healthland, common woodland and parkland. Primarily providing for informal recreation with some non-intensive active recreations. Car parking at strategic locations.
Metropolitan park Weekend and occasional visits by car or public transport	60 hectares 3.2 km but more when park is larger than 60 hectares	Either natural heath, common, woods or formal parks providing for active and passive recreation. May contain playing fields, provided at least 40 hectares remain for other pursuits. Adequate car parking.
District parks Weekend and occasional visits on foot, by cycle, car or short bus trip	20 hectares 1.2 km	Landscaped settings with a variety of natural features providing for a range of activities, including outdoor sports, children's play and informal pursuits. Some car parking.
Local parks For pedestrian visitors	2 hectares 0.4 km	Providing for court games, children's play, sitting out etc., in a landscaped environment. Playing fields if the park is large enough.
Small local parks Pedestrian visits especially by old people and children, particularly valuable in high-density areas	2 hectares 0.4 km	Gardens, sitting-out areas and children's play-grounds.
Linear open space Pedestrian visits	Variable Where feasible	Canal towpaths, footpaths, disused rail lines etc., providing opportunities for informal recreation.

Source: Williams (1995)

- *financial barriers* include direct economic constraints due to costs of participation such as admission or membership costs (e.g. golf club fees) which may raise issues related to the public sector's role in provision;
- *social barriers* often reinforce the financial barriers whereby lower socio-economic groups do not participate due to financial barriers. And even when such barriers are removed, the image of participation still has cultural and social barriers (e.g. opera-going);

- *transport* can be a deterrent to urban recreational participation where access is limited by car ownership or where a short journey by bus may be difficult and costly in time for public transport users.

Using the key variables, which reflect basic resource attributes, Williams (1995) devised a practical typology of urban recreational resources as illustrated in Table 5.4. The challenge for recreational provision in any urban context is

Table 5.3: Summary and explanation of key variables deployed within the recreation resource typology

Variable	Sub-categories	Explanation
Design	Purpose-built	Resource is designed for specific recreational uses
	Adapted	Resource has been converted to a recreational use from a previous function
	Annexed	Resource is not designed nor intended for recreational use, but will be used as such by some groups
Organisational	Formal	Resource has a structured design/layout and/or management
	Informal	Resource has no such structure
Function	Single	Resource has one intended recreational function
	Multi	Resource has a diversity of intended recreational functions
	Shared	Resource has a variety of functions of which recreation is one
Space/use characteristics	Extensive	Individual recreational functions range over large areas with generous use of space
	Intensive	Functions are concentrated with little or no unused/wasted space
Scale	Large	Over 10 acres in extent
	Medium	Between 2 and 10 acres in extent
	Small	Below 2 acres in extent
Catchment	City-wide	Resource draws use from across the urban area
	District	Resource draws use primarily from its district
	Local	Resource draws use primarily from its neighbourhood
Source of provision	Public	Funded/managed by government at either local or national level
	Private	Funded/managed by private individuals/groups for their own use
	Voluntary	Funded/managed by groups acting as cooperatives, clubs or societies, for the use of members

Source: Williams (1995)

the planning and management undertaken to ensure that principles of equity and equal access are permitted where possible.

URBAN RECREATIONAL PLANNING

According to Patmore (1983: 117–18):

It may be possible to view [urban recreation] provision in a rational, hierarchical frame, to develop

models for that precision that equate access and opportunity in a spatial pattern with mathematical precision, but reality rarely gives an empty canvas where such a model can be developed in an unfettered form. Rather, reality is conditioned by the accident of historic legacy, by the fashions of spending from the public purse and by the commercial dictates of the public sector.

In geographical terms, urban recreational provision in town and cities grew in an *ad hoc* fashion, and in many Western European contexts

Table 5.4: Basic typology of outdoor recreation facilities in urban areas

	Public facilities Formal	Private/voluntary facilities Informal	Formal	By particular groups Informal
Large scale city-wide catchment	Major parks Major sports fields/stadia Municipal golf courses	Major commons Major urban woodland Major water space Urban country parks	Private golf courses	Major shopping centres Major transport centres, e.g. airports, stations
Medium scale district catchment	Recreation grounds Small parks	Urban greenways Minor urban woodland Minor water space Cycleways	Sports clubs e.g. bowls or cricket	
Small scale local catchment	Children's play areas		Domestic gardens	Local streets/ pavements Waste ground Grass verges

Source: Williams (1995)

the task of city planners in the 1960s and 1970s was to tidy up the decades of incremental growth. In the UK, one solution used was to create 'leisure directorates' in city councils to amalgamate public recreation interests into one consolidated department. As Burtenshaw *et al.* (1991) argued, the consolidation of recreation activities in the public sector led to debates on the extent to which such activities should be a commercial or municipal enterprise. In fact, no one coherent philosophy has been developed, with individual cities deciding the precise range of activities which should be publicly funded.

Yet the 1980s and 1990s have seen the main changes in urban recreational provision and planning as the following case study shows. The case study of urban parks integrates many of the concepts and ideas already developed in the chapter, concluding with a discussion on

management and planning philosophy and the implementation of geographical principles.

URBAN TOURISM

The second part of this chapter examines the concept of urban tourism, reviewing the principal contributions towards its recognition as a tourism phenomena worthy of study, and it also emphasises the scope and range of environments classified as urban destinations together with some of the approaches towards its analysis. It then considers a framework for the analysis of the tourist's experience of urban tourism which is followed by a discussion of key aspects of urban tourist behaviour: where do urban tourists go in urban areas, what activities do they undertake, how do they perceive these places and learn about the spatial

CASE STUDY: The management, planning and provision of urban parks in the 1990s. The example of Newham, East London

There has been a comparative neglect of urban parks by leisure and recreation researchers. Much of the research undertaken in the UK pre-dates the legislation and changes introduced in the late 1980s. Previous research has not examined the realities facing public sector leisure provision in the late 1980s and early 1990s although previous studies of urban parks have established their significance in metropolitan areas. Duffield and Walker (1983) produced a detailed review of research on urban parks which included a number of notable studies (e.g. Greater London Council 1968; Balmer 1973; Bowler and Strachan 1976). Previous studies of urban park use indicated that their catchments were localised and informal, fulfilling short-distance and short-stay recreational needs (Patmore 1983). Since the early 1980s, research on urban parks has focused on: historical re-constructions of urban park development; user-based research (including behavioural and perception-type studies); research on park planning, access-related studies; and a growing interest in the application of management principles to parks.

The largest single area of research on urban parks has focused on the accessibility (Harrison 1983) and behavioural-type studies, exemplified by Burgess *et al.* (1988a, 1988b, 1988c) and those undertaken by Milton Keynes Development Corporation (1988, 1989). In addition, Gregory (1988) and Grahn (1991) examined the attitudes and psychological constructs of different socio-economic groups using parks and open spaces, while Grocott (1990) considered the role of public participation in the design and creation of community parks. There has also been a growing interest in the management issues associated with urban parks. One major development which has altered the philosophy and delivery of leisure services in local authorities concerns the management of services through a unified 'Leisure Services Department'. These departments have created a new organisational structure for leisure service provision to accommodate the additional administrative functions created by the *Local Government Act* (1988). However, critics have argued that this new organisational structure may actually lead to fragmentation and poor integration in service provision, owing to the increased bureaucracy and centralised management of service provision by administrators rather than practitioners, who had daily contact with clients.

Accompanying organisational changes in leisure service provision since 1988 is a new ethos of service quality and quality assurance. This has permeated the delivery of public services. Barber (1991) examined the significance of management plans of parks and the role of local accountability, identifying individual park managers as the most effective personnel to ensure that the delivery of park-based services contributed to the quality of life in the local area. However, being responsive to the local needs has an economic cost and this may not always be compatible with the pursuit of efficiency in service provision. Morgan (1991) acknowledged the growing importance of consumer orientation in the planning and management process for parks and open spaces, to ensure community needs and desires were adequately considered. The increased use of attitude surveys and monitoring of urban park planning and management by local authorities is a direct response to the new ethos pervading public service provision. Yet research monitoring has a significant resource implication at a time of public sector restrictions on local government expenditure. The growing interest in urban park management is reflected in

Welch's (1991) survey which documents many of the issues facing local authorities in the 1990s including park safety, Compulsory Competitive Tendering (CCT), park-related legislation, recreation management and risk management. Against this background, attention now turns to London in terms of open space provision and the London Borough of Newham as a context in which to understand the role of spatial analysis.

URBAN PARK PROVISION IN LONDON

Research on recreation and leisure in London has hitherto attracted little interest at a city-wide level following the abolition of the Greater London Council (GLC) in 1986, which had included leisure and recreation in its strategic planning function. Since 1986 each London Borough's Unitary Development Plan is the framework for the formulation of policies to guide the provision of parks and open spaces. Leisure and recreation still remain a neglected aspect of London's diverse economic, social and cultural activities. Major studies of London's urban geography and expanding service sector (e.g. Hoggart and Green 1991) fail to acknowledge the significance of leisure service provision, although Bennett (1991: 212–3) did examine the London Boroughs' statutory responsibility for leisure and recreation provision.

The scale and nature of open space provision in London was set out in the Greater London Development Plan (Greater London Council 1969). Provision was based on a hierarchical principle, with different parks fulfilling various functions according to their size and distance from the users' homes. The concept of variety in park supply was to be achieved by the diversity of functions offered by parks in the capital, emphasising the social principle that parks of equal status were to be accessible to all sections of London's population. According to Burgess et al. (1988a), research in Greenwich questioned the suitability of a hierarchical system of park provision at the local area level, arguing that local communities did not recognise parks in terms of the differing functions that the GLC park hierarchy assigned to them. They claimed that most people in their survey felt that open spaces closest to their home failed to meet their leisure needs. This is a considerable problem for local authority leisure service departments, when the scale of public expenditure on open space and parks provision is examined at a London-wide scale. The extent to which financial resources are meeting local recreational needs is an important issue in view of the prioritisation of open space and park budgets of different local authorities across the capital.

According to the Chartered Institute of Public Finance and Accountancy (1990) in 1990/91, local authority leisure expenditure in London amounted to almost £66 million gross expenditure on open space and park provision from a total leisure budget of £106 million. The scale and distribution of expenditure highlights the overriding importance and priority attached by local authorities to open spaces and park provision. Furthermore, in 1990–91, £48 million of the total £66 million expenditure by London's local authorities on open space and park provision was spent on hired or contracted-out services administered through CCT procedures (Audit Commission 1993). Clearly urban parks form a publicly-funded service, since only £6.5 million of the total expenditure on open space and park provision in London was generated as income. In view of the scale of public expenditure on open spaces and parks, it is appropriate to consider the extent to which the leisure needs of London's population are fulfilled beyond the amenity value of such resources. There is increasing concern by quangos, such as the Audit Commission, on cost effective ways of delivering public services, and local authority leisure service departments are no exception to this. Within this context, it is pertinent to consider the extent to which the delivery of park-based services are responsive to local needs in one area of London – the London Borough of Newham.

THE LONDON BOROUGH OF NEWHAM, LEISURE PROVISION AND URBAN PARKS

Newham is an east London Borough with a population of 212,170 (1991). As one of the larger London Boroughs, covering 3,637 ha, it comprises a number of distinct communities. The Borough is a diverse multiracial area (Figure 5.3 and Table 5.5) with a variety of economic and social contrasts, including part of London Docklands in the south, and pockets of deprivation and unemployment elsewhere (Hoggart and Green 1991). In many respects, Newham has a range of inner city characteristics with an outer London location. A large number of the Borough's main open spaces and parks were established in the Victorian and Edwardian period, with subsequent additions in the inter-war and post-war periods. The existing provision of open space and parks comprises 180 ha of

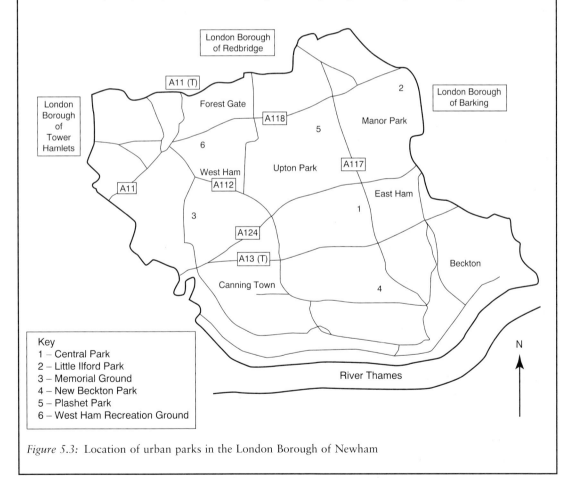

Figure 5.3: Location of urban parks in the London Borough of Newham

Table 5.5: Ethnic origins of Newham's population

	per cent
UK White	57.7
Black Caribbean	7.2
Black African	5.6
Black Other	1.6
Indian	13.0
Pakistani	5.9
Bangladeshi	3.7
Chinese	0.8
Other Groups	4.4
Total population in 1991	**212,170**

Source: OPCS (1992)

parks and open space, some 4.9 per cent of the total area of the Borough.

Newham Council performs a number of roles in terms of leisure provision, with responsibility based in the Leisure Services Department, established in 1984. Newham's Leisure Development Strategy 1990–94 sets out the Council's objectives for leisure in the 1990s, which are focused on partnership schemes to enhance leisure opportunities for both residents and visitors to Newham. To guide the development and implementation of the Leisure Development Strategy, a Leisure Services Development Plan 1990–94 has also been produced. This is to ensure that the main objectives and tasks associated with the delivery of leisure services by different units within the Leisure Services Department can be provided according to the following principles: equal opportunity, service quality, customer choice and value for money. Unfortunately, the Charted Institute of Public Finance and Accountancy (1990) report on leisure and recreation statistics does not contain any financial entries under Newham, making it difficult to assess the extent of local government expenditure on leisure services within the borough, particularly in terms of how its leisure budget is deployed.

As a local planning authority, Newham Council also establishes planning policies to determine the amount of land designated for open space. A variety of open space designations exist: green belt land to the north of the Borough (for example, Wanstead Flats and the City of London Cemetery); Metropolitan Open Land;

Table 5.6: London Borough of Newham Leisure Development Plan: Key objectives and actions for parks and open spaces

Parks and open spaces:
- Ensure the care and maintenance of Newham's parks and open spaces under the Compulsory Competitive Tendering legislation applicable to grounds maintenance.
- Increase the variety and quality of parks through landscape design, tree planting, ecological pilot schemes, bye-laws review and a systematic planned maintenance programme.
- Progress the development of parks at Newham Maternity Hospital site, East Beckton and the Thames Barrier.
- Introduce initiatives to encourage a greater use of parks for leisure, recreation and education.
- Review allotment provision in the borough with a view to improving allotment sites and addressing under-provision.
- Produce a comprehensive policy regarding usage, booking systems, fees and charges associated with leisure facilities located in parks.
- Introduce a policy and procedure for the adoption of open spaces.

Source: Newham Borough Council (1991b)

sites of borough-wide importance; sites of local importance and green corridors, complemented by urban parks (Archer and Yarman 1991). These policies are now incorporated in the unitary Development Plan for Newham, with urban parks forming one of the most widely available forms of open space either as large multi-purpose parks or smaller community based recreation grounds. In terms of the organisation and management of urban parks, Newham Leisure Services Department proposed a number of key objectives and actions for parks and open spaces (Table 5.6). The implementation of these objectives and actions, together with the day-to-day running and management of parks and open spaces, is based within a Park Client Unit. The Unit has its own devolved budget to purchase central council services through the internal trading system (see Walsh 1988), with responsibility for park maintenance contracts which are subject to CCT. Performance indicators are used to review the Park Client Unit's progress towards key objectives identified in the Leisure Services Development Plan. The Unit also has to recognise the implications of other Council policies and initiatives such as Newham's *Policy for the Environment: A Consultation Document* (Newham Borough Council, 1991a) which affects open space and park provision, since it aims to:

> preserve, develop and maintain a greener environment for Newham making it a more attractive, safer and cleaner place to live and work in. Parks, open spaces and play areas improve the local environment and provide people with opportunities for exercise, community and cultural activities, sport, quiet relaxation in natural surroundings. The protection of trees and other vegetation contributes to [sic] quality of the local environment and is an essential contribution to the reduction of global warming.
> (London Borough of Newham 1991a: 41)

In addition, the Park Client Unit must be aware of other Leisure Service Department policies such as the new ethos of customer care and satisfaction to ensure that 'everyone in Newham wants to be a customer of Leisure Services, and that every customer is a satisfied customer' (Newham Borough Council, 1991b: 9). However, for the Park Client Unit to translate such an objective into reality for leisure provision at the local area level required there must be a fundamental reassessment of the most appropriate organisational structure to deliver leisure services to local communities.

One of the key functions for the Park Client Unit is to undertake research to identify areas for service development and to ensure quality service provision is delivered in practice at the local level, as opposed to remaining an element of a broad leisure strategy. For this reason, the Park Client Unit explored their information needs prior to assessing and monitoring consumer satisfaction in the delivery of park services. It is within this context that a research project was undertaken to establish a source of systematically derived data on park use and satisfaction in the borough. The absence of existing information of park use in the borough reflects the current pressures facing local authorities who often lack adequate resources to deal with the expanding functions of local government. Therefore, the research reported here identifies areas of user concern and satisfaction within a number of park environments, to establish a baseline for further monitoring and research on parks and user groups.

NEWHAM URBAN PARK USER SURVEY

Methodology

The primary objective of the research for Newham's Park Client Unit was to examine a range of themes related to park use including: client type, patterns of weekly, seasonal and annual use, attitudes towards amenity value,

and management issues relating to the maintenance and development of the parks. One key
task was to compile a questionnaire survey
which was suitably sensitive to incorporate
the beliefs and attitudes of park users across
the borough. To achieve this objective, six
parks were selected (Figure 5.3) so that a
number of larger urban parks and smaller parks
and recreation grounds were included in
the review. The survey method, based on a
detailed questionnaire, was designed to interview users within the recreational environment
in which they felt at ease, by conducting a
random sample of users within the park rather
than to deter users with a closely monitored
entry/exit survey.

A total of 463 interviews were conducted
within the parks on a Saturday and Tuesday in
late March 1992. The majority of interviews
lasted between 15 and 40 minutes and were
undertaken between 09.00 and 17.00 hours,
achieving a reasonable distribution of responses
despite the variable weather conditions.

Results: Key Findings and Discussion

Of the 463 people interviewed, the sample was
drawn from Central Park (29.7 per cent),
Plashet Park (27 per cent), New Beckton Park
(2.3 per cent), Little Ilford Park (11.8 per cent),
West Ham Lane Recreation Ground (11.8 per
cent) and West Ham Memorial Ground (13
per cent). The parks selected yielded a useful
cross-section of opinions on a weekday and at
a weekend, with equal numbers of male and
female respondents drawn from a variety of age
groups (Table 5.7). The largest single group of
users (23.5 per cent) were aged 26–35 years,
following by the 17–25 age group (18 per cent)
and over 65 years of age (16 per cent) with
approximately 36 per cent aged 36–65 years of
age.

The ethnic origins of the respondents revealed
a particular bias towards people of UK origin

Table 5.7: Age group of respondents

	Male	Female
16 Years Old	1	0
17–25	45	37
26–35	48	61
36–45	33	34
46–55	23	30
56–65	27	28
over 65	43	30
Total	220	220

No response = 23

(71 per cent) followed by those of Afro-
Caribbean origin (11 per cent) and people of
Asian origin (8.5 per cent). A small number of
respondents were of Irish descent (2.5 per cent).
Only 1.5 per cent of respondents were from
other ethnic groups whilst a small number of
people did not respond to this question (5.5 per
cent). The sample was reasonably representative
of the UK born and Afro-Caribbean population.
It was the Asian population who were under
represented. One possible explanation of the
low number of Asian users in the sample is the
underlying racial tensions within the borough in
the weeks preceding the survey, a feature noted
by Burgess et al. (1988a) in another London
borough, where racial harassment constrained
park use among users of Asian descent.

The main user groups were young mothers
with children playing in a park, older age
groups and young people aged 16–21 years. A
significant number of users visited a park on a
daily basis in the spring (56 per cent) and during the summer (50 per cent). This indicates that
there were a regular group of users who made
extensive use of the parks. The length of time
spent in a park each day by 54 per cent of users
was between 15 minutes to one hour. Most
users visited the park alone (66 per cent), often

meeting other people within the park. The majority of users also visited urban parks within the borough on a regular basis, and a minority (7 per cent) also made extensive use of local recreation grounds. The reasons mentioned for visiting the parks among 35 per cent of users were: to go for a walk; to enjoy the flowers and scenery; to walk the dog; and to play with their children. A significant number of respondents chose to visit a park because of its facilities and location.

The parks sampled surveyed a distinct range of communities across the borough. For example, 91 per cent of users walked to the park, being located within five to ten minutes of their home. This is a feature noted in other urban park surveys (Patmore 1983). The majority of parks were located within easy access of the main centres of population in the borough. The postcode of the respondent indicated that their home address displayed a clear geographical bias towards the two largest parks within East Ham (Plashet and Central Park), which serve the major centres of population within the borough. This confirmed that the overwhelming pattern of use was local in relation to that catchment area.

Table 5.8 indicates that the recreational activities undertaken by the users reveal a bias towards passive leisure pursuits (walking the dog, going for a walk, and taking a short cut), compared to only 5.7 per cent of users who visited the park for active pursuits (sport or jogging). This illustrates one of the real functions of the parks – passive recreation, particularly in the older parks established in the late Victorian and Edwardian period. The establishment of Central and Plashet Park were primarily for walking and relaxation as the design principles embodied in their layout reinforce this type of use. Therefore, other active recreational pursuits, such as sports, cannot easily be integrated within the existing layout.

Those parks developed in Newham after 1945 (for example, New Beckton Park) overcome some of these potential constraints by developing innovative layouts to provide a clear zoning of uses. Path layouts do not constrain the integration of passive and active pursuits which sometimes cause conflict in the older parks. Therefore, the parks surveyed contained a variety of layouts, resources and facilities for both passive and, to a lesser degree, active recreation. Recreation grounds tended to provide more opportunities for sport and games.

Most users did not explicitly recognise the problems associated with the layout of specific parks, tending to emphasise other factors such as personal constraints. The most frequently mentioned reason (36 per cent) was the limited amount of time available to visit the park, indicating the extent to which leisure activities were accommodated within respondents' daily activities. Personal and child safety were also identified as potential constraints by only eight per cent of users, although this may conceal the problem of low usage rates by Asian groups due to the problem of perceived racial threats and harassment. Interestingly, 29 per cent of users claimed that there were no factors constraining their use.

Table 5.8: Recreational activities of park users

	Number	per cent
Walking the dog	131	29.0
Taking a short cut	119	26.0
Walking through	118	25.5
Playing with children	29	6.3
Playing sport/jogging	26	5.7
Sitting down	11	2.4
Meeting people	11	2.4
Other reasons	8	1.8
No response	10	2.2
Total	463	*

Note: * Total does not equal 100 owing to rounding error.

IMPLICATIONS FOR MANAGING URBAN PARKS AND LOCAL LEISURE PROVISION IN THE 1990s

Urban parks perform an important social role, with the potential to provide an accessible leisure resource for metropolitan populations regardless of gender, race, age and disability. As a non-profit making leisure resource, parks provide opportunities for planned and spontaneous leisure pursuits, being largely oriented towards passive rather than active forms of recreation. The results from the questionnaire survey have important implications for the management, development, planning and promotion of urban parks in Newham in terms of their ability to meet local leisure needs. The survey highlighted a number of potential problems related to the internal management process within Newham Council's Leisure Services Department and the external delivery of park services. The internal management of park services by the Park Client Unit would appear to be isolated from the central decision making process within the Leisure Services Department, which in turn is also distant from the actual delivery of services. Whilst the Park Client Unit is responsible for the day-to-day management of the parks and open spaces in Newham, there is little interaction between the users and provider of park services. To a certain extent this is a function of new management practices such as CCT, which devolve maintenance to contractors and remove opportunities for staff–user interaction and local park-based management. By reducing the Direct Service Organisation (DSO) input to park maintenance and management (see Welch 1991), Newham's urban parks are centrally planned and unable easily to incorporate the views and feelings of the users through a local park plan. This was one criticism which appeared in the questionnaire survey since different park users emphasised the importance of making improvements to parks in their locality. Within Newham there is no coherent and leisure-specific approach to park provision, with the Park Client Unit pulled in different directions by Council policies embodied in the Leisure Development Strategy 1990–94, the borough's Unitary Development Plan and the Newham Policy for the Environment. Thus the Park Client Unit is responsible for the immediate management issues although strategic planning and development functions are undertaken centrally. In practice there is no appropriate framework for local leisure planning since no specific management plans exist for individual parks. Therefore, park provision and management tends to accord with general principles of provision rather than innovative locally determined plans (see Grocott 1990).

In terms of maintenance, the survey intimated that CCT procedures had reduced the quality and knowledge of staff employed on maintenance contracts resulting in a de-skilling process to achieve cost savings. Many respondents also felt that staffing levels were now at a critical level and this may actually inhibit their use of parks. If the experience in Newham is typical of other London boroughs, maintenance consumes a large proportion of the budget with capital expenditure on facility development dealt with through the borough's Leisure Development Plan. Therefore, alterations to the park environment (for instance, safe-play surfaces for children) have to be dealt with from central budgets rather then devolved budgets for local park managers to deploy in whatever way they feel necessary to meet local leisure needs. Although Newham Council is aware of these issues through different policies, progress is piecemeal and not determined according to expressed demand in local parks, owing to the existing lack of research of park use and user satisfaction.

Significant progress towards improving the park environment and diversity of leisure uses could be achieved by improving the interpretation of wildlife, horticulture, educational uses and the development of organised children's events. Users do not perceive parks as a static recreational resource only for passive use: they recognised multiple use and some of the conflicts which arise from a lack of activity-based zoning within specific parks. In many cases, users requested additional leisure facilities within local parks to facilitate active leisure pursuits. The most contentious issue within the survey was the 'dog management problem'. It is evident that park use by dog owners should be identified as a discrete activity although it cannot easily be integrated within the existing layout of parks. Therefore, there need to be designated areas for dog walking which do not conflict with other uses. This will inevitably require a great deal of education of park users and changes in layout. The existing lack of dog management measures appears to erode the amenity value of many parks and actually deters some parents from taking children to open spaces.

A greater variety of park events also needs to be introduced to enhance the level of use and overcome inertia amongst non-park users. Promotion of the parks to provide leisure opportunities amongst non-users (for instance, ethnic minorities) is one area where action needs to be taken in view of the limited awareness of the Council's 'Parks for People' leaflet. Yet the extent to which these improvements can be implemented on a park-by-park basis ultimately depends on the Leisure Service Department's prioritisation of capital spending on this leisure resource. The existing plans by the Park Client Unit are for piecemeal changes to the structure and layout of individual parks as funds become available. Yet given the significance of urban parks in the leisure life-styles of urban populations, there seems to be some evidence to support a strategy of capital investment in existing parks to implement some of these changes, rather than the acquisition of additional open spaces which will inevitably

place pressure on the distribution of maintenance budgets.

Urban parks are clearly an important and accessible local resource, which need to be planned and managed at the local level in relation to the individual park catchments and their users. This has major resource implications, since it requires a re-evaluation of how park-based leisure services are planned and delivered, as well as the most appropriate organisational structure to manage these public resources. Although parks are a non-commercial leisure resource, their development and management consume a significant proportion of the total leisure budget of local authorities. In the existing climate of financial restrictions on local authority spending, one has to consider whether the administration, organisation and management should be devolved to individual park managers. The management structure and organisation of Newham's Leisure Services Department has meant that service provision is somewhat distant from the local needs of different client groups. Even though individual units (for example, the Park Client Unit) fulfil the role of an intermediary in the provision, delivery and management of park-based services, the power base and allocation of resources remain under central control. Therefore, expenditure on urban parks is carefully monitored through a central financial accounting system to ensure maintenance is carried out within strict financial guidelines.

The situation in Newham appears to follow the organisation and management structure developed for leisure service provision in other metropolitan local authorities with large areas of open space and urban parks. Urban park provision by these public sector organisations is still based on traditional service delivery practices, being supply-led rather than demand-led. The impact of CCT has created a culture of financial management in the maintenance and management of these resources as political ideology has altered the framework for local leisure policy (Bramham and Henry 1985).

In a demand-led environment, the emphasis is on the efficient allocation and prioritisation of scarce public resources to meet a limited range of leisure needs, with a user-pay philosophy affecting the provision of public services not deemed to be essential. These changes can be seen in Newham's Leisure Services Department and the Park Client Unit's approach to leisure provision, where it now has procedures in place for CCT and day-to-day management issues, and attention is now focusing on assessing user perceptions. Yet the full potential of urban parks is not being realised within the context of the rapid expansion of local authority leisure service departments (Veal and Travis 1979), if Newham's experience is representative of other localities. The major challenge facing local authority providers is to achieve financial savings in maintenance contracts for parks while devolving the management, planning and future development of the park infrastructure to a community-based form of planning which is adequately resourced and responsive to local needs.

Although parks are not as fashionable as capital intensive leisure facilities, they are operated on a non-commercial basis and offer access to the entire population. Therefore, their value within the urban environment should be given greater recognition as they contribute to the wider public good of metropolitan populations compared with more specialised and targeted sport and leisure facilities. It is clear that further research is needed to establish how local leisure needs can be met in terms of park provision, so that park management plans focus attention on local areas and communities. Urban parks and open spaces are an important sustainable leisure resource which can accommodate multiple uses, being accessible to local communities who may not have access to countryside areas. They are an integral feature of the urban landscape and assume an important part of the daily lives of local communities.

attributes of the locality, and how is this reflected in their patterns of behaviour? Having reviewed these features, the chapter concludes with a discussion of service quality issues for urban tourism.

UNDERSTANDING THE NEGLECT OF URBAN TOURISM BY RESEARCHERS

Ashworth's (1989) seminal study of urban tourism acknowledges that a double neglect has occurred. Those interested in the study of tourism 'have tended to neglect the urban context in which much of it is set, while those interested in urban studies . . . have been equally neglectful of the importance of the tourist function of cities' (Ashworth 1989: 33). While more recent tourism textbooks (e.g. Shaw and Williams 1994) have expanded upon earlier syntheses of urban tourism research in a spatial context (e.g. Pearce 1987a), it still remains a comparatively unresearched area despite the growing interest in the relationship between urban regeneration and tourism (see Law 1992 for a detailed review of the relationship of tourism and urban regeneration). The problem is also reiterated in a number of studies as one explanation of the neglect of urban tourism (see Vetter 1985; Page and Sinclair 1989). Despite this problem, which is more a function of perceived rather than real difficulties in understanding urban tourism phenomena, a range of studies now provide evidence of a growing body of literature on the topic (see Vetter 1985; Ashworth 1989, 1992a and b; Ashworth and Tunbridge 1990; Page 1995a and b). But even though more publications are now appearing in the academic literature, it does not imply that urban tourism is recognised as a distinct and notable area of research in tourism studies. This is due to the tendency for urban tourism research to be based on descriptive and empirical case studies which do not contribute to a greater theoretical or methodological understanding of urban tourism. In fact, such an approach is perpetuated by certain disciplines which contribute to the study of tourism, where the case study method of approach does little more than describe the situation in each instance and fails to relate the case to wider issues to derive generalisations and to test hypotheses and assumptions within the academic literature. In this respect, the limited understanding is a function of the lack of methodological sophis tication in tourism research noted in recent critiques of the subject (e.g. Pearce and Butler 1993).

According to Ashworth (1992a), urban tourism has not emerged as a distinct research focus: research is focused on tourism in cities. This strange paradox can be explained by the failure by planners, commercial interest and residents to recognise tourism as one of the main economic rationales for cities. Tourism is often seen as an adjunct or necessary evil to generate additional revenue, while the main economic activities of the locality are not perceived as tourism related. Such negative views of urban tourism have meant that the public and private sectors have used the temporary, seasonal and ephemeral nature of tourism to neglect serious research on this theme. Consequently, a vicious circle exists: the absence of public and private sector research makes access to research data difficult, and the large-scale funding for primary data collection using social survey techniques, necessary to break the vicious circle, is rarely available. The absence of large-scale funding for urban tourism research reflects the prevailing consensus in the 1980s that such studies were unnecessary. However, with the pressure posed by tourists in many European tourist cities in the 1990s (e.g. Canterbury, London, York, Venice and Florence), this perception is changing now that the public and

private sectors are belatedly acknowledging the necessity of visitor management (see English Tourist Board/Employment Department 1991 for a discussion of this issue) as a mechanism to enhance, manage and improve the tourist's experience of towns and places to visit. Nevertheless, as Ashworth (1992a: 5) argues:

> Urban tourism requires the development of a coherent body of theories, concepts, techniques and methods of analysis which allow comparable studies to contribute towards some common goal of understanding of either the particular role of cities within tourism or the place of tourism within the form and function of cities.

One way of assessing progress towards these objectives is to review the main approaches developed within the tourism literature.

APPROACHES TO URBAN TOURISM: GEOGRAPHICAL ANALYSIS

To understand how research on urban tourism has developed distinctive approaches and methodologies, one needs to recognise why tourists seek urban tourism experiences. Shaw and Williams (1994) argue that urban areas offer geographical concentration of facilities and attractions that are conveniently located to meet both visitor and resident needs alike. But the diversity and variety among urban tourist destinations has led researchers to examine the extent to which they display unique and similar features. Shaw and Williams (1994) identify three approaches:

- the diversity of urban areas means that their size, function, location and history contribute to their uniqueness;
- towns and cities are multi-functional areas, meaning that they simultaneously provide various functions for different groups of users; and
- the tourist functions of towns and cities are rarely produced or consumed solely by tourists, given the variety of user groups in urban areas.

Ashworth (1992a) conceptualises urban tourism by identifying three approaches towards its analysis, where researchers have focused on:

- the supply of tourism facilities in urban areas, involving inventories (e.g. the spatial distribution of accommodation, entertainment complexes and tourist related services), where urban ecological models have been used. In addition, the facility approach has been used to identify the tourism product offered by destinations;
- the demand generated by urban tourists, to examine how many people visit urban areas, why they choose to visit and their patterns of behaviour, perception and expectations in relation to their visit; and
- perspectives of urban tourism policy, where the public sector (e.g. planners) and private sector agencies have undertaken or commissioned research to investigate specific issues related to their own interests in urban tourism.

More recently, attempts to interpret urban tourism theoretically have been developed by Mullins (1991) and Roche (1992). Whilst these studies do not have a direct bearing on attempts to influence or affect the tourist experience of towns and cities, their importance should not be neglected in wider reviews of urban tourism: they offer explanations of the sudden desire of many towns and cities with a declining industrial base to look towards service sector activities such as tourism. Both studies examine urban tourism in the context of changes in post-industrial society and the relationship with structural changes in the mode of capitalist production. In other words, both studies question the types of process now shaping the operation and development of tourism in post-industrial cities, and the implications for public sector tourism and leisure policy. One outcome of such research is that it highlights the role of the state, especially local government in seeking to develop service industries based on

tourism and leisure production and consumption in urban areas, as a response to the restructuring of capitalism which has often led to employment loss in the locality. Mullins' (1991) concept of tourism urbanisation is also useful as it assists in developing the following typology of urban tourist destination:

- Capital cities;
- Metropolitan centres, walled historic cities and small fortress cities;
- Large historic cities;
- Inner city areas;
- Revitalised waterfront areas;
- Industrial cities;
- Seaside resorts and winter sport resorts;
- Purpose-built integrated tourist resorts;
- Tourist-entertainment complexes;
- Specialised tourist service centres; and
- Cultural/art cities.

(After Page 1995: 17)

This typology illustrates the diversity of destinations which provide an urban context for tourist visits, and highlights the problem of deriving generalisations from individual case studies without a suitable conceptual framework. For this reason, it is pertinent to focus on the concept of the 'tourist experience of urban tourism' as a framework to assess some as the experiential aspects of this phenomena.

THE TOURIST EXPERIENCE OF URBAN TOURISM

There is a growing literature on tourist satisfaction (e.g. Ryan 1995), and what constitutes the experiential aspects of a tourist visit to a locality. In the context of urban tourism, the innovative research by Graefe and Vaske (1987) offers a number of important insights as well as a useful framework. Graefe and Vaske (1987) acknowledge that the 'tourist experience' is a useful term to identify the experience of an individual which may be affected 'by individual, environmental, situational and personality-related factors as well as the degree of communication with other people. It is the outcome which researchers and the tourism industry constantly evaluate to establish if the actual experience met the tourist's expectations' (Page 1995a: 24). Operationalising such a concept may prove difficult in view of the complex array of factors which may affect the visitor experience (Figure 5.4). For example, where levels of overcrowding occurs at major tourist sites (e.g. Canterbury, Venice, St Paul's Cathedral, London and the Tower of London), this can have a negative effect on visitors who have a low tolerance threshold for overcrowding at major tourist sites. Yet conversely, other visitors may be less affected by use levels thereby illustrating the problem within tourism motivation research – predicting tourist behaviour and their responses to particular situations. In fact Graefe and Vaske (1987: 394) argue that 'the effects of increasing use levels on the recreation/ tourist experience can be explained only partially . . . as a function of use level'. Therefore, the individual tourists' ability to tolerate the behaviour of other people, level of use, the social situation and the context of the activity are all important determinants of the actual outcome. Thus, evaluating the quality of the tourist experience is a complex process which may require a careful consideration of the factors motivating a visit (i.e. how the tourist's perception of urban areas makes them predisposed to visit particular places), their actual patterns of activity and the extent to which their expectations associated with their perceptions are matched in reality (Page 1995a: 25). For this reason, attention now turns to some of the experiential aspects of urban tourists' visits and the significance of behavioural issues influencing visitor satisfaction. In view of the diversity of tourists visiting urban areas, it is useful to define the market for urban tourism.

- the weather conditions at the time of visit
- the standard and quality of accommodation available
- the cleanliness and upkeep of the city
- the city's aesthetic value (i.e. its setting and beauty)
- the tourists' personal safety from crime
- accessibility of attractions and points of interest in the city
- the extent to which local people welcome visitors in a warm manner
- the ability of tourism employees to speak foreign languages
- the range of cultural and artistic amenities
- the ambience of the city environment as a place to walk around
- the level of crowding and congestion
- the range of nightlife and entertainment available
- range of restaurants and eating establishments in the city
- the pleasurability of leisure shopping
- the price levels of goods and services in the city
- the level of helpfulness among local people
- the adequacy of emergency medical care

Figure 5.4: Factors to consider in evaluating the urban tourism experience
Source: Modified from Haywood and Muller (1988)

Plate 5.1: The Tower of London is a major drawcard in London for urban tourists.

Plate 5.2: The National Gallery in London: A tourist and recreational resource which is based on the arts.

THE URBAN TOURISM MARKET: DATA SOURCES

Identifying the scale, volume and different markets for urban tourism remains a perennial problem for researchers. Urban tourism is a major economic activity in many of Europe's capital cities but identifying the tourism markets in each area is problematic. Page (1995a) provides a detailed assessment of the principal international data sources on urban tourism, reviewing published statistics by the World Tourism Organisation and the Organisation for Economic Cooperation and Development. Such data sources commonly use the domestic and international tourist use of accommodation as one measure of the scale of tourism activity. In the context of urban tourism, it requires researchers to have an understanding of spatial distribution of tourist accommodation in each country to identify the scale and distribution of tourist visits. In countries where the majority of accommodation is urban-based, such statistics may provide preliminary sources of data for research. Whilst this may be relevant for certain categories of tourist (e.g. business travellers and holiday makers), those visitors staying with friends and relatives within an urban environment would not be included in the statistics. Even where statistics can be used, they only provide a preliminary

assessment of scale and volume and more detailed sources are needed to assess specific markets for urban tourism. For example, Page (1995a) reviews the different market segmentation techniques used by marketing researchers to analyse the tourism market for urban areas which helps one to understand the types of visitors and motives for visiting urban destinations. Table 5.9 highlights two typologies developed within the tourism literature to acknowledge the significance of individual motives for visiting urban destinations. However, Jansen-Verbeke (1986) does point to the methodological problem of distinguishing between the different users of the tourist city. For example, Burtenshaw *et al.* (1991) discuss the concept of functional areas (Figure 5.5) within the city, where different visitors seek certain attributes for their city visit (e.g. the historic city, the culture city, the night life city, the shopping city and the tourist city) where no one group has a monopoly over its use. In other words, residents of the city and its hinterland, visitors and workers all use the resources within the tourist city, but some user groups identify with certain areas more than others. Thus, the tourist city is a multi-functional area which complicates attempts to identify a definitive classification of users and the areas/facilities they visit.

Ashworth and Tunbridge (1990) prefer to

Table 5.9: Typologies of urban tourists

According to Blank and Petkovitch (1980) the motives for visiting urban areas can be classified thus:

- visiting friends and relatives
- business/convention visitation
- outdoor recreation activities
- entertainment and sightseeing activities
- personal reasons
- shopping
- other factors

while more recently Page (1995: 48) identified a broader range of motivations for visiting urban areas which includes:

- visiting friends and relatives
- for business travel
- conference and exhibition attendance
- educational reasons
- cultural and heritage tourism
- religious travel (e.g. pilgrimages)
- hallmark events attendance
- leisure shopping
- day trips

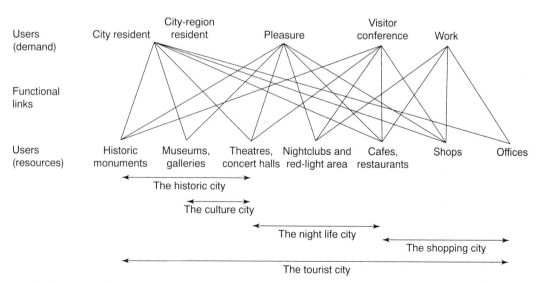

Figure 5.5: Functional areas in the tourist city
Source: After Burtenshaw *et al.* (1991), reproduced with permission from David Fulton Publishers

Plate 5.3: Conference travel is an extremely significant component of urban tourism. Singapore Convention Centre.

Plate 5.5: Casinos and associated entertainment complexes are an increasingly significant element of urban tourism. Crown Casino, Melbourne, Australia.

Plate 5.4: Tourism can be a major driving force behind urban regeneration. Street revitalisation programme, Victoria, Canada.

approach the market for urban tourism from the perspective of the consumers' motives, focusing on the purchasing intent of users, their attitudes, opinions and interests for specific urban tourism products. The most important distinction they make is between use/non-use of tourism resources, leading them to identify international users (who are motivated by the character of the city) and incidental users (who view the character of the city as irrelevant to their use). This two-fold typology is used by Ashworth and Tunbridge (1990) to identify four specific types of users:

- intentional users from outside the city-region (e.g. holiday makers and heritage tourists);
- intentional users from inside the city-region (e.g. those using recreational and entertainment facilities – recreating residents);
- incidental users from outside the city-region (e.g. business and conference/exhibition tourists and those on family visits – non-recreating visitors); and
- incidental users from inside the city-region (e.g. residents going about their daily activities – non-recreating residents).

Such an approach recognises the significance of attitudes and the use made of the city and services rather than the geographical origin of the visitor as the starting point for analysis. Although the practical problem with such an approach is that tourists tend to cite one main motive for visiting a city, any destination is likely to have a variety of user groups in line with Ashworth and Haan's (1986) examination of users of the tourist–historic city of Norwich. Their methodology involved tourists self-allocating the most important motives for visiting Norwich. While 50 per cent of holiday makers were intentional users of the historic city, significant variations occurred in the remaining markets using the historic city. But this does confirm the multi-use hypothesis advanced by Ashworth and Tunbridge (1990) which was subsequently developed in a geographical context by Getz (1993a). Having outlined some of the methodological issues associated with assessing the market for urban tourism, attention now turns to the behavioural issues associated with the analysis of tourist visits to urban areas.

URBAN TOURISM: BEHAVIOURAL ISSUES

Any assessment of urban tourist activities, patterns and perceptions of urban locations will be influenced by the supply of services, attractions and facilities in each location. Recent research has argued that one needs to understand the operation and organisation of tourism in terms of the production of tourism services and the ways in which tourists consume the products in relation to the locality, their reasons for consumption, what they consume and possible explanations of the consumption outcome as visitor behaviour. As Law (1993: 14) argues:

> tourism is the geography of consumption outside the home area; it is about how and why people travel to consume . . . on the production side it is concerned to understand where tourism activities develop and on what scale. It is concerned with the process or processes whereby some cities are able to create tourism resources and a tourism industry.

One framework developed in the Netherlands by Jansen-Verbeke (1986) to accommodate the analysis of tourism consumption and production in urban areas is that of the 'leisure product' (see pp. 99–100). The facilities in an urban environment can be divided into the 'primary elements', 'secondary elements' and 'additional elements' (see Jansen-Verbeke 1986 for a more detailed discussion of this approach). To distinguish between user groups, Jansen-Verbeke (1986) identified tourists' and recreationalists' first and second reasons for visiting three Dutch towns (Deneter, Kampen and Zwolle). The inner city environment provides a leisure function for various visitors regardless of the prime motivation for visiting. As Jansen-Verbeke (1986: 88–9) suggests:

> On an average day, the proportion of visitors coming from beyond the city-region (tourists) is about one-third of all visitors. A distinction that needs to be made is between week days, market days and Sundays. Weather conditions proved to be important . . . the hypothesis that inner cities have a role to play as a leisure substitute on a rainy day could not be supported.

Among the different user groups, tourists tend to stay longer, with a strong correlation between 'taking a day out', sightseeing and 'visiting a museum' as the main motivations to visit. Nevertheless, leisure shopping was also a major 'pull factor' for recreationalists and tourists, through it is of greater significance for the recreationalists. Using a scaling technique, Jansen-Verbeke (1986) asked visitors to evaluate how important different elements of the leisure product were to their visit. The results indicate that there is not a great degree of difference between tourists' and recreationalists' rating of elements and characteristics of the city's leisure product. While recreationalists attach more importance to shopping facilities than events and museums, the historical characteristics of the environment and decorative elements combined with other elements, such as markets, restaurants, and the compact nature of the inner city, to attract visitors. Thus, 'the conceptual approach to the system of inner-city tourism is inspired by common features of the inner-city environment, tourists' behaviour and appreciation and promotion activities' (Jansen-Verbeke 1986: 97). Such findings illustrate the value of relating empirical results to a conceptual framework for the analysis of urban tourism and the necessity of replicating similar studies in other urban environments to test the validity of the hypothesis, framework and interpretation of urban tourists' visitor behaviour. But how do tourists and other visitors to urban areas learn about, find their way around and perceive the tourism environment?

TOURIST PERCEPTION AND COGNITION OF THE URBAN ENVIRONMENT

How individual tourists interact and acquire information about the urban environment remains a relatively poorly researched area in tourism studies, particularly in relation to towns and cities. This area of research is traditionally seen as the forte of social psychologists with an interest in tourism, though much of the research by social psychologists has focused on motivation (e.g. Guy and Curtis 1986, on the development of perceptual maps). Reviews of the social psychology of tourism indicate that there has been a paucity of studies of tourist behaviour and adaptation to new environments they visit. This is somewhat surprising since 'tourists are people who temporarily visit areas less familiar to them than their home area' (Walmesley and Jenkins 1992: 269). Therefore, one needs to consider a number of fundamental questions related to:

- How will the tourists know the areas they visit?
- How do they find their way around unfamiliar environments?
- What features in the urban environment are used to structure their learning experience in unfamiliar environments?
- What type of mental maps and images do they develop?

These issues are important in a tourism planning context since the facilities which tourists use and the opportunities they seek will be conditioned by their environmental awareness. This may also affect the commercial operation of attractions and facilities, since a lack of awareness of the urban environment and the attractions within it may mean tourists fail to visit them. Understanding how tourists interact with the environment to create an image of the real world has been the focus of research into social psychology and behavioural geography (see Walmesley and Lewis 1993: 95–126). Geographers have developed a growing interest in the geographic space perception of all types of individuals (Downs 1970), without explicitly considering tourists in most instances. Behavioural geographers emphasise the need to examine how people store spatial information and 'their choice of different activities and locations within the environment' (Walmesley and Lewis 1993: 95). The process through which individuals perceive the urban environment is shown in Figure 5.6. Whilst this is a simplification, Haynes (1980) notes that no two individuals will have an identical image of the urban environment because the information they receive is subject to mental processing. This is conditioned by the information signals they receive through their senses (e.g. sight, hearing, smell, taste and touch) and this part of the process is known as perception. As our senses may only comprehend a small proportion of the total information received, the human brain sorts the information and relates it to the knowledge, values and attitudes of the individual through the process of cognition (Page 1995a: 222). The final outcome of the perception and cognition process is the formation of a mental image of a place. These images are an individual's own view of reality, but they are important to the individual and group when making decisions about their experience of a destination, whether to visit again, and their feelings in relation to the tourist experience of place.

As Walmesley and Lewis (1993: 96) suggest, 'the distinction between perception and cognition

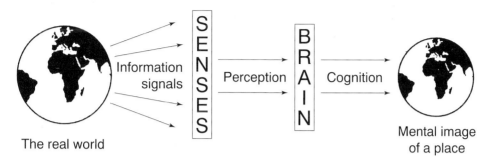

Figure 5.6: Perceptions of place

is, however, a heuristic device rather than a fundamental dichotomy because in many senses, the latter subsumes the former and both are mediated by experience, beliefs, values, attitudes, and personality such that, in interacting with their environment, humans only see what they want to see'. Consequently, an individual tourist's knowledge of the environment is created in their mind as they interact with the unfamiliar environment they are visiting (or a familiar environment on a return visit).

According to Powell (1978: 17–18) an image of the environment comprises ten key features which include:

a) a spatial component accounting for an individual's location in the world;
b) a personal component relating the individual to other people and organisations;
c) a temporal component concerned with the flow of time;
d) a relational component concerned with the individual's picture of the universe as a system of regularities;
e) conscious, subconscious, and unconscious elements;
f) a blend of certainty and uncertainty;
g) a mixture of reality and unreality;
h) a public and private component expressing the degree to which an image is shared;
i) a value component that orders parts of the image according to whether they are good or bad; and
j) an affectional component whereby the image is imbued with feeling.

Among geographers, the spatial component to behavioural research has attracted most interest, and they derive much of their inspiration from the pioneering research by Lynch (1960). Lynch's research asked respondents in North American cities to sketch maps of their individual cities, and by simplifying the sketches, derived images of the city. Lynch developed a specific technique to measure people's urban images in which respondents drew a map of the centre of the city from memory, marking on it the streets, parks, buildings, districts and features they considered important. 'Lynch found many common elements in these mental maps that appeared to be of fundamental importance to the way people collect information about the city' (Hollis and Burgess 1977: 155). Lynch (1960) found five elements in the resulting maps after simplifying the maps. These were:

a) *Paths* which are the channels along which individuals move.
b) *Edges* which are barriers (e.g. rivers) or lines separating one region from another.
c) *Districts* which are medium-to-large sections of the city with an identifiable character.
d) *Nodes* which are the strategic points in a city

which the individual can enter and which serve as foci for travel.

e) *Landmarks* which are points of reference used in navigation and way finding, into which an individual cannot enter.

(See Figure 5.7 for a schematic diagram of Lynchean landscape elements.)

The significance of such research for the tourist and visitor to the urban environment is that the information they collect during a visit will shape their image of the place, influencing their feelings and impressions of a place. Furthermore, this imageability of a place is closely related to the

legibility by which is meant the extent to which parts of the city can be recognised and interpreted by an individual as belonging to a coherent pattern. Thus a legible city would be one where the paths, edges, districts, nodes and landmarks are both clearly identifiable and clearly positioned relative to each other.

(Walmesley and Lewis 1993: 98)

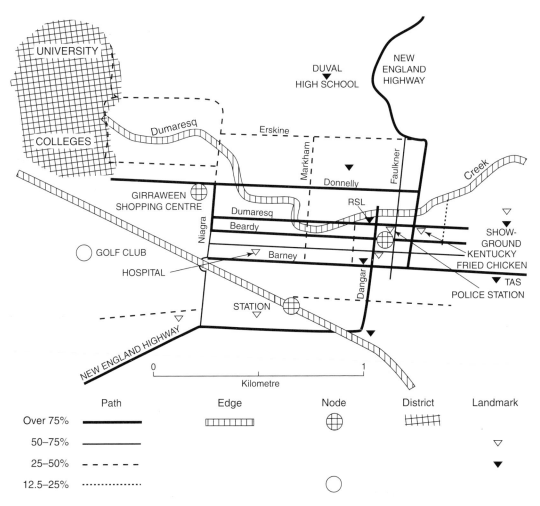

Figure 5.7: The Lynchean landscape of Armidale, New South Wales
Source: After Walmesley and Lewis (1993: 127)

Although there may sometimes be confusion among individuals regarding recognition of Lynchean urban landscape elements, it does help researchers to understand how individuals perceive the environment. Even so, Walmesley and Lewis (1993) review many of the issues associated with the methodology of imagery research and raise a range of concerns about deriving generalisations from such results. Such studies do have a role to play in understanding how people view, understand and synthesise the complexity of urban landscapes into images of the environment. Nevertheless, criticisms of spatial research of individual imagery of the environment are that it uses a 'borrowed methodology, a potpourri of concepts, and liberal doses of borrowed theory' (Stea and Downs 1979: 3, cited in Walmesley and Lewis 1993). In a tourism context, Walmesley and Jenkins (1992) observed that tourism cognitive mapping may offer a number of useful insights into how tourists learn about new environments and for this reason, it is pertinent to consider how visitor behaviour may be influenced by the ability to acquire spatial knowledge and synthesise it into meaningful images of the destination to assist them in finding their way around the area or region.

TOURISM COGNITIVE MAPPING

Walmesley and Lewis (1993: 214) review the factors that affect visitor behaviour in terms of five interrelated factors which may initially shape the decision to visit an urban environment. These are:

- antecedent conditions;
- user aspirations;
- intervening variables;
- user satisfaction; and
- real benefits.

These factors will, with experience, raise or reduce the individual's desire for recreational (and tourism) activity. The opportunities and constraints on visitors' behaviour are affected by income, disposable time available and a host of other socio-economic factors. Research by Stabler (1990) introduces the concept of 'opportunity sets' where the individual or family's knowledge of tourism opportunities is conditioned by their experience and the constraints on available time to partake in leisure and tourism activities. Thus, once the decision is taken to visit an urban environment, the tourist faces the problem of familiarity/unfamiliarity of the location. It is the latter which tends to characterise most urban tourist trips, though visitors are often less hesitant about visiting urban destinations if they live in a town or city environment.

P. Pearce (1977) produced one of the pioneering studies of cognitive maps of tourists. Using data from sketch maps from first-time visitors to Oxford, England, the role of landmarks, paths and districts were examined. The conclusion drawn indicated that visitors were quick to develop cognitive maps, often by the second day of the visit. The interesting feature of the study is that there is evidence of an environmental learning process at work. Walmesley and Jenkins' (1992: 272) critique of Pearce's (1977) findings note that:

- the number of landmarks, paths and districts increased over time;
- the number of landmarks identified increased over a period of 2–6 days, while recognition of the number of districts increased from 2 to 3;
- the resulting sketch maps were complex with no one element dominating them.

A further study by P. Pearce (1981), examined how tourists came to know a route in Northern Queensland (a 340 km strip from Townsville to Cairns). The study indicated that experiential variables are a major influence upon cognitive maps. For example, drivers had a better knowledge than passengers, while age and prior use of the route were important conditioning factors. But as Walmesley and Jenkins (1992: 273) argue, 'very little concern has been shown for the cognitive maps of tourists' except for the work by Aldskogius (1977) in Sweden and Mercer (1971a) in Australia.

SERVICE QUALITY ISSUES IN URBAN TOURISM

The competitive nature of urban tourism is increasingly being reflected in the growth in marketing and promotion efforts by towns and cities as they compete for a share of international and domestic tourism markets. Such competition has led to tourists' demands for higher standards of service provision and improved quality in the tourist experience. As Clewer *et al.* (1992) note, certain urban tourists (e.g. the German Market) have higher expectations of service quality than others. But developing an appropriate definition or concept of urban tourism quality is difficult due to the intangible nature of services as products which are purchased and consumed.

In the context of urban tourism, three key issues need to be addressed. First, place-marketing generates an image of a destination that may not be met in reality due to the problems of promoting places as tourist products. The image promoted through place-marketing may not necessarily be matched in reality through the services and goods which the tourism industry delivers. As a result, the gap between the customer's perception of a destination and the bundle of products they consume is reflected in their actual tourist experience, which has important implications for their assessment of quality in their experience. Secondly, the urban tourism product is largely produced by the private sector either as a package or a series of elements which are not easily controlled or influenced by the place-marketer. Thirdly, there are a large range of associated factors which affect a tourist's image of a destination, including less tangible elements like the environment and the ambience of the city which may shape the outcome of a tourist's experience. As a result, the customer's evaluation of the

quality of the services and products provided is a function of the difference (gap) between expected and perceived service. It is in this context that the concept of service quality is important for urban tourism. Gilbert and Joshi (1992) present an excellent review of the literature, including many of the concepts associated with service quality. In the case of urban tourism, it is the practical management of the 'gap' between the expected and the perceived service that requires attention by urban managers and the tourism industry. In reviewing Parasuraman *et al.*'s (1985) service quality model, Gilbert and Joshi (1992: 155) identify five gaps which exist between:

a) the expected service and the management's perceptions of the consumer experience (i.e. what they think the tourist wants) (Gap 1);
b) the management's perception of the tourist needs and the translation of those needs into service quality specifications (Gap 2);
c) the quality specifications and the actual delivery of the service (Gap 3);
d) the service delivery stage and the organisation/provider's communication with the consumer (Gap 4);
e) the consumer's perception of the service they received and experienced, and their initial expectations of the service (Gap 5).

Gilbert and Joshi (1992) argue that the effective utilisation of market research techniques could help to bridge some of the gaps. For:

Gap 1   by encouraging providers to elicit detailed information from consumers on what they require;
Gap 2   by the management providing realistic specifications for the services to be provided which are guided by clear quality standards;
Gap 3   by the employees being able to deliver the service according to the specifications; these need to be closely monitored and staff training and development is essential:

a service is only as good as the staff it employs;

Gap 4 by the promises made by service providers in their marketing and promotional messages being reflected in the actual quality offered. Therefore, if a city's promotional literature promises a warm welcome, human resource managers responsible for employees in front-line establishments need to ensure that this message is conveyed to its customers; and

Gap 5 by the major gap between the perceived service and delivered service being reduced through progressive improvements in the appropriate image which is marketed to visitors, and the private sector's ability to deliver the expected service in an efficient and professional manner.

Such an approach to service quality can be applied to urban tourism as it emphasises the importance of the marketing process in communicating and dealing with tourists. To obtain a better understanding of the service quality issues associated with the urban tourist's experience of urban tourism, Haywood and Muller (1988) identify a methodology for evaluating the quality of the urban tourism experience. This involves collecting data on visitors' expectations prior to, and after their city-visit by examining a range of variables (see Page 1995a for a fuller discussion). Such an approach may be costly to operate, but it does provide a better appreciation of the visiting process and they argue that cameras may also provide the day to day monitoring of city experiences. At a city-wide level, North American and European cities have responded to the problem of large visitor numbers and the consequences of mass tourism for the tourist experience by introducing Town Centre Management Schemes (see Page 1994a for further detail of this issue) and Visitor Management Schemes (see Page and Hardyman 1996 for more detail on the developments and application of such schemes).

Whilst there is insufficient space here to review

these new management tools to combat the unwieldy and damaging effect of mass tourism on key tourist centres in developed and developing countries, it is notable that many small historic cities in Europe are taking steps to manage, modify and in some cases deter tourist activities. Yet before such measures can be taken, to improve the tourist experience of urban tourism in different localities, Graefe and Vaske (1987) argue that the development of a management strategy is necessary to:

- deal with problem conditions which may impact on the tourist experience;
- identify the causes of such problems; and
- select appropriate management strategies to deal with these problems.
  (See Graefe and Vaske 1987 for more detail on the use of this approach to improve the tourist experience.)

THE SIGNIFICANCE OF URBAN TOURISM

Tourism's development in urban areas is not a new phenomenon. But its recognition as a significant activity to study in its own right is only belatedly gaining the recognition it deserves within tourism studies. The reasons why tourists visit urban environments, to consume a bundle of tourism products, continues to be overlooked by the private sector which often neglects the fundamental issue – cities are multi-functional places. Despite the growing interest in urban tourism research, the failure of many large and small cities which promote tourism, to understand the reasons why people visit, the links between the various motivations and the deeper reasons why people are attracted to cities remains a fertile area for theoretically informed and methodologically sound research. Many cities are beginning to recognise the importance of monitoring visitor perceptions and satisfaction (e.g. Brocx 1994) and the activity patterns and behaviour of tourists

(Survey Research Associates 1991). While such studies may have provided rich pickings for market research companies, all too often the surveys have been superficial, naive and devoid of any real understanding of urban tourism. For the public and private sector planners and managers with an interest, involvement or stake in urban tourism, the main concern continues to be the potential for harnessing the all-year-round appeal of urban tourism activity, despite the often short-stay nature of such visitors. Ensuring that such stays are part of a high quality experience, where visitor expectations are realistically met through well researched, targeted and innovative products continues to stimulate interest among tour operators and other stakeholders in urban tourism provision. Yet as the research reported in this chapter suggests, the urban tourism industry, which is so often fragmented and poorly co-ordinated, rarely understands many of the complex issues of visitor behaviour, the spatial learning process which tourists experience and the implications for making their visit as stress free as possible.

These concerns should force cities seeking to develop an urban tourism economy to reconsider the feasibility of pursuing a strategy to revitalise the city-region through tourism-led regeneration. All too often both the private and public sectors have moved headlong into economic regeneration strategies for urban areas, seeking a tourism component as a likely backup for property and commercial redevelopment (e.g. see Lutz and Ryan 1996). The implications here are that tourism issues are not given the serious treatment they deserve. Where the visitors needs and spatial behaviour are poorly understood and neglected in the decision making process, it affects the planning, development and eventual outcome of the urban tourism environment. Although the experience of waterfront areas in large cities has not been reviewed in this chapter, recent research which reviews the ambitious schemes to market

tourism in London Docklands, to pull the centre of gravity and development in London to the east from the central tourism district in the west, resulted in developers underestimating the role of tourist behaviour (e.g. the inertia of tourists who would not travel east from St Katherine's Dock to areas en route to Greenwich). The result is a series of missed business opportunities and a range of business failures (see pp. 115–120). Therefore, tourist behaviour, the tourism system and its constituent components need to be evaluated in the context of future growth in urban tourism to understand the visitor as a central component in the visitor experience. Managing the different elements of this experience in a realistic manner is requiring more attention among those towns and cities competing aggressively for visitors, using the quality experience approach as a new found marketing tool. Future research needs to focus on the behaviour, attitudes and needs of existing and prospective urban tourists to reduce the gap between their expectations and the service delivered. But ensuring that the tourism system within cities can deliver the service and experience marketed through promotional literature in a sensitive and meaningful way is now one of the major challenges for urban tourism managers. The approach adopted by the tourism industry needs to be more proactive in its pursuit of high quality visitor experiences rather than reactive towards individual problems that arise as a result of tourist dissatisfaction after a visit. Research has a vital role to play in understanding the increasingly complex reasons why tourists continue to visit urban environments and the factors which influence their behaviour and spatial activity patterns. While urban tourism continues to be a recognised and established form of tourism activity, research by the academic community and private sector has really only paid lip service to what is a central feature of the tourism system in most developed and developing countries.

CONCLUSION

This chapter has reviewed the role of recreation and tourism within the context of an urban environment, where recreationalists and tourists inevitably use some of the same resources. This is best summarised by Burtenshaw *et al.*'s (1991) conceptualisation of different users and functional areas of the city, where no one group has a monopoly over its use. The urban environment is still a neglected field of research in relation to the geographer's analysis of tourism and recreation, and yet the methodologies, techniques and skills they possess can help both the public and private sector to understand how a range of research issues affect the functioning of the recreational and tourism system. For example, in recreational

planning, issues of access, equality, need and social justice can easily be integrated into spatial analysis using secondary data. Where data does not exist, spatially orientated social surveys have proved to be extremely valuable in understanding the processes shaping and underpinning existing patterns of use and activity, provision and future development. However, this chapter has also demonstrated that applied geographical research (Sant 1982), for example as illustrated by the case study of urban recreational provision in the London Borough of Newham, can be used to pose questions and address problem-solving tasks for managerial solutions as well as providing a basis for raising more fundamental questions about the nature of tourism and recreation in contemporary capitalist society.

6

RURAL RECREATION AND TOURISM

As a focal point for geographical research, the recreational and tourism potential of rural areas is not a new theme for geographers to consider. The interest in rural areas has a long tradition (Owens 1984) but the problem remains that much of the research conducted, with a few exceptions (Getz and Page 1997; Sharpley and Sharpley 1997; Butler *et al.* 1998; D. Hall and O'Hanlon 1998) is now dated, fragmented and continues to view rural areas as either a recreational or a tourism resource. It fails to adopt a holistic view of the rural resource base as multifaceted environment capable of accommodating a wide range of uses (e.g. agriculture, industrialisation, recreation and tourism) and values. As Patmore (1983: 124) recognised 'recreation use must compete with agriculture, forestry, water abstraction, mineral extraction and military training' within the rural environment which has both spatial implications for competing and complementary land uses as well as for the identification of the ways in which recreation and tourism may be accommodated in an ever changing rural environment.

According to Coppock (1982: 8)

the contribution to research that geographers have made has been focused primarily on outdoor recreation in the countryside. No clear distinction has been made between tourism and recreation which is not surprising in a small, densely settled country [Britain] where there is considerable overlap between the two; in any case, geographical studies in tourism have been much less numerous than those in outdoor recreation.

This is an assertion that, to a certain extent still holds true for rural areas today. Butler *et al.* (1998: 2), argued that

In many cases, however, the specific activities which are engaged in during leisure, recreation and tourism are identical, the key differences being the setting or location of the activities, the duration of time involved, and, in some cases, the attitudes, motivations and perceptions of the participants. In recent years the differences between recreation and tourism in particular, except at a philosophical level, have become of decreasing significance and distinctions increasingly blurred.

In fact, Pigram (1983) observed that it is 'where [such] space consumption and spatial competition and conflict are most likely to occur . . . that spatial organisation and spatial concerns become paramount, and so the geographer has a valuable role to play in considering rural recreation and tourism as a process and phenomenon which has spatial implications'. Pigram (1983: 15) further argues that the geographer cannot only focus on the spatial organisation and interaction which occurs, but also the 'imbalance or discordance between population related demand and environmentally related supply of recreation [and tourism] opportunities and facilities'. This point is reiterated by Hall (1995) who felt that the rural areas now host a wide range of activities undertaken in people's leisure time and to determine whether the activity is tourism or recreation may seem irrelevant. In contrast, Patmore (1983: 123) argued that 'outdoor recreation in rural areas rapidly achieves a distinctive character of its own and needs separate consideration for more than convention'. Either way, recreation and tourism are increasingly important activities in rural areas throughout the Western world.

This chapter examines the growing interest from geographers in the way in which the rural environment is examined as a recreational and tourism resource together with some of the ways in which it has been conceptualised and researched. The chapter commences with a review of the concept of 'rural' and the ways in which geographers have debated its meaning and definition. This is followed by a discussion of the geographer's contribution to theoretical debate in relation to rural recreation and tourism. The contribution made by historical geography to the analysis of continuity and change in the rural environment and its consumption for leisure and tourism is briefly examined. The other contributions made by geographers to the analysis of recreation and tourism in rural environments is examined and a case study of tourism in Ireland is developed as a way of synthesising the geographer's interest in rural tourism.

IN PURSUIT OF THE CONCEPT OF 'RURAL'

Robinson's (1990) invaluable synthesis of rural change illustrates that the term 'rural' has remained an elusive one to define in academic research, even though popular conceptions of rural areas are based on images of rusticity and the idyllic village life. However, Robinson (1990: xxi) argued that:

> defining rural . . . in the past has tended to ignore common economic, social and political structures in both urban and rural areas . . . In simple terms, . . . 'rural' areas define themselves with respect to the presence of particular types of problems. A selective list of examples could include depopulation and deprivation in areas remote from major metropolitan centres; a reliance upon primary activity; conflicts between presentation of certain landscapes and development of a variety of economic activities;

and conflicts between local needs and legislation emanating from urban-based legislators. Key characteristics of 'rural' are taken to be extensive land uses, including large open spaces of under-developed land, and small settlements at the base of the settlement hierarchy, but including settlements thought of to be rural.

Therefore, research on rural recreation and tourism needs to recognise the essential qualities of what is 'rural'. While national governments use specific criteria to define 'rural', often based on the population density of settlements, there is no universal agreement on the critical population threshold which distinguishes between urban and rural populations. For the developed world, Robinson (1990) summarises the principal approaches used by sociologists, economists and other groups in establishing the basis of what is rural and this need not be reiterated here. What is important is the diversity of approaches used by many researchers who emphasise the concept of an urban–rural continuum as a means of establishing differing degrees of rurality and the essential characteristics of ruralness. Shaw and Williams (1994: 224) advocate the use of the concept of the rural opportunity spectrum, where the countryside is viewed as the location of a 'wide range of outdoor leisure and tourist activities, although over time the composition of these has changed'. Harrison (1991) highlighted the speed of change in rural areas, with the settings and activities undertaken in such settings changing rapidly in the 1970s and 1980s. Even so, such studies do little to establish a meaningful concept of what is meant by a rural setting. In contrast, Hoggart's (1990) provocative article 'Let's do away with rural' argues that 'there is too much laxity in the treatment of areas in empirical analysis . . . [and] that the undifferentiated use of 'rural' in a research context is detrimental to the advancement of social theory' (Hoggart 1990: 245), since the term rural is unsatisfactory due to inter-rural differences and urban–rural similarities. Hoggart (1990) argued that general classifications of urban and rural areas is of limited value. For this reason, recent advances in social theory may offer a number of important insights into conceptualising the rural environment and tourism-related activities.

According to Cloke (1992), rural places have been traditionally associated with specific rural functions: agriculture, sparsely populated areas, geographically dispersed settlement patterns; and rurality has been conceptualised in terms of peripherality (see Page 1994c for a discussion of tourism and peripherality), remoteness and dependence on rural economic activity. However, new approaches in social theory have argued that rural areas are inextricably linked to the national and international political economy. As Cloke (1992) rightly argues, changes in the way society and non-urban places are organised and function have rendered traditional definitions of rurality less meaningful due to the following changes:

(i)   increased mobility of people, goods and messages have eroded the autonomy of local communities;

(ii)   delocalisation of economic activity makes it impossible to define homogeneous economic regions;

(iii)   new specialised uses of rural spaces (as tourist sites, parks, and development zones) have created new specialised networks of relationships in the areas concerned, many of which are no longer localized;

(iv)   people who 'inhabit' a given rural area include a diversity of temporary visitors as well as residents; and

(v)   rural spaces increasingly perform functions for non-rural users and in these cases can be characterized by the fact that they exist independently of the action of rural populations.

(Mormont 1990: 31 cited in Cloke 1992)

Consequently, Mormont (1987) conceptualises rural areas as a set of overlapping social spaces, each with their own logic, institutions and network of actors (e.g. users and administrators). This reiterates many of the early ideas from behavioural scientists – that a rural space needs to

be defined in terms of how the occupants perceive it, as a social construct where the occupiers of rural spaces interact and participate in activities such as recreation and tourism. In this context, recent developments in social theory imply that the nature and use of rural areas for activities such as recreation and tourism is best explained by examining the processes by which their meaning of 'rural' is 'constructed, negotiated and experienced' (Cloke 1992: 55). One approach favoured by Cloke (1992) is the analysis of the way in which the commodification of the countryside has occurred, leading to the rise of markets for rural products where:

> the countryside . . . [is] an exclusive place to be lived in; rural communities [are considered] as a context to be bought and sold; rural lifestyle [is something] which can be colonized; icons of rural culture [are commodities] can be crafted, packed and marketed; rural landscapes [are imbued] with a new range of potential from 'pay-as-you-enter' national parks, to sites for the theme park explosion; rural production [ranges] from newly commodified food to the output of industrial plants whose potential or actual pollutive externalities have driven them from more urban localities.
>
> (Cloke 1992: 55)

In this respect, rural areas are places to be consumed and where production is based on establishing new commodities or in reimaging and rediscovering places for recreation and tourism. Cloke (1992) cites privatization in the UK as a major process stimulating this form of rural production focused on rural recreation and tourism. The new political economy influencing agriculture in the EC has also facilitated farm diversification into new forms of tourism accommodation (e.g. farm-stays) and attractions. Yet the critical processes stimulating the demand for the mass consumption of rural products have been essential in affecting such changes. Urry (1988) points to changes in taste, following the emergence of a new service class which have led to greater emphasis on consumption in rural environments. These tastes have also influenced other social groups who have adopted similar values in the consumption of rural areas including:

- the pursuit of a pastoral idyll;
- acceptance of cultural symbols related to the rural idyll; and
- a greater emphasis on outdoor pursuits in such environments.

While the detailed social and cultural interpretations of such trends are dealt with in detail by Urry (1988), Poon (1989) illustrates the practical implications of such changes for the tourism industry. Poon (1989) interprets these changes in terms of a 'shift from an 'old tourism' (e.g. the regimented and standardized holiday package) to a 'new tourism' which is segmented, customized and flexible in both time and space'. In fact recent research on services has analysed the change in society from a 'fordist' to 'Post-fordist' stage which has involved a shift in the form of demand for tourist services from a former pattern of mass consumption 'to more individual patterns, with greater differentiation and volatility of consumer preferences and a heightened need for producers to be consumer-driven and to segment markets more systematically' (Urry 1991: 52). While recreational use of the countryside may not exhibit such a high degree of marketing and reinterpretation to develop new, novel and profitable experiences, Butler *et al.* (1998) do point to the increasing use of rural areas for such purposes which are juxtaposed with more traditional recreational and tourist uses. Nevertheless, Hummelbrunner and Miglbauer (1994) support both Poon's (1989) and Urry's (1991) assessments, arguing that these changes to the demand and supply of tourism services have contributed to the emergence of a 'new rural tourism'. From a supply perspective, this has manifested itself in terms of 'an increasing interest in rural tourism among a better-off clientele, and also among some holidaymakers as a growing environmental awareness and a desire to be integrated with the residents in the areas they visit' (Bramwell 1994:

3). This not only questions the need to move beyond existing concepts such as core and periphery with rural tourism as a simplistic consumption of the countryside, but also raises the question of how rural areas are being used to provide tourism and recreational experiences and how businesses are pursuing market-oriented approaches to the new era of commodification in rural environments. If the 1990s is a 'new era of commodifying rural space, characterised by a speed and scale of development which far outstrip farm-based tourism and recreation of previous eras' (Cloke 1992: 59), then a critical review of this process at an international and national scale is timely, to assess the extent and significance of rural tourism and recreation in the 1990s and into the next millenium.

CONCEPTUALISING THE RURAL RECREATION–TOURISM DICHOTOMY

One of the problems within the literature in recreation and tourism is that the absence of a holistic and integrated view of each area has continued to encourage researchers to draw a distinction between recreation and tourism as complementary and yet semantically different activities, without providing a conceptual framework within which to view such issues. Cloke (1992) overcomes this difficulty by observing that the relationship between rural areas and tourism and leisure activities has changed, with the activities being the dominant elements in many rural landscapes which control and affect local communities to a much greater degree than in the past. Therefore, while a critical debate has occurred in the tourism and recreational literature in terms of the similarity and differences between tourists and recreationalists it is the social, economic and spatial outcomes that are probably the most significant feature to focus on in the rural environment. However, there is still a need to recognise the magnitude and effect of recreational

Plates 6.1 and 6.2: In recent years, literary images such as James Herriot's Yorkshire have been used to market rural tourism as the example of the fictitious Darrowby (Thirsk, North Yorkshire) implies.

and tourist use because of the timing, scale, resource impact and implication of each use. But ultimately each use is a consumption of resources and space in relation to the user's discretionary leisure time and income. According to Shaw and Williams (1984) there are a range of issues to consider in relation to this debate. For example in many countries, use of the countryside is a popular pastime (e.g. in 1990 the Countryside Commission found that 75 per cent of the population of England visited the countryside) and in such studies there is a clear attempt to avoid simplistic classifications of what constitutes tourist and recreationalist use. In fact Shaw and Williams (1994) prefer to use a more culturally determined definition to show that the use of rural landscapes for tourist and recreational purposes is conditioned by a wide range of social, economic and cultural meanings which affect the host area. Cultural definitions of urban and rural areas highlight not only the intrinsic qualities of the countryside which is significantly different from urban areas, but also the interpretation that 'there is nothing that is inherent in any part of the countryside that makes it a recreational resource' (Shaw and Williams 1994: 223). This recognises that there is a search for new meaning in a research context. In fact Butler *et al.* (1998: 8) would concur with this since:

One of the major elements of change in rural areas has been the changes within recreation and tourism. Until the last two decades or so, recreational and tourist activities in rural areas were mostly related closely to the rural character of the setting. They were primarily activities which were different to those engaged in urban centers … They could be characterised, at the risk of generalisation, by the following terms: relaxing, passive, nostalgic, traditional, low technological, and mostly non-competitive.

But in recent years this has been affected by changes to the meaning and use of rural environments, where the setting is no longer a passive component. Yet there is some support for not focusing on the rural setting, as Patmore (1983: 122) argued, 'there is no sharp discontinuity between urban and rural resources for recreation but rather a complete continuum from local park to remote mountain park'. If one maintains such an argument, it, to a certain extent, makes the geographer's role in classifying tourism and recreational environments and their uses for specific reasons and purposes rather meaningless if they are part of no more than a simple continuum of recreational and tourism resources; thereby denying new attempts to understand what motivates users to seek and consume such resources in a cultural context. To overcome this difficulty, Shaw and Williams (1994: 224) prefer to view 'rural areas as highly esteemed as locales for leisure and tourism' and their use is heavily contingent upon particular factors, especially social access, and the politics of countryside ownership. Yet these contingencies can only really be fully understood in the context of the developed world, according to Shaw and Williams (1994) by considering three critical concepts used by geographers: the rural opportunity spectrum, accessibility and time-space budgets. However, prior to any discussion of such key concepts, it is pertinent to consider the historical dimension to tourism and recreational pursuits in rural environments, since historical geographers emphasise both continuity, change and the role of spatial separation of social classes in past periods as factors which affected the past use of rural locales.

THE GEOGRAPHER'S CONTRIBUTION TO THEORETICAL DEBATE IN RURAL CONTEXTS

Within any research area, progress is often gauged in terms of the extent to which the subject contributes to the development of theory. As Perkins (1993: 116) argued, a

> social scientist's primary role is to develop theories about society. Theories are sets of logically inter-related statements about phenomena, such as recreation and leisure. The reason for developing such theories is to help us understand the world humans make for themselves. It is on the basis of the understanding reached in the development of these theories that we plan and manage particular social phenomena.

As Owens (1984: 174) argued 'during the mid-1970s there was a hiatus in leisure and recreation research which marked a profound change from the enthusiastic promotion of agency dependent *ad hoc* applied research to an evaluative phase characterised by introspection and self-criticism' since prior to 1975, the generation of empirical case studies dominated the literature. After 1975 calls from North American researchers for a

greater consideration of leisure behaviour and its contribution to theory was advocated. For example, critical reviews by researchers (e.g. Patmore 1977, 1978, 1979; Coppock 1980; Mercer 1979; Patmore and Collins 1980, 1981), to name but a few, reiterated these criticisms and Patmore (1977: 115) poignantly summarised the position where 'this review reveals continuing and glaring gaps in British research, not least in a better understanding of the nature and motivation of recreation demand and in the development of an effective body of integrative theory'.

A series of new texts in the 1980s (e.g. Kelly 1982, Smith 1983a; Torkildsen 1983) and the appearance of two major journals, *Leisure Studies and Leisure Sciences* raised the need for more theoretically determined research, but only a limited range of studies by geographers focused on theoretical and conceptual issues (e.g. Owens 1983) while other disciplines contributed to the debate in a more vigorous and central manner (e.g. Graefe *et al.* 1984a). Despite largescale research funding by government research agencies (e.g. the Social Science Research Council in the UK) in the 1970s and 1980s, a lack of concern for theory has meant that geographers have made little impact on the problem that

> the large body of rural outdoor recreation research has not been consolidated in more theoretical work but one wonders whether researchers have set themselves an intellectual challenge which they are unable to meet. Certainly, there is now a steady flow of publication, albeit mainly directed to traditional ends, and because of this the argument that lack of progress towards a theory of leisure and recreation simply reflects poor funding is now much less plausible.
>
> (Owens 1984: 176)

As a consequence, Perkins (1993: 116–17) suggests that 'there are four reasons for this neglect of theoretical geographical leisure research. The first is that within the discipline, leisure research is considered' to be unimportant when compared to the central concerns of economic, social and urban geography. The second reason is that very little research funding has been made available to geographers to pursue theoretical leisure research (see Perkins and Gidlow 1991). Third, much research has been British or North American in origin, 'where pressures between recreational uses of particular sites are very great ... geographers have worked closely with recreational site managers to develop short to medium term management strategies for these areas'. Finally, recreation geographers 'have hardly participated in the theoretical debates which have thrived in their discipline since the 1970s!'

In fact, Perkins (1993) offers one of the few attempts by geographers to rise to this challenge, using social theory, particularly structuration theory and his research is valuable in relation to the understanding of locales for the analysis of human and spatial interaction. *Locales* comprise a range of settings which are different and yet connected through interactions. The interactions result from 'the life path of individuals ... in ways that reflect patterns of production and consumption. These interactions result in a particular pattern of locales which have social and physical forms. Each life path is essentially an allocation of time between these different locales. A particular mode of production will emphasise dominant locales to which time must be allocated' (Perkins 1993: 126).

Within the theoretical literature on structuration, in a capitalist society, structure and human interaction are brought together through the concept of the locale. The dominant locales are:

- the home;
- work; and
- school;

and they are settings in which consumption occur. Thus a leisure locale is a setting for interaction whereby 'people pursue leisure within the context of their life commitments and access to resources. Leisure interactions, of course, occur in and are influenced by places, and to this extent the leisure locale includes a spatial component' (Perkins 1993: 126). In such theoretically determined analyses, Perkins (1993) calls for the geographers of recreation to consider the position and internal organisation of the leisure locale in a rural setting, in relation to the dominant locales (i.e. the home, work and school) and other institutional locales such as religion and the arts. One possible mechanism for pursuing such theoretically determined research may be to use new conceptualisations of geography using the new regional geography informed by structuration theory. Structuration theory and the new regional geography have emerged, emphasising producers of the interpenetration of structure and agency. Structure 'both constrains and enables people to take particular life paths, the collective effect of which is to produce and enable new members of society in their life paths ... [where] geographical behaviour [affects] people specific situations' (Perkins 1993: 125). Therefore, the geographer in a rural setting would need to consider both structure and human interaction and how it is all brought together in the context of the locale (see Thrift 1977; Giddens 1984 and Perkins 1993 for more detail).

In the context of rural tourism, the theoretical analysis advocated by Perkins (1993) for rural recreation also has a relevance, particularly when one considers the debate engendered by Bramwell (1994: 2):

> does the physical existence of tourism in rural areas create a rural tourism that has a significance beyond the self-evident combination of particular activities in a specific place? In other words, do the special characteristics of rural areas help shape the pattern of tourism so that there is a particular rural tourism?

While the comments by Bramwell (1994) certainly highlight the need for more attention to the concept of the locale, Cloke (1992) indicates that structuration theory does have a role to play, although, as Perkins (1993) indicates, geographers may need to consider the value of humanistic research to ask questions that can address the issues raised by Bramwell (1994): how do people value rural areas and the relationships between locales? Unfortunately, much of the research published to date remains theoretically uninformed and empirically driven. As a result, much of the research on rural tourism by geographers has, with a number of exceptions, failed to contribute to a growing awareness of its role, value and significance in the wider development of tourism studies and its importance as a mainstay of many rural economies. In this context, Butler and Clark's (1992) comments are relevant in that:

> The literature on rural tourism is sparse and . . . conceptual models and theories are lacking . . . Many of the references in tourism are case studies with little theoretical foundation . . . or they focus on specific problems . . . Some take a broader perspective focusing on issues and process . . . There is, therefore a lack of theory and models placing rural tourism in a conceptual framework.
>
> (Butler and Clark 1992: 167)

Much of the research on rural tourism has been published in a diverse range of social science journals (e.g. *Sociologia Ruralis*, *Tourism Recreation Research*), reports and edited collections of essays which have been poorly disseminated as well as one or two specific texts (e.g. Sharpley 1993). Consequently, rural tourism has remained peripheral to the focus of tourism research while remaining poorly defined. It continues to be a general term which encapsulates a wide range of interest groups not only from tourism studies, but also from economics, planning, anthropology, geography, sociology and business studies. There has also been a lack of integration between these interest groups, each cultivating their own view and approach to rural tourism. As a result few researchers have attempted to define the concept of rural tourism.

TOWARDS A CONCEPT OF RURAL TOURISM

Keane *et al.*'s (1992) innovative, but little known study on rural tourism offers a number of insights into the definition of rural tourism acknowledging that there are a variety of terms used to describe tourism activity in rural areas: agri-tourism, farm tourism, rural tourism, soft tourism, alternative tourism and many others which have different meanings from one country to another. Keane also points out that it is difficult to avoid some of this confusion in relation to labels and definitions because the term 'rural tourism' has been adopted by the European Community to refer to the entire tourism activity in a rural area (Keane *et al.* 1992). One way of addressing this seemingly tautological proposition, that tourism in rural areas is not necessarily rural tourism when so many typologies exist for types of tourism that may or may not be deemed rural tourism, is to examine what makes rural tourism distinctive.

WHAT MAKES RURAL TOURISM DISTINCTIVE?

Lane (1994) discusses the historical continuity in the development of rural tourism and examines some of the key issues which combine to make rural tourism distinctive. Bramwell (1994: 3) suggests that despite the problems of defining the concept of 'rural', 'it may be a mistake to deny our commonsense thoughts that rural areas can have distinctive characteristics or that these can have consequences for social and economic interactions in the countryside'.

The views and perceptions people hold of the countryside are different from those of urban areas which is an important starting point for establishing the distinctiveness of rural tourism. Lane (1994) actually lists the subtle differences between urban and rural tourism, in which individual social representations of the countryside are a critical component of how people interact with rural areas. In fact, Squire (1994) acknowledges that both the social representations and personal images of the countryside condition whether people wish to visit rural areas for tourism, and what they see and do during their visit.

Plate 6.3: Rural heritage is a significant attraction base for rural tourism. Sissinghurst, Kent, England.

Plate 6.4: Tourism may assist in the development of new rural industries through the creation of new markets. Vineyard development in Central Otago, New Zealand.

Plate 6.5: Hunters, fisherpersons and walkers serve as an important source of income for many small villages in Scandinavia. Elga, Norway.

Plate 6.6: Tourism has revitalised many former mining towns in the western United States through the development of resort and accommodation facilities. Telluride, Colorado.

Lane (1994) also highlights the impact of changes in rural tourism since the 1970s, with far greater numbers of recreationalists and tourists now visiting rural areas. As Patmore's (1983) seminal study on recreation and leisure acknowledges, the impact of car ownership has led to a geographical dispersion of recreationalists and tourists beyond existing fixed modes of transport (e.g. railways). Consequently, tourism has moved away from a traditional emphasis on resorts, small towns and villages to become truly rural, with all but the most inaccessible wilderness areas awaiting the impact of the more mobile tourist. Despite this strong growth in the demand for rural tourism, Lane (1994) acknowledges the absence of any systematic sources of data on rural tourism, since neither the World Tourism Organisation nor OECD have appropriate measures. In addition, there is no agreement among member countries on how to measure this phenomenon. One way of establishing the distinctive characteristics of rural tourism is to derive a working definition of rural tourism. Here the work by Lane (1994) is invaluable since it dismisses simplistic notions of rural tourism as tourism which occurs in the countryside. Lane (1994: 9) cites the following seven reasons why it is difficult to produce a complex definition of rural tourism to apply in all contexts:

1 Urban or resort-based tourism is not confined to urban areas, but spills out into rural areas.
2 Rural areas themselves are difficult to define, and the criteria used by different nations vary considerably.
3 Not all tourism which takes place in rural areas is strictly 'rural' – it can be 'urban' in form, and merely be located in a rural area. Many so-called holiday villages are of this type; in recent years, numerous large holiday complexes have been completed in the countryside. They may be 'theme parks', time shares, or leisure hotel developments. Their degree of rurality can be both an emotive and a technical question.
4 Historically, tourism has been an urban concept; the great majority of tourists live in urban areas. Tourism can be an urbanising influence on rural areas, encouraging cultural and economic change, and new construction.
5 Different forms of rural tourism have developed in different regions. Farm-based holidays are important in many parts of rural Germany and Austria. Farm-based holidays are much rarer in rural USA and Canada. In France, the self-catering cottage, or gîte, is an important component of the rural tourism product.
6 Rural areas themselves are in a complex process

of change. The impact of global markets, communications and telecommunication have changed market conditions and orientations for traditional products. The rise of environmentalism has led to increasing control by 'outsiders' over land use and resource development. Although some rural areas still experience depopulation, others are experiencing an inflow of people to retire or to develop new 'non-traditional' businesses. The once clear distinction between urban and rural is now blurred by suburbanisation, long distance commuting and second-home development.
7 Rural tourism is a complex multi-faceted activity: it is not just farm-based tourism. It includes farm-based holidays but also comprises special-interest nature holidays and ecotourism, walking, climbing and riding holidays, adventure, sport and health tourism, hunting and angling, educational travel, arts and heritage tourism, and, in some areas, ethnic tourism. There is also a large general-interest market for less specialised forms of rural tourism. This area is highlighted by studies of the German tourism market, where a major requirement of the main holiday is the ability to provide peace, quiet and relaxation in rural surroundings.

(Lane 1994: 9)

Consequently, rural tourism in its purest form should be:

1 Located in rural areas;
2 Functionally rural – built upon the rural world's special features of small-scale enterprise, open space, contact with nature and the natural world, heritage, 'traditional' societies and 'traditional' practices;
3 Rural in scale – both in terms of buildings and settlements – and, therefore, usually small-scale;
4 Traditional in character, growing slowly and organically, and connected with local families. It will often be very largely controlled locally and developed for the long-term good of the area; and

5 Of many different kinds, representing the complex pattern of rural environment, economy, history and location.

(After Lane 1994)

Lane (1994: 16) also argues that the following factors also have to be considered in defining rural tourism:

- holiday type;
- intensity of use;
- location;
- style of management; and
- degree of integration with the community.

Using the continuum-concept allows for the distinction to be made between those tourist visits which are specifically rural, and those which are urban, and those which fall in an intermediate category. Thus, any workable definition of rural tourism needs to establish the parameters of the demand for, and supply of, the tourism experience and the extent to which it is undertaken in the continuum of rural to urban environments. With these issues in mind, it is pertinent to examine the most influential studies published to date by historical geographers to illustrate how continuity and change in spatial patterns and processes of tourism and recreation activity contribute to the landscapes of rural leisure use in the present day.

RURAL RECREATION AND TOURISM IN HISTORICAL PERSPECTIVE

Rural environments, often referred to as the countryside or non-urban areas, have a long history of being used for tourism and recreational activities in both the developed and developing world, a feature frequently neglected in many reviews of rural areas. Towner (1996) documents many of the historical changes and factors which shaped tourism and leisure in the rural environment in Europe since 1540, observing how the rural landscape has been fashionable and developed for the use of social elites at certain times in history (e.g. the landed estates of the seventeenth and eighteenth century). Such a review provides an invaluable synthesis and point of reference on the history of tourism and recreation. For example, Towner (1996) reconstructs past geographies to show how the growth of towns and cities during the industrialisation of Europe led to an urbanised countryside around those nascent industrial centres (i.e. the construction of an urban fringe). Such patterns of recreational and tourism activity all combine to produce a wide variety of leisure and more belatedly, tourism environments which exhibit elements of continuity in use, but also have been in a constant state of change. For example, Towner (1996: 45–6) characterises the pre-industrial period where

> popular recreation in the countryside throughout much of Europe was rooted in the daily and seasonal rhythms of agricultural life . . . and took place in the setting of home, street, village green or surrounding fields and woods and throughout the year, a distinction can be made between ordinary everyday leisure and the major annual holiday events, and between activities that were centred around home and immediate locality and those which caused people to move.

The gradual transition towards more 'private rural landscapes for the more affluent and higher social classes' began a process of restricting access to the countryside which has remained a source of contention ever since. At the same time, the rise of rural retreats and landed estates, a feature of earlier leisure history, is complemented by the 'movement of the upper and middle classes into the countryside . . . During the nineteenth century, however, the scale of movement in Britain, Europe and North America increased considerably' (Towner 1996: 232–3).

While there is a debate as to whether such changes led to a rejection of urban environments and values in some cities (e.g. Paris), Green (1990) argues that a distinct cultural attitude developed whereby the town and country were viewed as a continuum rather than as two distinct resources juxtaposed to each other. Thus the rural environment was more than a simple playground for elites. In England, not only did the urban middle classes begin to visit the countryside in growing numbers in the nineteenth and early twentieth century as recreationalists and tourists, visiting scenic areas (e.g. the Lake District) and more remote areas (e.g. the Highlands of Scotland, see Butler and Wall 1985), but it raised spatial issues of access for increasing numbers of urbanites which were celebrated by the mass trespass of Kinderscout in the Yorkshire Moors in 1932, which anticipated the controversy over access to the countryside which continues in Britain to the present day. Such pressures certainly contributed to the establishment of the principle of access in the *National Parks and Access to the Countryside Act of 1949* in the UK, while similar legislative changes in other countries led to other measures to improve access to such resources (Jenkins and Prin 1998).

The 'Grand Tour' in Europe by the British landed classes in the mid-sixteenth to eighteenth centuries and thereafter by the middle classes, incorporated a specific interest in rural environments which contained elements of romanticism and scenery (Towner 1985), while innovations in transport technology facilitated a move away from a focus on urban centres to rural environments. Arguably, the advent of mass domestic tourism in the nineteenth century in England and Wales (Walton 1983) with the rise of the seaside resort, and in Europe (Towner 1996), was followed by the development of the rise of second homes in the early twentieth century, which all contributed to a greater use of rural landscapes for tourist consumption.

Rural areas have emerged as a new focus for recreational and tourism activities in the postwar period within most developed countries as their accessibility and attraction for the domestic population, and to a lesser degree, the international visitor, has earned them the reputation as the 'playground of the urban population'. For example, Ward and Hardy (1986) document the

development of the English holiday camp with its origins in the late nineteenth century and the rise of entrepreneurs such as Butlins, Warner and Pontins in the 1930s which led to an increasing consumption of rural and coastal locales for lower middle-class and skilled working-class tourism.

THE GEOGRAPHER'S APPROACH TO RURAL RECREATION AND TOURISM

Coppock (1982: 2) argues that 'much of the literature in the leisure field has been produced by multidisciplinary teams' of which geographers have been a part. According to Owens (1984: 157)

> until very recently at least, leisure and recreation have been overwhelmingly viewed as synonymous with the rural outdoors. Participation in rural leisure and recreation grew rapidly during the 1950s and 1960s and was accompanied by a surge of interest in applied research ... In the 1950s and 1960s two types of study became particularly important, national and regional demand surveys, and site studies which tackled a wide range of applied problems.

There was a tendency towards such studies being published quite rapidly in Europe and North America, though as Coppock (1982: 9) observed 'little attention has been paid to geographical aspects of leisure in developing countries', an area which still remains poorly researched in the 1990s.

In documenting the development of geographical research on rural recreation Coppock, (1980) points to books on leisure and recreation which appeared in five years from 1970, which were Patmore (1970 later updated in 1983), Lavery (1971), Cosgrove and Jackson (1972), Simmons (1974), Coppock and Duffield (1975), Robinson (1976) and Appleton (1974) may also be added to this list. These books highlight the breadth of focus in recreation and policy management with the spatial dimension being discussed within each text. Yet, according to Owens (1984), in the period

1975–84 few major contributions were published by geographers in the UK due to the slackening of government research funds for this area. At the same time overlapping areas of research emerged in terms of a behavioural focus and perception studies. The research by Lucas (1964) marks the early origins and development of work in recreational behaviour in human geography and it reflects a concern over the logical positivist tradition (Johnston 1991), and its inherent short-comings, particularly the focus on management-oriented and site-based empirical studies at the expense of the conceptual and theoretical studies.

STUDIES OF DEMAND

Demand for rural recreation grew at 10 per cent per annum in the period 1945–58 in the USA (Clawson 1958), and in the UK at a compound rate of 10–15 per cent per annum up to 1973 (Coppock 1980) and for researchers this heralded an era of rapid growth. As Robinson (1990) observes, the demand for rural recreation is strongly affected by social class and participation rates consistently show that the more affluent, better educated and more mobile people visit the countryside, while women have much lower rates. As long ago as 1965, Dower (1965) recognised leisure as the 'fourth wave' which compared the leisure phenomenon with three previous events in history that changed human activity and behaviour: the advent of industrialisation, the railway age, and urban sprawl, with leisure being the fourth wave. Patmore (1983: 124) commented that 'countryside recreation is no new phenome-non, but in the last two decades . . . consequent pressure on fragile environments, has fully justified Dower's vision of a great surge in towns-people breaking across the countryside, the fourth wave. By any measure, the phenomenon is of immense significance'. Patmore (1983) outlined the geographer's principal concerns with the demand for rural recreation in terms of research on the increasing participation among different

socio-economic groups using rural areas for recreational activities coupled with the impact of car ownership, and the resulting development of, and impact on, destinations. As a means of assessing the patterns and processes shaping recreational use in rural areas, Patmore examined the routes and range and impact of trips by users within the countryside, and at the micro level, the assessment of site patterns and activities yielded detailed insights into rural recreational behaviour. The interest in second homes was also developed, though arguably this is one clear area of overlap between rural tourism and recreation as it attracted a great of research in the 1970s (e.g. Coppock 1977a and 1982). In fact Robinson (1990: 260) summarises the main concerns for rural areas and how the geographer's interest in spatial concerns have largely remained unchanged since the 1960s and 1970s:

> various studies have shown that, increasingly, people's leisure time is being used in a space-extensive way: a move from passive recreation to participation. Growth has been fastest in informal pursuits taking the form of day or half-day trips to the countryside with the rise in the ownership of private cars, the urban population has discovered the recreational potential of both the countryside on its doorstep and also more remote and less occupied areas.

For managers, the challenge is in equating demand with supply. As Owens (1984: 159) rightly observed, 'research in terms of people's leisure behaviour [saw] . . . a need to emphasise social science perspectives as a means to providing a more explicit task of managing use with supply'. The development of participation studies (e.g. The Outdoor Recreation Resources Review Commission in the USA and the General Household Survey in Britain) provided a new direction. Here the argument developed was that specific factors such as socio-demographic variables like age, sex, income and education shaped the spatial patterns of participation. Yet many early surveys proved to be only snapshots of recreational use and were not replicated on a regular basis, making comparisons difficult while demand changed at such a rapid rate making forecasting exercises from such results difficult to sustain. Such studies also failed to acknowledge the role of latent demand where such opportunities do not currently exist.

Site studies

In terms of studies of demand for rural recreation, these appear to have been the most numerous among geographers, with the site a spatial entity and the source of supply and ultimate object of demand. Such microscale studies of demand and supply proliferated due to the tendency for research agencies to fund individual site studies, and the publication of results in research articles offered researchers convenient research programmes. Such studies can be classified in terms of studies of demand, in relation to economic evaluation, carrying capacity and user perception. In terms of demand such studies used a range of innovative techniques, including participant observation (e.g. Glyptis 1979), while the geographer's preoccupation with patterns of usage together with a concern for methodological issues such as sampling and respondent bias (e.g. Mercer 1979) also dominated the literature. The studies of economic evaluation has seen some geographers move into the realms of economics, with cost-benefit models developed and reviewed (e.g. Mansfield 1969), where demand is often conceptualised in terms of sensitivity to distance travelled, cost of travel and entrance fees to derive a simulated demand curve. Yet research has questioned the rationality of recreational users in spatial patterns of behaviour and activity in models which assume distance minimisation is the sole pursuit for satisfaction (see S.L. Smith 1983a, 1995 for more detail).

Carrying capacity

According to Owens (1984: 166)

the picture to emerge in the wake of the catalytic effect of demand-orientated site surveys is of a range of related but ill-coordinated empirical case studies.

It is none the less possible to pick out several broad and important themes in the accumulated body of research. Two of the most important are seen in the burgeoning literature on carrying capacity and user perception studies.

Carrying capacity studies developed from the geographer's interest in the recreationist's impact on resources, as increased participation and the need among managers for greater resource protection provided a ready made focus for applied geographical research. Yet, carrying capacity is among one of the most difficult concepts to put into practice (Patmore 1983; Graefe et al. 1984a). Often one rarely knows what the true carrying capacity is until it has been exceeded. Mercer (1979) acknowledges that any search for the concept of carrying capacity is futile, implying that a simple concept of carrying capacity can be developed which might be defined thus: 'recreation resources/facilities will only be suitable for use by a certain number of people beyond which figure carrying capacity will be exceeded to the detriment of the resources and/or the users' experience' (Owens 1984: 167). In trying to put the concept into practice, a range of studies were developed to measure capacity (e.g. Dower 1967; Stankey 1973), with the attempt to differentiate between ecological, physical, social and psychological (or perceptual) capacity.

The other area of study noted by Owens (1984) was user perception studies. The greatest impetus for such studies emerged in the USA, particularly in relation to perception of wilderness areas (Stone and Taves 1957) with a specific management objective – the extent to which policies could be developed which would not adversely affect users' perceptions. Lucas's (1964) landmark study of Boundary Waters Canoe area saw users' opinions being canvassed which showed that some respondents had a more restricted view of wilderness than others and this assisted managers in developing land use zoning measures.

The key perception studies undertaken have focused on the following range of themes, although in practice a number of the studies have often been dealt with under more than one theme:

- perception of scenery and evaluation of land-scape quality;
- perception of wilderness, wilderness management, and the psychology of wilderness experience;
- social and psychological carrying capacity;
- comparison of managers' and users' perceptions;
- social benefits of recreation, socialisation into leisure, quality of life elements in leisure experience;
- behaviour at sites and social meaning of recreation in relation to particular activities;
- perceived similarities between recreation activities and substitutability; and
- psychological structure of leisure, leisure activity types, typology of recreation activity preferences.
(See Owen 1984 for more detail of these studies)

Robinson (1990) also documented the behavioural differences between recreationalists in different countries, where there are cultural differences in the perception of rural aesthetics.

THE SUPPLY OF RURAL RECREATION

The types of studies developed and published reflect the geographer's interest in rural land use and the geographer's concern with the spatial distribution of resources which led to a range of studies of resource inventories and rural recreation. According to Pigram (1983)

> for many people, the concept of resources is commonly taken to refer only to tangible objects in nature. An alternative way is to see resources not so much as material substances, but as functions. In this sense resource functions are created by man through the selection and manipulation of certain attributes of the environment.

Resources are therefore constituted by society's subjective evaluation of their value and potential so that they satisfy recreational needs and wants. Earlier research by O'Riordan (1971: 4) still remains the most quoted definition of a resource: 'an attribute of the environment appraised by man to be of value over time within constraints imposed by his social, political, economic and institutional framework'. The recreational research by Clawson et al. (1960) still remains the popular conceptualisation of recreational resources, particularly in a rural context. Clawson et al. (1960) identified one of the standard approaches to recreational resources which has been developed and modified by geographers over the last 40 years: what constitutes a recreational resource, and how can you classify them, so that effective planning and management can be developed? Clawson et al. (1960) distinguished between recreation areas and opportunity using a range of factors: location, size, characteristics, degree of use and extent of artificial development of the recreation resource. The result was the development of a continuum of recreational opportunities from user-orientated to resource-based with rural areas falling into resource-based and intermediate areas (i.e. the urban fringe). While geographers have reworked and refined such ideas the resource-use remains one of the underlying tenets of the analysis of recreational resources (Simmons 1975). For example, Hockin et al. (1978) classified land-based recreational activities into:

- overnight activities (e.g. camping and caravanning);
- activities involving shooting;
- activities involving a significant element of organised competition (e.g. golf); and
- activities involving little or no organised competition (e.g. angling, cycling, rambling, picknicking and wildlife observation).

This has moved on a stage from the continuum zoning concept of Clawson et al. (1960) to recognise the diversity of demand and how it did not necessarily fit into any one particular zone.

Coppock and Duffield (1975) outlined their principal contribution in terms of understanding what resources were used and consumed by recreationalists, the levels and volume of use, the capacity of resources to absorb recreationalists, the range of potential resources available, the role of resource evaluation and the techniques of resource evaluation developed by geographers, though their own experience was largely confined to major studies undertaken in Lanarkshire and Greater Edinburgh. By comparing Coppock and Duffield's (1975) synthesis with Patmore (1983) assessment of the geographer's principal concern with recreational resources can be seen to concentrate around three themes:

> First there is the visual character of the resource itself, the very quality that gives stimulus and satisfaction. So much of the quality is intertwined with the theme of conservation and the composition of the rural landscape as a whole: for all its importance, however, that aspect is marginal to our purpose and will receive comparatively scant attention. The second theme is recreational opportunity, the direct use of the rural environment for recreational pursuits, both on sites with a uniquely recreational purpose and on those pursuits which recreation must compete directly and indirectly with other uses. The third theme is recreational variety, the variety of rural landscapes and the variety of recreational opportunity that each affords. It is that variety that is the geographer's concern; the frequent imbalance of recreational demand with resource supply, and the consequent compromises and patterns that such imbalance engenders.
>
> (Patmore 1983: 164)

It is evident that the range of issues which have guided research exhibit a large degree of commonality. Patmore (1983) outlined the main themes associated with the spatial analysis of rural recreational resources in terms of lost resources (to development and progress), preservation of resources, the active use and enjoyment of resources, the role of balancing conservation and use, and preservation and profit-recreation attractions. In addition, Patmore (1983) outlined the range of resources designed for rural recreation (e.g. forests, parks and the urban fringe), the use

of linear resources (e.g. roads and footpaths), water resources and the coastal fringe each of which have a significant rural dimension. Among the early research on some of these themes was Coppock's (1966) landmark study which sought to summarise information on recreational land and water in Britain, while Duffield and Owen (1973) and Goodall and Whittow (1975) examined forest resources and Tanner (1973, 1977) researched water resources.

A debate on the perception of scenery and its recreational value also emerged in the controversy over landscape evaluation (Penning-Rowsell 1973; Appleton 1974) which has an explicit recreational dimension and focused on the way people value the aesthetics of the landscape, and different methodologies to understand the value and meaning of landscapes. The compilation of resource inventories by geographers focused on the supply of rural recreation resources though there was little continuity in such research in the 1980s, with Pigram (1983) being critical of such studies where they had only a limited practical application.

THE IMPACT OF RURAL RECREATION

Robinson (1990: 270) observed that 'awareness and concern has grown over the environmental impact of recreational activity. In fact the growing severity of this impact reflects the concentrated form of rural recreation with distinctive foci upon a few "honey-pot" sites' where concentrated use may lead to adverse environmental impacts. In addition to direct impacts, the issue of conflict remains a consistent problem associated with recreational resources in the countryside. Many conflicts occur between recreation and agriculture which Shoard (1976) attributes to the *ad hoc* manner in which recreational use of agricultural land has developed. For example, farmers are frequently dissatisfied with recreationalists' use of rights of way across their land due to the damage and problems caused by a minority of recreationalists (e.g. litter, harassment of stock and pollution). One problem which has emerged in New Zealand is the rise in the prevalence of giardia, a water-borne disease spread by recreationalists and tourists defecating and urinating in streams and water sources. In contrast, in Wales the Countryside Commission estimate that 16 million people use paths covering a wide scale of use and there is great potential for adverse environmental impacts and conflict, aside from physical erosion and the subsequent need for on-going protection from this erosion and in some cases, the use of non-natural products (e.g. tarmac) to control it. However, as Owens (1984: 173) summarised:

> In general, research has been problem-orientated to meet specific managerial requirements, with the consequence that *ad hoc* site studies proliferated without there being any particular intention of making a contribution to the development of testable theory. Interest has tended to focus on concepts (e.g. social carrying capacity) and the intricacies of methodology (e.g. attitude scales and factor analysis). Of course conceptual and methodological development is a vital part of research, but the main criticism here relates to the degree to which there has been introspection.

In view of these comments, attention now turns to the geographer's contribution to the analysis of rural tourism.

RURAL TOURISM: SPATIAL ANALYTICAL APPROACHES

In the literature on rural tourism (e.g. Sharpley 1993; Getz and Page 1997; Sharpley and Sharpley 1997; Butler *et al.* 1998), there are few comparatively explicit spatial analytical approaches which make the geographer's perspective stand out above other social science contributions. While it is evident that research on demand, supply, impacts and management are evident, no well developed literature exists. Probably the nearest synthesis one finds is the occasional section on

tourism in rural geography texts (e.g. Robinson 1990) and a limited number of geography of tourism texts (e.g. Shaw and Williams 1994). For this reason, this section examines some of the more prominent contributions of geographers and is followed by a case study of tourism in Ireland.

THE IMPACT OF RURAL TOURISM

The literature on tourism impacts has long since assumed a central position within the emergence of tourism research, as early reviews by geographers confirm (e.g. Mathieson and Wall 1982). However, in a rural context, impact research has not been at the forefront of methodological and theoretical developments. One particular problem, as already noted, is the tendency for researchers to adopt well established theoretical constructs and concepts from their own disciplinary perspective and apply them to the analysis of rural tourism issues. Within the social and cultural dimensions of rural tourism, the influence of rural sociology in the 1960s and 1970s (e.g. Bracey 1970) dominated sociological research while V. Smith's (1977) influential collection of anthropological studies of tourism highlighted the approaches adopted by anthropologists. Probably the most influential statement on the social and cultural impacts is Bouquet and Winter's (1987a) diverse anthology of studies of the conflict and political debates associated with rural tourism. For example, Bouquet and Winter (1987b) consider the relationship between tourism, politics and the issue of policies to control and direct tourism (and recreation) in the countryside in the post-war period. Geographers have largely remained absent from this area of study as Hall and Jenkins (1998) and Jenkins *et al.* (1998) indicate. Even so, non-spatial studies, such as Winter's (1987) study of farming and tourism in the English and Welsh uplands, argues for circumspection in advocating farm tourism as a solution to the socio-economic development problems of 'less favoured areas', a conclusion which is widely endorsed by subsequent studies (e.g. Jenkins *et al.* 1998). Sociological studies offer an insight into the social implications of the spatially-determined activities of tourists and recreationalists in remote areas, where they may contribute to farm incomes.

More recently, a number of researchers have sought to diversify the focus of social and cultural impact research to include concerns about the way in which tourism development may change rural cultures (e.g. Byrne *et al.* 1993) and the consumption of rural environments and cultures in relation to late modernity or the post-modern society which has a specific relevance for studies in geography. The role of women in rural tourism has also belatedly attracted interest as a highly seasonal and unstable economic activity, since tourism offers one of the few employment opportunities to be taken up by women, which further contributes to the marginal status of women in the rural workforce. Similar arguments are also advanced by gender studies with a tourism component such as Redclift and Sinclair (1991) though few geographers have examined these issues. More recent studies by Edwards (1991) and Keane *et al.* (1992) also indicate the importance of community participation in tourism planning so that the local population, and women in particular, are not excluded from the benefits of rural tourism development. A particularly sensitive issue is that of indigenous people and traditional cultures, including land/resource rights and their roles as performers and entrepreneurs (Butler and Hinch 1996). Increasingly native people are becoming involved in tourism to help meet their own goals of independence and cultural survival, yet tourism development carries special risks for them (Hall 1996).

Considerable attention has been paid in the literature to residents' perceptions and attitudes towards tourism (in common with recreation research), including studies of small towns and rural areas (for example: Allen *et al.* 1988; Long *et al.* 1990; Getz 1994a; Johnson *et al.* 1994) but few geographers have undertaken longitudinal studies of rural tourism's impact on the way communities view, interact, accept or deny tourism, though examples in urban areas are also limited (see Page 1997). However, as Butler and Clark (1992: 180) conclude, an

> area where some research is needed is in the changing relationship between tourism and its host community. Rarely is tourism the sole rural economic activity. Over the last few decades the countryside has witnessed major changes in its social composition, the main symptoms being gentrification, new forms of social polarisation, and a domination by the service class. More research is needed on the relationship between the uneven social composition of the countryside, the spatially variable development of tourism, and the problematic relationship between the two.
>
> (Butler and Clark 1992: 180)

and it is somewhat ironic that with rural geographers making such a major contribution to rural studies, only a limited number have examined the implications in terms of social theory as well as the empirical dimensions of tourism development.

THE ECONOMIC IMPACT

The economic impact of rural tourism has been a fruitful area for research among a range of social scientists, often emphasising or challenging the role of tourism as a panacea for solving all the economic and social ills of the countryside although the major contribution of geographers has largely been in relation to the study of farm tourism. But as Butler and Clark (1992) rightly acknowledge, tourism in rural areas is not necessarily the magical solution to rural development, given its:

> income leakages, volatility, declining multipliers, low pay, imported labour and the conservatism of investors. The least favoured circumstance in which to promote tourism is when the rural economy is already weak, since tourism will create highly unbalanced income and employment distributions. It is a better supplement for a thriving and diverse economy than as a mainstay of rural development.
>
> (Butler and Clark 1992: 175)

In a longitudinal study of the Spey Valley, Scotland, Getz (1981, 1986b, 1993c, 1994a, b) documents a rural area in which tourism has remained the economic mainstay. In this respect, Butler and Clark's (1992) research is useful in that it identifies the principal concerns in rural economic research and the role of tourism in development in relation to:

- income leakage;
- multipliers;
- labour issues (local versus imported and low pay);
- the limited number of entrepreneurs in rural areas; and
- the proposition that tourism should be a supplement rather than the mainstay of rural economies.

The principal research in this area has been undertaken by economists such as Archer (1973, 1982) whose pioneering studies of multipliers have been used to establish the economic benefits of tourist expenditure in rural areas. While these studies have remained the baseline for subsequent research on rural tourism, few studies embrace a broad economic analysis to encompass the wide range of issues raised by Butler and Clark (1992). One possible explanation for this paucity of detailed economic studies of rural tourism may be related to the persistence of a 'farm tourism' focus.

Farm tourism

Farm tourism may offer one way of facilitating agricultural diversification. According to Evans (1992a) research on farm tourism can be divided into two categories. The first is an expanding literature concerned with 'differing types of farm diversification as a major option adapted by farm families to aid business restructuring, necessitated by falling farm incomes' (Evans 1992a: 140). The second is 'one devoted specifically to farm tourism and though these studies remain the

most detailed, they are becoming increasingly dated' (Evans 1992a: 140). Evans (1992a) cited those by Davies (1971), Jacobs (1973), DART (1974), Bull and Wibberley (1976), Denman (1978), and Frater (1982) which all use 1970s data.

Evans (1992a) is critical of the second group of studies for their lack of definitional clarity, since they fail to distinguish between the accommodation and recreational components of farm tourism (Evans and Ilbery 1989). Evans (1992a: 140) rightly considers the analytical components of the studies to be too simplistic, focusing on expected economic costs and benefits of these enterprises, and the characteristics and attitudes of farm families to such development. Despite these problems with the farm tourism literature and concerns with its marketing, a major impediment to developing more sophisticated understanding of farm tourism remains the absence of accurate national studies of the growth and development of farm tourism. However, Dernoi (1983) and Frater (1983) review the situation in Europe, Wrathall (1980) examines the development of France's gîtes ruraux, while Oppermann (1995) considers farm tourism in southern Germany, mapping and analysing the spatial distribution of the accommodation base. Vogeler (1977) discussed the situation in the United States, while Oppermann (1998) provided a valuable baseline survey of the New Zealand scene.

Evans and Ilbery's (1992) survey of England and Wales identified almost 6,000 farm businesses with accommodation. They also undertook a geographical analysis of the distribution of such accommodation, with South-West England, Cumbria, the Welsh border counties, North Yorkshire and the South-East coast of England popular locations for this activity. The upland areas and South-West England were the dominant locations, with a diversity of modes of operation (bed and breakfast, self-catering, camping and caravanning) and niche marketing used to satisfy particular forms of tourism demand (e.g. weekend breaks, week-long breaks and traditional two-week holidays). Evans (1992b) acknowledged the absence of national studies of why farm businesses have pursued this activity and the range of factors influencing their decision to undertake it. Evans and Ilbery (1992) also point to inherent contradictions in the existing literature, since their findings illustrate that larger farm businesses have also diversified into farm tourism (Ilbery 1991). Whilst this is at odds with Frater's (1982) research it illustrates that family labour is widely used to service farm-based accommodation. Such research also highlights the capital requirements of farm tourism ventures and the role of marketing, financial advice and the need for external agents in establishing networks to develop their business. Even so, Maude and van Rest (1985) argue that due to the limited returns for small farmers and the constraints of existing planning legislation it is not a significant means of tackling the serious problem of low farm incomes in upland areas (see also Jenkins *et al.* 1998). Thus, it is unlikely to improve the low-income problem of upland farmers in their Cumbria case study since they argue that farm tourism has been wrongly regarded as the main pillar in a diversified agricultural policy (Maude and van Rest 1985). Consequently, the continued debate and focus on farm tourism has detracted from a more critical debate on the wider significance of rural tourism within an economic context and the way it can be integrated into structuration theory and other contemporary theoretically-informed analyses.

THE ENVIRONMENTAL EFFECTS OF RURAL TOURISM

The environmental impact of tourism has been extensively reviewed in the tourism literature and rural tourism has emerged as a prominent element, with the usual caveat that tourism is destructive in different degrees of the actual qualities which attract tourists. In a rural context, the growing pressure emerging from the development-intensive nature of tourism, and the expansion of mass tourism has posed many new pressures as 'new tourism' discovers the qualities of rural environments. In fact, the construction of theme parks in rural environments, second homes (Gartner 1987), timeshare, conference centres, holiday villages, and designation of environments as special places to visit (e.g. National Parks) have all contributed to the insatiable tourism appetite for rural environments. Bramwell (1991) highlights the concern for more responsible and environmental forms of rural tourism as the 1990s with the sustainability debate firmly focused on the rural environment. Bramwell (1991) examines the extent to which rural tourism policy in Britain has been integrated with concepts of sustainability, outlining the role of the English Tourist Board and Countryside Commission policy formulation process. The Countryside Commission points to the need for improving the public's understanding and care of the rural environment as outlined in their consultation paper 'Visitors to the Countryside'. A number of recent special issues of Journals have also focused on sustainability and rural tourism (e.g. *Trends* 1994, *Tourism Recreation Research* 1991, *Journal of Sustainable Tourism* 1994) with geographers contributing to the debate (e.g. Butler and Hall 1998; Hall and Lew 1998). However, it is apparent that tourism in a rural context displays many of the features of the symbiotic relationship which exists between tourism and the environment and is a key component of its very attraction to tourists. In order to illustrate some of the major issues raised in the above discussion, attention now turns to a case study of rural tourism in Ireland.

CASE STUDY: Tourism in Ireland: Peripherality and the rural environment

This case study seeks to illustrate the concepts and approaches which geographers have used to examine rural tourism in Ireland (e.g. supply, demand and spatial patterns) emphasising how it may assist in understanding the organisation of tourism and its development. The literature on tourism in Ireland has expanded in recent years, following the growing recognition of the country's potential as a tourist destination (Page 1994c; Deegan and Dineen 1996; O'Connor and Cronin 1993). As a tourist destination, Ireland (which in this case study is confined to Eire, the Republic of Ireland – see Figure 6.1), is a largely rural environment at a national level and serves as a major example of tourism development in a largely rural environment, despite the expansion of urban and heritage tourism in small towns and cities (Page 1994d). In fact, Deegan and Dineen (1996: 111) aptly summarise the essential rural qualities of Ireland thus: 'to some international tourists it [Ireland] represents the essence of Irish tourism – the beautiful country-side, the clean air, the friendly people, the relative solitude. It can be effective also in serenading a greater geographical spread of tourists.'

Within the context of the European Community, Ireland is an interesting example of a country which is peripheral to the traditional spatial concentrations of tourism-related activities. Existing studies of tourism in these areas have emphasised the concept of peripherality in relation to economic disadvantage and the emergence of 'problem regions' within the EC. Explanations of 'problem regions' have been based on how regions develop within a capitalist society and the way in which inequalities occur between 'core' (urban) areas and their 'periphery'. Although research on the political economy of peripheral areas (e.g. Cooke 1986; Cooke 1989) has highlighted dependency relationships between core areas and their periphery, there has

been an absence of theoretical research on how tourism functions in peripheral areas of the EC.

Consequently, a strange paradox exists: previous research on economic potential and peripherality in the EC (e.g. Keeble et al. 1982) has implied that geographical isolation is an obstacle to economic development, although such research did not acknowledge the complexity of service industries and their varied location requirements. Yet tourism plays 'an important role in the economy of remote rural areas because of the dispersed nature of tourism expenditure' (Grimes 1992: 28) and its potential to assist in regional development is widely acknowledged (Pearce 1988b, 1989, 1992a). The relative geographical isolation of an area in the context of the European space economy does not necessarily imply that successful tourism development is precluded: the tourism potential of an area, region or country is not necessarily conditioned by peripherality even though research on economic potential has inferred that geographical isolation is a constraint on economic development. Understanding the concept of peripherality is dependent upon the scale at which it is considered, and this can range from the international level (e.g. within the EC), to the national level (e.g. a country such as Ireland), down to the regional level (i.e. regions within one country) and local scale (i.e. within different parts of a region). Various countries perceived as peripheral within the EC have benefited from a growing internationalisation of tourism and the search for new tourist destinations in areas characterised as rural. Even so, this has to be set against the potential social and cultural impacts which tourism may generate in more rural areas and against the economic dependence of an industry which is notoriously fickle and subject to seasonal fluctuations (Brunt 1988).

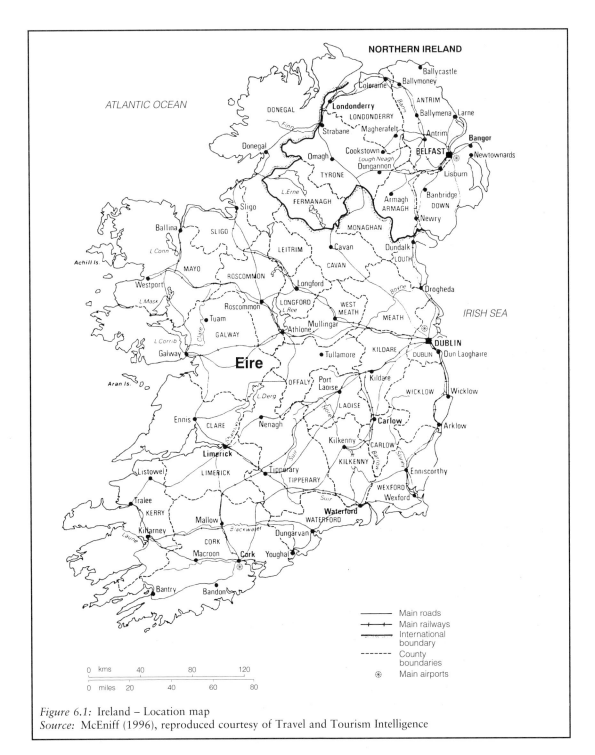

Figure 6.1: Ireland – Location map
Source: McEniff (1996), reproduced courtesy of Travel and Tourism Intelligence

THE GEOGRAPHER'S ANALYSIS OF PERIPHERALITY

The concept of peripherality is a useful starting point for the analysis of tourist destinations such as Ireland, although more detailed analysis of the context in which the tourism industry operates, recent trends and developments associated with tourism in the region, is equally important. Peripherality as a concept is not sufficiently developed within the existing literature on tourism in rural and marginal areas of the EC (see Seers et al. 1979; Seers and Ostrom 1983), since much of the research has focused on the significance of agricultural and manufacturing activities in terms of the dependency relationship between peripheral areas and core regions (Crotty 1979; Seers and Ostrom 1983; Barry 1991). According to Clout (1987: 12), within the EC, core areas are characterised by a 'high density of population, good reservoirs of expertise, efficient means of access to communication systems allowing contact with the wider world' while peripheral areas are 'fragmented in spatial, economic and organisational terms and tend to be more susceptible than core zones to economic dependence' (Clout 1987: 13). Shaw and Williams (1990) review the literature on tourism, economic development and dependence, which emphasised the role of the entrepreneur and transnational corporations in influencing the nature of dependency relationships between core and peripheral areas (de Kadt 1979; O'Hearn 1989). Shaw and Williams (1990) also discuss geographical models of tourism and the dependency relationship (see also Britton 1980b; Pearce 1989), and for this reason it is pertinent to highlight a number of key concepts which have dominated the analysis of tourism and economic development.

The concepts of core and periphery are used in tourism research on economic development to show how different areas expand and develop within a capitalist system. The origin and application of such concepts can be attributed to the work of Friedmann (1966) which considered economic development and the emergence of a polarised pattern of growth as core areas expanded and developed at the expense of peripheral areas. The theoretical basis of such research has been extensively reviewed, particularly the dynamics of economic change and development (e.g. Lloyd and Dicken 1987; Phelps 1992). Townsend (1991: 315), however, has argued that due to the lack of research on services and economic development, there is a 'need and scope for the refinement of economic base theory' in view of its inability to accommodate the role of services. Since the initial work by Friedmann (1966), Seers et al. (1979) have examined peripheral areas and economic development further in terms of countries in the European periphery, such as the Irish Republic, and emphasised their geographical characteristics, and the extent to which economic and social problems resulted from peripherality. However, the 'core–periphery' concepts remain in relation to research on economic development, since they form the basis for regional policy in the EC, which has aimed to reduce regional imbalances and economic disparities resulting from the historical pattern of economic development in the EC (Clout 1987). For example, the Commission of the European Community's *Fourth Periodic Report* (1991) differentiated between regions in the EC according to the nature of their 'regional problem', with the Irish Republic forming a 'lagging region'. But, even when the concepts of core and periphery are developed in a more pluralistic framework (Clout 1987), they still constitute an oversimplification of a highly complex situation.

One particular problem with the application of core–periphery concepts to tourism and service industries is related to the question of the scale at which you analyse the geographical patterns of economic development in terms of the advanced stages of capitalism in the EC, since in 'many service industries . . . there is a major problem of specifying the boundary and content of many services' (Urry 1991: 2). Tourism services are primarily concerned with the provision of an intangible product or experience to meet the perceived needs of tourists compared to the more tangible products supplied by the primary and secondary sectors of the economy. Thus, any attempt to theorise about the role of tourism, economic development and peripheral areas is notoriously difficult since core–periphery concepts cannot easily accommodate the complex role of tourism services in relation to changes in the organisation of contemporary society and the geographical preferences for different and varied tourist experiences. Recent research on services has analysed the change in society from a 'Fordist' to 'post-Fordist' stage or organisation (Esser and Hirsch 1989) which has involved a shift in the form of demand for tourist services from a former pattern of mass consumption 'to more individual patterns, with greater differentiation and volatility of consumer preferences and a heightened need for producers to be consumer-driven and to segment markets more systematically' (Urry 1991: 52). These changes had led to a shift from an 'old tourism' (e.g. the regimented and standardised holiday package) to a 'new tourism' (Poon 1989) which is segmented, customised and flexible. Therefore, any explanation of the role of tourism services and their role in peripheral areas needs to take account of new theoretical approaches to the production, consumption, and delivery of tourist services, the inter-relationships between these components and their impact on various localities. Consequently, while research on tourism urbanisation (Mullins 1991) has examined the consequences of concentrated tourist activity in urban areas, little theoretical work has been undertaken to examine the dispersed nature of tourist activity in relation to the growth of a new tourism, its development in peripheral areas and

the implications for economic dependency. Therefore, the development of new theoretical explanations will also need to move beyond the geographical concepts of core and periphery in understanding the process of tourism development in areas perceived as peripheral.

THE DIMENSIONS OF PERIPHERALITY IN THE REPUBLIC OF IRELAND

Despite a number of notable international research publications (e.g. Anon. 1983; McEniff 1987, 1991, 1996; Baum 1989a, 1989b; Deegan and Dineen, 1996; Euromonitor 1992; Pearce 1990b, 1992b), Ireland has been relatively neglected in the tourism literature. While the problem of peripherality has led certain researchers to observe that 'tourism . . . in Ireland would appear to be at an immediate and considerable disadvantage' (Pollard 1989: 301), significant progress has been made in overcoming this obstacle by expanding its international tourist arrivals in the late 1980s and early 1990s. By developing an expansionist policy towards inbound tourism and measures to redress the perceived 'peripherality' of Ireland's location in the EC, tourism has made a significant contribution to the national economy through tourist spending by building on the strengths and advantages of Ireland's geographical location and its distinctive tourism product (Bord Fáilte 1991a). Ireland's geographical position on the western margins of the EC is often viewed as peripheral (Mitchell 1970; Johnson 1987; Brunt 1988; Gillmore 1985; Carter and Parker 1989; Robinson 1991) and has been a powerful factor shaping the economic fortunes of the Irish economy according to the National Development Plan 1989–93. Grimes (1992), however, has argued that peripherality has been used as a mechanism to increase EC Structural Funds to address the perceived obstacles posed by relative geographical isolation and peripherality to economic development (Commission of the European Community 1991).

Ireland's role as a 'lagging region' in the EC is reflected in terms of its small population, estimated to be 3.6 million in 1996, equivalent to a population density of fifty per kilometre which is the lowest in the EC. However, 'between 1979 and 1986 Ireland had the biggest population growth rate' (Grimes 1992: 23) in the EC of 5.1 per cent, fuelled by a high birth rate of 1.7 per cent per annum, the second highest in the EC. Ireland was also characterised by high rates of net internal migration, with an annual average loss of population of 3.4 per 1000 induced in part by a high rate of unemployment of 14 per cent in 1990 (Economist Intelligence Unit 1991), which contributed to a continued outflow of skilled labour. Of the 1,120,000 people employed in Ireland in 1990, 15.4 per cent worked in agricultural-related activities, 26.9 per cent in manufacturing and 57.7 per cent in services, the latter having experienced a continued growth in the 1980s. As Grimes (1992: 25) acknowledged, 'economic performance in the Community has not been strong relative to that of other member countries', with GDP per head at 62.4 per cent of the EC average in 1989, which is combined with a large public debt in an economy characterised by a high degree of openness (O'Hagan and Mooney 1983). Employment in the service sector expanded at a rate of 2.3 per cent per annum between 1971 and 1981, generating some 129,000 jobs, which was significant as services 'use relatively few imports and most of their demand remains in the economy' (Grimes 1992: 28) which was beneficial for the Irish economy where substantial leakages occur due to imports and profit repatriation by foreign companies. Furthermore, O'Riordan (1986) also noted that within the context of Ireland, services create more income and employment than other sectors of the economy and, therefore, tourism

has assumed an important role as a service industry (Bord Fáilte 1985).

TOURISM DEMAND AND IRELAND'S ECONOMY

In 1994, the Irish tourism industry earned I£2.18 billion from domestic and international tourist spending, accounting for 6.8 per cent of GNP, with approximately 75 per cent of expenditure generated by overseas tourists. This made an important, though variable, contribution to the Irish economy within the context of the balance of payments (Gillmore 1985; Economist Intelligence Unit 1991) and employment generation (Deane 1987), where the number of full-time job equivalents in tourism rose from 69,000 in 1988 (Bord Fáilte 1989, Baum 1989b), to 82,000 in 1990 (McEniff 1991) and 94,000 in 1994 (McEniff 1996). The economic impact increased through a tourism multiplier effect of 1.72 (Fletcher and Snee 1989; Bord Fáilte 1900a). Baum (1989a: 141–2) examined the economic benefits of the tourism industry in the early 1980s.

The recent and sustained increase in tourist revenue is indicative of the Irish tourism industry's increased competitiveness, a higher quality of tourism product, the role of overseas marketing and promotion (Kassem 1987) and the development of Ireland's tourism infrastructure by Bord Fáilte and the private sector in the late 1980s, compared to a period of relative stagnation in the early 1980s (Gillmore 1985; Grimes 1992). A range of studies have described the historical development of tourism arrivals (e.g. Gillmore 1985; Brunt 1988; Pollard 1989), particularly in relation to improved accessibility (Brookfield 1955). According to McEniff (1996), in 1994, 68 per cent of Ireland's overseas visitors arrived by air, through the major gateways of Dublin, Shannon and Cork (see Figure 6.2). This tourist traffic comprised 1,488,000 visitors

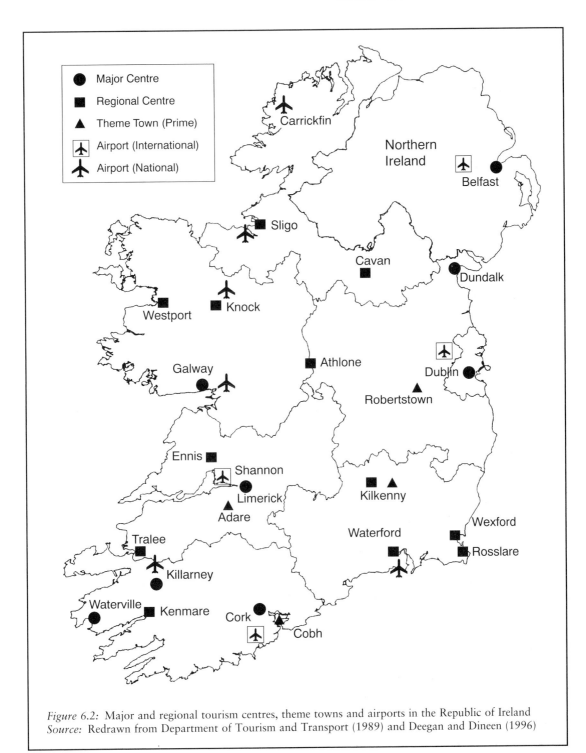

Figure 6.2: Major and regional tourism centres, theme towns and airports in the Republic of Ireland
Source: Redrawn from Department of Tourism and Transport (1989) and Deegan and Dineen (1996)

who travelled by cross-Channel air services (between the UK and Ireland), 726,000 visitors using continental European air services and 242,000 visitors on transatlantic flights through Shannon. In contrast, 1,225,000 visitors used sea crossings from the UK and continental Europe to travel to Ireland. The emphasis on air travel is indicative of the recent deregulation of air routes and competitively priced air fares, especially between the UK and Ireland, with the rise of Ryan Air. The state airline Aer Lingus is an important agent in the development of tourism (Aer Lingus 1991) as 'its role in the direct and indirect promotion of the tourist industry is . . . of great significance' (Brunt 1988, 33–4). Improvements to transport infrastructure are also evident with the investment of I£73.3 million between 1989 and 1993 from the EC-funded Operational Programme on Peripherality to upgrade Irish airports. In fact between 1994 and 1999, the EC-funded Operational Programme on Peripherality planned to spend I£370 million on upgrading tourism infrastructure, which will increase to I£652 million if other public and private sector contributions occur.

In 1989, Ireland received 1.3 per cent of the EC's total international arrivals, and research on the origin of visitors has underlined the country's dependence on two major source areas – Great Britain (including Northern Ireland, see Barry and O'Hagan 1972) and continental Europe (Gillmore 1985) which accounted for 85 per cent of arrivals in 1994 and 75 per cent of revenue (McEniff 1996). The number of arrivals from continental Europe has more than doubled since 1985 (see Table 6.1) whilst the North American Market has decreased in volume up to 1993 and then increased in 1994 (Grimes 1992; McEniff 1996), although it still forms an important source of revenue (O'Hagan and Harrison 1984a, 1984b). The importance of different motives for international tourists visiting Ireland have been discussed in detail by Gillmore

(1985), Brunt (1988), Pollard (1989) and McEniff (1991) and need not be reiterated here. More detailed studies have examined how special-interest tourism (Weiler and Hall 1992) has been developed in Ireland to diversity its tourism product and broaden the country's tourism appeal among niche markets such as social tourism (Champeaux 1987; McGrath 1989; Wilhelm 1990). Other forms of tourism, such as farm tourism (Fowler 1991), have been nurtured to develop alternative land uses, thereby diversifying the economic base in rural areas from agriculture to tourism despite the problems of seasonality and dependence (Ball 1989; McEniff 1991).

In contrast, domestic tourism (Gillmore 1985; Brunt 1988; Pollard 1989) and the role of outbound Irish tourism (Brunt 1988; Fitzpatrick and Montague 1989) has received comparatively little attention despite the economic contribution of the 5.1 million domestic trips made in 1990 which generated I£342 million for the Irish economy. Although the number of domestic trips doubled between 1985 and 1990, due in part to the growth in short breaks, 'revenue receipts from domestic holidays in 1990 were estimated to be worth I£342 million, an increase of 86% in nominal terms since 1985 . . . average expenditure per holidaymaker has decreased in nominal and real terms, falling in constant prices from I£99 per person in 1985 to I£81 in 1990' (McEniff 1991: 35). Brunt (1988: 86–7) examines the regional pattern of expenditure among the Irish population while Go (1991) emphasises the factors influencing outbound travel (e.g. social and work patterns, consumer tastes, leave entitlements and disposable income) and their sensitivity to fluctuations in the economic cycles, particularly in major urban areas (e.g. Dublin).

Table 6.1: Visitor arrivals in the Republic of Ireland by country of residence 1985–94 (000s)

Country	1985	1986	1987	1988	1989	1990	1991	1992	1993	1994
UK:	1,704	1,716	1,802	2,090	2,396	2,355	2,266	2,315	2,397	2,668
Great Britain	1,119	1,130	1,236	1,508	1,716	1,785	1,746	1,765	1,857	2,038
Northern Ireland	585	586	566	582	680	570	520	550	540	630
Continental Europe:	334	337	390	408	547	744	841	874	945	988
France	95	89	113	111	138	198	220	220	242	231
West Germany	98	100	103	113	154	178	203	230	265	269
Italy	16	17	22	21	37	73	96	101	116	121
Netherlands	33	33	40	38	46	72	83	73	69	80
Spain	15	23	34	34	38	54	62	56	57	59
Switzerland	17	17	17	24	31	41	46	52	40	62
Belgium/Luxembourg	22	21	20	20	28	37	33	40	41	41
Norway/Sweden	10	11	11	12	18	26	27	26	32	33
Denmark	17	14	13	14	22	16	19	18	17	19
Other European	11	12	17	21	35	49	–	–	–	–
North America:	422	343	398	419	427	443	356	417	422	494
USA	392	309	367	385	385	402	321	374	376	449
Canada	30	34	31	34	42	41	35	43	46	45
Australia/New Zealand	37	36	37	46	62	69	–	–	–	–
Others	32	35	37	44	52	54	–	–	–	–
Total tourist numbers	2,529	2,467	2,664	3,007	3,484	3,665	3,571	3,724	3,888	4,309

Source: Page (1994c); EIU (1996)

THE SUPPLY OF TOURISM RESOURCES IN IRELAND

Ireland's tourist product is based upon natural and man-made resources and an experience which is conditioned by the social and cultural environment (i.e. the people, their history, heritage, landscape and culture – see Keane 1972). The country's natural and man-made environment (Pollard 1989) reflects the aesthetic qualities of the Irish landscape (Foras Forbatha 1977), where 1.2 million ha of the landscape is classified as being of 'outstanding quality' (Mawhinney 1979), particularly in the more peripheral areas of the west of Ireland (Brunt 1988: 116) with its unpolluted, uncommercialised and scenic coastline, especially in the counties of Donegal, Clare and Kerry (Brady et al. 1972–73). Although urban tourism offers a contrast with the rural qualities of Ireland (Mawhinney 1979), Gillmore (1985: 312) identifies the principal preoccupations of visitors from a 1982 Bord Fáilte survey. The survey emphasised sightseeing, exploring the countryside and touring natural and cultural attractions as the main activities, highlighting the need to provide appropriate infrastructure and facilities to accommodate the rural and dispersed nature of many tourist activities (Plettner 1979). Mountain-based activities (Pollard 1989) and coastal-based activities also assumed an important role in tourists' use of rural environments. For example, Foras Forbatha's (1973) study of Brittas Bay highlighted the significance of coastal planning and the significance of 'carrying capacity' in these sensitive recreational and tourism environments and Carter and Parker (1989) examine some of the pressures posed by tourism in the coastal environment. Stevens (1987) also provided an interesting insight in the context of coastal environments, in terms of the tourist potential of subterranean caverns. Gillmore (1985) also identifies other natural resource-based forms of tourism such as parks and forests, as do Bagnall *et al.* (1978) and Murphy and Gardiner (1983, 1984), while rivers and water-based resources are highlighted by Deblock (1986) and the expansion of activity holidays is examined by Lucas (1986). Cultural and historical attractions also form an important component of Ireland's tourist product (Roche and Murray 1978; Brennan 1990) with the potential to form an integrated heritage zone at conservation sites (Tubridy 1987). Gillmore (1985) provides a detailed discussion of these heritage resources in terms of archaeological remains, religious sites, historic properties, museums and their geographical distribution throughout Ireland, although there is a marked absence of research on tourist transportation, tourist activity patterns and the spatial distribution of tourist travel in Ireland in relation to 'circuit tourism' (see Forer and Pearce 1984; Pearce 1987a). Nevertheless, there has been a renewed interest in 'heritage tourism' with the recent Visitor Attraction Survey in Ireland in 1991 (Tourism Development International 1992) which discusses trends and the profile of visitors and the proportion of heritage attractions among the stock of over 150 fee-paying attractions which received 4.5 million overseas and domestic visitors in 1991. Bord Fáilte (1990b) produced a strategy and action plan for heritage attractions and the analysis of their future development, marketing and management (Bord Fáilte 1992a, 1992b). These studies also highlighted potential gaps in the range of heritage themes presented to visitors, the need for greater quality assurance and the need for the integration of this form of tourism more fully into existing dispersed patterns of rural tourism, which are often based in remote, relatively inaccessible and peripheral locations outside the main towns and cities. In 1991 a network of twenty-five 'heritage towns' were designated in these peripheral areas (Page 1994d).

Accommodation also forms a critical component of tourism infrastructure in Ireland and according to Gillmore (1985: 323) it is 'a prerequisite for tourism development . . . [but] in the late 1950s its amount and quality . . . [in Ireland] were major restrictions on the expansion of the industry'. The public and private sector has, to a certain extent, addressed these weaknesses, as recent studies of Ireland's accommodation and lodging industry have shown (Blackwell 1970; Baum 1989a; Pollard 1989). For example, Baum (1989a) identified 4,383 lodging establishments in Ireland which employed 34,750 full and part-time people in the serviced accommodation sector. In addition, Baum (1989b) discussed the diversity and significance of small, family-run establishments in the serviced accommodation sector and the key issues facing this sector of the tourism industry as they were poised for growth in the 1980s. CERT, the State Training Industry for Tourism, also examined management training initiatives for the hotel industry based on research it had undertaken on the accommodation sector (CERT 1987a, 1987b, 1991), while it is also interesting to note that I£20 million from the EC European Social Fund between 1989 and 1993 was spent on tourism training.

Bord Fáilte also undertake such studies (e.g. its analysis of interhotel trends, Bord Fáilte 1986), and Simpson Xavier Horwath (1990) have undertaken a more detailed review of recent trends in Ireland's hotel sector. In the non-serviced accommodation sector (Plettner 1979), research identified the type of facilities sought by tourists and the opportunities for architects in building forest cabins and farm building conversion and the potential for caravans and camp-sites in Ireland and Northern Ireland. Fowler (1991) examined developments in farm tourism while Gillmore (1985) and Brunt (1988) focus on the largely unresearched issue of the impact of second homes in rural areas (see Coppock 1977a), particularly the ownership patterns, with the highest densities recorded in Wicklow–Wexford, Donegal, West Galway and South-West Ireland. Gillmore (1985) also examines the demand for second homes and the ownership patterns which were dominated by Dublin residents. In the case of second home ownership among Northern Ireland residents, there was a trend towards a significant concentration in the Donegal region while among continental European second home owners, their properties were mainly located in South-West Ireland. Glebe (1978), for example, observes the tendency in West Cork and South Kerry for abandoned farms in coastal areas to be converted to second homes or retirement cottages. Brunt (1988: 116) acknowledges that 'although tourism contributes positively to the development of rural areas, there are problems which have to be recognised . . . [including] the problems of seasonality, the potential and actual conflict between tourism and competing land uses' induced through second home development. Therefore, with those potential problems in mind, it is pertinent to consider how the tourism industry is organised and managed in Ireland in order to address potential conflicts generated by tourism.

POLICY ISSUES IN IRISH TOURISM: THE CASE OF RURAL TOURISM

According to McEniff (1991: 37) 'the stance of the Irish government in relation to tourism is relatively interventionist', with the Department of Tourism and Transport responsible for policy formulation and funding the national tourism organisation, Bord Fáilte (Heneghan 1976). Pearce's (1990b) review identified the organisational framework developed to manage, market, promote, plan, develop, research and regulate tourism in Ireland. As Pearce (1990b, 1992b) shows, Bord Fáilte's main expenditure is devoted to marketing and promotion, and McEniff (1991: 38) provides a useful analysis of state expenditure on tourism in the period 1987–90 which emphasises the drop in the real value of the government allocation and the privatisation of former state interests in tourism (e.g. the B & I Ferry line in 1991).

In terms of the politics of tourism (Fianna Fail 1987) various state and semi-state agencies have performed important roles both directly and indirectly in relation to tourism (for example, the Office of Public Works is responsible for national parks and monuments). The government's National Development Plan 1989–1993 (Anon. 1989) highlighted the underlying rationale for state involvement in tourism:

- to double the number of international tourist arrivals;
- to increase revenue from tourism by I£500 mn between 1989 and 1993; and
- to create an additional 25,000 jobs by 1993.

In order to achieve these objectives, the Irish government introduced an Operational Programme for Tourism 1989–1993 (Bord Fáilte 1991b) One of the main outcomes was the receipt of I£147 million of EC aid from the 'European Regional Development Fund and the European Social Fund for investment in infrastructure, marketing and training to help meet these objectives' (McEniff 1991: 37) which continued with the 1994–1999 Programme. Pearce (1992b) provides a useful analysis of the ERDF assistance made available to Ireland's tourism industry and the dramatic change in fortunes from the situation in 1984, where no assistance had been granted, to the one in 1988, where 80 per cent of the total appropriations received by Ireland's tourism industry through the ERDF were made in that year alone. In fact, Pearce (1992b: 48) argued that this 'substantial increase in tourism projects in Ireland in 1988 reflects a broader change in official policy to tourism which saw a more positive stance being taken with regard to its role in the Irish economy', with the state putting forward tourism projects to the EC for ERDF funding, which had not been the case prior to 1988. Ireland's 'lagging region' status greatly assisted its ability to attract ERDF funds for tourism which were directed towards a range of infrastructure and attraction-related developments, especially in relation to the nation's heritage. For example, Bord Fáilte, who administered ERDF funds for tourism projects in Ireland in 1989–93 (Bord Fáilte 1991b) and Stevens (1991) noted that over 33 per cent of this revenue was allocated to the development of Ireland's heritage resources although Bord Fáilte suggest that 'over 40 per cent of the ERDF funds for tourism development are earmarked for the history and culture product and over 100 significant projects have been proposed' (Bord Fáilte 1992a: 1).

Gillmore (1985: 306) argued that 'one of the most important developments in tourism administration was the measure of decentralisation adopted in 1964 when Bord Fáilte established eight Regional Tourism Organisations (RTO) and Mowat (1984) has examined the role of tourism administration in the development of tourist resources in North-West Ireland. Whilst

the eight RTOs were reduced to seven in 1984 to achieve economies in expenditure on tourism, this does reflect a regionalisation of tourism administration to address the 'growth in tourist traffic in the 1960s and the advent of the more mobile motoring holidaymaker following the widening of car ownership and the introduction of the first car ferries to the public in 1965' (Pearce 1990b: 138). In fact, the relationship between Bord Fáilte and the RTOs is indicative of a core–periphery relationship within the terms of the management and power base for tourism marketing, development and promotion, especially since the ERDF funds are an additional source of funding to allocate to appropriate projects. Pearce (1990b) discusses the rationale, organisation and activities of the RTOs and their relationship with Bord Fáilte, particularly in relation to funding, visitor servicing, planning, development, marketing and promotion, and therefore these issues need not be reiterated here.

In terms of planning (Mawhinney and Bagnall 1976), Pearce (1990b) highlights the spatial component in relation to the designation of areas for conservation, developing some 81 tourism planning zones. The role of tourism development in expanding, improving and diversifying Ireland's tourism plant in terms of accommodation, attractions and infrastructure is apparent from the incentive grants and funding available from Bord Fáilte and government schemes (Bord Fáilte 1991a; McEniff 1991). For example, Bord Fáilte approved 275 projects with a total capital cost of I£529 million between 1987 and June 1991 under the Business Expansion Scheme, which provided tax relief for investment in tourism. Bord Fáilte also promoted agri-tourism to 'provide incentives to farmers and other rural dwellers towards the cost of providing facilities which will enhance the attractiveness of an area for tourists and meet clearly identified tourist demand' (Bord Fáilte 1991b), a scheme administered by the

RTOs and Bord Fáilte to encourage rural economic development based on tourism. In addition, McEniff (1991) outlined the increased investment by licensed banks to the hospitality industry and the improvements made to accommodation facilities up to 1990. Pearce (1990b) also documents the marketing and promotional roles of Bord Fáilte and the RTOs and emphasises the significance of promoting the

> image of Ireland as a whole abroad ... it is a national image, sometimes directed at specific interest groups, which has been promoted, presumably because this is seen as the most effective method of marketing a small country in large and competitive markets such as the UK, the USA and West Germany with a comparatively modest total budget.
>
> (Pearce 1990b: 42)

This reflects some of the budgetary constraints faced by public sector tourism organisations at a time of expansion in the tourism industry.

Although public and private sector organisations are involved in the management of tourism in Ireland, various social, cultural and environmental impacts have resulted from tourist development. For example, Williams (1985) has examined the significance of native language-speaking in the Gaeltacht areas of Ireland, and Gillmore (1985: 329) pointed to the positive benefits of tourism in such areas, despite the 'social disruption and diminution of cultural identity'. In contrast, O'Cinneide and Keane (1990) cite the example of the Inishowen peninsula and the initial reluctance of local entrepreneurs and tourist businesses to plan strategically and to promote tourism on a local area basis. However, McDermott and Horner (1978) examined second home conversion and development, which were used for tourist and recreational purposes, and they noted its positive contribution to rural renewal in Western Connemara, although there is little agreement on the extent to which the advantages of second home ownership outweigh the

disadvantages (Robinson 1990). Within the context of Ireland's Gaeltacht areas, it is interesting to note Whyte's (1978) observation that in a similar remote context – the Isle of Skye – local residents perceived the influx of English-speaking second-home owners as a threat to the Gaelic-speaking tradition. In an urban context the social impact of tourism has been observed where 'tourists visiting Dublin are at risk of victimisation in the capital in relation to crime' (Rottman 1989: 97).

In terms of environmental impacts, Gillmore (1985: 329) suggested that 'concern for tourism has been a vital force in promoting interest in environmental conservation in general and the protection of the landscape in particular'. Carter and Parker (1989), however, placed more emphasis on the environmental costs of tourism and argued the 'value of Irish beaches and dunes to the economy makes it paradoxically [sic] that very little is done to manage the coast. In some places, management plans have been implemented, for example by the National Trust at Murlough, County Down but in far too many places, the beach environment has simply been allowed to deteriorate' (Carter and Parker 1989: 408). The recent designation of the Wicklow National Park has also seen a greater concern for the impact of tourism on the environment as the environmental impact statements for visitor centres in both Wicklow National Park (Brady et al. 1991) and Dun Chaoin, County Kerry (Environmental Impact Services Limited 1991) indicated. However, with the planned expansion of the volume of international tourism in Ireland, it is inevitable that the impacts generated by tourism will need further detailed research if the complexities of tourist–host interaction are to be more fully understood, especially regarding the extent to which Ireland's high-quality environmental attributes can be maintained through a careful policy of sustainable development in keeping with the character of the landscape and its acceptability to the local population.

Deegan and Dineen's (1996) recent synthesis of Irish tourism policy observes that there are examples of successful rural tourism initiatives in Ireland (Keane and Quinn 1990; Feehan 1992) particularly in relation to community development. Like the literature on rural tourism in general, Ireland exhibits many examples of a focus on farm tourism (O'Connor 1995, 1996) and accommodation initiatives such as 'Rent-an-Irish Cottage' (Share 1992). However, the LEADER programme in Ireland is an example of a policy initiative intended to assist with the development of rural tourism.

LEADER 1 PROGRAMME

LEADER is an EU programme intended to assist with alternative forms of development to replace declining agriculture incomes (Kearney *et al.* 1994; Jenkins *et al.* 1998). As Figure 6.3 shows, a number of LEADER I areas were designated covering 61 per cent of Ireland and 44 per cent of funded projects were associated with rural tourism. Some 50 per cent of the I£70 million funds for LEADER I were devoted to these tourism projects, and 35 per cent of the projects were associated with accommodation. The evaluation of the LEADER 1 programme observed that while net employment gains were targeted, major benefits were associated with qualitative improvements (e.g. capacity building in rural communities) since rural tourism development was identified by Deegan and Dineen (1996: 109) as a 'potent vehicle for local development, economic recovery, social progress and conservation of the rural heritage' although they note that the difference between LEADER I and other programmes which emphasised farm tourism were that they focused more on the process and confidence building process in rural communities prior to launching rural tourism programmes.

However, Keane and Quinn (1990) observe that rural tourism in Ireland remains a frag-

mented topic with the state tourism organisation (Bord Fáilte) only belatedly supporting what has been viewed as a marginal activity. Yet it is far from a niche market, since one of the very attractions of the Irish tourism product is its rural idyll, despite its recognition that 'it has a marginal though important contribution to make to regional income distribution in areas of the country which have undeveloped tourism resources and are not on recognised tourist routes' (Deegan and Dineen 1996: 111), though LEADER 1 is probably best noted for the qualitative rather than quantitative contribution it made to improving rural tourism in Ireland. McEniff (1996: 61) also noted that 'because of the popularity of LEADER 1, aims to limit the proportion of funding allocated to tourism projects' is now enshrined in LEADER 2, while a number of other government schemes now aim to assist rural tourism development (e.g. The Operational Programme for Agriculture, Rural Development and Forestry).

SUMMARY

It is apparent from the case study that the economic impact of tourism appears to have dominated the research agenda in Ireland, despite the growing interest in rural tourism, especially among geographers. Ireland is an interesting example of the way in which perceived inaccessibility, combined with the positive features of its remoteness and landscapes, have been harnessed through creative and innovative marketing to boost tourist arrivals. Air travel and increased sea routes from the UK and mainland Europe, together with more competitively priced air fares, have assisted in overcoming the geographical effects of peripherality whilst the country has benefited from EC funds to develop its tourism industry. The application of 'core–periphery' concepts to explain tourism development and activities in a

Figure 6.3: Distribution of LEADER 1 areas in the Republic of Ireland
Source: Deegan and Dineen (1996: 110)

country such as Ireland highlight a major weakness in the simple delimitation of urban and rural areas which research has criticised for failing to take account of the socio-economic conditions and processes at work (Hoggart 1988).

Both the public and private sector have emphasised the positive effects of tourism in terms of the increased volume of international arrivals and, to lesser degree, the benefits of domestic tourism. This imbalance in attention implies that other disciplines have either not publicised the results of their research to the same effect as those concerned with the economic impact or that there has been relatively little interest in the broader aspects of tourism. There is also a noticeable absence of research on the sustainability of tourism and its environmental effects to indicate the State's concern for this controversial issue. Although there have been some influential studies undertaken on tourism in Ireland, a greater emphasis is needed on rural tourism in order to understand the long-term effects of basing a significant element of the country's economy on tourism.

Managing tourism in a period of expansion during the 1990s requires a greater cooperation between the public and private sectors of tourism interest to ensure that critical components of the nation's heritage are not irrecoverably damaged. For example, the impact of tourism on Ireland's regional culture and the Gaelic language is a case in point. This is one of the distinctive characteristics of the Irish tourist product which needs to be protected and enhanced rather than eroded through the internationalisation of tourism. If 'Ireland is a tourist destination with a future . . . [with] its unspoilt environment . . . rich in the tourism resource of tomorrow . . . which the sophisticated tourist increasingly seeks . . . [and its] scenery, people and culture make for a unique holiday destination' (Bord Fáilte 1991b), it will need to sensitively manage the impact of the tourist and tourism in the 1990s to maintain a delicate balance between attaining economic benefits from tourism and minimising the potentially detrimental impact on the Irish population, its distinctive Gaelic culture and its largely unspoilt natural environment.

CONCLUSION

This chapter has emphasised the development of geographical research in rural recreation and tourism and the major philosophical changes in emphasis from empirically derived analyses through to more socially derived analyses. The geographer has sometimes found it hard to distinguish between the context of recreation and tourism, as users consume the same resources in the rural environment. The 1960s and 1970s saw the development of a strong recreational geography of the rural environment emerge from the leading research of noteworthy authors such as Coppock, Duffield, Lavery and Glyptis within the UK and in North America, followed by the

influential work of Smith (1983a). The disappointing feature is the lack of continuity and theoretical development after the 1970s to follow up and build upon the groundwork established in the 1960s and 1970s. One possible explanation may be derived from chapter 1 with the denial of mainstream geography and its reluctance to embrace such research as critical to the conceptual and theoretical development of the discipline. This is certainly true in tourism up until the 1990s when research by mainstream human geographers such as Cloke have began to cultivate critical social geographies of recreation and tourism in the countryside. Even so, one would expect that geographical research assessment exercises in countries such as the UK, would do little to foster a spirit of mainstream incorporation of tourism and recreation into the discipline as it may be assessed under business and management rather than as a sub-group of geography. The nearest inroad is through the study groups of professional bodies such as the IBG and AAG where these developments have not been discouraged. Human geography in particular has been less accepting of such fringe subject areas and a consequence is that even when notable researchers have emerged in these areas they have not fostered the same stature or influence of the human geographers of the 1960s and 1970s who cultivated and really established rural recreation and tourism as a rich area of spatially contingent research. The scope of the studies reviewed and discussed in this chapter have a common theme associated with some of the common problems associated with rural areas in general, namely peripherality. Yet, ironically, this can also be a major feature associated with place marketing of rural areas where the peaceful rural idyll is marketed and commodified around the concept of space and peripherality. The rural geographer has made some forays into this area of research but more often than not, many of the texts on rural geography only pay a limited attention to tourism and recreation despite its growing significance in economic, social and political terms.

7

TOURISM AND RECREATION IN THE PLEASURE PERIPHERY
Wilderness and National Parks

Historically, wilderness has been one of the main sources of 'the other' in Western society. Wilderness was what lay beyond the boundaries of a 'civilised', ordered landscape. Since the beginning of the nineteenth century however, wilderness and wild areas began to assume a more favourable impression under the influence of the romantic and transcendentalist movements which favoured wild nature as an antidote to an increasingly industrialised and technocratic society. More recently, the conservation and commodification of wilderness has become entwined with the growth of recreation and tourism which has seen national parks established not only for outdoor and adventure recreation enthusiasts but also one of the main sites in which eco-tourism occurs.

Geographers have long played a significant role in understanding and contributing to the conservation of natural resources and natural areas and their relationship with recreation and tourist activities (e.g. Graves 1920; Marsh and Wall 1982; Sewell and Dearden 1989). Indeed, recreation and tourism has long been used as an economic justification for the conservation and legal protection of such areas. Geographers have contributed to an understanding of a number of different dimensions of the relationship between wilderness and national park concepts and recreation and tourism:

• the changing meaning of wilderness in Western society;

• the environmental history of national parks and wilderness areas;
• the value of wilderness;
• the identification and inventory of wilderness;
• the demand for wilderness and natural areas, including visitor profiles, activities and behaviours;
• the development of wilderness and national park policy and the supply of wilderness and natural areas for recreation and tourist activities.

THE CHANGING MEANING OF WILDERNESS IN WESTERN SOCIETY

Definition presents a major problem in the identification of wilderness areas. Definition is important 'because it is the basis for common understanding and communication' and it 'provides a basis for putting a concept into action through creating and preserving a referent' (Gardner 1978: 7). However, wilderness is an elusive concept with many layers of meaning (Gardner 1978; Graber 1978). Tuan (1974: 112) has gone so far as to claim that, 'wilderness cannot be defined objectively: it is as much a state of mind as a description of nature'. Wilderness has now become 'a symbol of the orderly progress of nature. As a state of mind, true wilderness exists only in the great sprawling cities'.

The problem of defining wilderness was summarised by Nash (1967: 1):

'Wilderness' has a deceptive concreteness at first glance. The difficulty is that while the word is a noun it acts like an adjective. There is no specific material object that is wilderness. The term designates a quality (as the '-ness' suggests) that produces a certain mood or feeling in a given individual and, as a consequence, may be assigned by that person to a specific place. Because of this subjectivity a universally acceptable definition of wilderness is elusive . . . Wilderness, in short, is so heavily freighted with meaning of a personal, symbolic, and changing kind as to resist easy definition.

The meaning of wilderness has changed over time but several themes may be distinguished. The word wilderness is derived from the old English word *wilddeoren* meaning 'of wild beasts', which in turn is derived from the teutonic languages of northern Europe. In German, for example, *Wildnis* is a cognate verb, and *Wildor* signifies wild game (Nash 1967: 2).

The Romance languages have no single word which expresses the idea of wilderness but rely instead on its attributes. In French the equivalent terms are *lieu desert* (deserted place) and *solitude inculte*, while in Spanish wilderness is *la naturaleza, immensidad or falts da cultura* (lack of cultivation). 'Italian uses the vivid *scene di disordine o confusione*' (Nash 1967: 2). The Latin root of desert, *de* and *serere* (to break apart, becoming solitary) connotes not only the loneliness and fear associated with separation but also an arid, barren tract lacking cultivation (Mark 1984: 3). Both the north European and the Mediterranean traditions define and portray wilderness as a landscape of fear, which is outside the safer bounds of human settlement (Tuan 1971, 1979). An image that was taken up by Nash (1967: 2) who noted that the image of wilderness 'is that of a man [sic] in an alien environment where the civilization that normally orders and controls life is absent'.

The landscape of fear that dominated early attitudes towards wilderness was noted in the eighth-century classic *Beowulf* (Wright 1957), 'where *wildeor* appeared in reference to savage and fantastic beasts inhabiting a dismal region of forests, crags, and cliffs' (Nash 1967: 1). The translation of the scriptures into English from Greek and Hebrew led to the use of wilderness as a description of 'the uninhabited, arid land of the Near East' (Nash 1967: 2–3). It was at this point that wilderness came to be associated with spiritual values. Wilderness was seen as both a testing ground for man and an area in which man could draw closer to God.

The biblical attitude towards nature was an essential ingredient of the Judeo-Christian or Western attitude towards wilderness (Glacken 1967; Passmore 1974; Graber 1978; Attfield 1983; Pepper 1984; Short 1991). According to the dominant tradition within Judeo-Christianity concerning humankind's relationship with nature, it was 'God's intention that mankind multiply itself, spread out over the earth, make its domain over the creation secure' (Glacken 1967: 151). This relationship is best indicated in *Genesis* 1:28 where God said to man, 'Be fruitful and multiply, and fill the earth and subdue it; and have dominion over the fish of the sea and over the birds of the air and over every living thing that moves upon the earth.'

To the authors of the Bible, wilderness had a central position in their accounts as both a descriptive and as a symbolic concept. To the ancient Hebrews, wilderness was 'the environment of evil, a kind of hell' in which the wasteland was identified with God's curse (Nash 1967: 14–15). Paradise, or Eden, was the antithesis of wilderness. The story of Adam and Eve's dismissal from the Garden of Eden, from a watered, lush paradise to a 'cursed' land of 'thorns and thistles' (*Genesis* 2:4), reinforced in Western thought the notion that wilderness and paradise were both physical and spiritual opposites (Williams 1962). *Isaiah* (51:3), for instance, contains the promise that God will comfort Zion and 'make her wilderness like Eden, her desert like the garden of the Lord', while *Joel* (2:3) stated that 'the land is like the garden of Eden before them, but after them a desolate wilderness'.

The experience of the Israelites during the Exodus added another dimension to the Judeo-Christian attitude towards wilderness. For forty years the Jews, led by Moses, wandered in the 'howling waste of the wilderness' (*Deuteronomy* 32:10) that was the Sinai Peninsula (Funk 1959). The wilderness, in this instance, was not only a place where they were punished by God for their sins but also a place where they could prove themselves worthy of the Lord and make ready for the promised land. Indeed, it was precisely because it was unoccupied that it 'could be a refuge as well as a disciplinary force' (Nash 1967: 16).

The experience of the Exodus helped to establish a tradition of going to the wilderness 'for freedom and purification of faith' (Nash 1967: 16). Elijah spent forty days in the wilderness in order to draw guidance and inspiration from God (1 *Kings* 19: 4–18). John the Baptist was the voice crying in the wilderness to prepare for the coming of the Messiah (*Matthew* 4:1), while Christ himself 'was led by the spirit into the wilderness to be tempted by the devil' (*Matthew* 4:1; *Mark* 1:12ff). It was through the environment of evil and hardship, characteristic of the dominant Judeo-Christian perception of the wilderness, that spiritual catharsis could occur. A sentiment that exists through to this day (Graber 1976). (See chapter 6 on the role of wilderness areas in rural tourism.)

The example of the prophets venturing into the wilderness was followed by early Christian ascetics (Williams 1962). Hermits and monks established themselves in wilderness surroundings in order to avoid the temptations of earthly wealth and pleasure and to find a solitude conducive to spiritual ideals. As Tuan (1974: 148) recorded: 'The monastic community in the wilderness was a model of paradise set in an unredeemed world. Wilderness was often perceived as the haunt of demons but in the neighbourhood of the monastery it could acquire some of the harmony of redeemed nature and the animals in it, like their human suzerains in the monastery, lived in peace.'

The desert ascetics drew on an appreciation of nature that sprung from the Bible itself. As Glacken (1967: 151) observed, 'The intense otherworldliness and rejection of the beauties of nature because they turn men away from the contemplation of God are elaborated upon far more in theological writings than in the Bible itself'. The desert monks lived in the solitude of the wilderness to remove themselves from man, not from nature. Psalm 104 provides one of the clearest statements of the existence of a sympathetic attitude in Christianity towards nature, noting that everything in nature has its place in a divine order: 'the high mountains are for the wild goats; the rocks are a refuge for the badgers' (Ps. 104:18). 'O Lord, how manifold are thy works! In wisdom hast thou made them all' (Ps. 104: 24). As Glacken (1967: 157) noted:

> It is not to be wondered at that Psalm 104 has been quoted so often by thinkers sympathetic to the design argument and the physico-theological proof for the existence of God. The life, beauty, activity, order, and reasonableness in nature are described without mysteries, joyously – even triumphantly. God is separate from nature but he may be understood in part from it.

The theme of the wisdom of the Lord being shown in the order of nature was similarly indicated elsewhere in the Bible. The psalmist in Psalm 8:1 exclaimed 'O Lord, our Lord, how majestic is thy name in all the earth!' The notion that, 'The heavens are telling the glory of God; and the firmament proclaims his handiwork' (Psalm 19:1) proved to be influential throughout Christendom in the Dark and Middle Ages, although by no means enabling a universally sympathetic attitude towards nature. Nature came to be regarded as a book which could reveal the works of the Lord in a manner similar to the scriptures. In the early exegetical writings God was regarded as being made manifest in his works.

> There is a book of nature which when read along with the book of God, allows men to know and understand Him and his creation; not only man but nature suffered from the curse after the Fall; one may admire and love the beauty of the earth if this love and admiration is associated with the love of God.
> (Glacken 1967: 203)

This view of nature played an important role in establishing a favourable attitude towards wild country. St. Augustine (in Glacken 1967: 204) wrote, 'Some people in order to discover God, read books. But there is a great book: the very appearance of created things.' Pulpit eloquence, was 'adopted by medieval mystico-philosophical speculation, and finally passed into common usage' (Curtius 1953: 321, in Glacken 1957: 104).

Reading the book of nature for the word of God was eventually to lead to the reading of nature itself, but the notion of nature as a book was also to prepare the way for the development of a natural theology in the writings of St Francis of Assisi, St Bonaventura and Ramon Sibiude. To St Francis living creatures were not only symbols, but were also 'placed on earth for God's own purposes (not for man's), and they, like man, praise God' (Glacken 1967: 216). St Francis' theology represented a revolutionary change in Christian attitudes towards nature because of the distinct break that they make from the anthropocentric nature of earlier theology (White 1967). Upon the foundation built by the natural theologians and their intellectual heirs, such as John Ray and Gilbert White, came to be built the framework for the discovery of nature by the romantic movement. Nevertheless, despite a continuing appreciation of nature as part of God's divine presence by some theologians, the dominant attitude in the Judeo-Christian tradition until the seventeenth century was that true appreciation of God could only be gained by looking inwards, not out at nature. Nature was provided for man to utilise. Wilderness and wild lands were to be tamed and cultivated to display the divine order as interpreted by man.

The dominant Judeo-Christian view of wilderness may be contrasted with that of Eastern religions. In Eastern thought, wilderness 'did not have an unholy or evil connotation but was venerated as the symbol and even the very essence of the deity' (Nash 1967: 20). The aesthetic appreciation of wild land began to change far earlier in the Orient than in the West. By the fourth century AD, for instance, large numbers of people in China had began to find an aesthetic

appeal in mountains, whereas they were still seen as objects of fear in Europe (Nicholson 1962; Tuan 1974).

Eastern faiths such as Shinto and Taoism 'fostered love of wilderness rather than hatred' (Nash 1982: 21). Shinto deified nature in favour of pastoral scenes. The polarity that existed between city and wilderness in the Judeo-Christian experience did not exist outside European cultural tradition (Callicott 1982). Western civilization has tended to dominate, rather than adapt, to its surrounding landscape whereas traditional Eastern and non-European cultures have tended to attempt to blend into their surroundings. As Tuan (1974: 148) noted, 'In the traditions of Taoist China and pre-Dorian Greece, nature imparted virtue or power. In the Christian tradition sanctifying power is invested in man, God's vice regent, rather than nature.' However, it should be emphasised that Oriental civilisations, such as those of China, India and Japan, have had highly destructive impacts on the environment and will continue to do so.

The attitude of different cultures to nature and, hence, wilderness is important (Tuan 1976). As Eidsvik (1980, 1985) has recognised, wilderness has only recently taken on global meaning with the increasing dominance of Western culture throughout the world. The perception of wilderness as an alien landscape of fear is derived from the northern European set of attitudes towards nature, where the Judeo-Christian perception of nature became combined with the teutonic fear of the vast northern forests. It is perhaps of no coincidence therefore that the creation of designated wilderness areas began in lands occupied by peoples who have inherited European cultural attitudes. However, despite retaining something of its original attributes the meaning of wilderness has changed substantially over time and now incorporates wider scientific and conservation values. Table 7.1 portrays the development of the wilderness concept in the United States, Canada, New Zealand and Australia: those countries within which the idea of wilderness has been most

Table 7.1: The development of the wilderness concept in the United States, Canada, New Zealand and Australia

Date	United States	Canada	New Zealand	Australia
Pre 1860	Major romantic influence on American art and literature			A 'New Britannia'
1832	Joseph Catlin calls for the creation of a 'nation's Park'			Aesthetic and utilitarian visions of the Australian landscape
1832	Arkansas Hot Springs reserved			Rapid clearfelling of land for agriculture and mining
1851	Transcendentalism – Thoreau's Walking proclaims that 'in Wildness is the preservation of the World'	Development of a romantic perception of the Canadian landscape		
1860	Romantic Monumentalism			
1864	George Perkins Marsh's Man and Nature is published, heralds the start of 'economic conservation'; Yosemite State Park established			Marsh's book well received in Australia; 1866 Jenolan Caves reserved
1870	Wilderness perceived as 'worthless land'			The need to conserve forests argued by Clarke, Goyder and von Mueller 'Scientific Vision'; 1879 Royal National Park established in New South Wales
1872	Yellowstone National Park established; John Muir begins writing and campaigning for wilderness preservation		1878 T. Potts publishes National Domains; 1881 Thermal Springs Districts Act	
1880	Rise of 'Progressive Conservation' led by Gifford Pinchot	1885 Banff Hot Springs Reserve declared	1887 Tongariro deeded to the New Zealand Government	Rise of the 'Bush Idyll'; National Parks associated recreation and tourism 'Sydney or the Bush'; 1891 National Park Act (S.A.); 1892 Tower Hill National Park Act (Vic.)
1890	F.J. Turner declares the end of the American frontier; Yosemite National Park created with help of railroads; Forests Reserves Act 1891; Cult of the Wilderness	Strengthening of a romantic vision of nature in Canada and rise of progressive conservation; 1894 Algonquin Park established	1892 J. Matson calls for Australasian Indigenous Parks	
1900	Tourism a major motive for the establishment of parks in all four countries			
1905	U.S. Forest Service created			1905 State Forests and National Parks Act (Queensland); 1915 Scenery Preservation Act (Tas.); Growth of the 'Bushwalking Movement' under Myles Dunphy in NSW
1910		1911 Dominion Forest Reserves and Parks Act		
1913	Preservationists lose battle to prevent Hetch Hetchy being dammed			
1916	U.S. National Park Service created			
1920	Rise of Ecological Perspectives; Forest Service areas retained as 'primitive lands'		Negative reaction to introduced animals in National Parks begins	
1926	Forest Service Wilderness Inventory			

Year	USA / North America	Canada	New Zealand	Australia
1927				Formation of the National Parks and Primitive Areas Council
1928	Forest Service Regulation L-20			
1930			National Parks Act	
1934	Everglades National Park established			Greater Blue Mountains National Park Scheme
1937	Formation of the Wilderness Society			
1939	Forest Service 'U' Regulations			
1940				
1944				Development of Snowy-Indi Proposal (NSW); Kosciusko State Park Act
1949	Keyser Report			
1950	Dinosaur National Monument Campaign; First Wilderness Bill			
1952			National Parks Act	
1955		Wilderness Areas Act (Ontario)	Reserves and Domains Act	
1956				
1957				Victorian National Park Authority created
1960	ORCC Report			
1962	Wilderness Act becomes law; Agencies begin implementation			
1963				Kosciusko Primitive Area established (NSW)
1964	RARE I commences			
1967				N.S.W. National Parks and Wildlife Service created; Wilderness becomes a major policy issue: Little Desert, Great Barrier Reef, Fraser Island and Lake Pedder
1969			Study tour of National Parks Director to North America	
1970	Eastern Wilderness Act	Mounting pressure from tourists and commercial interests in national parks in all countries		
1974	RARE II commences; Bureau of Land Management			
1975				National Parks and Wildlife Service (Commonwealth) created
1977			Reserves Act	
1980	commences inventory 'Sagebrush Rebellion'; Provision for wilderness in Alaska; Major conflicts over wilderness preservation		National Parks Act	
1981			Wilderness Advisory Group established	
1982				National Conservation Strategy
1983				Franklin Dam Case
1984	South Moresby Island campaign		new wilderness areas established	Calls for establishment of National Wilderness System
1985				CONCOM discussion paper
1986			World Heritage listing for South Westland Park	
1987			Creation of Department of Conservation	Federal government acts to preserve the Wet Tropics, Kakadu, and the Lemonthyme and Southern Forests; NSW Wilderness Act passed
1990	Increased attention given to concept of ecotourism and sustainable tourism by governments and industry bodies			

influential in outdoor recreation and tourism policy and in the production and consumption of tourism experiences.

The classic example of changing popular attitudes towards wilderness is witnessed in the history of the evolution of the wilderness concept in the United States (Table 7.1). The founding fathers of the American colonies saw the wild lands before them in classical biblical terms and although attitudes towards wilderness did change gradually through the seventeenth and eighteenth centuries it was not until the late eighteenth century that positive appreciation of American nature began to emerge. The political independence of the American nation found cultural expression in the extolment of the virtues of American natural scenery. However, a similar cultural expression was not to be found in colonial Canada where untamed nature still assumed the guise of a landscape of fear (Kline 1970). Nevertheless, America's cultural independence from the Old World produced a desire to laud the moral purity of the wild forests and mountains of the New World, untainted as they were by the domination of things European. A cultural movement which, perhaps somewhat ironically, sprang from the romantic movement then sweeping Europe.

The American romantic movement laid the groundwork upon which a popular appreciation of the value of wild land would come to be based. Artistic, literary and political perceptions of the importance of contact with wild nature provided the stimulus for the creation of positive cultural attitudes towards the American wilderness. Once positive attitudes towards primitive, unordered nature had developed then the emergence of individuals and societies dedicated to the preservation of wilderness values was only a short step away. However, an appreciation of the aesthetic values of wild land was countered by the utilitarian ethic that dominated American society.

The majority of Americans saw the land as an object to be conquered and made productive. The first reservations for the preservation of scenery therefore tended to be established in areas that were judged to be waste lands that had no economic value in terms of agriculture, grazing, lumbering or mining. The aesthetic value of wilderness was protected by national parks and reserves which were intended to protect national scenic monuments that expressed the cultural independence of America in addition to providing for the development of the area through the tourist dollar. Monumentalism was characterised by the belief that natural sites, such as Niagara Falls or the Rockies, were grand, noble and elevated in idea and had something of the enduring, stable and timeless nature of the great architecture of Europe, and proved a significant theme in the establishment of American parks (Runte 1979).

Although the national parks in Australia, Canada and New Zealand did not assume the same importance as national monuments, their development nevertheless parallels that of the American park system. The themes of aesthetic romanticism, recreation and the development of 'worthless' or 'waste' lands through tourism characterised the creation of the first national parks in Australia, Canada and New Zealand. Banff National Park in Canada was developed by the Canadian Pacific Railroad as a tourist spa (Marsh 1985). New Zealand's first parks had lodges and hostels established within them that matched the tourist developments in the North American parks. Australia's first parks, particularly those of Queensland and Tasmania, were also marked by the influence of the desire of government to boost tourism. However, the Australian parks were also noted for their establishment, in unison with railway development, as areas where city-dwellers could find mental restoration in recreation and communion with nature (Hall 1985, 1992a).

With the closing of the American frontier at the end of the nineteenth century the preservation of America's remaining wilderness received new impetus. A massive but unsuccessful public campaign by wilderness preservationists led by

John Muir to protect Hetch Hetchy Valley in Yosemite National Park from a dam scheme, a conservation-minded President (Theodore Roosevelt) in the White House, and the emergence of economically oriented 'progressive conservation' under the leadership of Gifford Pinchot all led to wilderness preservation becoming a matter of public importance in the United States.

The United States Forest Service and National Park Service responded to pressures from recreationalists for the creation of designated wilderness areas. Contemporaneously, the development of the science of ecology led to a recognition of the scientific importance of preserving wilderness. The various elements of wilderness preservation blended together in the inter-war years to lay a framework for the establishment of legally protected wilderness areas.

Economic conservation and the development of a scientific perception of wilderness was also influential in Australia, Canada and New Zealand. In Australia, the publication of George Perkins Marsh's (1864 (1965)) book *Man and Nature* stimulated the colonial governments into establishing forest reserves. In addition, significant scientists, such as Baron von Mueller, and bodies such as the Australasian Association for the Advancement of Science argued for the preservation of native flora and fauna in both Australia and New Zealand. However, the first national parks in Australia were created for reasons of aesthetics, tourism and recreation with science gaining little recognition (Hall 1992a).

In Canada, progressive conservation proved influential in the creation of forest reserves and it is significant to note that many of the early Canadian parks were established under forestry legislation. However, the preservation of wilderness lagged behind the efforts of the United States (Nicol 1969).

The declaration of the *Wilderness Act* in 1964 marked the beginning of the current legislative era of wilderness preservation in the United States.

Under the *Wilderness Act* wilderness is defined as 'an area where the earth and its community of life are untrammelled by man, where man himself is the visitor that does not remain'. The four defining qualities of wilderness areas protected under the Act are that such areas:

a) generally appear to be affected by the forces of nature, with the imprint of man substantially unnoticeable;

b) have outstanding opportunities for solitude or a primitive and unconfined type of recreation;

c) have at least 5,000 acres or is of sufficient size as to make practical its preservation and use in an unimpaired condition; and

d) may also contain ecological, geological or features of scientific, educational, scenic or historical value.

The protection of wilderness through legal means gave new impetus to the task of improving the process of defining and compiling a wilderness inventory as well as providing for its management. A process that is still continuing today in America as well as in countries, such as Australia, which have tended to follow the American model for wilderness and national park protection. Although wilderness in New Zealand is given administrative protection under a variety of acts, there is no specific legislation for the preservation of wilderness. Similarly, until late 1987 with the passing of the New South Wales *Wilderness Act*, no wilderness legislation had been enacted in Australia (Hall 1992a). In Canada, wilderness areas have received a degree of protection under provincial legislation. However, as in Australia and New Zealand, there is no national wilderness act. But in recent years increasing attention has been given to the implications of international heritage agreements, such as the World Heritage Convention, as a mechanism for the preservation of wilderness and other natural areas of international significance (Hall 1992a).

THE ENVIRONMENTAL HISTORY OF NATIONAL PARKS AND WILDERNESS AREAS

Environmental history is a field concerned with the role and place of nature in human life (Worster 1977). Research and scholarship on the environmental history of national parks and wilderness lies at the intersection of a number of fields of geographic and academic endeavour. Within geography, as with history, the increased awareness of the environment as a social, economic and political issue has led to geographers and historians attempting to chart the history of land use of a given region or site in order to increase understanding of its significance, values and present-day use. Such research is not just an academic exercise. As well as assisting in understanding how current natural resource management problems or user conflicts have developed, such research can also be used to develop interpretive material for visitors as part of a programme of heritage management, an area in which geographers are becoming increasingly involved (e.g. Ashworth and Tunbridge 1990; Tunbridge and Ashworth 1996; Hall and McArthur 1996, 1998). Cronan (1990) asserts that good work in environmental history incorporates three levels of analysis. These are the dynamics of natural ecosystems in time (ecology), the political economies that people erect within these systems (economy), and the cognitive lenses through which people perceive those systems (the history of ideas). Geographers, with their integrative approach to environment, cultural landscapes and land use, would therefore seem to be ideally poised to work in this area. As Mark (1996: 153) observed, 'Widening the scope of historical narrative has frequently resulted in more complex interpretation of the past and should point the way toward greater understanding of the past in heritage management.'

National parks are a major focus of heritage management but have been a relatively quiet backwater in traditional historical narrative. Environmental history, however, can place them within the larger context of interaction between nature and culture (Griffiths 1991; Mark 1996). For example, a number of extremely valuable park histories which highlight the role of tourism and outdoor recreation in park development have been written on the Yellowstone (Haines 1977), Grand Canyon (Hughes 1978), Rocky Mountain (Buchholtz 1983), Olympic (Twight 1983), Sequoia and Kings Canyon National Parks (Dilsaver and Tweed 1990), and Yosemite (Runte 1990) national parks in the United States; the Albertan (Bella 1987) and the Ontario (Killan 1993) national park systems in Canada, and with useful national overviews being provided by Nelson (1970), Hall (1992a), Dearden and Rollins (1993).

Substantial methodological research is called for when undertaking research on environmental and park histories. In the New Worlds of North America and the Antipodes, travel accounts written during the period of initial European settlement have been utilised by scholars interested in historic environments (Powell 1978). They often hope to establish a pre-European settlement landscape as a baseline from which to assess subsequent environmental change. One difficulty with using travel accounts, however, is they are often written in places where the journalist is not actually travelling; instead the diarist is summarising past events at a convenient place (Mark 1996). Another problem is how to tie the usually limited detail (little of which could be utilised quantitatively) to specific localities. The paucity of locality information is often present in even the best accounts, such as those left by collectors of natural history specimens.

The only site-specific records available in many areas about presettlement landscapes are land survey notes. These have been helpful in establishing a historic condition of some forests, riparian habitats, and grasslands. Their reliability varies, however, because there can be limitations associated with insufficient description, bias in recording data, contract fraud, and land use prior to survey (Galatowitsch 1990). Another technique which is useful for developing an historical record of land use change or for reconstructing past environments or heritage sites is repeat photography (Rogers *et al.* 1984). However, while such techniques may be useful for specific sites or attractions the photographic record of 'ordinary' landscapes, i.e. those which were not subject to the interest of visitors as a view or panorama, is more difficult to construct because of incomplete records.

Cultural landscape documentation is somewhat narrower in scope than environmental history because the question of nature's character is not so central (Mark 1996). Nevertheless, it emphasises change over time and represents a way of integrating nature with culture. In a park setting, its emphasis becomes one of design, material, change, function, and use, with one of its main effects on heritage management being the broadening of the focus of historic preservation beyond buildings to the associated landscape and environmental context (Mark 1991).

THE VALUES OF WILDERNESS

Decisions affecting environmental policies grow out of a political process (Henning 1971; 1974), in which 'value choice, implicit and explicit . . . orders the priorities of government and determines the commitment of resources within the public jurisdiction' (Simmons *et al.* 1974: 457). Therefore, in order to consider the means by which wilderness is utilised, it is essential to understand what the values of wilderness are. As Henning (1987: 293) observed: 'In the end, the survival of the wilderness will depend upon values being a respected factor in the political and governmental process.'

The value of wilderness is not static. The value of a resource alters over time in accordance with changes in the needs and attitudes of society. As noted above, ideas of the values of primitive and wild land have shifted in relation to the changing perceptions of Western culture. Nevertheless, the dynamic nature of the wilderness resource does not prevent an assessment of its values as they are seen in present-day society. Indeed, such an evaluation is essential to arguments as to why wilderness should be conserved.

Broadly defined, the values of wilderness may be classified as being either anthropocentric or biocentric in nature. The principal emphasis of the anthropocentric approach is that the value of wilderness emerges in its potential for direct human use. In contrast, 'the biocentric perspective places primary emphasis on the preservation of the natural order'. The former approach places societal above ecological values and emphasises recreational and aesthetic rather than environmental qualities. Both perspectives focus on human benefits. However, 'the important distinction between them is the extent to which these benefits are viewed as being independent of the naturalness of wilderness ecosystems' (Hendee *et al.* 1978: 18).

A more radical, and increasingly popular, interpretation of the notion of the value of wilderness has been provided by what is often termed a deep ecology perspective (Godfrey-Smith 1979, 1980; Nash 1990; Oelschlaeger 1991). Deep ecologists argue that wilderness should be held as valuable not just because it satisfies a human need (instrumental value) but as an end in itself (intrinsically valuable). Instrumental anthropocentric values, derived from a Cartesian conception of nature, are regarded as being opposed to a holistic or systematic view 'in which we come to appreciate the symbiotic interdependencies of the natural world' (Godfrey-Smith 1979: 316). The holistic view broadly corresponds with the ecological conception of wilderness (Worster 1977; Nash 1990; Oelschlaeger 1991). However, it goes further by arguing that 'the philosophical task is to try and provide adequate justification . . . for a scheme of values according to which concern and sympathy for our environment is immediate and natural, and the desirability of protecting and preserving wilderness self-evident' (Godfrey-Smith 1979: 316), rather than justified purely according to human needs.

We can, however, provide – and it is important that we can provide – an answer to the question: 'What is the *use* of wilderness?' We certainly ought to preserve and protect wilderness areas as gymnasiums, as laboratories, as stockpiles of genetic diversity, and as cathedrals. Each of these reasons provides a powerful and sufficient instrumental justification for their preservation. But note how the very posing of this question about the *utility* of wilderness reflects an anthropocentric system of values. From a genuinely ecocentric point of view the question, 'What is the *use* of wilderness?' would be as absurd as the question, 'What is the *use* of happiness?'

(Godfrey-Smith 1979: 319)

Hendee *et al.* (1978) identified three consistent themes in the values associated with wilderness: experiental, mental and moral restorational,

Table 7.2: Components of the wilderness experience

Component	Nature of experience	Examples
Aesthetic appreciation	Appreciation of wild nature	Leopold 1921, 1925; Marshall 1930; McKenry 1972a; Smith 1977; Hamilton-Smith 1980; Alexander 1984; Nash 1990.
Religious	The experience of God in the wilderness	McKenry 1972a; Hendee *et al.* 1978; Wright 1980; Hamilton-Smith 1980; Nash 1990.
Escapist	Finding freedom away from the constraints of city living	McKenry 1972a; Smith 1977; Hendee *et al.* 1978; Hamilton-Smith 1980; Hawes 1981.
Challenge	The satisfaction that occurs in overcoming dangerous situations and fully utilising physical skills	McKenry 1972a; Smith 1977; Gardner 1978; Hamilton-Smith 1980; Warboys 1980.
Historic/Romantic	The opportunity to re-live or imagine the experiences of pioneers of the 'frontier' that formed national culture	Leopold 1925; Smith 1977; Hamilton-Smith 1980; Ride 1980; Alexander 1984; Johnston 1985
Solitude	The pleasure of being alone in a wild setting	Lee 1977; Smith 1977; Hamilton-Smith 1980; Hawes 1981; Sinclair 1986.
Companionship	Paradoxically, in relation to the previous category, the desire to share the setting with companions	Lee 1977; Smith, 1977; Hamilton-Smith, 1980.
Discovery/Learning	The thrill of discovering or learning about nature in a natural setting	Smith 1977; Gardner 1978; Hamilton-Smith 1980.
Vicarious appreciation	The pleasure of knowing that wilderness exists without actually ever having seen it	McKenry 1977; Smith 1977; Hawes 1981; Johnston 1985.
Technology	Influence of technological change on outdoor activities	Marsh and Wall 1982.

and scientific. Experiental values highlight the importance of the 'wilderness experience' for recreationists and tourists (Scott 1974; Hamilton-Smith 1980; McKenry 1980). Several themes emerge in an examination of the wilderness experience including the aesthetic, the spiritual and the escapist (Table 7.2). Given its essentially personal nature, the wilderness experience is extremely difficult to define (Scott 1974). Nevertheless, the values recorded from writings on wilderness listed in Table 7.2 do point to the various aspects of the wilderness experience that are realised in human contact with wild and primitive lands.

Associated with the values of the wilderness experience is the idea that wilderness can provide mental and moral restoration for the individual in the face of modern civilisation (Carhart 1920; Boyden and Harris 1978). This values wilderness as a 'reservoir for renewal of mind and spirit' and in some cases offering: 'an important sanctuary into which one can withdraw, either temporarily or permanently, to find respite' (Hendee *et al.* 1978: 12). This harks back to the biblical role of wilderness as a place of spiritual renewal (Funk 1959) and the simple life of Thoreau's *Walden Pond* (Thoreau 1854 (1968)). The encounter with wilderness is regarded as forcing the individual to rise to the physical challenge of wilderness with corresponding improvements in feelings of self-reliance and self worth. As Ovington and Fox (1980: 3) wrote: 'In the extreme', wilderness:

generates a feeling of absolute aloneness, a feeling of sole dependence on one's own capacities as new sights, smells and tastes are encountered . . . The challenge and the refreshing and recreating power of the unknown are provided by unadulterated natural

Table 7.3: The scientific values of wilderness

Value	Description
Genetic resources/biodiversity	Large natural communities such as those provided for in wilderness areas can serve as sources of genetic materials which are potentially useful to man. As more of the world's natural ecosystems are removed or simplified the remaining natural areas will assume even greater importance as storehouses of genetic material.
Ecological research and biological monitoring	Wilderness areas provide protection for large natural ecosystems. Within these areas a variety of research on ecological processes can occur. Research may consist of ecosystem dynamics, comparative ecology, ethology, surveys of fauna and flora, and the relationship of base ecological data to environmental change.
Environmental base-lines	Wilderness areas, representative of particular biomes, can be used as reference areas in the monitoring of environmental change both within the biome and on a global scale.
The evolutionary continuum	Wilderness areas provide the conditions in which the evolutionary continuum of adaptation, extinction and speciation can occur without the direct interference of humans.
Long-term	Wilderness areas provide conditions in which flora and fauna conservation can occur, particularly for those species which require large territories to reproduce and be preserved.

Sources: Smith (1977); Frankel (1978); Hendee *et al.* (1978); Hall (1992a)

wilderness large enough in space for us to get 'lost' in. Here it is possible once again to depend upon our own personal faculties and to hone our bodies and spirits.

The third major theme in the values associated with wilderness is that of the scientific values of wilderness. Table 7.3 identifies the various ways in which wilderness is of importance to science.

The preservation of wilderness is regarded as an essential component in the scientific study of the environment and man's impact on the environment. Furthermore, wilderness has increasingly come to assume tremendous economic importance because of the value of the genetic material that it contains. However, the multi-dimensional nature of the wilderness resource may lead to value conflicts over the use of wilderness areas.

A fourth theme which is inherent in the values of wilderness is that of economic worth. In addition to the economic significance of genetic resources, wilderness has importance as a tourist and recreation attraction. Indeed, the economic valuation of wilderness and natural areas has now become a critical factor in their designation (Hall 1992a), although it should be noted that the economic value of tourism has long been used to justify national park creation in areas that would otherwise be deemed worthless (Runte 1972a, 1972b, 1973, 1974a, 1974b, 1977, 1979). Such a value may be also enhanced through international recognition such as that achieved through listing as a World Heritage site (Mosley 1983).

McKenry (1977) has provided an analysis of the degree to which the values of wilderness are disrupted by activities such as forestry, mining, grazing and road construction. Table 7.4, based on McKenry's research, records the level of compatibility between wilderness values and common disruptive activities. The significant factor which emerges from Table 7.4 is that because of the intrinsic characteristics of wilderness as primitive and remote land the range of uses that can be occur within wilderness areas without diminishing the values of wilderness is extremely limited and will require careful management. As soon as the characteristics of the wilderness resource are infringed through the activities of Western man then wilderness values are reduced. Emphasis is placed upon the impacts of Western society, rather than those of technologically underdeveloped peoples, because as the following discussion will illustrate, the present-day concept of wilderness is a product of Western thought. Indeed, geographers such as Nelson (1982, 1986) have argued for the adoption of a human–ecological approach to wilderness and park management which sees the incorporation of the attitudes and practices of indigenous peoples as being an essential part of a contemporary perspective on the notion of wilderness.

IDENTIFYING WILDERNESS

Although the values of wilderness are well recognised, for management and legislative purposes such values need to be turned into a method by which wilderness values can be mapped in space. In addition, such a process can assist in the provision of conservation, scientific and tourism information, technical advice, recognition of management issues and objectives, the integration of conservation and development, and the design of a national conservation system.

According to Dasmann's (1973: 12) classification of national parks and equivalent reserves, wilderness areas have two principal purposes 'that of protecting nature (defined as primary) and that of providing recreation for those capable of enduring the vicissitudes of wilderness travel by primitive means'. These purposes reflect the values of wilderness identified in the previous section. 'The area is maintained in a state in which its wilderness or primitive appearance is not impaired by any form of development, and in which the continued existence of indigenous animal and plant species is assured' (Dasmann 1973: 12). However, unlike some of the use limitations of strict natural areas, wilderness is available to recreationists.

Dasmann's recognition of wilderness as a discrete land-use category did not appear in the IUCN's (1978) eventual categorisation of conservation areas. However, this does not imply that wilderness has only minimal value as a form of conservation land-use. Rather it is a recognition of the difficulties in transferring the notion of wilderness from a North American to a more universal setting (Eidsvik 1985). Nevertheless, increased public awareness of the environment, sustainable development, World Heritage areas,

Biosphere Reserves and other sites of international conservation significance, highlight the worldwide attention given to the preservation of the earth's remaining wilderness areas. Indeed, the IUCN General Assembly in 1984 recommended 'that all nations identify, designate and protect their wilderness areas on both public and private lands' (Resolution 16/34 in Eidsvik 1987: 19). Yet, such measures need to have a basis by which wilderness can be identified if it is to succeed. Although a wilderness inventory has

Table 7.4: Interactions between values associated with wilderness and common disruptive activities

Common disruptive activities	Water resources	Traditional aboriginal habitat	Wildlife resources and habitat	Plant resources and habitat	Research and education	Wilderness recreation resources	Vicarious appreciation of wilderness	Reserve resource pool
Hydro	1–2	5	3–4	3–4	4–5	4-5	4–5	4–5
Forestry	3–4	5	3–4	3–4	3–4	4–5	4–5	2–3
Mining	3–4	5	3–4	3–4	3–4	4–5	5	4–5
Agriculture	3–4	5	3–4	4–5	3–4	5	5	4–5
Grazing	3–4	4–5	2–3	3–4	2–3	3–4	3–4	2–3
Road	2–3	4–5	2–3	2–3	2–3	4–5	4–5	2–3
Tourism	3–4	5	3–4	2–3	2–3	4–5	4–5	2–3
Off-road	2–3	4–5	2–3	2–3	2–3	4–5	2–3	1–2

Scale of disruption to wilderness values
1 No incompatible interaction (i.e. mutually compatible)
2 Slightly incompatible
3 Substantial incompatibility
4 Slight compatibility only
5 Totally incompatible (i.e. mutually exclusive)

Source: Adapted from McKenry (1977: 209)

CASE STUDY: Wilderness inventory in Australia

One of the key elements in preserving wilderness is the identification of areas of high-quality wilderness that can be incorporated into a national wilderness system. In 1985 the Australian Conservation Foundation and other conservation groups, particularly the Wilderness Society, led the Working Group on Management

of National Parks of the Australian Council of Nature and Conservation Ministers (CONCOM) to examine the establishment of a nationwide system of wilderness areas. CONCOM (1985: 7) recommended that 'an inventory of potential wilderness areas should be compiled by all states and Territories, where possible in

Table 7.5: Australian wilderness inventories

Study and area	Definitions of wilderness	Dimensional criteria	Status of coastal areas	Status of roadworks	Data base
Helman et al. 1976: Eastern New South Wales and south-east Queensland	Large area of land perceived to be natural, where genetic diversity and natural cycles remain essentially unaltered.	• A minimum core area of 25,000 ha; • a core area free of major indentations; • a core area of at least 10 km in width; and • a management (buffer) zone surrounding the core of about 25,000 ha or more.	Coastal areas were not required to meet the dimensional criteria as rigidly as inland areas, due to their linear characteristics and the type of ecosystems and recreation they support.	If roads do not seriously impair the user's perception of the wilderness or the natural functioning of the ecosystem and use can be controlled by management, their presence to a limited degree should not preclude wilderness status.	Landsat images in conjunction with DNM 1:250,000 maps. Aerial reconnaissance to check results.
Stanton and Morgan 1977: Queensland	An extensive pristine area with extremely limited access.	Size based on a core area defined as a day's walk from any access point. A minimum wilderness area (with no core) of about 40,000 ha.	No specific criteria.	Roadworks are incompatible with the strict definition of wilderness.	Aerial photographs at approximately 1:84,000. 1:1,000,000 maps.
Feller et al. 1979: Victoria	As for Helman et al.	As for Helman et al., with special criteria for semi-arid and mountain wilderness, a minimum area of about 150,000 ha for semi-arid wilderness and 50,000 ha for mountain wilderness.	Minimum area as close as possible to 50,000 ha; it may be smaller if • the core area is free of major indentations; • there is a buffer on the landward side of the core; • there is a reasonable length of coast included in the core.	• All two-wheel drive roads and substantial four-wheel drive tracks were excluded from the core. Substantial tracks were included only if they were dead-end and not often used; • sealed and gravel roads were excluded from the core and buffer; and • an acceptable density of tracks was determined for each wilderness.	DNM 1:100,00 maps, aerial photographs at 1:20,000 to 1:50,000. Additional information from Forests Commission, National Parks Service and Land Conservation Council maps. Some field checking was carried out.

Russell et al. 1979: Tasmania	As for Helman et al.	As for Helman et al. with special attention to exclusion of intrusions and the use of natural topographic boundaries to determine core area boundaries. Minimum areas of approximately 10,000 ha were also identified and delineated.	The core of a wilderness area with a coastal boundary may extend to the coastline with an as yet undefined buffer zone extending into the surrounding coastal waters.	The buffer zone boundary excluded all formed access roads and high-density or high-impact vehicular tracks. Vehicular roads and tracks were excluded from the inner core wilderness areas.	Lands Department 1:500,000, 1:250,000 geographic and 1:100,000 topographic maps. Land tenure maps at 1:100,000 and 1:250,000. Aerial photographs at 1:50,000. Some field checking.
Kirkpatrick 1980: south-west Tasmania	An area of land remote from access by mechanised vehicles and within which there is little or no consciousness of the environmental disturbances of Western man.	Wilderness was assumed to exist in relatively undisturbed environments at places greater than 5 km or more from access point or human disturbance. Wilderness quality scores were derived from mathematical functions which represent the relationship between the intensity of the wilderness experience, the time/distance from the access point or nearest sign of human disturbance, and the proportion of the area of visibility occupied by signs of human disturbance.	No special consideration.	No roadworks are included in wilderness areas.	Lands Department 1:100,000 and 1:250,000 map series. Additional information from the National Parks and Wildlife Service and the South West Tasmanian Resource Survey.
Lesslie and Taylor 1983: South Australia	Land which is remote from and undisturbed by the presence and influences of settled people.	Wilderness quality was scaled according to four indicators: remoteness from settlement, remoteness from access, aesthetic primitiveness and bio-physical primitiveness. Wilderness quality was then expressed as classes: very high, high or moderately high. Additive and weighted additive procedures ranked sites according to their wilderness value. High-quality wilderness could then be distinguished.	No special consideration.	High-grade roads were regarded as access points while low-grade roads were treated as aesthetic disturbances. Wilderness quality relates to the density of linear structures (such as roadworks) per unit area. Four wheel drive transport was seen as an appropriate wilderness travel mode in arid and semi-arid areas.	DNM 1:250,000 and 1:100,000 topographic series, Department of Lands 1:50,000 topographic series and South Australian Royal Automobile Association Touring maps.

Study				Data sources
Hawes and Heatley 1985: Tasmania	• largely free of evidence of human artifacts, activity and disturbance; • remote from substantial human artifacts and areas where there is substantial human activity or disturbance; and • remote of access.	Land whose direct remoteness (the map distance between that point and the nearest intrusion) and access remoteness (the minimum time separation between that point and any access point) are d and t respectively, for a suitable choice of values d (km) and t (hours and days).	• Regular use of mechanised vehicles is regarded as a major intrusion; and • no special provision was made for the use of coastal areas by mechanized vehicles as it was assumed that use was still low due to the relative inaccessibility.	The following were regarded as major intrusions: • all roads, and all vehicular tracks accessible to and frequently used by off-road vehicles; • all areas where mechanised transport is intensively used or where the use of such transport has led or is likely to lead to the formation of permanent tracks or cause long-term environmental disturbance.	1:100,000 maps of Tasmania and 1:500,000 vegetation map of Tasmania; primitive country and wilderness were identified manually on 1:500,000 maps.
Lesslie et al. 1987; Preece and Lesslie 1987: Victoria	As for Lesslie and Taylor 1983.	Modification of Lesslie and Taylor methodology for ease of digitising, storing and spatially organising wilderness quality indicators through a grid cell framework. (National Wilderness Inventory State I).	No special consideration.	Three grades of road and track access were distinguished according to the level of access and the degree of use: major two-wheel-drive roads; minor two-wheel-drive roads; and four-wheel-drive tracks.	DNM 1:100,000 topographic maps, Department of Conservation Forests and Lands regional maps, RAC Victoria Guide maps, governmental reports, land tenure information and personal knowledge.
Lesslie et al. 1988: Tasmania	As for Lesslie et al. 1987.	National Wilderness Inventory Stage II, as for Lesslie et al. 1987.	No special consideration.	As for Lesslie et al. 1987.	National 1:250,000 topographic mapping grid, of Tasmania, 1:100,000 topographic maps, 1:25,000 1:100,000 vegetation map topographic series, RAC Tasmania touring information, Forestry Commission 1:100,000 maps, large-scale aerial photography, Forestry Commission Tasmania GIS Forest type database.

Lesslie, Abrahams and Maslen 1991: Cape York Peninsula, Queensland	As for Lesslie et al. 1987.	National Wilderness Inventory Stage III.	No special consideration.	As for Lesslie et al. 1987	National 1:250,000 topographical mapping grid.
Lesslie, Maslen, Canty, Goodwins and Shields 1991: Kangaroo Island, South Australia	As for Lesslie et al. 1987.	National Wilderness Inventory: South Australia.	Lakes, rivers and oceans included as natural bodies.	In addition to the three grades utilised in previous National Wilderness Inventory stages a fourth grade of access was distinguished: very low – 'established but unconstructed vehicle access routes (e.g. beach access) and cleared lines; established walking tracks; cleared land' (p.10)	National 1:250,000 topographical mapping grid, 1:100,000 map series, Department of Lands 1:50,000 map series.
Manidis Roberts Consultants 1991: Western New South Wales	A wilderness area is a large tract of land remote at its core from access and settlement, substantially unmodified by modern technological society or capable of being restored to that state, and of sufficient size to make practical the long term protection of its natural system.	Combination of Helman et al. and National Wilderness Inventory methodology in order to indicate prospective wilderness areas.	Not applicable.	A paved road excludes the surrounding land from a wilderness area classification. Tracks and loose surface roads are acceptable in small quantities, because it is possible to reduce the impact and restore the wilderness value. Walking tracks and maintenance tracks impacts are not considered to reduce wilderness value substantially.	Literature review, contacts within the network of conservation groups, 1:100,000 scale maps, by NATMAP and the Central Mapping Authority.

Source: Hall (1992a: 12–17)
DNM: Division of National Mapping
RAC: Royal Automobile Club

consultation with user groups. The inventory would assess areas within existing parks and extend to other land if appropriate. It would be desirable for a consistent approach to be adopted for the surveys'. However, the hopes of CONCOM were not met. Despite both the quality and quantity of research, no consistent approach to evaluating wilderness in Australia has been accepted by all participants in the process of wilderness identification and management, although the Australian Heritage Commission's National Wilderness Inventory Program came closest. This situation may be due to the academic nature of most wilderness research, the geographic differences between regions, the politics of wilderness preservation, or it may well derive from the intrinsic intangibility of wilderness (Hall 1987, 1992a). Nevertheless, the identification of primitive and remote areas will obviously be critical to the protection and management of wilderness.

WILDERNESS INVENTORIES

> Planners and managers now require detailed information to assist in the identification of areas suitable for designation and protection as wilderness, to monitor the status of the resource, and to develop appropriate and effective management prescriptions. There is also a need for the capacity to assess the impact on wilderness of various development proposals so that alternatives can be examined and a suitable response determined.
> (Lesslie et al. 1988: iv)

Definition is the major problem in the inventory of wilderness. The definition, and its accompanying criteria, provide the source from which all else flows. Two different conceptions of wilderness are generally recognised, one anthropocentric, the other biocentric or ecocentric (see above). From the anthropocentric view, wilderness is seen from a perspective in which human needs are considered paramount. Adherents of this approach tend to ascribe a recreational role

to wilderness. In contrast, the biocentric approach defines 'wilderness in ecological terms and [equates] wilderness quality with a relative lack of human disturbance' (Lesslie and Taylor 1983: 10).

The recreational values of wilderness have tended to be dominant in wilderness literature (Hendee et al. 1978). This is partly the result of the 'Americanisation' of the wilderness concept, where the predominantly recreational perspective of American research has coloured most other studies, but it is also probably related to the way in which the wilderness concept has developed (Nash 1963; Smith 1977; Stankey 1989; Oelschlaeger 1991). Nevertheless, over recent years the biocentric concept of wilderness has become increasingly important in research. This increased priority is most likely related to the growth of importance of ecological research relative to recreational research in national park and reserve management and to a recognition that fauna and flora have an intrinsic right to exist (Nash 1990).

Table 7.5 demonstrates the major features of the wilderness inventories that had been carried out in Australia to the early 1990s by when the methodology for the National Wilderness Inventory supported by the Australian Heritage Commission had become well developed. For each inventory the study area, wilderness definition, dimensional criteria, status of coastal areas, database, and status of roadworks is recorded. The status of roadworks criterion is included because it provides a basis of comparison with the 'roadless area' concept which permeates American notions of wilderness and also illustrates one of the major problems in standardising wilderness criteria (Bureau of Land Management 1978). As Lesslie and Taylor (1983: 23) observed, 'road definition is a major point of contention in the general wilderness literature. Controversy centres on the qualities which make a high grade road an unacceptable intrusion into wilderness and a low grade road a detrimental but nevertheless acceptable intrusion'.

The first Australian study of wilderness of any consequence, the wilderness study of eastern New South Wales and south-east Queensland by Helman *et al.* (1979) was designed as a model for future Australian wilderness inventories and it was applied in Victoria (Feller *et al.* 1979) and Tasmania (Russell *et al.* 1979). However, the inventory procedures may not be valid for arid and semi-arid environments because they were undertaken in relatively humid, forested and mountainous environments (Lesslie and Taylor 1983); also, they failed to recognise the remoteness and primitiveness which constitute the key qualities of wilderness (Mark 1985). Stanton and Morgan's (1977) study of Queensland identified four key areas as fitting rigid conservation-based criteria. Twenty-four other areas were identified as being 'equivalent to the wilderness areas delineated by Helman *et al.* (1979)' in their study of eastern Australia (Morgan 1980).

Kirkpatrick and Haney's (1980) study of south-west Tasmania identified wilderness as a recreational resource, 'as land remote from access by mechanised vehicles, and from within which there is little or no consciousness of the environmental disturbance of western man' (Kirkpatrick and Haney 1980: 331). Kirkpatrick and Haney assigned absolute wilderness quality scores, which had not been attempted in Australian wilderness inventories, although it was characteristic of American ones. However, unlike the United States inventories, Kirkpatrick and Haney focused on the more readily quantifiable characteristics of wilderness: remoteness and primitiveness.

Remoteness and primitiveness are the two essential attributes of wilderness (Helburn 1977). Remoteness is measured 'as the walking time from the nearest access point for mechanised vehicles' while primitiveness, which 'has visual, aural and mental components', is 'determined from measures of the arc of visibility of any disturbance . . . and the distance to the nearest disturbance' (Kirkpatrick and Haney 1980: 331). The identification of remoteness and primitiveness as the essential attributes of a wilderness area helped create the methodological basis for the wilderness inventory of South Australia by Lesslie and Taylor (1983, 1985) and provides the basis for a national survey of wilderness.

Lesslie and Taylor (1983) saw previous wilderness inventory procedures as unsatisfactory because they sought to express a relative concept in absolute terms. They identified four indicators of wilderness quality: remoteness from settlement, remoteness from access, aesthetic primitiveness (or naturalness) and biophysical primitiveness (or naturalness). These indicators were used to provide an inventory of relatively high-quality wilderness areas in South Australia. The attributes of remoteness and primitiveness may be expressed as part of a continuum which indicates the relative wilderness quality of a region (Figure 7.1). A continuum approach can accommodate the ecological and recreational characteristics of a far wider range of environments than the inventories formulated for the higher rainfall areas of Australia (Lesslie and Taylor 1983; Hall and Mark 1985; Hall 1987; Lesslie *et al.* 1987; Lesslie 1991; Manidis Roberts Consultants 1991).

The variation in approaches to wilderness inventory in Australia is 'systematic of confusion concerning the definition of wilderness, since areas which satisfy biocentric considerations need not be consistent with areas which satisfy anthropocentric considerations' (Lesslie and Taylor 1983: 11). The area required to satisfy recreational criteria for wilderness may be much smaller than the area required for maintaining the ecological balance of a region (Valentine 1980). Therefore, the experiential criterion for wilderness remains substantially different to the ecological criterion and the concept of 'wilderness experience' must be separated from

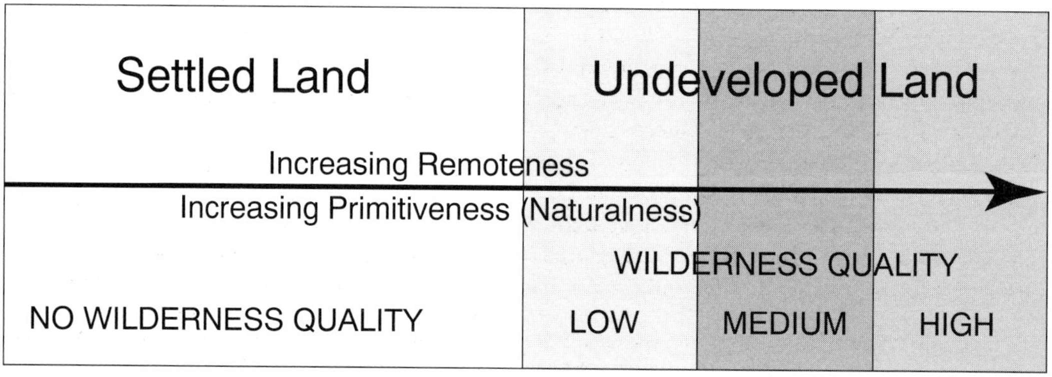

Settled Land	Undeveloped Land		
Increasing Remoteness →			
Increasing Primitiveness (Naturalness) →			
	WILDERNESS QUALITY		
NO WILDERNESS QUALITY	LOW	MEDIUM	HIGH

Figure 7.1: The wilderness continuum
Source: Hall (1992a)

that of 'wilderness area'. As Lesslie and Taylor (1983: 14) observed, there has been an 'almost universal tendency to confuse the *benefits derived from wilderness* with the *nature of wilderness itself*', a point of crucial importance in the delineation, inventory and management of wilderness. Hence, the two attributes which are definitive of wilderness, *remoteness* from the presence and influences of settled people and *primitiveness*, the absence of environmental disturbance by settled people, need to be based at the high-quality end of the wilderness continuum in order to accommodate the anthropocentric and biocentric dimensions of wilderness (Taylor 1990; Lesslie 1991). In Australia, the methodology of Lesslie and Taylor (1983), and modified in the 1987 Victorian inventory (Lesslie *et al.* 1987; Preece and Lesslie 1987), comes closest to achieving this goal and has served as the model for other studies within the Australian Heritage Commission's National Wilderness Inventory (see below). Furthermore, the Lesslie *et al.* (1987) methodology is able to indicate low-quality wilderness areas which are not indicated in an inventory along the lines of Helman *et al.* (1976), but which may nevertheless be of significant conservation and recreation value (Hall 1987).

In 1987 the Australian government, through the Australian Heritage Commission, initiated a National Wilderness Inventory (NWI) to provide information in order to improve decisions about wilderness conservation (Lesslie *et al.* 1991). This action was 'a result of its concern over the rapid decline in area and quality of relatively remote and natural lands in Australia and in recognition that an inventory of the remaining resource was the necessary first step in formulating appropriate measures for conservation and management' (Lesslie, Abrahams and Maslen 1991: 1). The NWI had three main emphases (Lesslie, Mackey and Shulmeister 1988): to compile a national wilderness database; to refine database maintenance procedures and analytical techniques; and to produce information relevant to policy and management issues. Several inventories were conducted under the auspices of the National Wilderness Inventory, including surveys of Victoria (Lesslie *et al.* 1987; Preece and Lesslie 1987); Tasmania (Lesslie *et al.* 1988); South Australia (Lesslie *et al.* 1991); and Queensland (Lesslie, Abrahams and Maslen 1991). In 1990 the NWI was accelerated to provide a comprehensive coverage for the whole of Australia.

'The evaluation of wilderness in the National Wilderness Inventory is based upon the notion of wilderness quality as a continuum of remote and natural conditions from pristine to urban' (Lesslie, Abrahams and Maslen 1991: 6). A spatial framework utilising the techniques of Geographic Information Systems (GIS) is used to sample variation in values of the four wilderness quality indicators. There are two major advantages in using a GIS to formulate wilderness evaluation databases. First, the approach is open-ended: new data can be added and current data modified. Indeed, in Australia,

> information about access and land use is often poorly recorded and lacking in currency. Even the most recently available information may be inaccurate and out of date. This makes the compilation of a reliable database difficult, particularly because of the necessary dependence on published sources for much of the required information.
> (Lesslie, Abrahams and Maslen 1991: 13)

Second, the process is spatially flexible, enabling scale to be matched to purpose. Furthermore, maps showing the distribution of wilderness identified in the inventory can be generated rapidly and efficiently in order to assist decision-making.

FROM IDENTIFICATION TO PRESERVATION

The purpose of wilderness inventory in Australia has, on the whole, been to identify areas of wilderness quality for the possible enactment of conservation measures by government. Inventories provide a systematic means of ensuring the designation areas of high environmental quality. 'Recognition of wilderness is the necessary first step towards protecting, appreciating and managing wilderness areas' (Manidis Roberts Consultants 1991: 2). However, identifying an area as wilderness does not, by itself, ensure that its wilderness qualities can be maintained; this can only be done through the appropriate legislation and management. 'Decisions of this kind are

inevitably judgemental, requiring comparative assessments of the social worth of alternative and often conflicting landuse opportunities' (Lesslie et al. 1988: v). Nevertheless, from a management perspective:

> The delimitation of wilderness management boundaries for any particular location is a separate question. The major point to be made here is that the commonly accepted practice of placing a wilderness management boundary around a location of high wilderness quality, and ensuring no wilderness degrading activities take place within, will not ensure the retention of high wilderness quality. For instance, a development in lesser quality wilderness on the margin of an area of higher quality wilderness will reduce wilderness quality within the higher quality area.
> The lesson to be drawn from this is that areas of lower quality wilderness which fringe areas of high quality are important in maintaining these quality areas. In order to ensure protection of wilderness quality a wilderness management area therefore must include all marginal areas.
> (Lesslie, Abrahams and Maslen 1991: 20)

CONCOM (1986: 8) proposed that the following key criteria be used to identify and evaluate land which has potential as a wilderness area:

- Remoteness and size: a large area, preferably in excess of 25,000 hectares, where visitors may experience remoteness from roads and other facilities.
- Evidence of people: an area with minimal evidence of alteration by modern technology.

However, CONCOM (1985) was not sure that these criteria would reflect differences in landscape and ecological diversity across Australia. The CONCOM criteria may be contrasted with the United States wilderness legislation which suggests a guideline for minimum wilderness size of an area of 5,000 acres (2,023 ha), and where impacted ecosystems may be included if they contribute to the viability and integrity of the wilderness area. One of the

ironies of the criteria for wilderness identification chosen by CONCOM is they exclude many
of the wilderness areas that have already been
established under state legislation! According
to CONCOM (1986: 4), 'Wilderness areas
are established to provide opportunities for the
visitor to enjoy solitude, inspiration and empa-
thy with his or her natural surroundings.' The
CONCOM position is to preserve the 'wilderness experience', not necessarily the intrinsic
qualities of wilderness. However, to preserve
wilderness mainly for recreation values is to
ignore the significant range of other values of a
wilderness area (see above).

Unlike the United States government, the
Australian government does not have vast
areas of federal land upon which wilderness

legislation would be readily enforceable. State
governments, which under the Australian constitution have primary control over land use,
regards the reservation of wilderness areas
under appropriate legislation as being a state
responsibility. This situation therefore means
that unless the Federal Government exercises
its constitutional powers in relation to the
environment, any national wilderness system
can be achieved only through consensus between
the Commonwealth and the various state and
Territory governments. Nevertheless, the NWI
still serves as a valuable management tool
by which to evaluate the potential loss of wilderness quality which new developments might
bring and the potential corresponding loss
of visitor satisfaction.

been undertaken in the United States, probably
the most sustained research programme on
wilderness identification occurred in Australia,
and it is to this case study which we will now
turn.

TOURIST AND RECREATIONAL DEMAND FOR WILDERNESS, NATIONAL PARKS AND NATURAL AREAS

Many values are attached to wilderness in
Western society. Tourism and recreation has
increasingly become significant as one of the main
values attached to wilderness and its conservation
with substantial increases in demands for access
to wilderness in recent years. Demand for tourist
or recreational experience of wild country or
wilderness can be related to two major factors.
First, changing attitudes towards the environment. Second, access to natural areas.

As discussed above, there has been the development of a more favourable response to wild
country in Western society over the last 200 years.

These positive responses have been reinforced
in recent years by the overall development of a
climate of environmental concern which has
served to influence recreation and tourism patterns in natural areas. Going hand-in-hand with
the increase in demand for personal contact with
nature has been the production of natural areas
for tourist consumption. While the setting of a
boundary for a national park may be appropriate
for assisting conservation management it can also
serve as a marker for tourist space on which it is
appropriate for the viewer to gaze. In the same
way that notions of rurality are complex spaces of
production and consumption (see chapter 6), so it
is that the ideas of wilderness and naturalness are
bound up in the commodification of landscapes
for tourist and recreational enjoyment (Olwig and
Olwig 1979; Short 1991; Evernden 1992). For
some, such a perspective is at odds with the
mythology that national parks are ecological
rather than cultural landscapes, but the cultural
idea of wilderness is implicit in the very notion of
wilderness itself. For example, Nash (1982: 1)
noted that wilderness is 'heavily freighted with
meaning of a personal, symbolic and changing

kind'. Although the personal meaning of wilderness may not be of great value when it comes to the designation of wilderness areas from a biocentric perspective which concentrates on actual rather than perceived naturalness (see above), it is of value in terms of the recreation and tourism values of wilderness.

The last decade has witnessed growing academic attention in the field of wilderness perception imagery (e.g. Kliskey and Kearsley 1993; Higham 1997). Stankey and Schreyer (1987), for example, demonstrate that wilderness perceptions may be shaped by a wide range of influences. These include social attitudes, cultural influences, recreational experiences, expectation and personal cognition. It is apparent, therefore, that 'while wilderness environments have an objective physical reality, what makes that reality 'wilderness' rests very much with personal cognition, emotion, values and experience' (Higham and Kearsley 1994: 508).

Kliskey and Kearsley (1993) argue that, while demand for access to wilderness increases, so too does the need to define the extent to which certain qualities of wilderness are sought. Kearsley (1990) illustrates this point with his proposal of a classification of natural areas based on degrees of naturalness, ease of access and the provision of facilities. Implementation of such a classification would facilitate the use of 'degrees of wilderness'. This would allow custodians of tourist facilities to provide for a wide range of wilderness preferences and utilise a wide range of natural settings. The wider spatial distribution of recreationists based upon an appreciation of wilderness perceptions, could contribute to the attainment of two fundamental goals; the maximising of visitor satisfaction and the mitigation of environmental impact at tourist sites. Kliskey and Kearsley (1993) also identified the need for a tourism development approach that does not impact upon the values sought by those who try to avoid the infrastructure of mass tourism, and to protect the social and environmental values that nature-based tourists, or ecotourists, seek. However, this demands that wilderness imagery assumes a role in the marketing and management of recreational and tourism resources in natural settings.

Higham (1997) examined the dimensions of wilderness imagery by international tourists in the South Island of New Zealand. This was done via a list of variables that may be considered appropriate or inappropriate to wilderness recreation and tourism. A five point Likert scale allowed respondents to express the extent to which each variable was considered acceptable or unacceptable. Higham noted that in 'classic' (i.e. high quality in terms of absence of human impact) wilderness terms it should be expected that these variables would be considered to violate or compromise qualities of wilderness recreation. However, only seven of the 21 variables listed received a generally negative response (a mean value less than 3.0). Thirteen variables returned mean values exceeding 3.0 indicating a generally favourable disposition within the sample frame (Table 7.6).

In Higham's (1997) study, 'Distance from civilisation' (mean = 4.0) is clearly an important aspect of wilderness recreation to most inbound tourists. The desire for remoteness is reinforced in the similar high regard for the scale of the location ('big enough to take at least two days to walk across' mean = 3.8). However, there is also a desire for the provision of safeguard mechanisms to reduce risk, with the provision of search and rescue operations receiving the highest mean score (4.3) of all listed variables. The desire for swing bridges and walkwires over watercourses, sign posting and well marked and maintained tracks confirm the widely held desire for wilderness recreation in a natural but relatively safe and humanised environment.

Furthermore, the placement of restrictions upon access and group size, again inconsistent with the notion of wilderness as free from human influences, were widely considered acceptable by inbound visitors. The variables 'restricted access . . .' and 'restricted group size' share a mean of 3.8 placing them favourably on Table 7.6. As

Table 7.6: Responses to variables listed in question 'Indicate whether you feel that the following activities/facilities are acceptable based on your perception of wilderness'

Variable list	1	2	3	4	5	Mean
Search and rescue operations	4.0	3.1	16.6	21.2	49.1	4.3
Distant from towns and cities	4.0	6.7	19.8	22.6	45.1	4.0
Swing bridges/walkwires over rivers or streams	5.2	6.8	21.8	28.3	36.9	3.9
Restricted group size	10.5	9.5	16.6	24.9	33.5	3.8
Restricted access to prevent crowding	10.5	8.0	17.5	25.2	34.2	3.8
Big enough to take at least two days to walk across	8.9	6.8	18.8	24.3	39.4	3.8
Water provided in huts	14.3	7.9	17.7	22.3	36.9	3.6
Maintained huts and shelters	9.5	11.0	22.7	27.9	26.4	3.6
Toilet facilities	14.0	8.5	18.6	22.9	34.5	3.6
Exotic plants/trees (pines, thistles and foxgloves)	11.2	11.6	20.4	20.7	33.4	3.6
Signposts/information	7.0	12.8	24.8	24.5	29.4	3.6
Road access to the start of track	12.5	11.6	27.1	22.0	25.0	3.4
Maintained tracks (e.g. tracks cleared of fallen trees)	13.1	18.3	21.7	27.2	18.0	3.2
Developed camping sites	20.2	14.4	25.2	24.2	14.1	3.0
Grazing of stock (cattle, sheep)	31.2	15.9	25.7	11.9	11.3	2.7
Gas provided in huts for cooking	33.7	16.7	21.3	10.3	16.7	2.6
Stocking of animals and fish not native to NZ	40.1	20.7	21.0	4.6	7.7	2.4
Hunting/trapping	38.6	18.8	21.9	9.3	8.0	2.4
Motorised transport (powered vehicles, boats)	44.9	22.5	15.7	6.2	8.3	2.2
Plantation logging/mining/hydro development	52.8	18.1	16.6	4.3	4.0	2.0
Commercial recreation (e.g. guided tours)	52.7	20.1	13.1	5.5	6.4	2.0

Non-essential/unacceptable 1–2–3–4–5 Essential/acceptable
Source: Higham (1997: 82).

Higham (1997: 83), observed, 'It is quite possible that positive disposition toward these variables derives from trampers visiting high profile tracks on which social carrying capacities are being approached and, at times, exceeded.'

Only seven listed variables returned a mean response which indicated a generally negative disposition (Table 7.6). Six of these seven variables described activities that were likely to present associated social or physical impacts. These included commercial recreation and motorised transport, and grazing of stock and hunting/trapping and plantation logging, respectively. The seventh such variable, 'gas provided in huts for cooking', is exceptional in that it described the provision of a facility that may ease the passage of visitors in backcountry locations. This was the only such variable that was generally rejected by inbound tourists, all other visitor provisions and facilities (huts, shelters, the provision of water and toilet facilities) being considered generally acceptable or compatible with wilderness recreation and tourism.

Higham's (1997) research raises important questions about the role of accessibility to wilderness areas. Indeed, issues of access are now presenting major management problems in wilderness and national parks. For many years access to wilderness was restricted by both the nature of the terrain and the capacity of individuals to travel there. Up until the Second World War the main means of access to most national parks was train, with many of the national parks in the New World actually being developed in association with the railroads (Runte 1974a, 1974b, 1979; Hall 1992a). However, in the post-war period there was a substantial increase in the proportion of personal car ownership, thereby increasing accessibility to parks. National park management agencies also promoted themselves to the public through 'parks for the people campaigns'. Herein though lies the critical situation which many parks and wilderness managers now find themselves in. National Parks were originally established to provide both recreational enjoyment and conservation (Hall 1992a). The founders of the park movement, though, such as John Muir, could never have imagined the almost continuous growth in demand for park access from tourists and recreationists seeking to escape the urban environment. The situation now sees traffic jams occuring in some parks, congestion on walking tracks, displacement of local users by tourists, increased pollution and other adverse environmental impacts and reduced visitor satisfaction (e.g. Hall and McArthur 1996; Higham 1997; Kearsley 1997). Within this context, therefore, park and wilderness managers are now seeking both a better understanding of their visitors and how they may be satisfied, and strategies to find a better match between visitor needs and the capacities of the resource to be used yet retain the values that attract people in the first place (Hall and McArthur 1998).

Historically, tourist profiles have been generated to assist in the planning and management of visitor demand at a particular destination, attraction or site. Analysing tourist demand has traditionally been based on one of two main approaches: a socio-economic approach and a psychological or psychographic approach (see chapter 2). The socio-economic approach attempts to establish a correlation between a visitor's actions at a particular destination and their social position (Lowyck *et al.* 1992). Mathieson and Wall (1982) argue that visitor attitudes, perceptions, and motivations at a destination are influenced by socio-economic characteristics such as age, education, income, residence, and family situation.

Representative of this form of research is Blamey's (1995) study of international ecotourists to Australia, a country which has paid particular attention to promoting its natural feature to tourists in recent years (Hall 1995).

According to Blamey (1995) Japanese and other Asian tourists are the most common inbound visitors to national parks on an absolute basis (21 and 19 per cent respectively of all such visitors), although they have the lowest propensities to do so on a per visit basis. Visitors from Switzerland have the highest propensity to visit natural areas (74 per cent) followed by Germany, Canada, Scandinavia and other European countries (all above 65 per cent). In addition, the economic expenditure of nature-based tourists may be substantial. Blamey (1995) reported that in 1993 the average expenditure per trip for international visitors undertaking bushwalks during their stay was Aus.$2,824 in 1993, or 58 per cent above the average expenditure of all inbound visitors (Aus.$1,788).

Psychographic or psychological approaches classify people into groups according to their lifestyles, including values, motivations and expectations (Blamey and Braithwaite 1997). Lifestyles are distinctions in people's behaviour which are identified and categorised to distinguish different types of respondents. In a comparative study of Canadian tourists, ecotourists were found to be more motivated by features such as wilderness and parks than the rest of the Canadian population in choosing a destination (Kretchmann and Eagles 1990; Eagles 1992).

Higham (1997) investigated a variety of wilderness motivations in an attempt to identify qualities of backcountry recreation that motivate tourists to visit tracks in the New Zealand conservation estate. Eighteen wilderness motivation variables were drawn from a review of the wilderness literature. The degree to which variables were supported or refuted by sample units is illustrated in Table 7.7. Motivation variables are listed on this table in order of mean response. Perhaps not surprisingly, natural beauty and

Table 7.7: Responses to variables listed in question 'Motivations for coming to this location'

Variable list	1	2	3	4	5	Mean
To appreciate the beauty of nature	85.6	11.4	1.8	0.3	0.6	1.2
Scenic beauty/naturalness	84.1	11.4	3.3	0.6	0.6	1.2
To encounter wilderness/untouched nature	61.6	25.5	7.2	3.6	1.2	1.6
To experience remoteness, peace and quiet	46.2	31.2	13.5	4.8	3.3	1.9
To see New Zealand's native birds and animals	38.9	30.7	18.8	8.5	2.1	2.1
To learn about NZ's flora/fauna/natural systems	28.3	32.5	21.7	12.3	4.8	2.3
For a totally new and different experience	30.9	21.6	23.7	14.4	9.0	2.5
To get away from life's pressures	34.2	22.8	16.2	9.6	15.3	2.5
To face the challenges of nature	24.9	24.9	21.6	13.8	12.6	2.7
To undertake strenuous physical exercise	22.8	23.7	23.4	15.6	12.0	2.8
To experience solitude	20.9	19.7	21.8	17.6	13.6	3.0
To meet people and make friends	12.9	18.0	30.2	21.6	16.8	3.1
Relax with family, friends or partner	23.1	17.4	17.1	10.5	30.3	3.1
Self awareness/contemplation	14.2	21.1	25.1	18.1	15.7	3.2
To feel rejuvenated	18.8	14.8	21.2	11.8	24.8	3.3
To learn more about conservation/ management issues	5.4	7.2	28.7	26.9	29.9	3.7
To confront hazards and take risks	5.7	8.7	21.0	24.6	37.5	3.9
To test mental skills (direction, mapping)	6.0	9.0	17.5	27.7	38.6	3.9

Strong motivation 1–2–3–4–5 No motivation
Where percentage figures do not total 100, the difference is explained by non-response to variables
Source: Higham (1997: 81)

outstanding scenery are primary motivations as identified by international visitors. Indeed, Higham (1997: 80) argued that

> this is a result that explains and entrenches the over-whelming popularity of the high status Great Walks [of New Zealand]. The reputations of the Milford, Routeburn, Kepler tracks are, in large part, explained by outstanding opportunities to experience alpine scenery. While these tracks remain those of unequalled scenic repute it is likely that inbound tourist interest in them will remain high.

The 18 variables listed appeared in random order in Higham's (1997) original questionnaire. It is thus interesting to note the order in which variables appear in Table 7.7 when listed by mean response. When paired sequentially, the first 10 listed variables demonstrate consistency in terms of both motivation and mean response. Table 7.7 presents a clear impression of the motivations that attracted

inbound tourists to visit the walking tracks. These, in decreasing strength of motivation, were:

1 To experience natural beauty and outstanding scenery;
2 To experience remote and relatively untouched nature;
3 To experience New Zealand's distinctive flora, fauna and natural systems;
4 To escape civilisation and engage in something completely new and different;
5 To engage in the physical challenge that natural areas present.

The desire to experience solitude, one of the classic principles of wilderness recreation (see above), represents the eleventh variable listed on Table 7.7. This variable receives a mean score of 3.0. The last seven listed variables returned mean scores that described a negative rather than positive disposition. The last two relate to the physical and mental challenges that classic wilderness recreation offers, yet these receive distinctly low levels of endorsement by tourists. Such a situation therefore raises fundamental questions about the benefits which people are seeking when they visit wilderness areas and the extent to which agencies should seek to supply such benefits.

Another major issue in terms of tourism and recreation in national parks and wilderness areas is the extent to which tourism economically benefits such peripheral areas. Researchers disagree on the economic impact of nature tourists on local communities (Hull 1998; Weaver 1998). On the one hand there is the argument that since these visitors spend most of their time out on the land or in the wilderness their economic impacts on local communities are minimal (e.g. Rudkin and Hall 1996). On the other, environmentalists have promoted tourism as a non-consumptive use of nature and a win–win development strategy for underdeveloped rural areas. As an influential World Wildlife Fund publication on ecotourism states:

> One alternative proposed as a means to link economic incentives with natural resources preservation is the promotion of nature tourism. With increased tourism to parks and reserves, which are often located in rural areas, the populations surrounding the protected areas can find employment through small-scale tourism enterprises. Greater levels of nature tourism can also have a substantial economic multiplier effect for the rest of the country. Therefore, tourism to protected areas demonstrates the value of natural resources to tourists, rural populations, park managers, government officials and tour operators.
>
> (Boo 1990: 3)

Indeed, Boo (1990) found that nature oriented tourists had higher daily expenditures than those tourists who were not nature oriented. Grekin and Milne (1996) also argued that ecotourism is an industry where the physical isolation of a destination may work to its economic advantage

by providing a taste of the unknown and the untouched. Similarly, Stoffle *et al.* (1979) in a study on indigenous tourism in the south-western United States also found that tourists who felt positive about residents at a particular destination were likely to purchase items to remember their experience. Hull (1998), in examining the average daily expenditure patterns of ecotourists on the North Shore of Quebec, found that package ecotourists had a substantially higher average daily expenditure than independent tourists. Accommodation was the area of largest expenditure with package tourists spending on average (Can$42.04) and independent tourist spending (Can.$11.76). For package tourists, accommodation costs represented 59.6 per cent of their average daily expenditure while for independent tourists accommodation costs represent only 23.8 per cent. Package tourists' second largest expenditure category was transportation at 22.2 per cent while for independent tourists meals were the second largest category at approximately 17.8 per cent (Hull 1998). Expenditure patterns show that over 75 per cent of the package tourists' costs are restricted to accommodation and transportation while independent tourists, even though they spend less overall, are spending more money in different sectors of the local economy and contributing more to the sustainability of the industry. Hull's findings are supported by those of Place (1998: 117) who also noted that

> Ecotourism can provide an economic base, but it does not happen automatically, or without social and environmental impacts. If it is to be sustainable, local populations must be allowed to capture a significant amount of the economic multipliers generated by tourism. Successful reduction of multiplier leakage requires local participation in development planning and outside assistance with the provision of necessary infrastructure, training and credit.

Ecotourism, tourism and recreation in natural environments, undoubtedly can bring economic benefits to both communities on the periphery and to the wholesalers and suppliers of such experiences, and it is for this reason that increasing attention is being given to the supply of the experience of wild nature.

SUPPLYING THE WILDERNESS AND OUTDOOR RECREATION EXPERIENCE

In many ways the idea that one can 'supply' a wilderness or outdoor recreation experience seems at odds with the implied freedom of wilderness. However, the tourism industry is in the business of producing such experiences, while national parks and wilderness areas, by virtue of their formal designation are places which have been defined as places where such experiences can be found. One of the most important transformations in the production of leisure on the periphery has been the way in which the initial construction of national parks as places of spectacular scenery and national monuments for the few were transformed into places of mass recreation in the 1950s and 1960s and to places of tourist commodification in the 1980s and 1990s, particularly through the notion of ecotourism.

A number of different meanings applied to the concept of 'ecotourism' (Valentine 1992; Hall 1995; Weaver 1998) which range from 'shallow' to 'deeper' statements of the tourism environment relationship:

- ecotourism as any form of tourism development which is regarded as environmentally friendly and has the capacity to act as a branding mechanism for some forms of tourist products;
- ecotourism as 'green' or 'nature-based' tourism which is essentially a form of *special interest* tourism and refers to a specific market segment and the products generated for that segment;
- ecotourism as a form of nature-based tourism that involves education and interpretation of the natural environment and is managed to be ecologically and culturally sustainable.

The Australian Office of National Tourism (1997), for example, defined ecotourism as 'nature-based tourism that involves interpretation of the natural and cultural environment and ecologically sustainable management of natural areas'.

> Ecotourism is seen as ecologically and socially responsible, and as fostering environmental appreciation and awareness. It is based on the enjoyment of nature with minimal environmental impact. The educational element of ecotourism, which enhances understanding of natural environments and ecological processes, distinguishes it from adventure travel and sightseeing.
>
> (Office of National Tourism 1997)

Many countries around the world are now focusing on the supply of an ecotourism product. Unfortunately, much of the ecotourism promotion best fits into the shallow end of the ecotourism spectrum, in that much of it revolves around the branding of a product or destination rather than seeking to ensure sustainability. Indeed, one of the greatest problems of ecotourism is the extent to which such experiences can be supplied without a limit on the number of people who visit natural areas, as visitation may not only lead to environmental damage, but also perceptions of crowding thereby reducing the quality of the experience. As Kearsley *et al.* (1997: 71) noted, 'From the viewpoint of tourism . . . it is the impact of tourists upon tourists that has increasingly led to concern. Issues of crowding, displacement and host community dissatisfaction have risen to prominence'.

Crowding is a logical consequence of rising participation in outdoor recreation and nature based tourism activities (Gramann 1982). It should therefore be of no great surprise that crowding is the most frequently studied aspect of wilderness recreation (Shelby *et al.* 1989). Indeed, many issues in wilderness management and outdoor recreation, such as satisfaction, desired experiences, carrying capacity and displacement are all related to the primary issue of crowding. Furthermore, social carrying capacity is increasingly being recognised

Plate 7.1: Mount Cook National Park, New Zealand – is it still within the perceived threshold of a wilderness experience given the large amount of people who visit it?

Plate 7.2: Erosion on a walking trail in Noosa Heads National Park, Queensland, Australia.

Plate 7.3: National parks are often under enormous pressure in terms of visitor numbers. The Grand Canyon National Park in the United States receives over five million visitors a year.

as being the most critical of all types of carrying capacity as ecological impacts can often be controlled by management actions other than limiting use levels; for example, facilities can be extended and made more effective, and physical capacities are usually high (Shelby and Heberlein 1984).

Importantly, crowding should not be confused with density. Density refers to the number of individuals in a given area while crowding refers to the evaluation of a certain density (Graefe *et al.* 1984a, 1984b). In a review of 35 studies of crowding, Shelby *et al.* (1989) identified four sources of variation in perceptions of crowding:

- *temporal variation* – either in terms of time or season within which outdoor recreation activities are taking place. For example, weekends and public holidays are likely to experience higher than average use densities thereby resulting in inflated perceptions of crowding;
- *resource availability* – variation of resource availability, e.g. the opening and closing of tracks in alpine areas, may act to alter the presence of people at recreational sites;
- *accessibility* – distance (expressed in terms of time, cost, spatial distance or perceived distance) will affect crowding and densities, particularly if there is little or no recreation resource substitution; and
- *management strategies* – management can intervene directly, e.g. use restrictions, or indirectly, e.g. demarketing, to reduce visitor numbers at recreation sites.

Shelby *et al.* (1989) also investigated the hypothesis that crowding perceptions would vary according to the type of recreational use. However, they were not able to resolve this hypothesis. However, recent research by Higham (1996) indicates that recreational use history is a substantial factor in influencing perceptions of crowding.

Concerns over crowding are closely related to issues of social carrying capacity in wilderness and outdoor recreation areas. Social carrying capacity in recreation areas 'has typically been defined as a use level beyond which some measure of experiential quality becomes impaired' (Graefe *et al.* 1984b: 500). However, as chapter 6 noted, there is no 'absolute value' of social carrying capacity, there is no single response to specific levels of use in a particular area. Instead, indicators of social or behavioural capacity will be dependent on the management objectives for a given recreation site (Greafe *et al.* 1984a). Shelby and Heberlein (1986: 21) therefore refined this definition to read: 'Social carrying capacity is the level of use beyond which social impacts exceed acceptable levels specified by evaluative standards.'

Several factors have been identified as influencing crowding norms, with a number of variables contributing to the interpretation of increasing recreational use density as perceived crowding (Manning 1985):

- visitor characteristics: motivations, preferences and expectations, previous use experiences, visitors' attitudes towards wilderness;
- characteristics of those encountered: type and size of groups encountered, behaviour of those encountered, perceptions of alikeness;
- situational variables: type of area and location within an area.

Manning (1985) concluded that crowding norms are extremely diverse, yet the significance of visitor characteristics as a factor and the psychographic variables which comprise this factor indicate the possibility of a high degree of agreement being reached on crowding norms within particular subsets of the recreational population. This latter possibility highlights the importance of managers having a good understanding of the psychographic and demographic profiles of their visitor base in order to optimise levels of visitor satisfaction and attainment of management objectives (Hall and McArthur 1998).

Density alone provides no measure of visitor

satisfaction. Satisfaction will be determined by expectations, prior experiences, and commitment to the recreational activity. Perceptions of crowding are therefore influenced by use densities, but this relationship is mediated by a range of other factors and variables (Graefe *et al.* 1984a). Indeed, a range of reactions or coping strategies are possible in recreationalist response to decreased recreational satisfaction, which may result not only from crowding, but also from such factors as littering, noise and worn campsites (e.g. Anderson and Brown 1984). Such reactions include:

- modifying behavioural patterns, e.g. by camping rather than using developed facilities;
- changing time of visit or use, e.g. visiting in shoulder or off-peak periods in order to avoid conflicts with other users;
- changing perceptions, expectations and recreation priorities (also referred to as product shift (Shelby *et al.* 1988), e.g. developing a new set of expectations about a recreational setting in order to maintain satisfaction;
- recreational displacement, where those who are most sensitive to recreational conflicts seek alternative sites to achieve desired outcomes.

Of the above strategies, recreational displacement is probably the most serious from the manager's perspective as displacement appears to be a reality of wilderness use regardless of the level of recreational experience (Becker 1981; Anderson and Brown 1984). Therefore, increases in numbers of visitors to wilderness and other natural areas, particularly at a time when such areas have to cope with their promotion as places for ecotourism experiences as well as the pressures of traditional recreation users may lead to a decline in wilderness qualities as users are displaced from site to site. For example, in the

Plate 7.4: Access to national parks and other places of scenic beauty is a major area. Should cars be allowed within national parks or should they be kept outside? Many national parks now suffer problems of traffic congestion more typically associated with urban centres. Rocky Mountain National Park, United States.

Plate 7.5: In order to minimise erosion caused by large visitor numbers in natural areas, substantial site and trail hardening may have to be undertaken as here in the Waitakere Regional Park, Auckland, New Zealand. However, what effects does such work have on the visitor experience and does the increased ease of access actually encourage yet more visitation?

case of major walking tracks in the South Island of New Zealand, Kearsley (1997: 95) observes:

> In a context where there is a clear hierarchy of sites, as in Southern New Zealand, displacement down the hierarchy is an all-too-likely possibility . . . the very large increase in overseas users of the Routeburn has displaced some domestic recreationists (and perhaps some tourists) to second tier tracks such as the Hollyford or Dart-Rees, or, indeed, out of tramping altogether. Similarly, their arrival might displace others yet further down the hierarchy to even less well known places, and there is a danger that trampers might be forced into wild and remote environments that are beyond their safe capacity . . .
>
> One consequence of this, if it is happening, is increased visitor pressure on more remote locations and displacement of moderate wilderness purists to a limited reservoir of pristine sites . . . with obvious physical impacts. A second consequence is the effect upon host community satisfaction, as domestic recreationists are displaced by overseas visitors. Both of these consequences have serious implications for the sustainability of tourism.

The case of crowding and other variables which influence visitor satisfaction and behaviour, including displacement, highlights the significance of understanding the factors of supply and demand of the recreation and tourist experience (see chapters 2 and 3). Just as importantly they indicate the need for sound planning and management practice in trying to achieve a balance between the production and consumption of tourism and recreation, particularly in environmentally sensitive areas. And it is to the geographer's substantial contribution to these areas that the next chapter will turn.

CONCLUSION

This chapter has highlighted a number of areas in which geographers have contributed to research and scholarship in the tourism and recreation periphery. From the *Topophilia* of Tuan (1974), the sacred space of Graber (1978) and the breathtaking historical analysis of Glacken (1967), geographers have been at the forefront not only of understanding the human relationship to the natural environment and wild lands in particular, but also to the behaviours of tourists and recreationists in the wilderness. In addition geographers have assisted in developing techniques to identify wilderness areas, undertake environmental histories and to cast light on their values.

As a resource analyst, the geographer therefore 'seeks to understand the fundamental characteristics of natural resources and the processes through which they are allocated and utilised' (Mitchell 1979: 3). The geographer's task is also relayed by Coppock (1970: 25), who has made remarks of direct relevance to a better understanding of the relationship between tourism, recreation and wilderness conservation: 'A concern with problem solving and with the processes of human interaction with resources, particularly in respect of decision making, will powerfully assist a more effective geographical contribution to conservation.'

8

TOURISM AND RECREATION PLANNING AND POLICY

Geographers have long been interested in planning. Indeed, a number of academic departments combine geography and planning, while many geography students have gone on to specialise in planning as a professional career. Planning and the associated area of policy analysis are therefore substantive areas of applied geographical research, particularly as geographers have sought to make their work more relevant to the society in which they work (Johnston 1991).

It should therefore come as no surprise that tourism and recreation planning and policy have long been major areas of interest for geographers. This chapter examines the nature of recreation and tourism planning and policy and then goes on to discuss the contributions that geographers have made in these fields, particularly with respect to the role that planning and policy makes at a regional or destination level. More specific applications in recreational and tourism planning have been introduced in earlier chapters and so this chapter discusses many of the principles, concepts and geographical contributions to the field as a whole.

RECREATION AND TOURISM PLANNING AND POLICY

Planning for tourism has traditionally focused on land-use zoning, site development, accommodation and building regulations, the density of tourist development, the presentation of cultural, historical and natural tourist features, and the provision of infrastructure including roads and sewage (Getz 1987). However, in recent years, tourism planning has adapted and expanded to include broader environmental and socio-cultural concerns, and the need to develop and promote economic development strategies at local, regional and national scales, particularly within an increasingly globalised tourism environment (Pearce 1989; Hall 1995; Hall *et al.* 1997).

The diverse nature of recreation and tourism has meant that the industry is difficult for policy makers and planners to define and grasp conceptually. This has meant that there have been substantial difficulties for policy makers to develop appropriate policies, while the coordination of the various elements of the recreation and tourism product has been extremely difficult (Hall 1994; Hall and Jenkins 1995). Yet, somewhat paradoxically, it is the very nature of the industry, particularly the way in which local communities, their culture and lifestyles, and the environment are part of the broad leisure product, which makes planning so important (Murphy 1985) and, perhaps, academically appealing (Hall *et al.* 1997).

What is planning? 'Planning is a process, a process of human thought and action based upon that thought – in point of fact, forethought, thought for the future – nothing more or less than this is planning, which is a very general human activity' (Chadwick 1971: 24). Similarly, according to Hall (1982a: 303), planning, 'should aim to provide a resource for democratic and informed decision-making. This is all planning can legitimately do, and all it can pretend to do. Properly understood, this is the real message of the systems revolution in planning and its aftermath.' Hall's (1982a) observation, reflects Johnston's (1991: 209) comment that underlying the geographer's involvement in planning and policy is 'the basic thesis that geographers should be much more involved in the creation and monitoring and policies', yet, as he went on to note, 'what sort of involvement?', a point discussed in chapter 1.

As a general field of research, tourism planning has mirrored broader trends within the urban and regional planning traditions (e.g. Getz 1986a, 1987; Hall 1999) primarily because it has been focused on destination planning rather than individual tourism business planning. Moreover, planning for tourism tends to reflect the economic, environmental and social goals of government and, increasingly, industry interests, at whichever level the planning process is being carried out (Hall *et al.* 1997).

Planning for tourism occurs in a number of forms (development, infrastructure, promotion and marketing); structures (different government and non-government organisations); scales (international, national, regional, local and sectoral) and times (different time scales for development, implementation and evaluation). However, planning is rarely exclusively devoted to tourism *per se*. Instead, planning for tourism tends to be 'an amalgam of economic, social and environmental considerations' which reflect the diversity of the factors which influence tourism development (Heeley 1981: 61). In contrast, recreational planning has assumed a more integrated form, being an integral part of most public sector planning schemes alongside other fundamental themes such as housing. This is very evident in urban areas as chapter 5 shows. In this respect, recreation is often a local need-based activity or a regional planning function to deal with the impacts, needs and effects of visitors on the host community. The contribution of recreation to quality of life issues in the local and visitor population, particularly in park, national park and natural areas remains a well developed planning activity as described by Patmore (1983) and contributions in Lavery (1971) (also see chapter 5 which notes the contribution of geographers to wilderness planning activities). Therefore, recreational activity has

Table 8.1: International tourism policies 1945–present

Phase	Characteristics
1945–55	The dismantling and streamlining of the police, customs, currency, and health regulations that had been put into place following the second world war.
1955–70	Greater government involvement in tourism marketing in order to increase tourism earning potential.
1970–85	Government involvement in the supply of tourism infrastructure and in the use of tourism as a tool of regional development.
1985–present	Continued use of tourism as a tool for regional development, increased focus on environmental issues, reduced direct government involvement in the supply of tourism infrastructure, greater emphasis on the development of public–private partnerships and industry self-regulation, and the development of tourism business networks to meet policy goals.

Source: After Hall (1994a), (1999)

emerged as largely a public sector exercise where geographers have not made major contributions to the methodology, activities and actions associated with this concept. Where geographers have made major contributions, they have been in the area of policy in the 1970s (e.g. Coppock (1976) and Patmore (1973)) advising government on sport and recreation policy. For this reason, this chapter focuses on tourism as recreational planning is more accepted as a public sector activity (see pp. 151–52) and geographers have made fewer lasting methodological or critical contributions to recreational planning and policy in the 1980s and 1990s. Furthermore, much of what is considered as tourism outside urban areas also subsumes recreational activity in natural and wilderness areas (see chapter 7).

Tourism planning does not just refer specifically to tourism development and promotion, although these are certainly important. The focus and methods of tourism planning have evolved to meet the demands which have been placed on government with respect to tourism. For example, international tourism policies amongst the developed nations can be divided into four distinct phases (Table 8.1). Of particular importance, has been the increased direct involvement of government in regional development, environmental regulation and the marketing of tourism, although more recently there has been reduced direct government involvement in the supply of tourism infrastructure, greater emphasis on the development of public–private partnerships and industry self-regulation.

The attention of government to the potential economic benefits of tourism and recreation has provided the main driving force for tourism planning (Richards 1995; Charlton and Essex 1996). The result has often been 'top-down planning and promotion that leaves destination communities with little input or control over their own destinies' (Murphy 1985: 153). However, attention is gradually becoming focused on the need to integrate social and environmental concerns into the economic thrust of much tourism

development (Pearce 1989). Tourism must be integrated within the wider planning processes in order to promote certain goals of economic, social and environmental enhancement or maximisation that may be achieved through appropriate tourism development (Hall 1995). As Murphy (1985: 156) observed, 'planning is concerned with anticipating and regulating change in a system, to promote orderly development so as to increase the social, economic, and environmental benefits of the development process'. Therefore, tourism planning must be 'a process, based on research and evaluation, which seeks to optimize the potential contribution of tourism to human welfare and environmental quality' (Getz 1987: 3).

APPROACHES TO TOURISM PLANNING

Getz (1987) identified four broad traditions or approaches to tourism planning: 'boosterism', an economic, industry-oriented approach, a physical/spatial approach, and a community-oriented approach which emphasises the role that the destination community plays in the tourism experience. As Getz (1987: 5) noted, 'the four traditions are not mutually exclusive, nor are they necessarily sequential. Nevertheless, this categorisation is a convenient way to examine the different and sometimes overlapping ways in which tourism is planned, and the research and planning methods, problems and models associated with each'. To these four approaches, Hall (1995) added a further approach, that of sustainable tourism planning. Table 8.2 provides a detailed overview of the components of each tourism planning approach. Different planning approaches, while not mutually exclusive, conceptualise tourism planning in distinct ways. Each perspective differs in its underlying assumptions about planning, problem definition, the appropriate level of analysis, and research methods. Researchers therefore choose their perspective/s according to their profession, education, values, the organisational

Table 8.2: Tourism planning approaches: assumptions, problem definition, methods and models

Planning tradition	Underlying assumptions and related attitudes	Definition of the tourism planning problem	Some examples of related methods	Some examples of related models
Boosterism	• tourism is inherently good • tourism should be developed • cultural and natural resources should be exploited • industry as expert • development defined in business/corporate terms	• how many tourists can be attracted and accommodated? • how can obstacles be overcome? • convincing hosts to be good to tourists	• promotion • public relations • advertising • growth targets	• demand forecasting models
Economic	• tourism equal to other industries • use tourism to: create employment, earn foreign revenue and improve terms of trade, encourage regional development, overcome regional economic disparities • planner as expert • development defined in economic terms	• can tourism be used as a growth pole? • maximisation of income and employment multipliers • influencing consumer choice • providing economic values for externalities • providing economic values for conservation purposes	• supply–demand analysis • benefit–cost analysis • product–market matching • development incentives • market segmentation	• management processes • tourism master plans • motivation • economic impact • economic multipliers • hedonistic pricing
Physical/spatial	• tourism as a resource user • ecological basis to development • tourism as a spatial and regional phenomenon • environmental conservation • development defined in environmental terms • preservation of genetic diversity	• physical carrying capacity • manipulating travel patterns and visitor flows • visitor management • concentration or dispersal of visitors • perceptions of natural environment • wilderness and national park management • designation of environmentally sensitive areas	• ecological studies • environmental impact assessment • regional planning • perceptual studies	• spatial patterns and processes • physical impacts • resort morphology • LAC (limits of acceptable change) • ROS (recreational opportunity spectrum) • TOS (tourism opportunity spectrum) • destination life cycles

Community	• need for local control • search for balanced development • search for alternatives to 'mass' tourism development • planner as facilitator rather than expert • development defined in socio-cultural terms	• how to foster community control? • understanding community attitudes towards tourism • understanding the impacts of tourism on a community • social impact	• community development • awareness and education • attitudinal surveys • social impact assessment	• ecological view of community • social/perceptual carrying capacity • attitudinal change • social multiplier
Sustainable	• integration of economic, environmental and socio-cultural values • tourism planning integrated with other planning processes • holistic planning • preservation of essential ecological processes • protection of human heritage and biodiversity • inter and intra-generational equity • achievement of a better balance of fairness and opportunity between nations • planning and policy as argument • planning as process • planning and implement-ation as two sides of the same coin • recognition of political dimension of tourism	• understanding the tourism system • setting goals, objectives and priorities • achieving policy and administrative coordination in and between the public and private sectors • cooperative and integrated control systems • understanding the political dimensions of tourism • planning for tourism that meets local needs and trades successfully in a competitive marketplace	• strategic planning to supersede conventional approaches • raising producer awareness • raising consumer awareness • raising community awareness • stakeholder input • policy analysis • evaluative research • political economy • aspirations analysis • stakeholder audit • environmental analysis and audit • interpretation	• systems models • integrated models focused on places and links and relationships between such places • resources as culturally constituted • environmental perception • business ecology • learning organisations

Sources: After Getz (1987); Hall et al. (1997); Hall (1999)

context within which they work, and the nature of the planning problem.

Boosterism is the simplistic attitude that tourism development is inherently good and of automatic benefit to the hosts. Residents of tourist destinations are not involved in the decision-making, planning and policy processes surrounding tourism development. According to Getz (1987: 10):

> Boosterism is still practised, and always will be, by two groups of people: politicians who philosophically or pragmatically believe that economic growth is always to be promoted, and by others who will gain financially by tourism. They will go on promoting it until the evidence mounts that they have run out of resources to exploit, that the real or opportunity costs are too high, or that political opposition to growth can no longer be countered. By then the real damage has usually been done.

In contrast, an economic planning approach towards tourism aims to promote growth and development in specific areas. The planning emphasis is on the economic impacts of tourism and its most efficient use to create income and employment benefits for regions or communities.

One of the main areas to which geographers have contributed is the physical/spatial approach under which tourism is regarded as having an ecological base with a resultant need for development to be based upon certain spatial patterns, capacities or thresholds that would minimise the negative impacts of tourism on the physical environment (Getz 1983, 1987). Indeed, much of the concern with the physical and behavioural carrying capacities of specific locations discussed in the previous chapter falls into this particular approach. Research by Page and Thorn (1997) in New Zealand reviewed the impact of a market-led approach to tourism planning at the national level where a lack of rational national policy or planning advice has significant implications for local areas which are required to deal with the micro scale issues. The ability to incorporate sustainable planning principles and to manage visitors was also a notable problem for many public sector planning agencies highlighted by

Page and Thorn (1997). A more preferable focus for local areas is the contribution which a community approach can make.

A community approach emphasises the social and political context within which tourism occurs and advocates greater local control over the development process. Geographers have also been active in this area as it builds upon a strong urban and regional planning tradition that is concerned with being relevant to community needs. The most well known exemplar of this approach is the work of Murphy (1985).

A community approach to tourism planning is as an attempt to formulate a 'bottom up' form of planning, which emphasises development *in* the community rather than development *of* the community. Under this approach, residents are regarded as the focal point of the tourism planning exercise not the tourists, and the community, which is often equated with a region of local government, is usually used as the basic planning unit. Nevertheless, substantial difficulties will arise in attempting to implement the concept of community planning in tourist destinations. As Dowling (1993: 53) noted 'research into community attitudes towards tourism is reasonably well developed, although incorporation of such views into the planning process is far less common'. For example, Jenkins (1993) identified seven impediments to incorporating public participation in tourism planning:

- the public generally has difficulty in comprehending complex and technical planning issues;
- the public is not always aware of or understands the decision-making process;
- the difficulty in attaining and maintaining representativeness in the decision-making process;
- the apathy of citizens;
- the increased costs in terms of staff and money;
- the prolonging of the decision-making process;
- adverse effects on the efficiency of decision-making.

One notable exception here is the research reported by Page and Lawton (1997) which sought to incorporate residents' views as part of the planning process for tourism in a local area.

As the above discussion indicates, one of the major difficulties in implementing a community approach to tourism planning is the political nature of the planning process. Community planning implies a high degree of public participation in the planning process. However, public participation implies that the local community will have a degree of control over the planning and decision-making process. Therefore, a community approach to tourism planning implies that there will be a need for partnership in, or community control of, the tourism development process. Yet power is not evenly distributed within a community and some groups and individuals will therefore have the ability to exert greater influence over the planning process than others (Hall and Jenkins 1995). Therefore, in some circumstances, the level of public involvement in tourism planning can be more accurately described as a form of tokenism in which decisions or the direction of decisions has already been prescribed by government. Communities rarely have the opportunity to say 'no' (Hall 1995). Nevertheless, as Murphy (1985: 153) argued: 'If tourism is to become the successful and self-perpetuating industry many have advocated, it needs to be planned and managed as a renewable resource industry, based on local capacities and community decision making', with an increased emphasis being given to the interrelated and evolutionary nature of tourist development.

More recently geographers have become concerned with the development of sustainable approaches towards tourism (Hall and Lew 1998). Sustainable tourism planning is therefore an integrative form of tourism planning, which bears much similarity to the many of the traditional applied concerns of the geographer as resource manager (Mitchell 1979). Sustainable tourism planning seeks to provide lasting and secure livelihoods with minimal resource depletion, environmental degradation, cultural disruption and social instability. The approach therefore tends to integrate features of the economic, physical/spatial and community traditions.

Dutton and Hall (1989) identified five key elements of sustainable tourism planning: cooperative and integrated control systems, development of industry coordination mechanisms, raising consumer awareness, raising producer awareness, and strategic planning to supersede conventional approaches.

COOPERATIVE AND INTEGRATED CONTROL SYSTEMS

In a typical planning process, stakeholders are consulted minimally, near the end of the process, and often via formal public meetings. 'The plan that results under these conditions tends to be a prescriptive statement by the professionals rather than an agreement among the various parties'; by contrast, an interactive style 'assumes that better decisions result from open, participative processes' (Lang 1988 in Wight 1998: 87). An integrative planning approach to tourism planning and management at all levels (from the regional plan to individual resort projects) would assist in the distribution of the benefits and costs of tourism development more equitably, while focusing on improved relationships and understanding between stakeholders may also assist in agreement on planning directions and goals. However, cooperation alone will not foster commitment to sustainable development without the incentive of increased mutual benefits.

One of the most important aspects of cooperative and integrated control systems is the selection of indicators of sustainability. The role of an indicator is to make complex systems understandable. An effective indicator or set of indicators helps a destination, community or organisation determine where it is, where it is going, and how far it is from chosen goals. Sustainability indicators provide a measure of the long-term viability of a destination or community based on the degree to which its economic, environmental, and social systems are efficient and integrated (Gill and Williams 1994; Hall 1999). However, indicators are only useful in the context of appropriately framed questions (Hall and McArthur 1998). In choosing indicators, one must have a clear understanding of planning goals and objectives. For example, a typology of indicators might include:

- economic, environmental and social indicators (measuring changes in the state of the economy, environment and society);
- sustainability indicators (measuring distance between that change and a sustainable state of the environment);
- sustainable development indicators (measuring progress to the broader goal of sustainable development in a national context).

There has been a tendency to pick indicators that are easiest to measure and reflect most visible change, therefore important concerns from a holistic perspective of tourism development, such as the social and cultural impacts of tourism, may be dropped. In addition, appropriate indicators may not be selected because organisations may not want to be held accountable for the results of evaluations (Hall and McArthur 1998). According to Wight (1998) indicators to reflect desired conditions and use should ideally:

- be directly observable;
- be relatively easy to measure;
- reflect understanding that some change is normal, particularly in ecological systems, and be sensitive to changing use conditions;
- reflect appropriate scales (spatial and temporal);
- have ecological, not just institutional or administrative boundaries;
- encompass relevant structural, functional, and compositional attributes of the ecosystem;
- include social, cultural, economic and ecological components;
- reflect understanding of indicator function/

type (e.g. baseline/reference, stress, impact, management, system diagnostic);
- relate to the vision, goals and objectives for the destination region; and
- be amenable to management.

DEVELOPMENT OF INDUSTRY COORDINATION MECHANISMS

While a range of formal and informal tourism industry bodies exist in almost every country in the world, few of these address such complex issues such as sustainable development. The support by industry groups of environmental codes is perhaps indicative of possible directions if common needs can be agreed upon. However, for such guidelines to be effective, it must be ensured that they do not constitute a 'lowest common denominator' approach to development and implementation (Hall 1995). Therefore, government and public interest groups tend to use their influence to encourage greater industry coordination on planning issues by creating structures and processes which enable stakeholders to talk to each other and create effective relationships and partnerships. In many ways such measures are easier to achieve at a local level because the range of stakeholders which need to be incorporated in coordinating bodies will be narrower. In addition contact at the local level provides a greater capacity for face-to-face contact to occur and therefore trust building to develop (Hall 1999).

RAISING CONSUMER AWARENESS

One of the hallmarks of tourism, and other industries, in recent years has been the increased consumer demand for 'green' or 'environmentally-friendly' products; such demand is often related to increased consumer awareness of environmental and social issues associated with trade and tourism. However, in many cases, the difference between a sustainable and non-sustainable tourism operation can be difficult for consumers to detect, particularly if the greening of tourism is regarded more as a branding device rather than a fundamental change in product development.

One development which is usually regarded as an indicator of increased consumer awareness is the development of tourist codes of behaviour in order to minimise the negative impacts of tourists on the social and physical environment (Hall and Lew 1998). For example, Valentine (1992) cites the example of the Audubon Society, one of the largest conservation groups in the United States, which has developed the Audubon Travel Ethic in order to draw attention to the appropriate behaviours and ethics to which individuals travelling with the Society should follow:

1 The biota shall not be disturbed.
2 Audubon tours to natural areas will be sustainable.
3 The sensibilities of other cultures will be respected.
4 Waste disposal shall have neither environmental nor aesthetic impacts.
5 The experience a tourist gains in travelling with Audubon shall enrich his or her appreciation of nature, conservation, and the environment.
6 The effect of an Audubon tour shall be to strengthen the conservation effort and enhance the natural integrity of places visited.
7 Traffic in products that threaten wildlife and plant populations shall not occur.

However, while consumer awareness is important and may result in shifts in tourism product, particularly if one believes the old adage that the consumer is king, fundamental changes are also required on the supply side of the tourism equation.

RAISING PRODUCER AWARENESS

According to Hall (1995) greater attention has been given to meeting the demands of different consumer segments than the needs of the supplier of the tourist product. As with the raising of consumer awareness, much attention has been given to the production of environmental codes of conduct or practice for tourism associations (Hall and McArthur 1998). For example, extensive guidelines have been developed for tourism operators in the Antarctic (Hall and Johnston 1995). However, such guidelines, while undoubtedly influencing the actions of some tourism operators, may need to be backed up by government regulation and environmental planning legislation if they are to have any overall affect on development practices. For example, where such codes of conduct are voluntary what practical measures exist to punish operators who do not subscribe to them?

STRATEGIC PLANNING TO SUPERSEDE CONVENTIONAL APPROACHES

Strategic planning is becoming increasingly important in tourism (e.g. Dowling 1993). Strategic planning aims to be proactive, responsive to community needs, to incorporate implementation within a single planning process, and be ongoing. A 'strategy' is a means to achieve a desired end. Strategic planning is the process by which an organisation effectively adapts to its management environment over time by integrating planning and management in a single process. The strategic plan is the document which is the output of a strategic planning process, it is the template by which progress is measured and which serves to guide future directions, activities, programmes and actions. The outcome of the strategic planning process is the impact that the process has on the organisation and its activities. Such impacts are then monitored and evaluated through the selection of appropriate indicators as part of the ongoing revision and readjustment of the organisation to its environment. Strategic planning therefore emphasises the process of continuous improvement as a cornerstone of organisational activity in which strategic planning is linked to management and operational decision making. According to Hall and McArthur (1998) there are three key mechanisms to achieve strategic planning which differentiate it from conventional planning approaches:

- a planning framework which extends beyond organisational boundaries and focuses on strategic decisions concerning stakeholders and resources;
- a planning process that stimulates entrepreneurial and innovative thinking; and
- an organisational values system that reinforces managers and staff commitment to the organisational strategy.

Effective strategic planning for sustainable tourism recognises the importance of factors which affect the broad framework within which strategies are generated, such as institutional arrangements, institutional culture and stakeholder values and attitudes. These factors are significant because it is important to recognise that strategic plans will be in line with the legislative powers and organisational structures of the implementing organisation(s) and the political goals of government. However, it may also be the case that once the strategic planning process is underway, goals and objectives formulated, and the process evaluated, the institutional arrangements may be recognised as being inadequate for the successful achievement of sustainable goals and objectives. In addition, it must be recognised that in order to be effective, the strategic planning process needs to be integrated with the development of appropriate organisational values (see Hall and Jenkins 1995 on the role of values in planning and policy). Indeed, with respect to the significance of values it may be noted that the strategic planning process is as important as its output, i.e. a plan. By having an inclusive planning process by which those responsible for implementing the plan are also those who helped formulate it, the likelihood of 'ownership' of the plan and, hence, effective

implementation will be dramatically increased (Heath and Wall 1992; Hall and McArthur 1996).

A strategic planning process may be initiated for a number of reasons (Hall and McArthur 1998), including:

- *Stakeholder demands* Demand for the undertaking of a strategic plan may come from the pressure of stakeholders, e.g. environmental conservation groups or government.
- *Perceived need* The lack of appropriate information by which to make decisions or an appropriate framework with which to implement legislative requirements may give rise to a perception that new management and planning approaches are required.
- *Response to crisis* The undertaking of strategic planning exercises are often the result of a crisis in the sense that the management and planning system has failed to adapt to aspects of the management environment, e.g. failure to conserve the values of an environmentally significant site from visitor pressures.
- *Best practice* Visitor managers can be proactive with respect to the adoption of new ideas and techniques. Therefore, a strategic planning process can become a way of doing things better.
- *Adaptation, innovation and the diffusion of ideas* Individuals within an organisation can encourage strategic planning processes as part of the diffusion of ideas within and between responsible management agencies.

Strategic planning is rarely initiated for a single reason. However, it is important to understand as much as possible why a particular planning process is being initiated as this helps the participants understand the expectations which have been created. Once underway, strategic planning is designed to be iterative. In other words, planning systems are meant to be able to adapt and change; they *learn* how to be effective in terms of the most appropriate set of goals, objectives, actions, indicators, institutional arrangements, and practices. In this sense, strategic planning from the perspective of sustainable tourism seeks to reflect in an organisational context the principles of appropriate adaptation and change which exist in the ecological relationships they are, so often, attempting to maintain. In addition, strategic approaches place great store on understanding the policy environment within which tourism planning operates, and it is to this that we will now briefly turn.

TOURISM POLICY

As with planning, geographers have long held a substantial interest in policy making, although such concerns have only recently found substantial expression in the tourism sphere (e.g. Fagence 1990, 1991; Pearce 1992a, 1992b; Hall and Jenkins 1995). Public policy is the focal point of government activity. Public policy 'is whatever governments choose to do or not to do' (Dye 1992: 2). This definition covers government action, inaction, decisions and non-decisions as it implies a deliberate choice between alternatives. For a policy to be regarded as public policy, at the very least it must have been processed, even if only authorised or ratified, by public agencies (Hall *et al.* 1997). Public policy making, including tourism policy making, is first and foremost a political activity. Public policy is influenced by the economic, social, and cultural characteristics of society, as well as by the formal structures of government and other features of the political system. Policy is therefore a consequence of the political environment, values and ideologies, the distribution of power, institutional frameworks, and of decision-making processes (Hall and Jenkins 1995; Hall *et al.* 1997) (Figure 8.1).

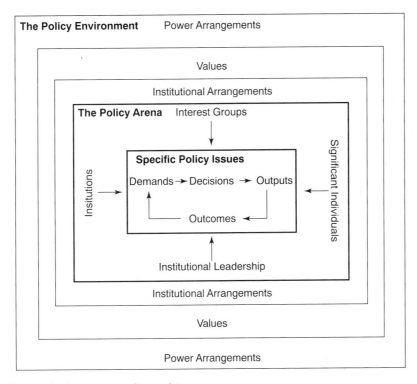

Figure 8.1: Elements in the tourism policy making process

Tourism public policy is whatever governments choose to do or not to do with respect to tourism (Hall and Jenkins 1995). However, as a number of studies by geographers have indicated (e.g. McKercher 1993c, 1997; Jenkins 1997), pressure groups (e.g. tourism industry associations, conservation groups, community groups), community leaders and significant individuals (e.g. local government councillors), members of the bureaucracy (e.g. employees within tourism commissions or regional development agencies) and others (e.g. academics and consultants), influence and perceive public policies in significant and often markedly different ways.

Research on tourism policy research can generally be divided into two main types of theory: that which adopts prescriptive models and that which adopts descriptive models (Mitchell 1989; Hall 1994; Hall and Jenkins 1995). 'Prescriptive or normative models seek to demonstrate how [planning and] policy making should occur relative to pre-established standards', whereas 'descriptive models document the way in which the policy process actually occurs' (Mitchell 1989: 264). Prescriptive (normative) models serve as a guide to an ideal situation. The majority of references to policy and decision making in the tourism literature have tended to utilise a prescriptive model of policy making which demonstrate how tourism policy and decision making should occur relative to pre-established standards (e.g. Murphy 1985). The prescriptive–rational approach assumes that a dichotomy exists between the policy-making process and administration and the existence of 'Economic Man [sic]', whereby individuals can 'identify and rank goals, values and objectives', and 'can choose consistently among them after having collected all the necessary data and systematically evaluated them' (Mitchell 1979: 296). However, while these may be useful rational models against which to compare reality, they do not provide detailed insights into the real world of planning and its associated set of values, power and interests. Instead, approaches, methods and techniques need to be evaluated within the con-

text of the goals, objectives and outcomes of tourism planning and development (Hall and Jenkins 1995; Hall et al. 1997).

Descriptive approaches give rise to explanations about what happened during the decision-making, planning and policy-making processes. Case studies are an important component of descriptive tourism research as they help analysts understand the effects that such factors as choice, power, perception, values and process have on tourism planning and policy making. As Mitchell (1979: 42) recorded, 'much research in resource analysis has been based upon one-shot case studies'. The main criticism of the case study method is 'claimed to be its reliance upon historical–descriptive chronology and lack of consistency in scope, context and conceptual cohesiveness' (Davis 1981: 8). However, although a single case study 'will rarely be sufficient for a full inquiry', the duplication of studies may well suggest fundamental relationships and generalizations (Mitchell 1979: 43). Indeed, 'it cannot be claimed that the case evidence is entirely definitive or utterly representative' (Davis 1981: 7), but case studies do present the researcher with the capacity to highlight certain problem areas within the scope of the objectives to be gained in this thesis. An attitude reflected in the recreation research of La Page (cited in Mercer 1973: 42): 'For sound research planning, I would gladly swap all the "highly significant" correlation coefficients of the past 10 years for a couple of good case studies that yielded some solid conceptual insight to build on.'

Under a descriptive approach, emphasis is therefore placed on understanding the various elements of the policy process and how it arrives at certain outputs and outcomes, As Jenkins (W. 1978: 16) argued, 'for many process is a central, if not the central, focus, to the extent that they argue that a conceptual understanding of the policy process is fundamental to an analysis of public policy'. Therefore, for the descriptive analysis of tourism policy

to explain policy maintenance and policy change, one needs to explore the socio-political conditions in which the political system operates, examining in particular the extent to which outputs are conditioned by external influences. Thus ... the vital task of the policy analyst is to explore the links between the environment, the political system and policy outputs and impacts.

(Jenkins W., 1978: 26–7)

Unfortunately, the understanding of the tourism policy process is rather limited as the area has not received a great deal of emphasis until recently, although geographers have been making a substantial contribution to the field (e.g. Pearce 1992b; Hall and Jenkins 1995). Nevertheless, an understanding of the way in which government utilises tourism as a policy mechanism may be extremely valuable not only in terms of improving the policy-making and planning process, but also in terms of improving the conditions of the people who are affected by such policies.

For example, tourism as a policy response to the economic problems of rural areas in developed countries has gone through a number of phases in recent years (Jenkins *et al.* 1998). Until the mid-1980s rural tourism was primarily concerned with commercial opportunities, multiplier effects and employment creation (e.g. Canadian Council on Rural Development 1975). In the late 1980s policy guidance shifted to the message that the environment is a key component for the tourism industry. Under this notion, 'tourism is an additive rather than extractive force for rural communities' (Curry 1994: 146). Tourism was regarded as 'sustainable', stressing the intrinsic value of the environment and, in some countries, the rural community as a tourist resource. (Although in Australia sustainability was defined primarily in ecological terms (Hall 1995).)

In the late 1980s and early 1990s an additional layer to the policy responses of government to tourism and regional development has been added which returns to the earlier economic concerns (e.g. Pearce 1992a). This is the perception of rural tourism as a major mechanism for arresting the decline of agricultural employment and therefore as a mechanism for agricultural diversification

(Rural Development Commission 1991a, 1991b). In the case of Europe, for example, we see the identification of specific rural development areas (Pearce 1992a; Jenkins *et al.* 1998). Rural tourism has also been given substantial emphasis in Australia, New Zealand and North America because of its development potential (Butler *et al.* 1998). For example, as the Australian Commonwealth Department of Tourism (1993: 24) noted

Diversification of traditional rural enterprises into tourism would provide considerable benefits to local rural economies including:
• wider employment opportunities;
• diversifying the income base of farmers and rural towns;
• additional justification for the development of infrastructure;
• a broader base for the establishment, maintenance and/or expansion of local services;
• scope for the integration of regional development strategies; and
• an enhanced quality of life through extended leisure and cultural opportunities.

Yet despite government enthusiasm for tourism as a mechanism to counter problems arising out of rural restructuring and depopulation, the success of these policies has been only marginally successful, with the greatest growth from tourism and recreation related industries occurring in the larger rural service centres and the rural–urban fringe, arguably those areas which least need the benefits that tourism can bring (Butler *et al.* 1998; Jenkins *et al.* 1998). Why has this occurred?

To a great extent it relates to a failure by government to understand the nature of tourism and its relationship with other sectors of the economy and the policy and planning process itself. First, all the dimensions of development need to be considered. Second, it implies the need for us to be aware of the various linkages that exist between the elements of development. Third, it also implies that 'successful' regional development will require coordination and, at times, intervention, in order to achieve desired outcomes. Fourth, it also means that tourism should not be seen as the be all and end all of regional development, but instead should be utilised as an appropriate response to the real needs of rural regions. As Getz (1987: 3–4) stated, tourism 'can be a tool in regional development or an agent of disruption or destruction'. Or, to put it another way, to quote an article from Canada: 'Those who think a bit of Victorian architecture and an overpriced cappuccino bar are going to turn their community into a gold mine are in for a disappointment' (Threndyle 1994). However, the problems of rural tourism and recreation development have long been recognised. For example, as Baum and More (1966: 5) stated with respect to the American experience in the early 1960s:

> there are and there will be increasing opportunities for [tourism] development, but this industry should not be considered to be a panacea for the longstanding problems of substantial and persistent unemployment and underemployment besetting low-income rural areas . . . The successful development of a particular [tourism] enterprise or complex of enterprises requires the same economic considerations as the planning and development of economic activities in other sectors.

The starting point with respect to determining successful regional tourism development is deciding in the first place what the objectives should be and how a community is going to get there. Such a decision should not be made by the tourism industry alone. As Long and Nuckolls (1994: 19) noted:

> Pro-active, community-driven planning, that goes beyond developing and promoting the static supply side of tourism, is essential for successful development of a sustainable tourism industry. Furthermore, tourism plans must be integrated into broader strategies for community, economic and regional development and management. Communities that fail to organise resources and strategically plan for tourism will likely be faced with short term, haphazard development, resulting in long term, negative economic, social and environmental impacts.

An understanding of tourism policy processes therefore lies at the heart of broader goals of rural and regional development. Yet, as Hall and Jenkins (1998) argued, the formulation and implementation of rural tourism and recreation public policies present several conundrums. Unrealistic expectations of tourism's potential are unfortunately combined with ignorance or wilful neglect by decision-makers of the potentially adverse economic, environmental and social consequences of tourist development that threaten to curtail its benefits. Yet, as Duffield and Long (1981: 409) observed, 'Ironically, the very consequences of lack of development, the unspoilt character of the landscape and distinctive local cultures, become positive resources as far as tourism is concerned.' Government involvement in rural tourism development is therefore quite unsuccessful:

> Management decisions for the allocation of related outdoor recreation resources are seldom guided by strategic policy frameworks. Decisions are typically made in a reactive manner in response to various pressures from groups competing for the same resource or lobbying for different management of a particular resource . . . Even in Europe, where rural tourism has been increasingly promoted over the last decade as an important mechanism for regional economic development and European integration, substantial problems have emerged with respect to policy formulation and implementation.
>
> (Hall and Jenkins 1998)

The reason for such failures lie in a lack of understanding of policy processes: 'while the goals of rural tourism development are fairly clear at the regional level, little research has been conducted on the most appropriate policy mix to achieve such objectives and there is often minimal monitoring and evaluation of policy measures' (Hall and Jenkins 1998). Therefore, for each location within which regional development objectives are being sought through the development of tourism, there are a range of policy measures available (Table 8.3). Five different measures were identified:

Table 8.3: Rural tourism development policy instruments

Categories	Instruments	Examples
Regulatory instruments	1 Laws	Planning laws can give considerable power to government to encourage particular types of rural tourism development through, for example, land use zoning
	2 Licences, permits and standards	Regulatory instruments can be used for a wide variety of purposes especially at local government level, e.g. they may set materials standards for tourism developments, or they can be used to set architectural standards for heritage streetscapes or properties
	3 Tradeable permits	Often used in the United States to limit resource use or pollution. However, the instrument requires effective monitoring for it to work
	4 Quid pro quos	Government may require businesses to do something in exchange for certain rights, e.g. land may be given to a developer below market rates, or a development is of a particular type or design
Voluntary instruments	1 Information	Expenditure on educating the local public, businesses or tourists to achieve specific goals, e.g. appropriate recreational behaviour
	2 Volunteer associations and non-governmental organisations	Government support of community tourism organisations is very common in tourism. Support may come from direct grants and/or by provision of office facilities. Examples of this type of development include local or regional tourist organisations, heritage conservation groups, mainstreet groups, tour guide programmes, or helping to establish a local farmstay or homestay association
	3 Technical assistance	Government can provide technical assistance and information to businesses with regard to planning and development requirements
Expenditure	1 Expenditure and contracting	This is a common method for government to achieve policy objectives as government can spend money directly on specific activities. This may include the development of infrastructure, such as roads, or it may include mainstreet beautification programs. Contracting can be used as a means of supporting existing local businesses or encouraging new ones
	2 Investment or procurement	Investment may be directed into specific businesses or projects, while procurement can be used to help provide businesses with a secure customer for their products
	3 Public enterprise	When the market fails to provide desired outcomes, governments may operate their own businesses, e.g. rural or regional development corporations or enterprise boards. If successful, such businesses may then be sold off to the private sector
	4 Public–private partnerships	Government may enter into partnership with the private sector in order to develop certain products or regions. These may take the form of a corporation which has a specific mandate to attract business to a certain region for example

Table 8.3: continued

Categories	Instruments	Examples
	5 Monitoring and evaluation	Government may allocate financial resources to monitor rural economic, environmental and socio-economic indicators. Such measures may not only be valuable to government to evaluate the effectiveness and efficiency of rural tourism development objectives but can also be a valuable source of information to the private sector as well
	6 Promotion	Government may spend money on promoting a region to visitors either with or without financial input from the private sector. Such promotional activities may allow individual businesses to reallocate their own budgets, reducing planned expenditure on promotion
Financial incentives	1 Pricing	Pricing measures may be used to encourage appropriate behaviour or to stimulate demand, e.g. use of particular walking trails, lower camping or permit costs
	2 Taxes and charges	Governments may use these to encourage appropriate behaviours by both individuals and businesses, i.e. pollution charges. Taxes and charges may also be used to help fund infrastructure development, e.g. regional airports
	3 Grants and loans	Seeding money may be provided to businesses to encourage product development or to encourage the retention of heritage and landscape features
	4 Subsidies and tax incentives	Although subsidies are often regarded as creating inefficiencies in markets they may also be used to encourage certain types of behaviour with respect to social and environmental externalities, e.g. heritage and landscape conservation, that are not taken into account by conventional economics
	5 Rebates, rewards and surety bonds	Rebates and rewards are a form of financial incentive to encourage individuals and businesses to act in certain ways. Similarly, surety bonds can be used to ensure that businesses act in agreed ways, if they don't then the government will spend the money for the same purpose
	6 Vouchers	Vouchers are a mechanism to affect consumer behaviour by providing a discount on a specific product or activity, e.g. to shop in a rural centre
Non-intervention	1 Non-intervention (deliberate)	Government deciding not to directly intervene in sectoral or regional development is also a policy instrument, in that public policy is what government decides to do and not do. In some cases the situation may be such that government may decide that policy objectives are being met so that their intervention may not add any net value to the rural development process and that resources could be better spent elsewhere

Source: Hall and Jenkins (1998: 29–32)

- *regulatory instruments* – regulations, permits and licences that have a legal basis and which require monitoring and enforcement;
- *voluntary instruments* – actions or mechanisms that do not require expenditure;
- *expenditure* – direct government expenditure to achieve policy outcomes;
- *financial incentives* – including taxes, subsidies, grants and loans, which are incentives to undertake certain activities or behaviours and which tend to require minimal enforcement; and
- *non-intervention* – where government deliberately avoids intervention in order to achieve its policy objectives.

With the selection of the most appropriate measure or, more likely, a range of measures, being dependent on the particular circumstances of each region. There is no universal 'best way', each region or locale needs to select the appropriate policy mix for its own development requirements. However, this does not mean that the policy and planning process occurs in a vacuum. Rather the attention to policy and planning processes has the intent of making such processes as overt as possible, so that the values, influence and interests of various stakeholders are relatively transparent. There is no perfect planning or policy process, yet we can, through the geographer's contribution, help make it more relevant to the people who are affected by tourism development and continually strive for improvement.

CONCLUSION

This chapter has provided a broad overview of the tourism planning and policy process. It has noted the various strands of tourism planning, and emphasised the particular contribution of geographers to the physical/spatial, community and sustainable approaches to tourism planning. The reasons for focusing on tourism which is not as well developed or articulated in local, regional and national development plans beyond statements and broad objectives contrasts with recreational planning which has a much longer history of development and application. In fact if the experience of urban areas is considered, then one can see the emergence of recreational planning in the nineteenth century in the UK with the role of the public sector in park development, the provision of libraries and other items to meet the wider public good. What geographers have contributed to recreational planning is the synthesis and analysis of good practice, rather than being actively involved as academics, beyond a research role, to assist public and private sector bodies in locational analysis and land use planning. This chapter has therefore placed a great deal of emphasis on the importance of policy analysis, especially from a descriptive approach, and on the role of case studies as an appropriate methodology. This does not mean that prescription is without value, rather it argues that prescription must be seen in context, with particular reference to those who are in any way affected by policy statements.

In looking at the application of policy analysis to tourism issues we have therefore almost come full circle. The interests which have long concerned tourism and recreation geographers, that are applied and relevant to the needs of the subjects of our research remain, and it is to these issues which we shall return in the final chapter.

9

THE FUTURE

Speaking only as one individual, I feel strongly that I should not go into research unless it promises results that would advance the aims of the people affected and unless I am prepared to take all practicable steps to help translate the results into action.

(White 1972: 102)

As the various chapters in this book have indicated, geographers have made substantial contributions to the understanding of tourism and recreation. However, as noted in chapter 1, the geographers who are working in the field are, increasingly, not based in geography departments but instead are located in departments of tourism and recreation or leisure, environmental studies, or business. Indeed, the authors, while still regarding themselves as geographers, were working in faculties of business as this manuscript was being completed.

Such a situation is a reflection of several things: the growth of tourism and recreation as a separate, legitimate area of academic endeavour; the poor standing in which studies of tourism and recreation have generally been held within academic geography, and the applied nature of much work in tourism and recreation geography, which has meant a professional career in the public and private sectors for many geography graduates in the field. Such a situation clearly raises substantial questions about what the future of the sub-discipline will be. As Johnston recognised: 'It is the advancement of knowledge – through the conduct of fundamental research and the publication of its original findings – which identifies an academic d iscipline; the nature of its teaching follows from the nature of its research' (Johnston 1991: 2).

This final chapter will briefly revisit the place of tourism and recreation geography in the applied geography tradition. It will then discuss the contributions that geography can bring to the study of tourism and recreation and highlight a possible future for the field.

REVISITING APPLIED GEOGRAPHY

Within the literature on the geography of recreation and tourism there have been comparatively few studies which have emphasised how the tourism and recreation geographer has made a valuable contribution to the wider development of 'applied geography'. According to Sant (1982) the scope of applied geography comprises a concern with policy making and the monitoring of problems. More specifically it focuses on 'the sense of the problem, the contribution to decision making and policy, the monitoring of actions and the evaluation of plans. But these are common to all applied social sciences' (Sant 1982: 3) and so the geographer must ensure that s/he can make a distinctive contribution through the use of approaches, tools, techniques or skills which other social scientists, consultants and policy makers do not possess, if it is regarded as important that a geographical approach survives.

All too often the application of geographical skills in commercial and non-commercial contexts has been poorly developed. There are notable exceptions in the history of geographical thought where the skills of spatial analysis have been used for practical and commercial purposes, particularly in colonial times where the pursuit of resource inventories and mapping assisted in imperialist expansion in new territories (see Johnston 1991). In the post-war period some aspects of geography clearly dissipated to new disciplines such as town planning while the greater social science involvement and expansion of geographical subject matter saw geographers lose some of their competitive edge which had been gained in the pre and inter-war years. In recent times, some geographers have made transitions into the public and private sector where their skills have been in high demand (e.g. GIS), and some have made major contributions to public policy formulation and analysis in recreation and tourism (e.g. Patmore 1983). There has been the development of new specialisms which have emerged from a geographical tradition with an explicit public and commercial dimension. Recreation and tourism are two examples which have furnished many opportunities for the geographer to apply their skills in a wider context than academia, although this has not always meant that they have been particularly successful in capitalising on such opportunities.

While geographers still make a substantial contribution to planning this contribution is perhaps not widely acknowledged by society at large. Similarly, GIS is increasingly being usurped by marketers, while the contribution of geographers to tourism and recreation is now adding far more of an academic base for the field of tourism and recreation studies than it is for geography. Should we care? The answer we believe is 'yes'. As the book stated at the outset by imitating the title of Massey and Allen's (1984) work: *Geography Matters!*, the geography of tourism and recreation also matters. One of the problems is though that we are often not very good at convincing other people that we do. In fact declining enrolments in geography at university level in the UK have been attributed to the growth of interest in cognate subjects like tourism and recreation, though this is part of a growing interest in vocational subjects such as business studies. Given increasing demands for the development of sustainable forms of tourism on the one hand and a relevant academic geography on the other, geography and geographers have an important role to play. In some senses those geographers who have moved to business schools to pursue their interest in tourism and recreation have at least managed to retain a spatial component to such curricula.

CONTRIBUTIONS

According to Stamp (1960: 9) 'the unique contribution of the geographer is the holistic approach in which he sees the relationship between man and his [sic] environment'. This statement is just as relevant to the application of geography to problem solving today as it was when originally written. Indeed, perhaps more so given the size of the environmental, social and economic problems we face. Doornkamp (1982) posed a range of questions related to the role of applied geography and two of these are of significance to tourism and recreation:

- Is the geographical contribution sufficiently unique to make it worth pursuing?
- How, in the commercial world, can the work of the applied geographer be sold?

These two questions highlight the need for the geographer to assess what inherent skills they have which may be of value in an applied context. While accepting that the nature of geographical training in the 1990s may be somewhat different from that in the 1970s and 1980s, Table 9.1 does still provide a useful assessment of how the geographer can contribute to problem solving.

Whilst skills are important in addressing problems, Doornkamp (1982) and Dawson and Doornkamp's (1973) research in applied geography provides many key pointers to the value of a spatial approach. He highlights the need to separate knowledge from the ability to use skills.

Table 9.1: The skills of a geographer

* To think in spatial terms.
* To be able to assess the implications of the distribution of any one 'landscape' characteristic.
* To be able to think about more than one distribution at a time – and to perceive from this any likely generic links between the items under study.
* To be able to change the scale of thinking according to the needs of the phenomena or problems being analysed.
* To be able to add the dimension of time as appropriate.
* To be able to place phenomena within a 'model' or 'systems' framework.
* To be able to comprehend and initiate thinking that links the human and physical systems operating in the landscape.
* To 'read' and 'understand' landscape.
* To be able to use certain techniques, for example:
  – To acquire information through fieldwork, map analysis or from remote sensing sources – with an emphasis on spatial distributions and relationships.
  – To be able to handle and analyse large data sets, incomplete data sets, spatial data or time-based data, through quantitative methods using computer technology.
  – To be equally at home in a literary search amongst archives and historical records.
  – To be able to monitor landscape components, and to be able to submit them to further analyses as appropriate.
  – To present information with clarity, and especially in map form.
  – To utilise technological developments such as GIS to assist in gaining a holistic view of the problem in hand.
* To be able to provide a statement of one's findings which integrates one's own knowledge with that of allied disciplines.

Source: After Doornkamp (1982: 7)

During a geographical education, exposure to the systematic elements of the discipline in human and physical geography combines with practical and fieldwork in spatial techniques, which, together with regional studies, is where many of the former elements can be synthesised. This continues to provide the core of knowledge for the geographer and more advanced training then focuses on a specialised study in a particular sub-discipline of geography. It is often at this point that the crossover between geography and other social science disciplines occurs when the knowledge base becomes shared. The problem within business schools, is that the spatial component is extremely watered down to a basic conceptualisation of place, space and environment. At the same time, the inquisitive nature of geographical research, particularly the interest in human–environment relationships at a variety of spatial scales, often means that the geographer pursues an holistic perspective not often found in other disciplines. Yet conveying this to the new generation of students interested in the business applications of recreation and tourism requires the geographer to not only sell the value of a synthesising holistic approach, but to also move forward to meet the new challenge for applied geography in the late 1990s. Equally, the geographer also has a formidable challenge in convincing colleagues and researchers in mainstream geography of the validity and intellectual rigour associated with research in recreation and tourism.

But harnessing this training and the range of skills acquired in order to apply them in a problem solving context requires one important prerequisite. According to Doornkamp (1982: 9) this is an ability to see the problem from the point of view of the person who needs a solution. Having convinced this person of their ability to conceptualise the problem in their terms, in order to provide a solution three principal factors need to be considered:

> The research must be framed and reported in a manner which the client requires: it needs to be as concise and as thorough as possible. It is not to be a thesis or academic research paper. Otherwise the client will simply not recommend or use the organisation again. This is a principal failing for many academics who are unable to bridge the industry–academic interface;
> Personal relationships of trust and respect need to be built up in a commercial environment, often framed around numerous meetings and regular interfacing; and the work must be professionally presented, being easy to read, targeted at the audience intending to read it, and precise and unambiguous.

Even where the client is a non-paying customer (i.e. if the research is undertaken as a contribution to the local community), such criteria are equally important. Otherwise, the outside world's image of the geographer will remain one of the ivory tower academic perceived as being distant from the real world and problem solving contributions they can make. Likewise, academics need to be willing to incorporate changes on drafts and to recognise that in this environment their view is not necessarily without reproach. This is nowhere more the case than in recreation and tourism where an explicit business dimension is incorporated in such research.

It is fair to agree with Doornkamp's (1982: 26) analogy that practising geographers left the discipline in the immediate post-war period and joined the commercial world, calling themselves planners. A similar move may be occurring in recreation and tourism, with the movement of staff to business schools. The 'professional practice' side

of the discipline of geography has continued to lose out to other disciplines even when its skills are more relevant and analytical. Interfacing with the real world has meant that a small proportion of recreation and tourism geographers have made a steady transition to professional practice without compromising their academic integrity and reputation. While payment for their services may have filled some of their peers and contemporaries with horror, recreation and tourism are commercial activities. In some cases, not using the label 'geographer' can have a great deal of benefit when interfacing with recreation and tourism businesses since the public perception of geographers is not of practitioners making commercial or social contributions to society. So in summary, it is clear that applied geography problem solving in recreation and tourism contexts can enhance the geographer's skills and relationship with society. In the longer term, it may help address the public image of the discipline as one of major value to research in applied fields such as tourism. But ultimately the main barrier to the geographer using their skills for an applied purpose is their own willingness and ability to interface in commercial and public contexts where they can be heard, listened to, taken seriously and their skills can be harnessed. In many cases, there is often a belated recognition of the value of such skills when a client uses such a person. Therefore, the public face of geography can only be enhanced if it embraces recreation and tourism as legitimate sub-disciplines of a post-industrial society/geography which can have a major contribution to make in various applied contexts.

TRANSFORMATIONS?

As this book has indicated, the geography of tourism and recreation, as with the discipline as whole, has undergone considerable change since it began in the 1930s. This is to be expected as geography, as with any discipline, adapts and reacts in relation to the society and culture within which it operates (see chapter 1). The case for understanding the changing nature of tourism and recreation, 'contextually closely parallels the case made by realists for appreciating all human activity; the operation of human agency must be analysed within the constraining and enabling conditions provided by its environment' (Johnston 1991: 280). In this sense the environment for the study of tourism and recreation must be positive given the growth of international tourism and the role it now plays within government policy making. Given the significance of globalisation, postmodernism, post-fordism and localisation to contemporary social theory it should also be no surprise that many human geographers and other social scientists are now discovering tourism and recreation as having some significance for social change. However, previous work in the area is often ignored while many authors discussing contemporary tourism phenomena, particularly in an urban or rural setting, seem to think that all tourists and tourism are the same and fail to perceive the complexity of the phenomenon they are investigating.

It would also be true to note that many tourism and recreation geographers find the discovery of 'their' field by social theory somewhat amusing. Others will also find it threatening given that their own work bears all the hallmarks of traditional spatial science, excellent maps, flows and patterns but little role for more critical examination of tourism phenomenon.

The geography of tourism and recreation therefore bears the hallmarks of much Anglo-American geography in terms of the tensions that exist between the different approaches that there are within the discipline. Such tensions, if well managed, can be extremely healthy in terms of the debate they generate and the 'freshness' of the subject matter. However, if not well managed and if external influences become too attractive, splits will occur. Research and scholarship in the geography of tourism and recreation are now at this stage. Unless greater links are built between the sub-discipline and the discipline as a whole then, potentially, much of the field will be swallowed up by the rapidly expanding field of tourism studies. Even if only in terms of student numbers, such a shift would have substantial implications for geography as already mentioned above.

The geography of tourism and recreation is at a crossroads. It is to be hoped that a situation will not develop where those concerned with social theory will stay in geography and those who do not will go to the business and tourism schools. An understanding of social theory by itself will not provide geography graduates with jobs. However, the integration of some of the central concerns of social theory, and the central concerns of the geographer – sites, places, landscapes, regions and national configurations, and the spatial arrangements and relationships that interconnect them – with the subject of tourism and recreation will lead to the development of a more relevant applied area of geography that can better contribute to all its stakeholders.

REFERENCES

Aaker, D. and Day, G. (1986) *Marketing Research*, New York: Wiley.

Ackerman, E.A. (1963) 'Where is a research frontier?', *Annals of The Association of American Geographers*, 53: 429–440.

Aer Lingus (1991) *Report and Accounts for the Year Ended March 1991*, Dublin: Aer Lingus Group.

Aldskogius, H. (1977) 'A conceptual framework and a Swedish case study of recreational behaviour and environmental cognition', *Economic Geography*, 53: 163–83.

Alexander, K. (1984) 'In search of the spirit of wilderness', *Habitat*, 12(5): 3–5.

Allen, L.R., Long, P.T., Perdue, R.R. and Kieselbach, S. (1988) 'The impact of tourism development on residents' perceptions of community life', *Journal of Travel and Research*, 27(1): 16–21.

Anderson, D.H. and Brown, P.J. (1984) 'The displacement process in recreation', *Journal of Leisure Research*, 16(1): 61–73.

Anon. (1983) 'National Report No. 86, Ireland', *International Tourism Quarterly*, 3: 27–36.

Anon. (1989) *National Development Plan 1989–1992*, Dublin: Stationery Office.

Anon. (1994) Special issue on sustainable rural tourism development, *Trends* 31(1).

Appleton, I. (1974), *Leisure Research and Policy*, Scottish Academic Press: Edinburgh.

Arbel, A. and Pizam, A. (1977), 'Some determinants of hotel location: the tourists' inclination', *Journal of Travel Research*, 15 (Winter): 18–22.

Archer, B. (1973) *The Impact of Domestic Tourism*, Cardiff: University of Wales Press.

Archer, B.H. (1976) 'Uses and abuses of multipliers', in W.W. Swart and T. Var (eds) *Planning For Tourism Development: Quantitative Approaches*, New York: Praeger, pp. 115–32.

Archer, B.H. (1977a) 'The economic costs and benefits of tourism', in B.S. Duffield (ed.) *Tourism a Tool for Regional Development*, Leisure Studies Association Conference, Edinburgh, 1977, Edinburgh: Tourism and Recreation Research Unit, University of Edinburgh, pp. 5.1–5.11.

Archer, B.H. (1977b) *Tourism Multipliers: The State of the Art*, Occasional Papers in Economics, No. 11. Bangor: University of Wales Press.

Archer, B.H. (1978) 'Tourism as a development factor', *Annals of Tourism Research*, 5: 126–41.

Archer, B.H. (1982) 'The value of multipliers and their policy implications', *Tourism Management*, 3: 236–41.

Archer, B.H. (1984) 'Economic impact: misleading multiplier', *Annals of Tourism Research*, 11: 517–18.

Archer, J. and Yarman, I. (1991) *Nature Conservation in Newham*, London Ecology Unit: Ecology Handbook 17.

Argyle, M. (1996) *The Social Psychology of Leisure*, London: Penguin.

Ashworth, G. (1989) 'Urban tourism: an imbalance in attention', in C.P. Cooper (ed.) *Progress in Tourism, Recreation and Hospitality Management*, Vol. 1, London: Belhaven, pp. 33–54.

Ashworth, G.J. (1992a) ' Is there an urban tourism?', *Tourism Recreation Research*, 17(2): 3–8.

Ashworth, G.J. (1992b) 'Planning for sustainable tourism: a review article', *Town and Planning Review*, 63, 3: 325–29.

Ashworth, G. and Dietvorst, A. (eds) (1995) *Tourism and Spatial Transformations*, Wallingford: CAB International.

Ashworth, G.J. and de Haan, T.Z. (1986) 'Uses and users of the tourist–historic city', *Field Studies 10*, Groningen: Faculty of Spatial Sciences.

Ashworth, G.J. and Tunbridge, J.E. (1990) *The Tourist–Historic City*, London: Belhaven.

Ashworth, G.J. and Voogd, H. (1988) 'Marketing the city: concepts, processes and Dutch applications', *Town Planning Review*, 59(1): 65–80.

Ashworth, G.J. and Voogd, H. (1990a) *Selling the City*, London: Belhaven.

Ashworth, G.J. and Voogd, H. (1990b) 'Can places be sold for tourism?', in G.J. Ashworth and B. Goodall (eds) *Marketing Tourism Places*, London: Routledge, pp. 1–16.

Ashworth G.J. and Voogd, H. (1994) 'Marketing of tourism places: what are we doing?, in M. Uysal (ed.) *Global Tourist Behaviour*. New York: International Press, pp. 5–20.

Ashworth, G.J., White, P.E. and Winchester, H.P. (1988) 'The red light district in the West-European City: a neglected aspect of the urban landscape', *Geoforum*, 19(2): 201–12.

Attfield, R. (1983) *The Ethics of Environmental Concern*, Oxford: Basil Blackwell.

Audit Commission (1993) *Realising the Benefits of Competition: The Client for Contracted Services*, London: HMSO.

Austin, M. (1974) 'The evaluation of urban public facility location: an alternative to cost-benefit analysis', *Geographical Analysis*, 6: 135–46.

Bagnall, U., Gillmore, D. and Phipps, J. (1978) 'The recreational use of forest land', *Irish Forestry*, 35: 19–34.

Bailie, J.G. (1980) 'Recent international travel trends in Canada, *Canadian Geographer* 24(1): 13–21.

Baines, G.B.K. (1987) 'Manipulation of islands and men: sand-cay tourism in the South Pacific', in S. Britton and W.C. Clarke (eds) *Ambiguous Alternative: Tourism in Small Developing Countries*, Suva: University of the South Pacific, pp. 16–24.

Baldridge, J.V. and Burnham, R.A. (1975) 'Organizational innovation: individual, organizational, and environmental impacts', *Administrative Science Quarterly*, 20: 165–76.

Bailie, J.G. (1980) 'Recent international travel trends in Canada', *Canadian Geographer*, 24(1): 13–21.

Ball, R.M. (1989) 'Some aspects of tourism, seasonality and local labour markets', *Area*, 21: 35–45.

Balmer, K. (1971) 'Urban open space and outdoor recreation' in P. Lavery (ed.) *Recreation Geography*, Newton Abbot: David and Charles.

Balmer, K. (1973) *Open Space in Liverpool*, Liverpool: Liverpool Corporation.

Bandura, A. (1977) 'Self-efficacy: toward a unifying theory of behavioural change', *Psychological Review*, 84: 191–215.

Barber, A. (1991) *Guide to Management Plans for Parks and Open Spaces*, Reading: Institute of Leisure and Amenity Management.

Baretje, R. (1982) 'Tourism's external account and the balance of payments', *Annals of Tourism Research*, 9(1): 57–67.

Barke, M., Towner, J. and Newton, M. (1966) *Tourism in Spain*, Wallingford: CAB International.

Barnes, B. (1982) *T.S. Kuhn and Social Science*, London: Macmillan.

BarOn, R. (1984) 'Tourism terminology and standard definitions', *Tourist Review*, 39(1): 2–4.

BarOn, R. (1989) *Travel and Tourism Data: A Comprehensive Research Handbook on the World Travel Industry*, London: Euromonitor.

Barrett, J. (1958) The Seaside Resort Towns of England and Wales, unpublished Ph.D. thesis, London: University of London.

Barry, F. (1991) 'Industrialisation strategies for developing countries: lessons from the Irish experience', *Development Policy Review*, 9: 85–98.

Barry, K. and O'Hagan, J. (1972) 'An econometric study of British expenditure in Ireland', *Economic and Social Review*, 3: 143–61.

Baum, E.L. and Moore, E.J. (1966) 'Some economic opportunities and limitations of outdoor recreation enterprises', in G.W. Cornwall, and C.J. Holcomb, (eds) *Guidelines to the Planning, Developing, and Managing of Rural Recreation Enterprises*, Bulletin 301, Blacksburg: Cooperative Extension Service, Virginia Polytechnic Institute, pp. 52–64.

Baum, T. (1989a) 'Managing hotels in Ireland: research and development for change', *International Journal Hospitality Management*, 8: 131–44.

Baum, T. (1989b) 'Scope for the tourism industry and its employment impact in Ireland', *Service Industries Journal*, 9: 140–51.

Baum, T. (ed.) (1993) *Human Resource Issues in International Tourism*, Oxford: Butterworth Heinemann.

Becker, R.H. (1981) 'Displacement of recreational users between the Lower St. Croix and Upper Mississippi

Rivers', *Journal of Environmental Management*, 13(3): 259–67.

Belford, S. (1983) 'Rural tourism', *Architects Journal*, 178: 59–71.

Bell, M. (1977) 'The spatial distribution of second homes: a modified gravity model', *Journal of Leisure Research*, 9(3): 225–32.

Bella, L. (1987) *Parks for Profit*, Montreal: Harvest House.

Benko, G. and Strohmmayer, U. (1997) *Space and Social Theory: Interpreting Modernity and Postmodernity*, Oxford: Blackwell.

Bennett, R. (1991) 'Rethinking London government', in K. Hoggart and D. Green (eds) *London: A New Metropolitan Geography*, London: Edward Arnold.

Bennington, J. and White, J. (1988) *The Future of Leisure Services*, Harlow: Longman.

Bevins, M., Brown, T., Cole, G., Hock, K. and LaPage, W. (1974) Analysis of the Campground Market in the Northeast, Burlington, Vermont: USDA, Forest Service Bulletin 679, University of Vermont Agricultural Experimental Station.

Bitner, M.J. (1992) 'Servicescapes: The impact of physical surroundings on customers and employees', *Journal of Marketing*, 56(2): 57–71.

Bitner, M.J., Booms, B.H. and Tetreault, M.S. (1990) 'The service encounter: diagnosing favourable and unfavourable incidents', *Journal of Marketing*, 71–84.

Blackwell, J. (1970) 'Tourist traffic and the demand for accommodation: some projections', *Economic and Social Review*, 1: 323–43.

Blamey, R. (1995) *The Nature of Ecotourism*, Occasional Paper No.21, Canberra: Bureau of Tourism Research.

Blamey, R.K. and Braithwaite, V.A. (1997) 'A social values segmentation of the potential ecotourism market', *Journal of Sustainable Tourism*, 5(1): 29–45.

Blank, U. and Petkovich, M. (1980) 'The metropolitan area: A multifaceted travel destination complex' in D. Hawkins, E. Shafer and J. Ravelstad (eds) *Tourism Planning and Development*, Washington: George Washington University, 393–405.

Bodewes, T. (1981) 'Development of advanced tourism studies in Holland', *Annals of Tourism Research*, 8(1): 35–51.

Boo, E. (1990) *Ecotourism: The Potentials and Pitfalls*, 2 Vols., Washington D.C.: World Wildlife Fund.

Bord Fáilte (1985) *Employment in Tourism*, Dublin: Bord Fáilte.

Bord Fáilte (1986) *The Irish Hotel Industry, 1985 Manual for Inter Hotel Comparison*, Dublin: Bord Fáilte.

Bord Fáilte (1988a) *Bord Fáilte's Strategy for Growth*, Dublin: Bord Fáilte.

Bord Fáilte (1988b) *The Regional Tourism Organisations*, Dublin: Bord Fáilte.

Bord Fáilte (1989) *Tourism and the Economy*, Dublin: Bord Fáilte.

Bord Fáilte (1990a) *Economic Benefits of Tourism*, Dublin: Bord Fáilte.

Bord Fáilte (1990b) *Developing Heritage Attractions*, Dun Laoghaire Conference, Dublin: Bord Fáilte.

Bord Fáilte (1991a) *Co-Operative Marketing Guide 1992: Targeting Irish Tourism Opportunities at Home and Overseas*, Dublin: Bord Fáilte.

Bord Fáilte (1991b) *Investment Opportunities in the Irish Tourism and Leisure Industry*, Dublin: Bord Fáilte.

Bord Fáilte (1992a) *Heritage Attraction Development: A Strategy to Interpret Ireland's History and Culture for Tourism*, Dublin: Bord Fáilte.

Bord Fáilte (1992b) *Heritage and Tourism: Second Conference on the Development of Heritage Attractions in Ireland*, Dublin: Bord Fáilte.

Bouquet, M. (1987) 'Bed, breakfast and an evening meal: commensality in the nineteenth and twentieth century farm household in Hartland', in M. Bouquet and M. Winter (eds) *Who From Their Labours Rest? Conflict and Practice in Rural Tourism*, Aldershot: Avebury.

Bouquet, M. and Winter, M. (eds) (1987a) *Who From Their Labours Rests? Conflict and Practice in Rural Tourism*, Aldershot: Avebury.

Bouquet, M. and Winter, M. (1987b) 'Tourism, politics and practice', in M. Bouquet and M. Winter (eds) *Who From Their Labours Rests? Conflict and Practice in Rural Tourism*, Aldershot: Avebury.

Bowler, I. and Strachan, A. (1976) *Parks and Gardens in Leicester*, Leicester: Recreation and Cultural Services Department, Leicester City Council.

Boyden, S.V. and Harris, J.A. (1978) 'Contribution of the wilderness to health and wellbeing', in G. Mosley (ed.) *Australia's Wilderness: Conservation Progress and Plans*, Proceedings of the First National Wilderness Conference, Australian Academy of Science, Canberra, 21–3 October, 1977, Hawthorn: Australian Conservation Foundation, 34–7.

Bracey, H. (1970) *People and the Countryside*, London: Routledge and Kegan Paul.

Bradshaw, J. (1972) 'The concept of social need', *New Society*, 30(3): 640–3.

Brady, Shipman and Martin (1991) *Wicklow Mountain's National Park Visitor Centre Environmental Impact Statement*, Dublin: Brady, Shipman and Martin.

Brady, Shipman, Martin and Hyde, N. (1972–73) *National Coastline Study*, Dublin: Bord Fáilte and Foras Forbartha.

Bramham, P. and Henry, I. (1985) 'Political ideology and leisure policy in the United Kingdom', *Leisure Studies*, 4: 1–19.

Bramwell, B. (1991) 'Sustainability and rural tourism policy in Britain', *Tourism Recreation Research*, 16 (2): 49–51.

Bramwell, B. (1993) *Tourism Strategies and Rural Development*. Paris: OECD.

Bramwell, B. (1994) 'Rural tourism and sustainable rural tourism', *Journal of Sustainable Tourism*, 2: 1–6.

Brennan, E. (ed.) (1990) *Heritage: A Visitor's Guide*, Dublin: Stationery Office.

Briggs, A. (1969), *Victorian Cities*, Pelham: Middlesex.

British Tourist Authority (1993) *Guidelines for Tourism to Britain 1993–97*, London: British Tourist Authority.

British Travel Association and University of Keele (1967 and 1969) *Pilot National Recreation Survey*, Keele: University of Keele.

Britton, S.G. (1980a) 'A conceptual model of tourism in a peripheral economy', *South Pacific: The Contribution of Research to Development and Planning*, N.Z. MAB Report No. 6, Christchurch: NZ National Commission for UNESCO/Department of Geography, 1–12.

Britton, S.G. (1980b) 'The spatial organisation of tourism in a neo-colonial economy: a Fiji case study', *Pacific Viewpoint*, 21: 144–65.

Britton, S.G. (1982) 'The political economy of tourism in the Third World', *Annals of Tourism Research*, 9(3): 331–58.

Britton, S.G. (1991) 'Tourism, capital and place: towards a critical geography of tourism', *Environment and Planning D: Society and Space*, 9: 451–78.

Brocx, M. (1994) *Visitor Perceptions and Satisfaction Study Winter 1993*, Auckland: Tourism Auckland.

Brookfield, H. (1955) 'Ireland and the Atlantic ferry', *Irish Geography* 3: 69–78.

Brougham, J.E. and Butler, R.W. (1981) 'A segmenta-tion analysis of resident attitudes to the social impacts of tourism', *Annals of Tourism Research*, 8: 569–90.

Brown, R.M. (1935) 'The business of recreation', *Geographical Review*, 25: 467–75.

Brunt, B. (1988) *The Republic of Ireland*, London: Paul Chapman Publishing.

Buchholtz, C.W. (1983) *Rocky Mountain National Park: A History*, Boulder: Colorado Associated University Press.

Bull, A. (1991) *The Economics of Travel and Tourism*, London: Pitman.

Bull, C. and Wibberley, G. (1976) *Farm Based Recreation in South-East England: Studies in Rural Land Use Report 12*, London: Wye College, University of London.

Bull, P. and Church, A. (1994) 'The hotel and catering industry of Great Britain during the 1980s: sub-regional employment change, specialisation and dominance', in C.P. Cooper and A. Lockwood (eds) *Progress in Tourism, Recreation and Hospitality Management*, Vol. 5, Chichester: Wiley, pp. 248–69.

Bureau of Land Management (1978) *Wilderness Inventory Handbook: Policy, Direction, Procedures, and Evidence for Conducting Wilderness Inventory on the Public Lands*, Washington D.C.: US Department of the Interior, Bureau of Land Management.

Burgess, J., Harrison, C. and Limb, M. (1988a) 'People, parks and the urban green: A study of popular meanings and values for open spaces in the city', *Urban Studies*, 26: 455–73.

Burgess, J., Harrison, C. and Limb, M. (1988b) 'Exploring environmental values through the medium of small groups: part one: theory and practice', *Environmental and Planning A*, 20: 309–26.

Burgess, J., Harrison, C. and Limb, M. (1988c) 'Exploring environmental values through the medium of small groups. Part Two: Illustrations of a group at work', *Environment and Planning A*, 20: 457–76.

Burkart, A. and Medlik, S. (1974) *Tourism, Past, Present and Future*, Oxford: Heinemann.

Burkart, A. and Medlik, S. (1981) *Tourism, Past Present and Future*, 2nd edition. London: Heinemann.

Burns, J.P.A. and Mules, T.L. (1986) 'A framework for the analysis of major special events', pp. 5–38 in *The Adelaide Grand Prix: The Impact of a Special Event*, Eds. J.P.A. Burns, J.H. Hatch, T.L. Mules, The

Centre for South Australian Economic Studies, Adelaide.

Burns, J.P.A. and Mules, T.L. (1986) 'A framework for the analysis of major special events' in J.P.A. Burns, J.H. Hatch, T.L. Mules (eds) *The Adelaide Grand Prix: The Impact Of A Special Event*, Adelaide: The Centre for South Australian Economic Studies, 5–38.

Burtenshaw, D., Bateman, M. and Ashworth, G.J. (1991) *The City in West Europe*, 2nd edn, Chichester: Wiley.

Burton, R. (1974) *The Recreational Carrying Capacity of the Countryside*, Occasional Publication No. 11: Keele University Library, Keele, Staffordshire.

Burton, T. (1966) 'A day in the country – a survey of leisure activity at Box Hill in Surrey', *Chartered Surveyor* 98.

Burton, T. (1971) *Experiments in Recreation Research*, London: Allen and Unwin.

Burton, T.L. (1982) 'A framework for leisure policy research', *Leisure Studies*, 1: 323–35.

Butler, R.W. (1974) 'The social implications of tourist developments', *Annals of Tourism Research*, 2: 100–11.

Butler, R.W. (1975) 'Tourism as an agent of social change', in F. Helleiner (ed.) *Tourism as a Factor in National and Regional Development*, Occasional Papers in Geography, No. 4. Peterborough: Trent University, 89–50.

Butler, R.W. (1980) 'The concept of the tourist area cycle of evolution: implications for management of resources', *Canadian Geographer*, 24: 5–12.

Butler, R.W. (1990) 'Alternative tourism: pious hope or Trojan horse', *Journal of Travel Research*, 28(3): 40–5.

Butler, R.W. (1991) 'Tourism, environment, and sustainable development', *Environmental Conservation*, 18(3): 201–9.

Butler, R.W. (1992) 'Alternative tourism: the thin edge of the wedge', in V.L. Smith and W.R. Eadington (eds) *Tourism Alternatives: Potentials and Problems in the Development of Tourism*, Philadelphia: University of Pennsylvania Press, pp. 31–46.

Butler, R.W. (1998) 'Sustainable tourism – looking backwards in order to progress?', in C.M. Hall and A. Lew (eds) *Sustainable Tourism Development: A Geographical Perspective*, London: Addison Wesley Longman.

Butler, R. and Clark, G. (1992) 'Tourism in rural areas: Canada and the UK', in I. Bowler, C. Bryant and M.

Nellis (eds) *Contemporary Rural Systems in Transition, Volume 2: Economy and Society*, Wallingford: CAB International.

Butler, R.W. and Hall, C.M. (1998) 'Conclusion: the sustainability of tourism and recreation in rural areas', in R. Butler, C.M. Hall and J. Jenkins (eds) *Tourism and Recreation in Rural Areas*, Chichester: Wiley, pp. 249–58.

Butler, R.W. and Hinch, T. (eds) (1996) *Tourism and Indigenous Peoples*, London: International Thomson Publishing.

Butler, R.W. and Wall, G. (1985) 'Themes in research on the evolution of tourism', *Annals of Tourism Research*, 12: 287–96.

Butler, R.W., Hall, C.M. and Jenkins, J. (eds) (1998) *Tourism and Recreation in Rural Areas*, Chichester: Wiley.

Byrne, A., Edmondson, R. and Fahy, K. (1993) 'Rural tourism and cultural identity in the West of Ireland', in B. O'Connor and M. Cronin (eds) *Tourism in Ireland: A Critical Analysis*, Cork: Cork University Press.

Calais, S.S. and Kirkpatrick, J.B. (1986) 'The impact of trampling on the natural ecosystems of the Cradle Mt. Lake St. Claire National Park', *Australian Geographer*, 17: 6–15.

Callicott, J.B. (1982) 'Traditional American Indian and Western European attitudes toward nature: an overview', *Environmental Ethics*, 4: 293–318.

Campbell, C.K. (1966) An Approach to Recreational Geography, *B.C. Occasional Papers No. 7*.

Canadian Council on Rural Development (1975) *Economic Significance of Tourism and Outdoor Recreation for Rural Development*, Working paper, Ottawa: Canadian Council on Rural Development.

Cannon, J. (1987) 'Issues in sampling and sample design – a managerial perspective', in J.B. Ritchie and C. Goeldner (eds) *Travel, Tourism and Hospitality Research: A Handbook for Managers and Researchers*, New York: Wiley, pp. 101–16.

Carhart, A.H. (1920) 'Recreation in the forests', *American Forests*, 26: 268–72.

Carlson, A.S. (1938) 'Recreation industry of New Hampshire', *Economic Geography*, 14: 255–70.

Carlson, A.W. (1978) 'The spatial behaviour involved in honeymoons: the case of two areas in Wisconsin and North Dakota', *Journal of Popular Culture*, 11: 977–88.

Carter, R. and Parker, A. (1989) 'Resources and

management of Irish coastal waters and adjacent coasts', in R. Carter and A. Parker (eds) *Ireland: Contemporary Perspectives on Land and its People*, London: Routledge, pp. 393–420.

Carter, R.W.G. and Parker, A.J. (eds) (1989) *Ireland: Contemporary Perspectives on a Land and its People*, London: Routledge.

Cater, E.A. (1993) 'Ecotourism in the third world: problems for sustainable development', *Tourism Management*, 14(2): 85–90.

Cater, E.A. and Lowman, G. (eds) (1994) *Ecotourism: A Sustainable Option?* Chichester: Wiley.

CERT (1987a) *Management in the hotel industry*, Dublin: Bord Fáilte.

CERT (1987b) *Scope of the tourism industry in Ireland*, Dublin: CERT.

CERT (1991) *A profile of employment in the tourism industry in Ireland: non food/accommodation sectors*, Dublin: CERT.

Chadwick, G. (1971) *A Systems View of Planning*, Oxford: Pergamon Press.

Chadwick, R. (1987) 'Concepts, definitions and measures used in travel and tourism research', in J.R. Brent Ritchie and C. Goeldner (eds) *Travel, Tourism and Hospitality Research: A Handbook for Managers and Researchers*, New York: Wiley.

Chadwick, R. (1994) 'Concepts, definitions and measures used in travel and tourism research', in J.R. Brent Ritchie and C. Goeldner (eds) *Travel, Tourism and Hospitality Research: A Handbook for Managers and Researchers*, 2nd ed., New York: Wiley.

Champeaux, J.P. (1987) 'Le marché du tourisme social en Europe', *Espaces*, 86: 17–20.

Chang, T.C., Milne, S., Fallon, D. and Pohlmann, C. (1996) 'Urban heritage tourism: the global–local nexus', *Annals of Tourism Research*, 23: 1–19.

Chapin, F. (1974) *Human Activity Patterns in the City*, New York: Wiley.

Charlton, C. and Essex, S. (1996) 'The involvement of District Councils in tourism in England and Wales', *Geoforum* 27 (2): 175–92.

Chartered Institute of Public Finance and Accountancy (1990) *Leisure and Recreation Statistics 1990–91 Estimates*, London: Chartered Institute of Public Finance and Accountancy.

Christaller, W. (1933) *Die Zentralen Orte in Söddentschland*, Jena.

Christaller, W. (1963) 'Some considerations of tourism location in Europe: the peripheral regions – underde-veloped countries – recreation areas', *Regional Science Association Papers*, 12: 95–105.

Chubb, M. and Chubb, H. (1981) *One Third of Our Time? An Introduction to Recreation Behaviour and Resources*, New York: Wiley.

Church, A. (1988) 'Urban regeneration in London's Docklands: a five year policy review', *Environment and Planning C: Government and Policy*, 6: 187–208.

Church, A. (1990) 'Transport and urban regeneration in London Docklands', *Cities: The International Journal of Urban Policy and Planning*, 7(4): 289–303.

Cichetti, C. (1971) 'Some economic issues in planning urban recreation facilities', *Land Economics*, 47: 14–23.

Clark, J. and Crichter, C. (1985) *The Devil Makes Work: Leisure in Capitalist Britain*, Basingstoke: Macmillan.

Clark, P. (ed.) (1981) *Country Towns in Pre-industrial England*, Leicester: Leicester University Press.

Clarke, W.C. (1991) 'Time and tourism: an ecological perspective', in M.L. Miller and J. Auyong (eds) *Proceedings of the 1990 Congress on Coastal and Marine Tourism*, Honolulu: National Coastal Research and Development Institute, pp. 387–93.

Clary, D. (1984) 'The impact of social change on a leisure region, 1960–1982: a study of Nord Pays D'Auge', in J. Long and R. Hecock (eds) *Leisure, Tourism and Social Change*, Dunfermline: Centre for Leisure Research, Dunfermline College of Physical Education, pp. 51–6.

Clawson, M. (1958) *Statistics on Outdoor Recreation*, Washington D.C.: Resources for the Future.

Clawson, M. and Knetsch, J. (1968) *The Economics of Outdoor Recreation*, Baltimore: John Hopkins Press.

Clawson, M., Held, R. and Stoddart, C. (1960) *Land for the Future*, Baltimore: John Hopkins Press.

Clewer, A., Pack, A. and Sinclair, M.T. (1992) 'Price competitiveness and inclusive tour holidays', in P. Johnson and B. Thomas (eds) *Choice and Demand in Tourism*, London: Mansell, pp. 123–44.

Clift, S. and Page, S.J. (eds) (1996) *Health and the International Tourist*, London: Routledge.

Cloke, P. (1992) 'The countryside', in P. Cloke (ed.) *Policy and Change in Thatcher's Britain*, Oxford: Pergamon Press.

Clout, H.D. (1987) 'Western Europe in context', in H.D. Clout (ed.) *Regional Development in Western Europe*, 3rd edn, London: David Fulton, pp. 3–18.

Coalter, F. (1993) 'Sports participation: price or priorities?' *Leisure Studies*, 12: 171–82.

Cohen, E. (1972) 'Towards a sociology of international tourism', *Social Research*, 39: 164–82.

Cohen, E. (1974) 'Who is a tourist? A conceptual clarification', *Sociological Review*, 22: 527–55.

Cohen, E. (1979a) 'Rethinking the sociology of tourism', *Annals of Tourism Research*, 6: 18–35.

Cohen, E. (1979b) 'A phenomenology of tourist experiences', *Sociology*, 13: 179–201.

Cohen, E. (1983) 'Thai girls and farang men', *Annals of Tourism Research*, 9: 403–8.

Cole, D.N., Petersen, M.E. and Lucas, R.C. (1987) *Managing Wilderness Recreation Use: Common Problems and Potential Solutions*, USDA Forest Service General Technical Report INT–230, Utah: Intermountain Forest and Range Experiment Station.

Commission of the European Community (1991) *Fourth Periodic Report on the Social and Economic Situation and Development of the Regions of the Community*, Luxembourg: Commission of the European Community.

Connell, J. (1988) *Sovereignty and Survival: Island Microstates in the Third World*, Research Monograph No.3, Sydney: Department of Geography, University of Sydney.

Conway, H. (1991) *People's Parks: The Design and Development of Victorian Parks in Britain*, Cambridge: Cambridge University Press.

Cooke, K. (1982) 'Guidelines for socially appropriate tourism development in British Columbia', *Journal of Travel Research*, 21(1): 22–8.

Cooke, P. (ed.) (1986) *Global Restructuring, Local Responses*, London: Economic and Social Research Council.

Cooke, P. (1989) *Localities: The Changing Face of Urban Britain*, London: Unwin Hyman.

Cooper, C.E. (1947) 'Tourism', *Journal of Geography*, 46: 115–20.

Cooper, C.P. (1981) 'Spatial and temporal patterns of tourist behaviour', *Regional Studies*, 15: 359–71.

Cooper, C.P. (1987) 'The changing administration of tourism in Britain', *Area*, 19(3): 249–53.

Cooper, C.P. and Jackson, S. (1989) 'Destination life cycle: the Island of Man case study', *Annals of Tourism Research*, 16(3): 377–98.

Cooper, C.P., Fletcher, J., Gilbert, D.G. and Wanhill, S. (1993) *Tourism: Principles and Practice*, London: Pitman.

Cooper, M.J. and Pigram, J.J. (1984) 'Tourism and the Australian economy', *Tourism Management*, 5(1): 2–12.

Coppock, J.T. (1966) 'The recreational use of land and water in rural Britain', *Tidschrift voor Economische en Sociale Geografie* 57: 81–96.

Coppock, J.T. (1970) 'Geographers and conservation', *Area*, 2, 24–26.

Coppock, J.T. (1974) 'Geography and public policy: Challenges, opportunities and implications', *Transactions of the Institute of British Geographers*, 63: 1–16.

Coppock, J.T. (1976) 'Geography and public policy: Challenge, opportunities and implications' in J.T. Coppock and W. Sewell *Spatial Dimensions of Public Policy*, Oxford: Pergamon.

Coppock, J.T. (ed.) (1977a) *Second Homes: Curse or blessing?*, Oxford: Pergamon Press.

Coppock, J.T. (1977b) 'Tourism as a tool for regional development', in B.S. Duffield (ed.) *Tourism: A Tool for Regional Development*, Edinburgh: Tourism and Recreation Research Unit, University of Edinburgh, pp. 1.2–1.5.

Coppock, J.T. (1980) 'The geography of leisure and recreation', in E.H. Brown (ed.) *Geography Yesterday and Tomorrow*, Royal Geographical Society: London.

Coppock, J.T. (1982) 'Geographical contributions to the study of leisure', *Leisure Studies*, 1: 1–27.

Coppock, J.T. and Duffield, B. (1975) *Outdoor Recreation in the Countryside: A Spatial Analysis*, London: Macmillan.

Coppock, J.T. and Sewell, W.R.D. (1976) *Spatial Dimensions of Public Policy*, Oxford: Pergamon.

Cornwall, G.W. and Holcomb, C.J. (eds) (1966) *Guidelines to the Planning, Developing, and Managing of Rural Recreation Enterprises*, Bulletin 301, Blacksburg: Cooperative Extension Service, Virginia Polytechnic Institute.

Corsi, T.M. and Harvey, M.E. (1979) 'Changes in vacation travel in response to motor fuel shortages and higher prices', *Journal of Travel Research*, 17(4): 6–11.

Cosgrove, I. and Jackson, R. (1972) *The Geography of Recreation and Leisure*, London: Hutchinson.

Council of Nature Conservation Ministers (CONCOM) Working Group on Management of National Parks (1985) *Identification and Management of Wilderness Areas in Australia, Discussion Paper*, Canberra: CONCOM.

Council of Nature Conservation Ministers (CONCOM) Working Group on Management of National Parks (1986) *Guidelines for Reservation and Management of Wilderness Areas in Australia*, Canberra: CONCOM.

Countryside Commission (1974) *Advice Note on Country Parks*, Cheltenham: Countryside Commission.

Countryside Commission (1983) *A Management Plan for the Green Belt Area in Barnet and South Havering, CCP 147*, Cheltenham: Countryside Commission.

Coventry, N. (1998) 'December dive', *Inside Tourism*, March: 1.

Cowie, I. (1985) 'Housing policy options in relation to the America's Cup', *Urban Policy and Research*, 3: 40–1.

Crandall, R. (1980) 'Motivations for leisure', *Journal of Leisure Research*, 12: 45–54.

Crisler, R.M. and Hunt, M.S. (1952) 'Recreation regions in Missouri', *Journal of Geography*, 51(1): 30–9.

Crompton, J.L. (1979) 'An assessment of the image of Mexico as a vacation destination', *Journal of Travel Research*, 17(Fall): 18–23.

Crompton, J.L. and Richardson, S.L. (1986) 'The tourism connection where public and private leisure services merge', *Parks and Recreation*, October: 38–44, 67.

Crompton, J. and Van Doren, C. (1976) 'Amusement parks, theme parks, and municipal leisure services: Contrasts in adaption to cultural change', *Journal of Physical Education and Recreation*, 47: 18–22.

Cronan, W. (1990) 'Modes of prophecy and production: placing nature in history,' *Journal of American History*, 76(4): 1122–31.

Crotty, R. (1979) 'Capitalist colonialism and peripheralisation: the Irish case', in D. Seers, B. Schaffer and M.L. Kiljunen (eds) *Under-developed Europe: Studies in Core–Periphery Relations*, New Jersey: Humanities Press, pp. 225–35.

Csikszentmihalyi, M. (1975) *Beyond Boredom and Anxiety*, San Francisco: Jossey Bass.

Curry, N. (1994) *Countryside Recreation: Access and Land Use Planning*, London: E&FN Spon.

Damette, F. (1980) 'The regional framework of monopoly exploitation: new problems and trends', in J. Carney, R. Hudson and J.R. Lewis (eds) *Regions in Crisis*, London: Croom Helm.

Dann, G. (1981) 'Tourist motivation: an appraisal', *Annals of Tourism Research*, 8 (2): 187–219.

Dann, G. (1993) 'Limitations in the use of nationality and country of residence variable', in D. Pearce and R. Butler (eds) *Tourism Research: Critique and Challenges*, Routledge: London.

DART (1974) *Farm Recreation and Tourism in England and Wales*, Report to the Countryside Commission, English Tourist Board and Wales Tourist Board, Publication No. 14, CCP 83, Cheltenham: Countryside Commission.

Dasmann, R.F. (1973) *Classification and Use of Protected Natural and Cultural Areas*, IUCN Occasional Paper No.4, Morges: International Union for Conservation of Nature and Natural Resources.

Davies, E. (1971) *Farm Tourism in Cornwall and Devon – Some Economic and Physical Considerations*, Report No. 184, Exeter: Agricultural Economics Unit, University of Exeter.

Davies, E. (1987) 'Planning in the New Zealand National Parks', *New Zealand Geographer*, 43(2): 73–8.

Davis, B. (1981) *Characteristics and Influence of the Australian Conservation Movement*, unpublished PhD thesis, Hobart: University of Tasmania.

Dawson, J. and Doornkamp, J. (eds) *Evaluating the Human Environment: Essays in Applied Geography*, London: Edward Arnold.

Deane, B. (1987) 'Tourism in Ireland: an employment growth area', *Administration*, 35: 337–49.

Dearden, P. (1993) 'Cultural aspects of tourism and sustainable development: tourism and the hilltribes of Northern Thailand', in J.G. Nelson, R. Butler and G. Wall (eds) *Tourism and Sustainable Development: Monitoring, Planning and Managing*, Waterloo: Department of Geography, University of Waterloo.

Dearden, P. and Rollins, R. (eds) (1993) *Parks and Protected Areas in Canada: Planning and Management*, Toronto: Oxford University Press.

Deasy, G. (1949) 'The tourist industry in a north woods county', *Economic Geography*, 25(2): 240–59.

Deasy, G.F. and Griess, P.R. (1966) 'Impact of a tourist facility on its hinterland', *Annals of the Association of American Geographers*, 56(2): 290–306.

Debbage, K.G. (1990) 'Oligopoly and the resort cycle in the Bahamas', *Annals of Tourism Research*, 18(2): 251–68.

Debbage, K.G. (1991) 'Spatial behaviour in a Bahamian resort', *Annals of Tourism Research*, 18: 251–68.

Debbage, K. and Iaonnides, D. (eds) (1998) *The Economic Geography of Tourism*, London: Routledge.

Deblock, A. (1986) 'Tourisme et pàche', *Espaces*, 82: 22–5.

Deegan, J. and Dineen, D. (1996) *Tourism Policy and Performance*, London: International Thomson Publishing.

Deem, R. (1986) *All Work and No Play? The Sociology of Women and Leisure*, Milton Keynes: Open University Press.

De Kadt, E. (ed.) (1979) *Tourism – Passport to Development?*, Oxford: Oxford University Press.

Denman, R. (1978) *Recreation and Tourism in Farms, Crofts and Estates*, Report to the Highlands and Islands Development Board and the Scottish Tourist Board, Edinburgh.

Department of the Environment (1990) *Tourism and the Inner City*, London: HMSO.

Department of Regional Economic Expansion (1972) *The Canada Land Inventory: Land Capability Classification for Outdoor Recreation*, Report No. 6, Ottawa: Queens Printer for Canada.

Department of Tourism (1993) *Rural Tourism, Tourism Discussion Paper No.1*, Canberra: Department of Tourism.

Department of Tourism and Transport (1989) *Improving the Performance of Irish Tourism: A Summary Report*, Dublin: Stationery Office.

Dernoi, L.A. (1983) 'Farm tourism in Europe', *Tourism Management*, 4(3): 155–66.

d'Hauteserre, A. (1996) 'A response to Dimitri Ioannides, "Strengthening the ties between tourism and economic geography: a theoretical agenda"', *Professional Geographer*, 48(2): 218–19.

Dilley, R.S. (1986) 'Tourist brochures and tourist images', *The Canadian Geographer*, 30(1): 59–65.

Dilsaver, L.M. and Tweed, W.C. (1990) *Challenge of the Big Trees: A Resource History of Sequoia and Kings Canyon National Parks*, Three Rivers: Sequoia Natural History Association.

Ding, P. and Pigram, J. (1995) 'Environmental audits: an emerging concept for sustainable tourism development', *Journal of Tourism Studies*, 2: 2–10.

Dingsdale, A. (1986) 'Ideology and leisure under socialism: The geography of second homes in Hungary', *Leisure Studies*, 5: 35–55.

Doering, T.R. (1976) 'A reexamination of the relative importance of tourism to state economies', *Journal of Travel Research*, 15(1): 13–17.

Donajgrodski, A. (ed.) (1978) *Social Control in Nineteenth Century Britain*, London: Croom Helm.

Doorne, S. (1998) The Last Resort: A Study of Power and Participation on the Wellington Waterfront, Unpublished Ph.D. thesis, Department of Tourism and Services Management, Victoria University of Wellington.

Doornkamp, J. (1982) *Applied Geography*, Nottingham Monographs in Applied Geography No. 1, Department of Geography, University of Nottingham.

Douglas, N. and Douglas, N. (1996) 'Tourism in the Pacific: historical factors', in C.M. Hall and S. Page (eds) *Tourism in the Pacific: Issues and Cases*, London: International Thomson Business Press, pp. 19–35.

Dower, M. (1965) *The Challenge of Leisure*, London: Civic Trust.

Dowling, R.K. (1993) 'Tourism planning, people and the environment in Western Australia', *Journal of Travel Research*, 31(4): 52–58.

Dowling, R.K. (1997) 'Plans for the development of regional ecotourism: theory and practice', in C.M. Hall, J. Jenkins and G. Kearsley (eds) *Tourism Planning and Policy in Australia and New Zealand: Cases, Issues and Practice*, Sydney: Irwin Publishers, pp. 110–26.

Downs, R. (1970) 'Geographic space perception: past approaches and future prospects', *Progress in Geography*, 2: 65–108.

Downs, R.M. and Stea, D. (1973) *Image and Environment*, New York: Aldine.

Doxey, G.V. (1975) 'A causation theory of visitor–resident irritants: methodology and research inferences', in *Proceedings of the Travel Research Association 6th Annual Conference*, San Diego: Travel Research Association, pp. 195–8.

Dubaniewicz, H. (1976) 'An appraisal of the natural environment of the Ködz Region for the needs of economic development and recreation', *Geographica Polonica*, 34: 265–71.

Duffield, B. and Long, J. (1981) 'Tourism in the Highlands and Islands of Scotland: Rewards and conflicts', *Annals of Tourism Research*, 8(3): 403–31.

Duffield, B. and Owen, M. (1970) *Leisure + Countryside = : A Geographical Appraisal of Countryside Recreation in Lanarkshire*, Edinburgh: University of Edinburgh.

Duffield, B. and Walker, S. (1983) *Urban Parks and*

Open Spaces: A Review, Edinburgh: Tourism and Recreation Research Unit.

Dunning, J. and McQueen, M. (1982) *Transnational Corporations in International Tourism*, New York: United Nations.

Dutton, I. and Hall, C.M. (1989) 'Making tourism sustainable: the policy/practice conundrum', in *Proceedings of the Environment Institute of Australia Second National Conference*, Melbourne: Environment Institute of Australia, pp. 196–296.

Dye, T. (1992) *Understanding Public Policy*, 7th edn, Englewood Cliffs: Prentice Hall.

Eagles, P. (1992) 'The travel motivations of Canadian ecotourists', *Journal of Travel Research*, 31(2), 3–7.

Economist Intelligence Unit (1991) *Ireland Country Profile*, London: Economist Intelligence Unit.

Edington, J.M. and Edington, M.A. (1986) *Ecology, Recreation and Tourism*, Cambridge: Cambridge University Press.

Edwards J. (1991) 'Guest–host perceptions of rural tourism in England and Portugal', in M.T. Sinclair and M.J. Stabler (eds) *The Tourism Industry: An International Analysis*, Wallingford: CAB International.

Eidsvik, H.K. (1980) 'National parks and other protected areas: some reflections on the past and prescriptions for the future', *Environmental Conservation*, 7(3): 185–90.

Eidsvik, H.K. (1985) 'Wilderness policy – an international perspective', paper presented at the National Wilderness Resources Conference, Fort Collins, Colorado, July.

Eidsvik, H.K. (1987) *Categories Revision – A Review and a Proposal*, Commission on National Parks and Protected Areas, International Union for the Conservation of Nature and Natural Resources, Morges.

Eiselen, E. (1945) 'The tourist industry of a modern highway, US16 in South Dakota', *Economic Geography*, 21: 221–30.

Ellerbrook, M.J. and Hite, J.C. (1980) 'Factors affecting regional employment in tourism in the United States', *Journal of Travel Research*, 18(3): 26–32.

Elson, M. (1977) *A Review and Evaluation of Countryside Recreation Site Surveys*, Cheltenham: Countryside Commission.

Elson, M. (1979) *The Leisure Use of Green Belts and Urban Fringes*, London: Sports Council and Social Science Research Council.

Elson, M. (1986) *Green Belts: Conflict Mediation in the Urban Fringe*, London: Heinemann.

Elson, M. (1993) 'Sport and recreation in the green belt countryside', in S. Glyptis (ed.) *Leisure and the Environment: Essays in Honour of Professor J.A. Patmore*, London: Belhaven.

English Historic Towns Forum (1993) *Retailing in Historic Towns: Research Study 1992*, London: Donaldsons.

English Tourist Board/Employment Department (1991) *Tourism and the Environment: Maintaining the Balance*, London: English Tourist Board.

Environmental Impact Services Limited (1991) *Great Blasket Island National Park Visitor Centre, Dun Chaoirsn, Co. Kerry*, Dublin: Environmental Impact Services Limited.

Esser, J. and Hirsch, J. (1989) 'The crisis of fordism and the dimensions of a "post-fordist" regional and urban structure', *International Journal of Urban and Regional Research*, 13: 417–37.

Euromonitor, (1992) *European Tourism Report*, Euromonitor, London.

Evans, N.J. (1992a) 'Advertising and farm-based accommodation: a British case study', *Tourism Management*, 13(4): 415–22.

Evans, N.J. (1992b) 'The distribution of farm-based accommodation in England and Wales', *Journal of the Royal Agricultural Society of England*, 153: 67–80.

Evans, N.J. (1992c) 'Towards an understanding of farm-based tourism in Britain', in A.W. Gilg (ed.) *Progress in Rural Policy and Planning*, vol. 2, London: Belhaven Press.

Evans, N.J. and Ilbery, B.W. (1989) 'A conceptual framework for investigating farm-based accommodation and tourism in Britain', *Journal of Rural Studies*, 5(3): 257–66.

Evans, N. and Ilbery, B. (1992) 'The distribution of farm-based accommodation in England and Wales', *Journal of the Royal Agricultural Society of England* 153: 67–80.

Evernden, N. (1992) *The Social Creation of Nature*, Baltimore: John Hopkins University Press.

Ewert, A. and Hollenhurst, S. (1989) 'Testing the adventure model: empirical support for a model of risk recreational participation', *Journal of Leisure Research*, 21: 124–9.

Fabbri, P. (ed.) (1990) *Recreational Use of Coastal Areas: A Research Project of the Commission on the*

Coastal Environment, International Geographical Union, Dordrecht: Kluwer.

Fagence, M. (1990) 'Geographically-referenced planning strategies', *Journal of Environmental Management*, 3(1): 1–18.

Fagence, M. (1991) 'Geographic referencing of public policies in tourism', *Revue de Tourisme*, 3(3): 8–19.

Farrell, B.H. (ed.) (1978) *The Social and Economic Impact of Tourism on Pacific Communities*, Santa Cruz: Centre for South Pacific Studies, University of California.

Faulkner, B. and Tidesswell, C. (1996) 'Gold Coast resident attitudes toward tourism: the influence of involvement in tourism, residential proximity, and period of residence', in G. Prosser (ed.) *Tourism and Hospitality Research: Australian and International Perspectives*, Canberra: Bureau of Tourism Research.

Featherstone, M. (1987) 'Leisure, symbolic power and the life course', in J. Horne, D. Jary and A. Tomlinson (eds) *Sport, Leisure and Social Relations*, London: Routledge and Kegan Paul.

Fedler, A. (1987) 'Introduction: are leisure, recreation and tourism interrelated?', *Annals of Tourism Research*, 14(3): 311–13.

Feehan, J. (ed.) (1992) *Tourism on the Farm*, Dublin: Environmental Institute, University College.

Feller, M., Hooley, D., Dreher, T., East, I. and Jung, R. (1979) *Wilderness in Victoria: An Inventory*, Monash Publications in Geography No. 21, Clayton: Department of Geography, Monash University.

Ferguson, M. and Munton, R. (1978) *Informal Recreation in the Urban Fringe: Provision and Management of Sites in London's Green Belt*, working paper No. 2 Land for Informal Recreation, London: Department of Geography, University College.

Ferguson M. and Munton, R. (1979) 'Informal recreation sites in London's green belt', *Area*, 11: 196–205.

Ferrario, F.F. (1979a) 'The evaluation of tourist resources: an applied methodology part I', *Journal of Travel Research*, 17(3): 18–22.

Ferrario, F.F. (1979b) 'The evaluation of tourist resources: an applied methodology part II', *Journal of Travel Research*, 17(4): 24–29.

Fesenmaier, D.R. and Lieber, S.R. (1987) 'Outdoor recreation expenditure and the effects of spatial structure', *Leisure Sciences*, 9(1): 27–40.

Fianna Fail (1987) *Putting Growth Back into Tourism*, Dublin: Fianna Fail.

Filoppovich, L. (1979) 'Mapping of recreational development around a large city', *Soviet Geography*, 20: 361–69.

Fines, K. (1968) 'Landscape evaluation: a research project in East Sussex', *Regional Studies*, 2(1): 41–5.

Fitton, M. (1976) 'The urban fringe and the less privileged', *Countryside Recreation Review*, 1: 25–34.

Fitton, M. (1979) 'Countryside recreation – the problems of opportunity', *Local Government Studies* 5: 57–90.

Fitzpatrick, J. and Montague, M. (1989) 'Irish Republic outbound', *Travel and Tourism Analyst*, 6: 40–55.

Fletcher, J. and Snee, H.R. (1989) 'Tourism multiplier efforts', in S.F. Witt and L. Moutinho (eds) *Tourism Marketing and Management Handbook*, Hemel Hempstead: Prentice Hall, pp. 529–31.

Floor, H. (1990) *Aktiviteten Systemen en Bereikboaheid*, Amsterdam: Siswo.

Foras Forbartha (1973) *Brittas Bay: A Planning and Conservation Study*, Dublin: Foras Forbartha.

Foras Forbartha (1977) *Inventory of Outstanding Landscapes in Ireland*, Dublin: Foras Forbartha.

Forer, P. and Pearce, D.G. (1984) 'Spatial patterns of package tourism in New Zealand', *New Zealand Geographer*, 40: 34–42.

Forster, J. (1964) 'The sociological consequences of tourism', *International Journal of Comparative Sociology*, 5: 217–27.

Fowler, J. (1991) 'Farm house holidays in Ireland', *Tourism Recreation Research*, 16: 72–5.

Frankel, O.H. (1978) 'The value of wilderness to science', in G. Mosley (ed.) *Australia's Wilderness: Conservation Progress and Plans*, Proceedings of the First National Wilderness Conference, Australian Academy of Science, Canberra, 21–23 October, 1977, Hawthorn: Australian Conservation Foundation, pp. 101–105.

Frater, J. (1982) *Farm Tourism in England and Overseas*, Research Memorandum 93, Birmingham: Centre for Urban and Regional Studies, University of Birmingham.

Frater, J. (1983) 'Farm tourism in England', *Tourism Management*, 4(3): 167–79.

Frechtling, D. (1976) 'Proposed standard definitions and classifications for travel research', Marketing Travel and Tourism, *Seventh Annual Conference Proceedings*, Boca Raton: Travel Research Association, pp. 59–74.

Frechtling, D.C. (1977) 'Travel as an employer in the

state economy', *Journal of Travel Research*, 15(4): 8–12.

Frechtling, D.C. (1987) 'Assessing the impacts of travel and tourism – introduction to travel impact estimation', in J.R.B. Ritchie and C.R. Goeldner (eds) *Travel, Tourism and Hospitality Research: A Handbook for Managers and Researchers*, New York: Wiley, pp. 325–31.

Frechtling, D. (1996) *Practical Tourism Forecasting*, Oxford: Butterworth Heinemann.

Freeman, T.W. (1961) *A Hundred Years Of Geography*, London: Gerald Dockworth.

Fretter, A.D. (1993) 'Place marketing: a local authority perspective', in G. Kearns and C. Philo (eds) *Selling Places: The City as Cultural Capital, Past and Present*, Oxford: Pergamon Press, pp. 163–74.

Friedmann, J. (1966) *Regional Development Policy: A case study of Venezuela*, Massachusetts: MIT Press.

Fukaz, G. (1989) 'Hungary: more work, less leisure', in A. Olszewska and K. Roberts (eds) *Leisure and Lifestyle: A Comparative Analysis of Free Time*, London: Sage.

Funk, R.W. (1959) 'The wilderness', *Journal of Biblical Literature*, 78: 205–14.

Furnham, A. (1984) 'Tourism and culture shock', *Annals of Tourism Research*, 11: 41–58.

Galatowitsch, S.M. (1990) 'Using the original land survey notes to reconstruct presettlement landscapes of the American West', *Great Basin Naturalist*, 50(2): 181–91.

Gale, F. and Jacobs, J.M. (1987) *Tourists and the National Estate Procedures to Protect Australia's Heritage*, Australian Heritage Commission Special Australian Heritage Publication Series No.6, Canberra: Australian Government Publishing Service.

Gannon, J. and Johnston, K. (1995) 'The global hotel industry: the emergence of continental hotel companies', *Progress in Tourism and Hospitality Research*, 1: 31–42.

Gardner, J.S. (1978) 'The meaning of wilderness: a problem of definition', *Contact – Journal of Urban and Environmental Affairs*, 10(1): 7–33.

Gartner, W.C. (1986) 'Temporal influences on image change', *Annals of Tourism Research*, 13: 635–44.

Gartner, W.C. (1987) 'Environmental impacts of recreational home developments', *Annals of Tourism Research*, 14(1): 38–57.

Gaviria, M. (1975) *Turismo de Playa en Espana*, Madrid: Edicione S. Turner.

Getz, D. (1977) 'The impact of tourism on host communities a research approach', in B.S. Duffield (ed.) *Tourism: A Tool for Regional Development*, Edinburgh: Tourism and Recreation Research Unit, University of Edinburgh, pp. 9.1–9.13.

Getz, D. (1981) 'Tourism and rural settlement policy', *Scottish Geographical Magazine*, 97 (December): 158–68.

Getz, D. (1983) 'Capacity to absorb tourism: concepts and implications for strategic planning', *Annals of Tourism Research*, 10: 239–63.

Getz, D. (1984) 'Tourism, community organisation and the social multiplier', in J. Long and R. Hecock (eds) *Leisure, Tourism and Social Change*, Dunfermline: Centre for Leisure Research, Dunfermline College of Physical Education, pp. 85–100.

Getz, D. (1986a) 'Models in tourism planning towards integration of theory and practice', *Tourism Management*, 7(1): 21–32.

Getz, D. (1986b) 'Tourism and population change: long term impacts of tourism in the Badenoch–Strathspey District of the Scottish Highlands', *Scottish Geographical Magazine*, 102(2): 113–26.

Getz, D. (1987) *Tourism Planning and Research: Traditions, Models and Futures*, Paper presented at the Australian Travel Research Workshop, Bunbury, Western Australia, November 5–6.

Getz, D. (1991a) *Festivals, Special Events, and Tourism*, New York: Van Nostrand Reinhold.

Getz, D. (1991b) 'Assessing the economic impacts of festivals and events: research issues', *Journal of Applied Recreation Research*, 16(1): 61–77.

Getz, D. (1993a) 'Planning for tourism business districts', *Annals of Tourism Research* 20: 583–600.

Getz, D. (1993b) 'Tourist shopping villages: Development and planning strategies', *Tourism Management* 14(1): 15–26.

Getz, D. (1993c) 'Impacts of tourism on residents' leisure: concepts, and a longitudinal case study of Spey Valley, Scotland', *Journal of Tourism Studies*, 4(2): 33–44.

Getz, D. (1994a) 'Students' work experiences, perceptions and attitudes towards careers in hospitality and tourism: a longitudinal case study in Spey Valley, Scotland', *International Journal of Hospitality Management*, 13(1): 25–37.

Getz, D. (1994b) 'Residents' attitudes towards tourism: a longitudinal study in Spey Valley, Scotland', *Tourism Management*, 15(4): 247–58.

Getz, D. (1997) *Event Management and Tourism*, New York: Cognizant.

Getz, D. and Page, S.J. (eds) (1997) *The Business of Rural Tourism: International Perspectives*, London: International Thomson Publishing.

Giddens, A. (1984) *The Constitution of Society: Outline of the Theory of Structuration*, Cambridge: Polity Press.

Gilbert, D. and Joshi, I. (1992) 'Quality management and the tourism and hospitality industry', in C. Cooper and A. Lockwood (eds) *Progress in Tourism, Recreation and Hospitality Management*, vol. 4, London: Belhaven, pp. 149–68.

Gilbert, E.W. (1939) 'The growth of inland and seaside health resorts in England', *Scottish Geographical Magazine*, 55: 16–35.

Gilbert, E.W. (1949) 'The growth of Brighton', *Geographical Journal*, 114: 30–52.

Gilbert, E. (1951) 'Geography and regionalism', in G. Taylor (ed.) *Geography in the Twentieth Century*, London: Methuen.

Gill, A. and Williams, P.W. (1994) 'Managing growth in mountain tourism communities', *Tourism Management*, 15(3): 212–20.

Gillmore, D.A. (1985) *Economic Activities in the Republic of Ireland: A Geographical Perspective*, Dublin: Gill and Macmillan.

Glacken, C. (1967) *Traces on the Rhodian Shore, Nature and Culture in Western Thought from Ancient Times to the End of the Eighteenth Century*, Berkeley: University of California Press.

Glansberg, A. (1991) 'Revitalizing tourism in Northern Ireland', *Cornell Hotel and Restaurant Administration Quarterly*, 31: 28–30.

Glebe, G. (1978) 'Recent settlement desertion on the Beara and Iveragh peninsulas; a methodological approach', *Irish Geography*, 11: 171–6.

Glyptis, S. (1979) *Countryside Visitors: Site Use and Leisure Lifestyles*, unpublished PhD thesis, Hull: University of Hull.

Glyptis, S. (1981a) 'Leisure life-styles', *Regional Studies*, 15: 311–26.

Glyptis, S. (1981b) 'People at play in the countryside', *Geography*, 66(4): 277–85.

Glyptis, S. (1981c) Room to relax in the countryside', *The Planner*, 67(5): 120–22.

Glyptis, S. (1989) 'Recreational resource management' in C. Cooper (ed.) *Progress in Tourism, Recreation and Hospitality Management, Vol. 1*, London: Belhaven, 135–53.

Glyptis, S. (1991) *Countryside Recreation*, Harlow: Longman.

Glyptis, S. (1993) 'Leisure and the environment', in S. Glyptis (ed.) *Essays in Honour of Professor J.A. Patmore*, Belhaven: London.

Go, F. (1991) *Competitive Strategies for the International Hotel Industry*, Economist Intelligence Unit Special Report, London.

Go, F. and Pine, R. (1995) *Globalization Strategy in the Hotel Industry*, London: Routledge.

Godbey, G. (1976) *Recreation and Park Planning: The Exercise of Values*, Ontario: University of Waterloo.

Godfrey-Smith, W. (1979) 'The value of wilderness', *Environmental Ethics*, 1: 309–19.

Godfrey-Smith, W. (1980) 'The value of wilderness: a philosophical approach', in R.W. Robertson, P. Helman and A. Davey (eds) *Wilderness Management in Australia*, proceedings of a symposium held at the Canberra College of Advanced Education 19–23 July 1978, Canberra: School of Applied Science, Canberra College of Advanced Education, pp. 56–71.

Gold, J. (1980) *An Introduction to Behavioural Geography*, Oxford: Oxford University Press.

Goodall, B. (ed.) (1989) 'Tourism accommodation: Special issue', *Built Environment* 15(2).

Goodall, B. (1990) 'The dynamics of tourism place marketing', in G.J. Ashworth and B. Goodall (eds) *Marketing Tourism Places*, London: Routledge: pp. 259–79.

Goodall, B. and Whittow, J. (1975) 'Recreation requirements and forest opportunities', *Geographical Paper No. 378*, Reading: Department of Geography, University of Reading.

Goodenough, R. and Page, S.J. (1994) 'Evaluating the environmental impact of a major transport infra-structure project: the Channel Tunnel high speed rail link', *Applied Geography*, 14(1): 26–50.

Goodhead, T. and Johnson, D. (ed.) (1996) *Coastal Recreation Management*, London: E and F N Spon.

Graber, L.H. (1978) *Wilderness as Sacred Space*, Monograph No. 8, Washington D.C.: The Association of American Geographers.

Graburn, N.H.H. (1983) 'The anthropology of tourism', *Annals of Tourism Research*, 10: 9–33.

Graefe, A.R. and Vaske, J.J. (1987) 'A framework for managing quality in the tourist experience', *Annals of Tourism Research*, 14: 389–404.

Graefe, A.R., Vaske, J.J. and Kuss, F.R. (1984a) 'Social carrying capacity: an integration and synthesis of twenty years of research', *Leisure Sciences*, 6(4): 395–431.

Graefe, A.R., Vaske, J.J. and Kuss, F.R. (1984b) 'Resolving issues and remaining questions about social carrying capacity', *Leisure Sciences*, 6(4): 497–507.

Grahn, P. (1991) 'Landscaped in our minds: people choice of recreative places in towns', *Landscape Research*, 16: 11–19.

Gramann, J.H. (1982) 'Toward a behavioural theory of crowding in outdoor recreation: an evaluation and synthesis of research', *Leisure Sciences*, 5(2): 109–26.

Grano, O. (1981) 'External influence and internal change in the development of geography', in D.R. Stoddart (ed.) *Geography, Ideology and Social Concern*, Oxford: Blackwell, pp. 17–36.

Graves, H.S. (1920) 'A crisis in national recreation', *American Forestry*, 26(July): 391–400.

Greater London Council (1968) *Surveys of the Use of Open Space*, vol. 1, Greater London Council Research Paper 3, London: Greater London Council.

Greater London Council (1975) *Greater London Recreation Study*, London: Greater London Council.

Greater London Council (GLC) (1976) *Greater London Recreation Study: Part 1, Demand*, London: Greater London Council.

Green, B. (1990) *Countryside Conservation*, London: Unwin Hyman.

Greenhut, M. (1956) *Plant Location in Theory and Practice*, Chapel Hill: University of North Carolina Press.

Gregory, J. (1988) *Perceptions of Open Space: A Report on Research Undertaken by the Urban Wildlife Group*, Birmingham: Urban Wildlife Trust.

Grekin, J. and Milne, S. (1996) 'Toward sustainable tourism development: the case of Pond Inlet, NWT', in R.W. Butler and T. Hinch (eds) *Tourism and Indigenous Peoples*, London: Routledge, pp. 76–106.

Griffith, D. and Elliot, D. (1988) *Sampling Errors on the IPS*, London: OPCS New Methodology Series.

Griffiths, T. (1991) 'History and natural history: conservation movements in conflict', in D.J. Mulvaney (ed.) *The Humanities and the Australian Environment*, Canberra: Australian Academy of the Humanities, pp. 87–109.

Grimes, S. (1992) 'Ireland: the challenge of development in the European periphery', *Geography*, 77: 22–32.

Grinstein, A. (1955) 'Vacations: a psycho-analytic study', *International Journal of Psycho-Analysis*, 36: 177–86.

Grocott, A. (1990) 'Parks for people', *Leisure Management*, 8: 31–2.

Groome, D. and Tarrant, C. (1984) 'Countryside recreation: Achieving access for all?', *Countryside Planning Yearbook 1984*: 77–98.

Groundwork Foundation (1986) *Putting Wasteland to Good Use*, Birmingham: Groundwork Foundation.

Gunn, C. (1972) *Vacationscape: Designing Tourist Regions*, Austin: University of Texas.

Gunn, C. (1988) *Tourism Planning*, 2nd edn, London: Taylor and Francis.

Guthrie, H.W. (1961) 'Demand for goods and services in a world market', *Regional Science Association Papers*, 7: 159–75.

Guy, B.S. and Curtis, W.W. (1986) 'Consumer learning or retail environment: a tourism and travel approach', Conference paper presented at the American Academy of Marketing Conference, Cleveland University, W. Benoy Joseph (ed.) *Tourism Services Marketing: Advances in Theory and Practice*, American Academy of Marketing Conference, Cleveland University.

Haggett, P. (1986) 'Geography', in R.J. Johnston, D. Gregory, D.M. Smith (eds) *The Dictionary of Human Geography*, Oxford: Blackwell, pp. 175–8.

Haines, A.L. (1977) *The Yellowstone Story*, 2 vols, Yellowstone National Park: Yellowstone Library and Museum Association/Colorado Associated University Press.

Haley, A. (1979) 'Municipal recreation and park standards in the United States: central cities and suburbs', *Leisure Sciences*, 2: 277–91.

Hall, C.M. (1985) 'Outdoor recreation and national identity: a comparative study of Australia and Canada', *Journal of Canadian Culture*, 2(2): 25–39.

Hall, C.M. (1987) 'Wilderness inventories in Australia', in A. Conacher (ed.) *Readings in Australian Geography*, Proceedings of the 21st Institute of Australian Geographers' Conference, Perth, 10–18 May 1986, Nedlands: Department of Geography, University of Western Australia, pp. 466–76.

Hall, C.M. (1989) 'The definition and analysis of hallmark tourist events', *GeoJournal*, 19(3): 263–8.

Hall, C.M. (1990) 'From cottage to condominium: recreation, tourism and regional development in northern New South Wales', in D.J. Walmesley (ed.) *Change and Adjustment in Northern New South*

Wales, Armidale: Department of Geography and Planning, University of New England, pp. 85–99.

Hall, C.M. (1992a) *Wasteland to World Heritage: Preserving Australia's Wilderness*, Carlton: Melbourne University Press.

Hall, C.M. (1992b) *Hallmark Events: Impacts, Management and Planning*, London: Belhaven Press.

Hall, C.M. (1994) *Tourism and Politics: Policy, Power and Place*, London: John Wiley.

Hall, C.M. (1995) *Introduction to Tourism in Australia*, 2nd edn, South Melbourne: Longman Australia.

Hall, C.M. (1996) 'Tourism and the Maori of Aoteroa/New Zealand', in R.W. Butler and T. Hinch (eds) *Tourism and Indigenous Peoples*, London: International Thomson Publishing.

Hall, C.M. (1997) *Tourism in the Pacific: Development, Impacts and Markets*, 2nd edn, South Melbourne: Addison Wesley Longman.

Hall, C.M. (1998) *Introduction to Tourism: Development, Dimensions and Issues*, 3rd edn, South Melbourne: Addison Wesley Longman.

Hall, C.M. (1999) *Tourism Planning: Destinations, Organisations, People and the Environment*, Harlow: Addison Wesley Longman.

Hall, C.M. and Hodges, J. (1996) 'The party's great, but what about the hangover?: the housing and social impacts of mega-events with special reference to the Sydney 2000 Olympics', *Festival Management and Event Tourism*, 4(1/2): 13–20.

Hall, C.M. and Jenkins, J. (1995) *Tourism and Public Policy*, London: Routledge.

Hall, C.M. and Jenkins, J. (1998) 'The policy dimensions of rural tourism and recreation', in R. Butler, C.M. Hall and J. Jenkins (eds) *Tourism and Recreation in Rural Areas*, Chichester: Wiley, pp. 19–42.

Hall, C.M. and Johnston, M. (eds) (1995) *Polar Tourism: Tourism in the Arctic and Antarctic Regions*, Chichester: Wiley.

Hall, C.M. and Lew, A.A. (eds) (1998) *Sustainable Tourism Development: Geographical Perspectives*, Harlow: Addison Wesley Longman.

Hall, C.M. and McArthur, S. (1994) 'Commercial whitewater rafting in Australia', in D. Mercer (ed.) *New Viewpoints in Australian Outdoor Recreation Research and Planning*, Williamstown: Hepper Marriot and Associates Publishers, pp. 109–18.

Hall, C.M. and McArthur, S. (eds) (1996) *Heritage Management in Australia and New Zealand: The Human Dimension*, Sydney: Oxford University Press.

Hall, C.M. and McArthur, S. (1998) *Integrated Heritage Management*, London: The Stationery Office.

Hall, C.M. and Mark, S.R. (1985) *Saving All the Pieces: Wilderness and Inventory and Prospect in Western Australia*, A Working Paper, Nedlands: Department of Geography, University of Western Australia.

Hall, C.M. and Page, S.J. (eds) (1996) *Tourism in the Pacific: Cases and Issues*, London: International Thomson Business Press.

Hall, C.M. and Page, S.J. (eds) (1999) *Tourism in South and South-East Asia: Cases and Issues*, Oxford: Butterworth Heinemann.

Hall, C.M. and Selwood, H.J. (1987) 'Cup gained, paradise lost? a case study of the 1987 America's Cup as a hallmark event', in *Proceedings of the New Zealand Geography Society Conference*, Palmerston North: Department of Geography, Massey University.

Hall, C.M., Selwood, H.J. and McKewon, E. (1995) 'Hedonists, ladies and larrikins: crime, prostitution and the 1987 America's Cup', *Visions in Leisure and Business*, 14(3): 28–51.

Hall, C.M., Jenkins, J.M. and Kearsley, G. (eds) (1997) *Tourism Planning and Policy in Australia and New Zealand: Cases and Issues*, Sydney: Irwin Publishers.

Hall, D.R. (ed.) (1991) *Tourism and Economic Development in Eastern Europe and the Soviet Union*, London: Belhaven Press.

Hall, D.R. and O'Hanlan, L. (eds) (1998) *Rural Tourism Management: Sustainable Options*, Proceedings of an International Conference, 9–12 September 1998, Scottish Agricultural College Auchincruire, Ayr.

Hall, J. (1974) 'The capacity to adsorb tourists', *Built Environment*, 3: 392–7.

Hall, P. (1982a) *Urban and Regional Planning*, 2nd edn, Penguin: Harmondsworth.

Hall, P. (1982b) *Great Planning Disasters*. Penguin: Harmondsworth.

Hamilton-Smith, E. (1980) 'Wilderness: experience or land use', in R.W. Robertson, P. Helman and A. Davey (eds) *Wilderness Management in Australia*, Proceedings of a symposium held at the Canberra College of Advanced Education 19–23 July 1978, Canberra: School of Applied Science, Canberra College of Advanced Education, pp. 72–81.

Harmston, F.K. (1980) 'A case study of secondary impacts comparing through and vacationing travelers', *Journal of Travel Research*, 18(3): 33–6.

Harris, C.C., McLaughlin, W.J. and Ham, S.H. (1987) 'Integration of recreation and tourism in Idaho', *Annals of Tourism Research*, 14(3): 405–19.

Harrison, C. (1980–81) 'Recovery of lowland grassland and heathland in Southern England from disturbance by trampling', *Biological Conservation* 19: 119–30.

Harrison, C. (1981), *Preliminary Results of a Survey of Site Use in the South London Green Belt*, Working Paper No. 9, Land for Informal Recreation, London: Department of Geography, University College.

Harrison, C. (1983), 'Countryside recreation and London's urban fringe', *Transactions of the Institute of British Geographers*, 8: 295–313.

Harrison, C. (1991) *Countryside Recreation in a Changing Society*, London: TML Partnership.

Hartmann, R. (1984) 'Tourism, seasonality and social change', in J. Long and R. Hecock (eds) *Leisure, Tourism and Social Change*, Dunfermline: Centre for Leisure Research, Dunfermline College of Physical Education, pp. 101–12.

Harvey, D. (1974) 'What kind of geography, for what kind of public policy', *Transactions of the Institute of British Geographers*, 63: 18–24.

Harvey, D. (1987) 'Flexible accumulation through urbanisation', *Antipode*, 19: 260–86.

Harvey, D. (1988) 'Voodoo cities', *New Statesman and Society*, 30 September: 33–5.

Harvey, D. (1989a) 'From managerialism to entrepreneurialism: the transformation in urban governance in late capitalism', *Geografiska Annaler*, 71B: 3–17.

Harvey, D. (1989b) *The Condition of Postmodernity: An Enquiry into the Origins of Cultural Change*, Oxford: Basil Blackwell.

Harvey, D. (1990) 'Between space and time: reflection on the geographic information', *Annals Association of American Geographers*, 80: 418–34.

Harvey, D. (1993) 'From space to place and back again: reflections on the condition of postmodernity', in J. Bird, B. Curtis, T. Putnam, G. Robertson and L. Tickner (eds) *Mapping the Futures: Local Cultures, Global Change*, London: Routledge, pp. 3–29.

Harwood, C. and Kirkpatrick, J.B. (1980) *Forestry and Wilderness in the South West*, rev. edn, Hobart: Tasmanian Conservation Trust.

Hawes, M. (1981) 'In search of wilderness that speaks to the heart', *Habitat*, 9(6): 3.

Hawes, M. and Heatley, D. (1985) *Wilderness Assessment and Management*, A Discussion Paper, Hobart: The Wilderness Society.

Haynes, R. (1980) *Geographical Images and Mental Maps*, London: Macmillan.

Haywood, K.M. and Muller, T.E. (1988) 'The urban tourist experience: evaluating satisfaction', *Hospitality Education and Research Journal*: 453–9.

Heath, E. and Wall, G. (1992) *Marketing Tourism Destinations: A Strategic Planning Approach*, Chichester: Wiley.

Heeley, J. (1981) 'Planning for tourism in Britain', *Town Planning Review*, 52: 61–79.

Helber, L.E. (1988) 'The roles of government in planning in tourism with special regard for the cultural and environmental impact of tourism', in D. McSwan (ed.) *The Roles of Government in the Development of Tourism as an Economic Resource*, Seminar Series No.1, Townsville: Centre for Studies in Travel and Tourism, James Cook University, pp. 17–23.

Helburn, N. (1977) 'The wilderness continuum', *Professional Geographer*, 29: 337–47.

Helman, P. (1979) *Wild and Scenic Rivers: A Preliminary Study of New South Wales*, Occasional Paper No. 2, Sydney: New South Wales National Parks and Wildlife Service.

Helman, P.H., Jones, A.D., Pigram, J.J.J. and Smith, J.M.B. (1976) *Wilderness in Australia: Eastern New South Wales and South-East Queensland*, Armidale: Department of Geography, University of New England.

Hendee, J.C., Stankey, G.H. and Lucas, R.C. (1978) *Wilderness Management*, Miscellaneous Publication No. 1365, Washington: U.S. Department of Agriculture, Forest Service.

Hendry, L., Shucksmith, J., Love, J. and Glendinning, A. (1993) *Young People's Leisure and Lifestyles*, London: Routledge.

Heneghan, P. (1976) 'The changing role of Bord Fáilte 1960–1975', *Administration*, 24: 394–406.

Henning, D.H. (1971) 'The ecology of the political/administrative process for wilderness classification', *Natural Resources Journal*, 11: 69–75.

Henning, D. (1974) *Environmental Policy and Administration*, New York: American Elsevier Publishing Company.

Henning, D. (1987) 'Wilderness politics: public participation and values', *Environmental Management*, 11(3): 283–93.

Henry, I. (1988) 'Alternative futures for the public leisure service' in J. Benington and J. White (eds) *The Future of Leisure Services*, Harlow: Longman, 207–44.

Henry, I. (ed.) (1990) *Management and Planning in the Leisure Industries*, Basingstoke: Macmillan.

Herbert, D.T. (1987) 'Exploring the work–leisure relationship: an empirical study of south Wales', *Leisure Studies*, 6: 147–65.

Herbert, D.T. (1988) 'Work and leisure: exploring a relationship', *Area*, 20 (3): 241–52.

Herbertson, A.J. (1905) 'The major natural regions', *Geographical Journal*, 25: 300–310.

Higham, J.E.S. (1996) *Wilderness Perceptions of International Visitors to New Zealand: The Perceptual Approach to the Management of International Tourists Visiting Wilderness Areas within New Zealand's Conservation Estate*, unpublished PhD thesis, Dunedin: Centre for Tourism, University of Otago.

Higham, J.E.S. (1997) 'Visitors to New Zealand's back-country conservation estate', in C.M. Hall, J. Jenkins and G. Kearsley (eds) *Tourism Planning and Policy in Australia and New Zealand*, Sydney: Irwin Publishers, pp. 75–86.

Higham, J.E.S. and Kearsley, G.W. (1994) 'Wilderness perception and its implications for the management of the impacts of international tourism on natural areas in New Zealand', in C. Ryan (ed.) *Tourism Down-under: A Tourism Research Conference, 6–9 December 1994*, Palmerston North: Department of Management Systems, Massey University, pp. 505–29.

Hillman, M. and Whalley, A. (1977) *Fair Play for All: A Study of Access to Sport and Informed Recreation*, London: Political and Economic Planning Broadsheet No. 571.

Hinch, T.D. (1990) 'A spatial analysis of tourist accommodation in Ontario: 1974–1988', *Journal of Applied Recreation Research*, 15(4): 239–64.

Hinch, T.D. (1996) 'Urban tourism: perspectives on sustainability', *Journal of Sustainable Tourism*, 4(2): 95–110.

Hockin, R., Goodall, B. and Whitlow, J. (1978) 'The site requirements and planning of outdoor recreation activities', *Geographical Paper No. 54*, Reading: University of Reading.

Hoggart, K. (1988) 'Not a definition of rural', *Area*, 20: 35–40.

Hoggart, K. (1990) 'Let's do away with rural', *Journal of Rural Studies*, 6: 245–57.

Hoggart, K. and Green D. (eds) (1991) *London: A New Metropolitan Geography*, London: Edward Arnold.

Hollis, G.E. and Burgess, J.A. (1977) 'Personal London: students perceive the urban scene', *Geographical Magazine*, 50(3): 155–61.

Horwath and Horwath (1986) *London's Tourism Accommodation in the 1990s*, London: Horwath and Horwath.

Hoyle, B.S. and Pinder, D. (eds) (1992) *European Port Cities in Transition*, London: Belhaven.

Hudman, L. (1978) 'Tourist impacts: the need for regional planning', *Annals of Tourism Research*, 9: 563–83.

Hudson, P. (1990a) 'Stresses in small towns in north-western Australia: the impact of tourism and development', paper presented at the 24th Institute of Australian Geographers Conference, University of New England, Armidale, September.

Hudson, P. (1990b) 'Structural changes in three small north-western Australian communities: the relationship between development and local quality of life', Paper presented at Annual Conference of Regional Science Association, Australian and New Zealand section, Perth, December.

Hudson, R. and Townsend, A. (1992) 'Tourism employment and policy choices for local government', in P. Johnson and B. Thomas (eds) *Perspectives on Tourism Policy*, London: Mansell, pp. 49–68.

Hughes, H.L. (1984) 'Government support for tourism in the UK: a different perspective', *Tourism Management*, 5(1): 13–19.

Hughes, J.D. (1978) *In the House of Stone and Light: A Human History of the Grand Canyon*, Grand Canyon: Grand Canyon Natural History Association.

Hull, J. (1988) 'How sustainable is ecotourism in Costa Rica?' in C.M. Hall and A.A. Lew (eds) *Sustainable Tourism Development: Geographical Perspectives*, Harlow: Addison Wesley Longman, pp. 107–18.

Hummelbrunner, R. and Miglbauer, E. (1994) 'Tourism promotion and potential in peripheral areas: the Austrian case', *Journal of Sustainable Tourism*, 2: 41–50.

Hurst, F. (1987) 'Enroute surveys', in J.B. Ritchie and C. Goeldner (eds) *Travel Tourism and Hospitality Research: A Handbook for Managers and*

Researchers, 1st edition, New York: John Wiley and Sons, 401–16.

Ilbery, B.W. (1991) 'Farm diversification as an adjustment strategy on the urban fringe of the West Midlands', *Journal of Rural Studies*, 7(3): 2–18.

Industry Commission (1995) *Tourism Accommmodation and Training*, Melbourne; Industry Commission.

Inskeep, E. (1991) *Tourism Planning: An Integrated and Sustainable Development Approach*, New York: Van Nostrand Reinhold.

International Union for the Conservation of Nature and Natural Resources (IUCN) (1978) *Categories, Objectives and Criteria for Protected Areas*, A Final Report prepared by Committee on Criteria and Nomenclature Commission on National Parks and Protected Areas (CNPPA), Morges: International Union for Conservation of Nature and Natural Resources.

International Union of Tourism Organizations (IUOTO) (1974) 'The role of the state in tourism', *Annals of Tourism Research*, 1(3): 66–72.

Ioannides, D. (1995) 'Strengthening the ties between tourism and economic geography: a theoretical agenda', *Professional Geographer*, 47(1): 49–60.

Ioannides, D. (1996) 'Tourism and economic geography nexus: a response to Anne-Marie d'Hauteserre', *Professional Geographer*, 48(2): 219–21.

Isard, W. (1956) *Location and Space Economy*, Massachusetts: Massachusetts Institute of Technology Press.

Iso-Ahola, S. (1980) *The Social Psychology of Leisure and Recreation*, C. Thomas: Springfield, Illinois.

Jackson, P. and Smith, S.J. (1984) *Exploring Social Geography*, London: George Allen and Unwin.

Jacobs, C. (1973) *Farms and Tourism in Upland Denbighshire*, Tourism and Recreation Report 4, Denbighshire County Council.

James, P.E. (1972) *All Possible Worlds: A History Of Geographical Ideas*, 1st edition., Indianapolis: The Odyssey Press.

Janiskee, R. and Mitchell, L. (1989), 'Applied recreation geography' in M. Kenzer (ed.) *Applied Geography Issues, Questions and Concerns*, Dordrecht: Kluwer Academic Publishers.

Jansen-Verbeke, M. (1986) 'Inner-city tourism: resources, tourists and promoters', *Annals of Tourism Research* 13(1): 79–100.

Jansen-Verbeke, M. (1988) *Leisure, Recreation and Tourism in Inner Cities. Explorative Case Studies*, Amsterdam 1 Nijmegen: Netherlands Geographical Studies 58.

Jansen-Verbeke, M. (1989) 'Inner cities and urban tourism in the Netherlands: new challenges for local authorities', in P. Bramham, I. Henry, H. Mommass, and H. van der Poel (eds) *Leisure and Urban Processes: Critical Studies of Leisure Policy in Western European Cities*, London: Routledge, pp. 233–53.

Jansen-Verbeke, M., (1990) 'Leisure and shopping – tourism product mix', in G.J. Ashworth and B. Goodall (eds) *Marketing Tourism Places*, London: Routledge, pp. 128–37.

Jansen-Verbeke, M. (1991), 'Leisure shopping: a magic concept for the tourism industry', *Tourism Management*, 12 (1): 9–14.

Jansen-Verbeke, M. (1992) 'Urban recreation and tourism: physical planning issues', *Tourism Recreation Research*, 17(2): 33–45.

Jansen-Verbeke, M. and Ashworth G.J. (1990) 'Environmental integration of recreation and tourism', *Annals of Tourism Research*, 17(4): 618–22.

Jansen-Verbeke, M. and Dietvorst, A. (1987) 'Leisure, recreation and tourism: a geographic view on integration', *Annals of Tourism Research*, 14: 361–75.

Jenkins, J. (1993) 'Tourism policy in rural New South Wales – policy and research priorities', *GeoJournal*, 29(3): 281–90.

Jenkins, J. (1997) 'The role of the Commonwealth Government in rural tourism and regional development in Australia', in C.M. Hall, J. Jenkins and G. Kearsley (eds) *Tourism Planning and Policy in Australia and New Zealand: Cases, Issues and Practice*, Sydney: Irwin Publishers, pp. 181–91.

Jenkins, J. and Prin, E. (1998) 'Rural landholder attitudes: the case of public recreational access to 'private' lands', in R. Butler, C.M. Hall and J. Jenkins (eds) *Tourism and Recreation in Rural Areas*, Chichester: Wiley, pp. 179–96.

Jenkins, J. and Walmesley, D.J. (1993) 'Mental maps of tourists: a study of Coffs Harbour, New South Wales', *GeoJournal*, 29(3): 233–41.

Jenkins, J., Hall, C.M. and Troughton, M. (1998) 'The restructuring of rural economies: rural tourism and recreation as a government response', in R. Butler, C.M. Hall and J. Jenkins (eds) *Tourism and Recreation in Rural Areas*, Chichester: Wiley, pp. 43–68.

Jenkins, R.L. (1978) 'Family vacation decision-making', *Journal of Travel Research*, 16(Spring): 2–7.

Jenkins, W.I. (1978) *Policy Analysis: A Political and Organizational Perspective*, New York: St. Martin's Press.

Johnson, D., Snepenger, J. and Akis, S. (1994), 'Residents' perceptions of tourism development', *Annals of Tourism Research*, 21(3): 629–42.

Johnson, J.W. (1987) 'Republic of Ireland', in H.D. Clout (ed.) *Regional Development in Western Europe*, 3rd edn, London: David Fulton, pp. 285–306.

Johnston, R.J. (1983a) 'On geography and the history of geography', *History of Geography Newsletter*, 3: 1–7.

Johnston, R.J. (1983b) 'Resource analysis, resource management and the integration of human and physical geography', *Progress in Physical Geography*, 7: 127–46.

Johnston, R.J. (1986) 'Applied geography', in R.J. Johnston, D. Gregory, D.M. Smith (eds) *The Dictionary of Human Geography*, Oxford: Blackwell, pp. 17–20.

Johnston, R.J. (1991) *Geography and Geographers: Anglo-American Human Geography Since 1945*, 4th edn, London: Edward Arnold.

Johnston, R.J., Gregory, D. and Smith, D.M. (eds) (1986) *The Dictionary of Human Geography*, 2nd edn, Oxford: Basil Blackwell.

Johnston, R.J., Gregory, D. and Smith, D.M. (eds) (1994) *The Dictionary of Human Geography*, 4th edn, Oxford: Basil Blackwell.

Johnston, S. (1985) 'The beauty and significance of wild places', *Habitat*, 13(1), February, 27–28.

Jones, A.D. (1978) 'Measuring our wilderness', *Habitat*, 6(2): 16–9.

Jones, D.R.W. (1986) 'Prostitution and tourism', in J.S. Marsh (ed.) *Canadian Studies of Parks, Recreation and Tourism in Foreign Lands*, Occasional Paper 11, Peterborough: Department of Geography, Trent University, pp. 241–8.

Jones, S.B. (1933) 'Mining tourist towns in the Canadian Rockies', *Economic Geography*, 9: 368–78.

Jones, T. (1994) 'Theme park development in Japan' in C. Cooper and A. Lockwood (eds) *Progress in Tourism, Recreation and Hospitality Management*, Vol. 6, Chichester: Wiley, 111–25.

Jones Lang Wooten (1989) *Retail, Leisure and Tourism*, London: English Tourist Board.

Kabanoff, B. (1982) 'Occupational and sex differences in leisure needs and leisure satisfaction', *Journal of Occupational Behaviour*, 3: 233–45.

Kassem, M. (1987) *Marketing of Tourism: an Investigation of the Application of Marketing Concepts and Practices in Promoting Egypt as a Tourist Destination in Britain and Ireland*, unpublished PhD thesis, University of Strathclyde.

Kay, T. and Jackson, G. (1991) 'Leisure despite constraint: the impact of leisure constraints on leisure particpation', *Journal of Leisure Research*, 23: 301–13.

Keane, E.F. (1972) *Irish Tourism: Industry in Strategic Change*, Dublin: Bord Fáilte.

Keane, M. and Quinn, J. (1990) *Rural Development and Rural Tourism*, SSRC, University College, Galway.

Keane, M.J., Briassoulis, H. and van der Stratten, J. (1992) ' Rural tourism and rural development', in H. Briassoulis, and J. van der Stratten (eds) *Tourism and the Environment: Regional, Economic and Policy Issues, Environment and Assessment*, vol. 2, Dordrecht: Kluwer Academic Publishers.

Kearney, B., Boyle, G. and Walsh, J. (1994) *EU Leader and Initiative in Ireland: Evaluation and Recommendations*, Department of Agriculture, Food and Forestry, Dublin: Commission of the European Communities.

Kearns, G. and Philo, C. (eds) (1993) *Selling Places: The City as Cultural Capital, Past and Present*, Oxford: Pergamon Press.

Kearsley, G.W. (1990) 'Tourism development and the user's perceptions of wilderness in Southern New Zealand', *Australian Geographer*, 21(2): 127–40.

Kearsley, G.W. (1997) 'Managing the consequences of over-use by tourists of New Zealand's conservation estate', in C.M. Hall, J. Jenkins and G. Kearsley (eds) *Tourism Planning and Policy in Australia and New Zealand*, Sydney: Irwin Publishers, pp. 87–98.

Kearsley, G.W., Hall, C.M. and J. Jenkins (1997) 'Tourism planning and policy in natural areas: introductory comments', in C.M. Hall, J. Jenkins and G. Kearsley (eds) *Tourism Planning and Policy in Australia and New Zealand*, Sydney: Irwin Publishers, pp. 66–86.

Keeble, D., Owens, P. and Thompson, C. (1982) 'Regional accessibility and economic potential in the European Community', *Regional Studies*, 16: 419–32.

Keller, C.P. (1984) 'Centre–periphery tourism development and control', in J. Long and R. Hecock (eds) *Leisure, Tourism and Social Change*, Dunfermline: Centre for Leisure Research, Dunfermline College of Physical Education, pp. 77–84.

Kelly, J. (1982) *Leisure*, Englewood Cliffs: Prentice Hall.

Ken, S. and Rappoport, R. (1975) Beyond Palpable Mass Demand – Leisure Provision and Human Demands: The Life Cycle Approach, Paper presented to Planning and Transport Research and Computation (International) Company Ltd, Summer Annual Meeting.

Kent, W.E., Meyer, R.A. and Reddam, T.M. (1987) 'Reassessing wholesaler marketing strategies: the role of travel research', *Journal of Travel Research*, 25(3): 31–3.

Kenzer, M. (ed.) (1989) *Applied Geography Issues, Questions and Concerns*, Dordrecht: Kluwer Academic Publishers.

Keogh, B. (1984) 'The measurement of spatial variations in tourist activity', *Annals of Tourism Research*, 11: 267–82.

Keown, C. (1989) 'A model of tourists propensity to buy: The case of Japanese visitors to Hawaii', *Journal of Travel Research*, Winter: 31–4.

Killan, G. (1993) *Protected Places: A History of Ontario's Provincial Parks System*, Toronto: Dundurn Press

Kinnaird, V. and Hall, D. (eds) (1994) *Tourism: A Gender Analysis*, Chichester: John Wiley.

Kirkpatrick, J. (1980) 'Hydro-Electric development and wilderness: report to the Department of the Environment', attachment to Department of the Environment (Tas.), *Assessment of the HEC Report on the Lower Gordon River Development Stage Two*, Hobart: Department of the Environment.

Kirkpatrick, J.B. and Haney, R.A. (1980) 'The quantification of developmental wilderness loss: the case of forestry in Tasmania', *Search*, 11(10): 331–5.

Kissling, C. (1989) 'International tourism and civil aviation in the South Pacific: Issues and innovations', *GeoJournal* 19(3): 309–16.

Kline, M.B. (1970) *Beyond the Land Itself: Views of Nature in Canada and the United States*, Cambridge: Harvard University Press.

Kliskey A.D. and Kearsley G.W. (1993) 'Mapping multiple perceptions of wilderness in southern New Zealand', *Applied Geography*, 13: 203–23.

Knetsch, J. (1969) 'Assessing the demand for outdoor recreation', *Journal of Leisure Research*, 1(2): 85.

Konrad, V.A. (1982) 'Historical artifacts as recreational resources', in G. Wall and J. Marsh (eds) *Recreational Land Use*, Ottawa: Carleton University Press, pp. 393–416.

Kosters, M.J. (1984) 'The deficiencies of tourism social science without political science: Comment on Richter', *Annals of Tourism Research*, 11: 609–613.

Kretchmann, J. and Eagles, P. (1990) 'An analysis of the motives of ecotourists in comparison to the general Canadian population', *Society and Leisure*, 13(2): 499–507.

Lane, B. (1994) 'What is rural tourism?', *Journal of Sustainable Tourism* 2: 7–21.

Lang, R. (1988) 'Planning for integrated development', in F.W. Dykeman (ed.) *Integrated Rural Planning and Development*, Sackville: Mount Allison University, pp. 81–104.

Latham, J. (1989) 'The statistical measurement of tourism' in C.P. Cooper (ed.) *Progress in Tourism, Recreation and Hospitality Management*, vol. 1, London: Belhaven, pp. 57–76.

Lavery, P. (ed.) (1971) *Recreational Geography*, Newton Abbott: David and Charles.

Lavery, P. (1975) 'The demand for leisure: a review of studies', *Town Planning Review*: 185–200.

Law, C. (1988) 'Conference and exhibition tourism', *Built Environment* 13(2): 85–92.

Law, C.M. (1992) 'Urban tourism and its contribution to economic regeneration', *Urban Studies*, 29 (3/4), 599–618.

Law, C.M. (1993) *Urban Tourism: Attracting Visitors to Large Cities*, London: Mansell.

Law, C.M. (ed.) (1996) *Tourism in Major Cities*, London: International Thomson Business Publishing.

Law, S. (1967) 'Planning for outdoor recreation', *Journal of the Town Planning Institute* 53: 383–86.

Lawton, G. and Page, S.J. (1997b) 'Health advice to the travellers to the Pacific Islands: Whose responsibility?', in M. Oppermann (ed.) *Pacific Rim Tourism*, Wallingford: CAB International, 184–95.

Lawton, G., Page, S. and Hall, C.M. (1996) 'The provision of health advice to tourists', Paper presented at the International Geographical Union Conference, The Hague, August.

Lawton, R. (1978), 'Population and Society 1730–1900', in R. Dodgson and R. Butlin (eds) *An Historical Geography of England and Wales*, London: Academic Press, pp. 291–366.

Lawton, R. and Page, S.J. (1997a) 'Evaluating travel

agents' provision of health advice to tourists, *Tourism Management*, 18(2): 89–104.

Lea, J. (1988) *Tourism and Development in the Third World*, London: Routledge.

Lee, R.G. (1977) 'Alone with others: the paradox of privacy in the wilderness', *Leisure Services*, 1, 3–19.

Leiper, N. (1984) 'Tourism and leisure: The significance of tourism in the leisure spectrum', Proceedings of the 12th New Zealand Geography Conference, New Zealand Geographical Society, Christchurch, 249–53.

Leiper, N. (1990) *Tourism Systems: An Interdisciplinary Perspective*, Palmerston North, New Zealand: Department of Management Systems Occasional Paper 2, Massey University.

Leopold, A. (1921) 'The wilderness and its place in forest recreational policy', *Journal of Forestry*, 19(7): 718–721.

Leopold, A. (1925) 'Wilderness as a form of land use', *Journal of Land and Public Utility Economics*, 1(4):398–404.

Lesslie, R. (1991) 'Wilderness survey and evaluation in Australia', *Australian Geographer*, 22: 35–43.

Lesslie, R.G. and Taylor, S.G. (1983) *Wilderness in South Australia*, Occasional Paper No. 1, Adelaide: Centre for Environmental Studies, University of Adelaide.

Lesslie, R.G. and Taylor, S.G. (1985) 'The wilderness continuum concept and its implications for Australian wilderness preservation policy', *Biological Conservation*, 32: 309–33.

Lesslie, R.G., Mackey, B.G. and Preece, K.M. (1987) *National Wilderness Inventory: A Computer Based Methodology for the Survey of Wilderness in Australia*, prepared for the Australian Heritage Commission, Canberra: Australian Heritage Commission.

Lesslie, R.G., Mackey, B.G. and Preece, K.M. (1988) 'A computer-based method for the evaluation of wilderness, *Environmental Conservation*, 15(3): 225–32.

Lesslie, R G., Mackey, B.G. and Shulmeister, J. (1988) *Wilderness Quality in Tasmania, National Wilderness Inventory: Stage II*, A report to the Australian Heritage Commission, Canberra: Australian Heritage Commission.

Lesslie, R., Abrahams, H. and Maslen, M. (1991) *Wilderness Quality on Cape York Peninsula, National Wilderness Inventory: Stage III*, Canberra: Australian Heritage Commission.

Lesslie, R.G., Maslen, M., Canty, D., Goodwins, D. and

Shields, R. (1991) *Wilderness on Kangaroo Island, National Wilderness Inventory: South Australia*, Canberra: Australian Heritage Commission.

Lew, A.A. (1985) 'Bringing tourists to town', *Small Town*, 16: 4–10.

Lew, A.A. (1987) 'A framework for tourist attraction research', *Annals of Tourism Research* 14(4): 553–75.

Lew, A.A. (1989) 'Authenticity and sense of place in the tourism development experience of older retail districts', *Journal of Travel Research*, 27(4): 15–22.

Lew, A.A. and van Otten, G.A. (eds) (1997) *Tourism on American Indian Lands*, New York: Cognizant Communications Corporation.

Lew, A.A. and Wu, L. (eds) (1995) *Tourism in China: Geographic, Political and Economic Perspectives*, Boulder: Westview Press.

Ley, D. and Olds, K. (1988) 'Landscape as spectacle: World's Fairs and the culture of heroic consumption', *Environment and Planning D*, 6: 191–212.

Limb, M. (1986) *Community Involvement in the Management of Open Space for Recreation in the Urban Fringe*, unpublished PhD thesis, University of London, London.

Lindberg, K. and McKercher, B. (1997) 'Ecotourism: a critical overview', *Pacific Tourism Review*, 1: 65–79.

Linton, D. (1968) 'The assessment of scenery as a recreation resource', *Scottish Geographical Magazine*, 84 (3): 219–38.

Llewelyn-Davis Planning/Leisureworks (1987) *Tourism Development in London Docklands: Themes and Facts*, London: London Docklands Development Corporation.

Lloyd, P. and Dicken, P. (1987) *Location in Space: A Theoretical Approach to Human Geography*, 2nd edn, London: Harper and Row.

Locke, S. (1985) *Country Park Visitor Surveys: Lessons from a Study at Sherwood Forest and Rufford Country Parks, Nottinghamshire*, Cheltenham: Countryside Commission, CCP 180.

London Tourist Board (1987) *The Tourism Strategy for London*, London: London Tourist Board.

London Tourist Board (1988) *London Tourism Statistics*, London: London Tourist Board.

Long, J.A. (1984) 'Introduction – tourism and social change', in J. Long and R. Hecock (eds) *Leisure, Tourism and Social Change*, Dunfermline: Centre for Leisure Research, Dunfermline College of Physical Education, pp. 69–76.

Long, J. (1987) 'Continuity as a basis for change: Leisure and male retirement', *Leisure Studies* 6: 55–70.

Long, P.T. and Nuckolls, J.S. (1994) 'Organising resources for rural tourism development: the importance of leadership, planning and technical assistance', *Tourism Recreation Research*, 19(2): 19–34.

Long, P., Perdue, R. and Allen, L. (1990) 'Rural residents perception and attitudes by community level of tourism', *Journal of Travel Research* 29: 3–9.

Lösch, A. (1944) *Die Raümliche Ordnung der Wirtschaft*, Jena: Gustar Fischer.

Lovingwood, P. and Mitchell, L. (1978) 'The structure of public and private recreational systems: Columbia, South Carolina', *Journal of Leisure Research* 10: 21–36.

Lowenthal, D. (1975) 'Past time, present place: landscape and memory', *The Geographical Review*, 65: 1–36.

Lowenthal, D. (1985) *The Past is a Foreign Country*, Cambridge: Cambridge University Press.

Lowyck, E., Van Langenhove, L. and Bollaert, L. (1992) 'Typologies of tourist roles', in P. Johnson and T. Barry (eds) *Tourism Policy*, London: Mansell, pp. 13–32.

Lucas P. (1986) 'Fishy business', *Leisure Manager*, 4: 18–19.

Lucas, R. (1964) 'Wilderness perception and use: the example of the Boundary Waters Canoe Area', *Natural Resources Journal* 3(1): 394–411.

Lutz, R.J. and Ryan, C. (1996) 'The impact inner city tourism projects: the case of the International Convention Centre, Birmingham, UK', in P. Murphy (ed.) *Quality Management in Urban Tourism*, London: John Wiley.

Lynch, K. (1960), *The Image of the City*, Cambridge, Mass: MIT Press.

MacCannell, D. (1973) 'Staged authenticity: arrangements of social space in tourist settings', *American Journal of Sociology*, 69: 578–603.

MacCannell, D. (1976) *The Tourist: A New Theory of the Leisure Class*, London: Macmillan.

McAlvoy, L. (1977) 'Needs and the elderly: An overview', *Parks and Recreation*, 12(3): 31–5.

McCool, S. (1978) 'Recreation use limits: issues for the tourism industry', *Journal of Travel Research*, 17(2): 2–7.

McDermott, D. and Horner, A. (1978) 'Aspects of rural renewal in Western Connemara', *Irish Geography*, 11: 176–9.

McEniff, J. (1987) 'Republic of Ireland', *International Tourism Reports*: 5–26.

McEniff, J. (1991) 'Republic of Ireland', *International Tourism Reports*: 25–45.

McEniff, J. (1996) 'Ireland', *International Tourism Reports* 1: 45–66.

McGahey, S. (1996) 'South Korea outbound', *EIU Travel and Tourism Analyst*, 1: 17–35.

McGrath, F. (1989) 'Characteristics of pilgrims to Lough Derg', *Irish Geography*, 22: 44–7.

McIntosh, R.W. and Goeldner, C. (1990) *Tourism: Principles, Practices and Philosophies*, New York: Wiley.

McKenry, K. (1972a) *Value Analysis of Wilderness Areas*, Combined Universities Recreation Research Group, Monograph 2, Clayton: Monash University.

McKenry, K. (1972b) 'A history and critical analysis of the controversy concerning the Gordon River Power Scheme', in Australian Conservation Foundation, *Pedder Papers Anatomy of a Decision*, Parkville: Australian Conservation Foundation, Parkville, 9–30.

McKenry, K. (1977) 'Value analysis of wilderness areas', in D. Mercer (ed.) *Leisure and Recreation in Australia*, Malvern: Sorrett Publishing, 209–21.

McKenry, K. (1980) 'The beneficiaries of wilderness', in R.W. Robertson, P. Helman and A. Davey (eds) *Wilderness Management in Australia*, Proceedings of a symposium held at the Canberra College of Advanced Education 19–23 July 1978, Canberra: School of Applied Science, Canberra College of Advanced Education, pp. 82–91.

McKercher, B. (1993a) 'Some fundamental truths about tourism: understanding tourism's social and environmental impacts', *Journal of Sustainable Tourism*, 1(1): 6–16.

McKercher, B. (1993b) 'The unrecognized threat to tourism: can tourism survive sustainability', *Tourism Management*, 14(2): 131–36.

McKercher, B. (1993c) 'Australian conservation organisations' perspectives on tourism in National Parks: a critique', *GeoJournal*, 29(3): 307–13.

McKercher, B. (1997) 'Benefits and costs of tourism in Victoria's Alpine National Park: comparing attitudes of tour operators, management staff and public interest group leaders', in C.M. Hall, J. Jenkins and G. Kearsley (eds) *Tourism Planning and Policy in*

Australia and New Zealand: Cases, Issues and Practice, Sydney: Irwin Publishers, pp. 99–109.

McMurray, K.C. (1930) 'The use of land for recreation', *Annals of the Association of American Geographers*, 20: 7–20.

McMurray, K.C. (1954) 'Recreational geography', in P.E. James and C.F. Jones (eds) *American Geography: Inventory and Prospect*, Syracruse: Syracruse University Press.

McVey, M. (1986) 'International hotel chains in Europe: survey of expansion plans as Europe is rediscovered', *Travel and Tourism Analyst*, September: 3–23.

Madsen, H. (1992) 'Place-marketing in Liverpool: a review', *International Journal of Urban and Regional Research*, 16(4): 633–40.

Malamud, B. (1973) 'Gravity model calibration of tourist travel to Las Vegas', *Journal of Leisure Research*, 5(1): 13–33.

Manidis Roberts Consultants (1991) *National Estate NSW Wilderness Review*, Sydney: National Estate Grants Program, Department of Planning.

Manning, R.E. (1985) 'Crowding norms in backcountry settings: a review and synthesis', *Journal of Leisure Research*, 17(2): 75–89.

Mansfeld, Y. (1992) 'Industrial landscapes as positive settings for tourism development in declining industrial cities – the case of Haifa, Israel', *GeoJournal*, 28(4): 457–63.

Mansfield, N. (1969) 'Recreational trip generation: a cross-section analysis of weekend pleasure trips to the Lake District National Park', *Journal of Transport and Economic Policy*, 3: 152–64.

Mark, S.R. (1984) Wilderness review in the East Mojave National Scenic Area, California, unpublished MSc thesis, South Oregon State College.

Mark, S.R. (1985) 'Wilderness inventory of Western Australia', *Environment W.A.*, 7(3): 30–2.

Mark, S. (1991) 'Planning and development at Rim Village', in *Administrative History, Crater Lake National Park, Oregon*, Seattle: US Department of the Interior, National Park Service.

Mark, S. (1996) 'Writing environmental and park histories', in C.M. Hall and S. McArthur (eds) *Heritage Management in Australia and New Zealand: The Human Dimension*, Melbourne: Oxford University Press, 153–9.

Market Power (1991) *A Report on the Structure of the UK Catering Industry*, London: Market Power Ltd.

Marsh, G.P. (1864 (1965)) *Man and Nature; or, Physical Geography as Modified by Human Action*, D. Lowenthal (ed.), Cambridge, Mass: Belknap Press of Harvard University Press.

Marsh, J.G. (1983) 'Canada's parks and tourism: a problematic relationship', in P.E. Murphy (ed.) *Tourism in Canada: Selected Issues and Options*, Western Geographical Series, vol. 21, Victoria: Department of Geography, University of Victoria, 271–307.

Marsh, J.G. (1985) 'The Rocky and Selkirk Mountains and the Swiss connection 1885–1914', *Annals of Tourism Research*, 12: 417–33.

Marsh, J.G. and Wall, G. (1982) 'Themes in the investigation of the evolution of outdoor recreation', G. Wall and J. Marsh (eds) *Recreational Land Use, Perspectives on its Evolution in Canada*, Ottawa: Carleton University Press, pp. 1–12.

Martin, W. and Mason, S. (1979) *Broad Patterns of Leisure Expenditure*, London: Sports Council and Social Science Research Council.

Marshall, R. (1930) 'The problem of the wilderness', *Scientific Monthly*, 30: 141–148.

Maslow, A. (1954) *Motivation and Personality*, New York: Harper and Row.

Massey, D. and Allen, J. (eds) (1984) *Geography Matters! A Reader*, Cambridge: Cambridge University Press.

Mathieson, A. and Wall, G. (1982) *Tourism, Economic, Physical and Social Impacts*, Harlow: Longman.

Matley, I.M. (1976) *The Geography of International Tourism*, Resource paper No.76–1, Washington, D.C.: Association of American Geographers.

Matthews, H.G. (1983) 'Editor's page: on tourism and political science', *Annals of Tourism Research*, 10(4): 303–6.

Maude, A.J.S. and van Rest, D. J. (1985) 'The social and economic effects of farm tourism in the United Kingdom', *Agricultural Administration*, 20: 85–99.

Mawhinney, K. A. (1979) 'Recreation', in D.A. Gilmore (ed.) *Irish Resources and Land Use*, Dublin: Institute of Public Administration.

Mawhinney, K. A. and Bagnall, G. (1976) 'The integrated social economic and environmental planning of tourism', Administration, 24: 383–93.

Medlik, S. (1993) *Dictionary of Travel, Tourism and Hospitality*, Oxford: Butterworth-Heinemann.

Meleghy, T., Preglau, M. and Tafertsofer, A. (1985) 'Tourism development and value change', *Annals of Tourism Research*, 12: 201–19.

Mercer, D.C. (1970) 'The geography of leisure: a contemporary growth point', *Geography*, 55(3): 261–73.

Mercer, D. (1971a) 'Perception in outdoor recreation' in P. Lavery (ed.) *Recreational Geography*, Newton Abbot: David and Charles.

Mercer, D. (1971b) 'Discretionary travel behaviour and the urban mental map', *Australian Geographical Studies*, 9: 133–43.

Mercer, D. (1973) 'The concept of recreational need', *Journal of Leisure Research*, 5: 37–50.

Mercer, D. (1979) 'Outdoor recreation: contemporary research and policy issues', in T. O'Riordan and R.D. Arge (eds) *Progress in Resource Management and Environmental Planning*, vol. 1, New York: Wiley.

Mercer, D.C. (1994) 'Native peoples and tourism: conflict and compromise', in W.F. Theobald (ed.) *Global Tourism: The Next Decade*, Boston: Butterworth Heinemann, pp. 124–45.

Meyer-Arendt, K. (1990) 'Recreational Business Districts in Gulf of Mexico seaside resorts', *Journal of Cultural Geography*, 11: 39–55.

Middleton, V. (1988) *Marketing in Travel and Tourism*, Oxford: Butterworth Heinemann.

Milne, S. (1990) 'The impact of tourism development in small Pacific Island states', *New Zealand Journal of Geography*, 89: 16–21.

Milne, S. (1998) 'Tourism and sustainable development: the global–local nexus' in C.M. Hall and A.A. Lew (eds) *Sustainable Tourism Development: Geographical Perspectives*, Harlow: Addison Wesley Longman, pp. 35–48.

Milton Keynes Development Corporation (1988) *Study of the Use and Perception of Parks in Milton Keynes*, Milton Keynes: Milton Keynes Recreation Unit Study 18.

Milton Keynes Development Corporation (1989) *Parks Visitor Survey*, Milton Keynes: Milton Keynes Recreation Unit Study 18.

Minerbi, L. (1992) *Impacts of Tourism Development in Pacific Islands*, San Francisco: Greenpeace Pacific Campaign.

Mings, R.C. (1978) 'The importance of more research on the impacts of tourism', *Annals of Tourism Research*, July/September: 340–4.

Ministry of Housing and Local Government (1955) Green Belts, HMSO: Circular 42/55.

Mitchell, B. (1989) *Geography and Resource Analysis*, 2nd Ed., Harlow: Longman.

Mitchell, L. (1969a) 'Recreational geography: evolution and research needs', *Professional Geographer*, 21(2): 117–19.

Mitchell, L. (1969b) 'Towards a theory of public urban recreation', *Proceedings of the Association of American Geographers*, 1: 103–8.

Mitchell, L. and Lovingwood, P. (1976) 'Public urban recreation: An investigation of spatial relationships', *Journal of Leisure Research* 8: 6–20.

Mitchell, L.S. (1979) 'The geography of tourism: an introduction', *Annals of Tourism Research*, 9 (3): 235–44.

Mitchell, L.S. (1984) 'Tourism research in the United States: a geographical perspective', *GeoJournal*, 9: 5–15.

Mitchell, L.S. (1991) *A Conceptual Matrix for the Study of Tourism*, Les Cahiers du Tourisme, Aix en Provence: Centre des Haute Études Touristiques.

Mitchell, L.S. (1997) 'Rediscovering geography (i.e. RTS)', personal communication to Michael Hall, Friday 13 June.

Mitchell, L.S. and Lovingwood, P. (1976) 'Public urban recreation: an investigation of spatial relationships', *Journal of Leisure Research*, 8: 6–20.

Mitchell, L.S. and Murphy, P.E. (1991) 'Geography and tourism', *Annals of Tourism Research*, 18: 57–70.

Mitchell, N. C. (1970) 'Irish ports, recent developments', in N. Stephens and R. Glassock (eds). *Irish Geographical Studies in Honour of E. Estyn Evans*, Belfast: Queen's University of Belfast, Belfast, pp. 325–41.

Montanari, A. and Williams, A.M. (eds) (1995) *European Tourism: Regions, Spaces and Restructuring*, Chichester: Wiley.

Moore, K., Cushman, G. and Simmons, D. (1995) 'Behavioural conceptualisation of tourism and leisure', *Annals of Tourism Research*, 22(1): 67–85.

Morgan, C. and King, J. (1966) *Introduction to Psychology*, McGraw Hill: New York.

Morgan, G. (1980) 'Wilderness areas in Queensland: The rakes approach', 103–107 in R.W. Robertson, P. Helman, A. Davey (eds) *Wilderness Management in Australia*, Proceedings of a symposium held at the Canberra College of Advanced Education, 19–23 July 1978, Natural Resources, School of Applied Science, Canberra College of Advanced Education, Canberra.

Morgan, G. (1991) *A Strategic Approach to the Planning and Management of Parks and Open Space*,

Reading: Institute of Leisure and Amenity Management.

Mormont, M. (1987) 'Tourism and rural change', in M. Bouquet and M. Winter (eds). *Who From Their Labours Rest? Conflict and Practice in Rural Tourism*, Aldershot: Avebury.

Mosley, J.G. (1983) 'Australia's World Heritage areas', *Habitat*, 11(1): 16–26.

Mountinho, L. (1987) 'Consumer behaviour in tourism', *European Journal of Marketing* 21(10): 3–44.

Mowat, P. (1984) *The Administrative Factor in the Development of Tourist Resources and Markets in North-West Ireland*, unpublished D Phil thesis, New University of Ulster, Coleraine.

Mowforth, M. and Munt, I. (1997) *Tourism and Sustainability*, London: Routledge.

Mullins, G. and Heywood, J. (1984) 'Unobtrusive observation: A visitor survey technique', Columbus, Ohio: Ohio Agricultural Research Development Circular, Ohio Agricultural Development Centre No 20.

Mullins, P. (1984) 'Hedonism and real estate: resort tourism and Gold Coast development', in P. Williams (ed.) *Conflict and Development*, Sydney: Allen and Unwin.

Mullins, P. (1990) 'Tourist cities as new cities: Australia's Gold Coast and Sunshine Coast', *Australian Planner*, 28(3): 37–41.

Mullins, P. (1991) 'Tourism urbanization', *International Journal of Urban and Regional Research*, 15: 326–43.

Murphy, P.E. (1982) 'Tourism planning in London: an exercise in spatial and seasonal management', *Tourist Review*, 37: 19–23.

Murphy, P.E. (1985) *Tourism: A Community Approach*, New York: Methuen.

Murphy, P.E. (1988) 'Community driven tourism planning', *Tourism Management*, 9(2): 96–104.

Murphy, P.E. (1994) 'Tourism and sustainable development', in W. Theobold (ed.) *Global Tourism: The Next Decade*, Oxford: Butterworth Heinemann, pp. 274–90.

Murphy, P.E. (ed.) (1997) *Quality Management in Urban Tourism*, International Western Geographical Series, Chichester: Wiley.

Murphy, P.E. and Keller, C.P. (1990) 'Destination travel patterns: an examination and modelling of tourism patterns on Vancouver Island, British Columbia', *Leisure Sciences*, 12(1): 49–65.

Murphy, P.E. and Rosenblood, L. (1974) 'Tourism: an exercise in spatial search', *Canadian Geographer*, 18(3): 201–10.

Murphy, P.E. and Staples, W.A. (1979) 'Life cycle concept in marketing research', *Journal of Consumer Research*: 12–22.

Murphy, R.E. (1963) 'Geography and outdoor recreation: an opportunity and an obligation', *Professional Geographer*, 15(5): 33–4.

Murphy, W. and Gardiner, J.J. (1983) 'Forest recreating economics', *Irish Forestry*, 40: 12–19.

Nash, R. (1963) 'The American wilderness in historical perspective', *Journal of Forest History*, 6(4): 2–13.

Nash, R. (1967) *Wilderness and the American Mind*, New Haven: Yale University Press.

Nash, R. (1982) *Wilderness and the American Mind*, 3rd edn, New Haven: Yale University Press.

Nash, R. (1990) *The Rights of Nature: A History of Environmental Ethics*, Leichhardt: Primavera Press.

Naylon, J. (1967) 'Tourism – Spain's most important industry', *Geography* 52: 23–40.

Nelson, J.G. (ed.) (1970) *Canadian Parks in Perspective*, Montreal: Harvest House.

Nelson, J.G. (1973) 'Canada's national parks – past, present and future', *Canadian Geographical Journal*, 86(3): 68–89.

Nelson, J.G. (1982) 'Canada's national parks: past, present and future', in G. Wall and J.S. Marsh (eds) *Recreational Land Use Perspectives on its Evolution in Canada*, Carleton Library Series, Ottawa: Carleton University Press, pp. 41–61.

Nelson, J.G. (1986) *An External Perspective on Parks Canada Strategies*, Occasional Paper No.2, Waterloo: University of Waterloo Parks Canada Liaison Committee, University of Waterloo.

Neulinger, J. (1981) *The Psychology of Leisure*, Springfield: C. Thomas.

New Zealand Tourism Board (1991a) *Tourism in the 90s*, Wellington: New Zealand Tourism Board.

New Zealand Tourism Board (1991b) *New Zealand Domestic Tourism Study*, Wellington: New Zealand Tourism Board.

New Zealand Tourism Board (1995) *New Zealand Tourism in the 90s*, Wellington: New Zealand Tourism Board.

Newham Borough Council (1991a) *Newham's Policy for the Environment: A Consultation Document*, London: Borough of Newham.

Newham Borough Council (1991b) *Shaped for Success:*

Leisure Development Strategy 1990–94, London: Borough of Newham.

Ngoh, T. (1985) 'Guidelines for the harmonisation of international tourism statistics among PATA member countries', in *The Battle for Market Share: Strategies in Research and Marketing*, 16th Annual Conference Tourism and Travel Research Association, Salt Lake City: Graduate School of Business, University of Utah, pp. 291–306.

Nichols, L.L. (1976) 'Tourism and crime', *Annals of Tourism Research*, 3: 176–81.

Nicholson, M.H. (1962) *Mountain Gloom and Mountain Glory*, New York: Norton.

Nickels, S., Milne, S. and Wenzel, G. (1991) 'Inuit perceptions of tourism development: the case of Clyde River, Baffin Island, NWT', *Etudes/Inuit/Studies*, 15(1): 157–69.

Nicol, J.I. (1969) 'The National Parks movement in Canada', in J.G. Nelson and R.C. Scace (eds) *The Canadian National Parks: Today and Tomorrow*, vol. 1, Studies in Land Use History and Landscape Change National Park Series, Calgary: Department of Geography, University of Calgary, pp. 35–52.

O'Cinneide, M. and Keane, M.J. (1990) 'Applying strategic planning to local economic development: the case of the Connemara Gaeltacht, Ireland', *Town Planning Review*, 61: 475–86.

O'Connor, B. and Cronin, M. (eds) (1993) *Tourism in Ireland: A Critical Analysis*, Cork: Cork University Press.

O'Connor, P. (1995) 'Tourism and development in Ballyhoura: women's business?' *Economic and Social Review*, 26(4): 369–401.

O'Connor, P. (1996) *Invisible Players? Women, Tourism and Development in Ballyhoura*, Limerick: Women's Studies, Department of Government and Society, University of Limerick.

Oelschlaeger, M. (1991) *The Idea of Wilderness: From Prehistory to the Age of Ecology*, New Haven: Yale University Press.

Office of National Tourism (1997) *Ecotourism*, Tourism Facts No. 16, May (http://www.tourism.gov.au/new/cfa/cfa_fs16.html (accesssed 31/12/97)).

Office of Population censuses and surveys (OPCS) (1992) *1991 Census: Inner London*, London: OPCS.

Oglethorpe, M. (1984) 'Tourism and development in the Maltese Islands', in J. Long and R. Hecock (eds) *Leisure, Tourism and Social Change*, Dunfermline:

Centre for Leisure Research, Dunfermline College of Physical Education, 121–34.

O'Hagan, J. and Harrison, M. (1984a) 'UK and US visitor expenditure in Ireland: some econometric findings', *Economic and Social Review*, 15: 195–207.

O'Hagan, J. and Harrison, M. (1984b) 'Market share of US tourist expenditure in Europe: an econometric analysis', *Applied Economics*, 16: 919–31.

O'Hagan, J. and Mooney, D. (1983) 'Input–output multipliers in a small open economy: an application to tourism', *Economic and Social Review*, 14: 273–9.

O'Hearn, D. (1989) 'The Irish case of dependency, an exception to exceptions?', *American Sociological Review* 54: 578–96.

O'Leary, J.T. (1976) 'Land use definition and the rural community: disruption of community leisure space', *Journal of Leisure Research*, 8: 263–74.

Olszewska, A. (1989) 'Poland: the impact of the crisis on leisure patterns', in A. Olszewska and K. Roberts (eds) *Leisure and Lifestyle: A Comparative Analysis of Free Time*, London: Sage.

Olwig, K. and Olwig, K. (1979) 'Underdevelopment and the development of "natural" parks ideology', *Antipode*, 11(2): 16–25.

Oppermann, M. (1992) 'International tourist flows in Malaysia', *Annals of Tourism Research*, 19(3): 482–500.

Oppermann, M. (1993) 'German tourists in New Zealand', *The New Zealand Geographer*, 49(1): 31–4.

Oppermann, M. (1994) 'Regional aspects of tourism in New Zealand', *Regional Studies*, 28: 155–67.

Oppermann, M. (1995) 'Holidays on the farm: a case study of German hosts and guests', *Journal of Travel Research*, 33: 57–61.

Oppermann, M. (1998) 'Farm tourism in New Zealand', in R. Butler, C.M. Hall and J. Jenkins (eds) *Tourism and Recreation in Rural Areas*, Chichester: Wiley, pp. 225–35.

Oppermann, M. and Chon, K. (1997) *Tourism in Developing Countries*, London: International Thomson Publishing.

Organisation for Economic Co-operation and Development (1980) *The Impact of Tourism on the Environment*, Paris: Organisation for Economic Co-operation and Development.

O'Riordan, T. (1971) *Perspectives on Resource Management*, London: Pion Press.

O'Riordan, T. and Turner, R.K. (eds) (1984) *An*

Annotated Reader in Environmental Planning and Management, Oxford: Pergamon Press.

O'Riordan, W.K. (1986) 'Service sector multipliers', *Irish Banking Review*: 30–40.

Ovington, J.D. and Fox, A.M. (1980) 'Wilderness – a natural asset', *Parks*, 5(3): 1–4.

Owens, C. (1990) 'Tourism and urban regeneration', *Cities: The International Journal of Urban Policy and Planning*, August: 194–201.

Owens, P. (1984) 'Rural leisure and recreation research: a retrospective evaluation', *Progress in Human Geography*, 8: 157–85.

Page, S.J. (1988) *Poverty in Leicester 1881–1911: A Geographical Perspective*, unpublished PhD thesis, Department of Geography, University of Leicester.

Page, S.J. (1989) 'Tourist development in London Docklands in the 1980s and 1990's', *GeoJournal*, 19(3): 291–5.

Page, S.J. (1992) 'Perspectives on the environmental impact of the Channel Tunnel on tourism', in C. Cooper and A. Lockwood (eds) *Progess in Tourism, Recreation and Hospitality Management*, vol. 4, London: Belhaven, pp. 82–102.

Page, S.J. (1994a) 'European bus and coach travel', *Travel and Tourism Analyst*, 1: 19–39.

Page, S.J. (1994b) *Transport for Tourism*, London: Routledge.

Page, S.J. (1994c) 'Perspectives on tourism and peripherality: A review of tourism in the Republic of Ireland', in C. Cooper and A. Lockwood (eds) *Progress in Tourism, Recreation and Hospitality Management, Volume Five*, Chichester: Wiley, 26–53.

Page, S.J. (1994d) 'Developing heritage tourism in Ireland in the 1990's', *Tourism Recreation Research*, 19(2): 79–90.

Page, S.J. (1995a) *Urban Tourism*, London: Routledge.

Page, S.J. (1995b) 'Waterfront revitalisation in London: market-led planning and tourism in London Docklands', in S. Craig-Smith and M. Fagence (eds) *Recreation and Tourism as a Catalyst for Urban Waterfront Development*, Westport: Greenwood Publishing.

Page, S.J. (1997) 'Urban tourism: Analysing and evaluating the tourist experience', in C. Ryan (ed.) *The Tourist Experience: A New Introduction*, London: Cassell, pp. 112–35.

Page, S.J. (1999) *Transport and Tourism*, 2nd edn, London: Addison Wesley Longmann.

Page, S.J., Forer, P. and Lawton, G. (1999) 'Tourism and small business development: *Terra incognita*', *Tourism Management* 20(3).

Page, S.J. and Hardyman, R. (1996) 'Place marketing and town centre management: A new tool for urban revitalisation', *Cities: The International Journal of Urban Policy and Planning*, 13 (3): 153–64.

Page, S.J. and Lawton, G. (1997) 'The impact of urban tourism on destination communities: implications for community tourism planning in Auckland', in C.M. Hall, J. Jenkins and G. Kearsley (eds) *Tourism Planning and Policy in Australia and New Zealand: Cases, Issues and Practice*, Sydney: Irwin Publishers, pp. 209–26.

Page, S.J. and Sinclair, M.T. (1989) 'Tourism accommodation in London: alternative policies and the Docklands experience', *Built Environment*, 15(2): 125–37.

Page, S.J. and Thorn, K. (1997) 'Towards sustainable tourism planning in New Zealand: Public sector planning responses', *Journal of Sustainable Tourism* 5(1): 59–78.

Page, S.J., Nielsen, K. and Goodenough, R. (1994) 'Managing urban parks: user perspectives and local leisure needs in the 1990s', *Service Industries Journal*, 14(2): 216–37.

Pahl, R.E. (1975) *Whose City? And Further Essays in Urban Society*, Harmondsworth: Penguin.

Papson, S. (1981) 'Spuriousness and tourism: politics of two Canadian provincial governments', *Annals of Tourism Research*, 8: 220–35.

Parasuraman, A., Zeithmal, V. and Berry, L. (1985) 'A conceptual model of service quality and its implications for future research', *Journal of Marketing* 49(4): 41–50.

Parliamentary Commissioner for the Environment (1997) *Management of the Environmental Effects Associated With the Tourism Sector*, Wellington: Office of the Parliamentary Commissioner for the Environment.

Passmore, J. (1974) *Man's Responsibility for Nature*, London: Duckworth.

Patmore, J. (1970) *Land and Leisure*, Newton Abbot: David & Charles.

Patmore, J. (1973) 'Recreation', in J. Dawson and J. Doornkamp (eds) *Evaluating the Human Environment: Essays in Applied Geography*, London: Edward Arnold, 224–48.

Patmore, J. (1977) 'Recreation and leisure', *Progress in Human Geography*, 1: 111–17.

Patmore, J. (1978) 'Recreation and leisure', *Progress in Human Geography*, 2: 141–7.

Patmore, J. (1979) 'Recreation and leisure', *Progress in Human Geography*, 3: 126–32.

Patmore, J.A. (1983) *Recreation and Resources: Leisure Patterns and Leisure Places*, Oxford: Blackwell.

Patmore, J.A. and Collins, M. (1980) 'Recreation and leisure', *Progress in Human Geography* 4(1): 91–7.

Patmore, J.A. and Collins, M. (1981) 'Recreation and leisure', *Progress in Human Geography* 5(1): 87–92.

Patmore, J.A. and Rodgers, J. (eds) (1972) *Leisure in the North-West*, Salford: North-West Sports Council.

Pearce, D.G. (1978) 'Form and function in French resorts', *Annals of Tourism Research*, 5: 142–56.

Pearce, D.G. (1979) 'Towards a geography of tourism', *Annals of Tourism Research*, 6: 245–72.

Pearce, D.G. (1981) *Tourist Development*, Harlow: Longman.

Pearce, D. (1986) 'The spatial structure of coastal tourism: a behavioural approach', Paper presented at the International Geographical Union Commission on the Geography of Tourism and Leisure, Palma de Mallorca.

Pearce, D.G. (1987a) *Tourism Today: A Geographical Analysis*, Harlow: Longman.

Pearce, D.G. (1987b) Motel location and choice in Christchurch, *New Zealand Geographer*, 43(1): 10–17.

Pearce, D.G. (1988a) 'Tourist time-budgets', *Annals of Tourism Research*, 15: 106–21.

Pearce, D.G. (1988b) 'Tourism and regional development in the European Community', *Tourism Management*, 9: 11–22.

Pearce, D.G. (1989) *Tourist Development*, 2nd edn, Harlow: Longman.

Pearce, D.G. (1990a) 'Tourism, the regions and restructuring in New Zealand', *Journal of Tourism Studies*, 1(2): 33–42.

Pearce, D.G. (1990b) 'Tourism in Ireland: questions of scale and organisation', *Tourism Management*, 11: 133–51.

Pearce, D.G. (1992a) 'Tourism and the European regional development fund: the first fourteen years', *Journal of Travel Research*, 30: 44–51.

Pearce, D.G. (1992b) *Tourist Organisations*, Harlow: Longman.

Pearce, D.G. (1993a) 'Comparative studies in tourism research', in D. Pearce and R. Butler (eds) *Tourism Research: Critiques and Challenges*, London: Routledge.

Pearce, D.G. (1993b) 'Domestic tourist travel patterns in New Zealand', *GeoJournal*, 29(3): 225–32.

Pearce, D.G. (1995a) *Tourism Today: A Geographical Analysis*. 2nd edn, Harlow: Longman.

Pearce, D.G. (1995b) 'Planning for tourism in the 90s: an integrated, dynamic, multi-scale approach', in R.W. Butler and D.G. Pearce (eds) *Change in Tourism: People, Places, Processes*, London: Routledge, pp. 229–44.

Pearce, D.G. and Butler, R.W. (eds) (1993) *Tourism Research: Critiques and Challenges*, London: Routledge.

Pearce, J.A. (1980) 'Host community acceptance of foreign tourists: strategic considerations', *Annals of Tourism Research*, 7: 224–33.

Pearce, P.L. (1977) 'Mental souvenirs: a study of tourists and their city maps', *Australian Journal of Psychology*, 29: 203–10.

Pearce, P.L. (1981) 'Route maps: a study of travellers' perceptions of a section of countryside', *Journal of Environmental Psychology*, 1: 141–55.

Pearce, P. (1982) *The Social Psychology of Tourist Behaviour*, Oxford: Pergamon.

Pearce, P.L. (1984) 'Tourist guide interaction', *Annals of Tourism Research*, 11: 129–46.

Pearce, P. (1993) 'The fundamentals of tourist motivation' in D. Pearce and R. Butler (eds) *Tourism Research: Critique and Challenges*, London: Routledge.

Peet, R. (ed.) (1977) *Radical Geography: Alternative Viewpoints on Contemporary Social Issues*, London: Methuen.

Penning-Rowsell, E. (1973) *Alternative Approaches to Landscape Appraisal and Evaluation*, Planning Research Group, Report No. 11, Enfield: Middlesex Polytechnic.

Pepper, D. (1984) *The Roots of Modern Environmentalism*, London: Croom Helm.

Perdue, R. (1985) 'The 1983 Nebraska Visitor Survey: Achieving a high response rate', *Journal of Travel Research* 24(2): 23–6.

Perkins, H. (1993) 'Human geography, recreation and leisure', in H. Perkins and G. Cushman (eds) *Leisure, Recreation and Tourism*, Auckland: Longman Paul.

Perkins, H. and Gidlow, B. (1991) 'Leisure research in New Zealand: Patterns, problems and prospects', *Leisure Studies*, 10: 93–104.

Phelps, N. (1992) 'External economies, agglomeration and flexible accumulation', *Transactions of the Institute of British Geographers*, 17: 35–46.

Pigram, J.J. (1977) 'Beach resort morphology', *Habitat International*, 2(5–6): 525–41.

Pigram, J.J. (1980) 'Environmental implications of tourism development', *Annals of Tourism Research*, 7: 554–83.

Pigram, J.J. (1983) *Outdoor Recreation and Resource Management*, Beckenham: Croom Helm.

Pigram, J.J. (1985) *Outdoor Recreation and Resource Management*, 2nd edn, London: Croom Helm.

Pigram, J.J. (1987) *Tourism in Coffs Harbour: Attitudes, Perceptions and Implications*, Coffs Harbour: North Coast Regional Office, Department of Continuing Education, University of New England.

Pigram, J.J. (1990) 'Sustainable tourism: policy considerations', *Journal of Tourism Studies*, 1(2): 2–9.

Piperoglou, J. (1966) 'Identification and definition of regions in Greek tourist planning', *Regional Science Association Papers*, pp. 169–76.

Pizam, A. (1978) 'Tourism's impacts: the social costs to the destination community as perceived by its residents', *Journal of Travel Research*, 16(4): 8–12.

Place, S.E. (1998) 'How sustainable is ecotourism in Costa Rica?' in C.M. Hall and A.A. Lew (eds) *Sustainable Tourism Development: Geographical Perspectives*, Harlow: Addison Wesley Longman, pp. 107–18.

Plettner, H. J. (1979) *Geographical Aspects of Tourism in the Republic of Ireland*, Research paper 9, Galway: Social Sciences Research Centre, University College.

Plog, S. (1974) 'Why destination areas rise and fall in popularity', *The Cornell Hotel and Restaurant Administration Quarterly*, 15(November): 13–16.

Plog, S. (1977) 'Why destination areas rise and fall in popularity' in E. Kelly (ed.) *Domestic and International Tourism*, Wellesey, Massachusetts: Institute of Certified Travel Agents.

Pollard, J. (1989) 'Patterns in Irish tourism', in R.W.G. Carter and A.J. Parker (eds) *Ireland: Contemporary Perspectives on a Land and its People*, London: Routledge, pp. 301–30.

Pompl, W. and Lavery, P. (eds) *Tourism in Europe: Structures and Development*, Wallingford: CAB International.

Poon, A. (1989) *Tourism, Technology and Competitive Strategies*, Wallingford: CAB International.

Porter, M. (1980) *Competition in Global Industries*, Boston: Harvard Business School Press.

Powell, J.M. (1978) *Mirrors of the New World: Images and Image – Makers in the Settlement Process*, Canberra: Australian National University Press.

Pred, A. (1981) 'Production, family and free-time projects: a time-geographic perspective on the individual and societal changes in nineteenth century US cities', *Journal of Historical Geography*, 7: 3–86.

Preece, K.M. and Lesslie, R.G. (1987) *A Survey of Wilderness Quality in Victoria*, Melbourne/ Canberra: Ministry for Planning and Environment (Vic) and Australian Heritage Commission.

Pritchard, R. (1976) *Housing and the Spatial Structure of the City*, Cambridge: Cambridge University Press.

Rapoport, R. N. and Rapoport, R. (1975) *Leisure and the Family Life Cycle*, London: Routledge and Kegan Paul.

Redclift, N. and Sinclair, M.T. (eds) (1991) *Working Women: International Perspectives on Labour and Gender Ideology*, London: Routledge.

Reilly, W. (1931) *The Law of Retail Gravitation*, New York: Putnam Press.

Relph, E. (1976) *Place and Placelessness*. London: Pion.

Restaurant Brands (1997) *Restaurant Brands New Zealand Ltd. Prospectus 1997*, Auckland: F R Partners Limited and Merrill Lynch and Company.

Richards, G. (1995) 'Politics of national tourism policy in Britain', *Leisure Studies* 14(3): 153–73.

Ride, W.D.L. (1980) 'Wilderness: an Australian perspective', in R.W. Robertson, P. Helman and A. Davey (eds) *Wilderness Management in Australia*, Proceedings of a symposium held at the Canberra College of Advanced Education 19–23 July 1978, Occasional Papers in Recreational Planning, Natural Resources, School of Applied Science, Canberra: Canberra College of Advanced Education, pp. 35–45.

Ritchie, J.B. (1975) 'Some critical aspects of measurement theory and practice in travel research', in R. McIntosh and C. Goeldner, *Tourism Principles, Practices and Philosophies*, New York: Wiley, pp. 437–51.

Ritchie, J.R.B. (1984) 'Assessing the impact of hallmark events: conceptual and research issues', *Journal of Travel Research*, 23(1): 2–11.

Ritchie, J.B. and Aiken, C. (1984) 'Assessing the impacts of the 1988 Olympic Winter Games: the research program and initial results', *Journal of Travel Research*, 22(3): 17–25.

Ritchie, J.R.B. and Beliveau, D. (1974) 'Hallmark events: an evaluation of a strategic response to seasonality in the travel market', *Journal of Travel Research*, 14(Fall): 14–20.

Ritchie, J.R.B., Aitken, C.E. (1984) 'Assessing the Impacts of the 1988 Olympic Winter Games: The Research Program and Initial Results', *Journal of Travel Research*, 22(3): 17–25.

Ritchie, J.R.B. and Yangzhou, H. (1987) 'The role and impact of mega-events and attractions on national and regional tourism: a conceptual and methodological overview', Calgary: 37th Annual Congress of the International Association of Scientific Experts in Tourism.

Roberts, R. (1971) *The Classic Slum: Salford Life in the First Quarter of the Century*, Harmondsworth: Penguin.

Roberts, R. (1976) *A Ragged Schooling: Growing Up in the Classic Slum*, London: Fontanna.

Robinson, D. (1991) 'Living with peripherality', *Transport*, November/December: 177–85.

Robinson, G. M. (1990) *Conflict and Change in the Countryside*, London: Belhaven Press.

Robinson, H. (1976) *A Geography of Tourism*, Harlow: Longman.

Roche, F. W. and Murray, J. A. (1978) *Tourism and Archaeology: A Study of Wood Quay*, Dublin: McIver.

Roche, M. (1992) 'Mega-events and micro-modernisation: on the sociology of the new urban tourism', *British Journal of Sociology*, 43(4): 563–600.

Rodgers, H. (1969) *British Pilot National Recreation Survey Report No 1*, London: British Travel Association/University of Keele.

Rodgers, H. (1977) 'The leisure future: Problems of prediction' in J. Settle (ed) *Leisure in the North-West: A Tool for Forecasting*, Manchester: Sports Council Study No 11.

Rodgers, H. (1993) 'Estimating local leisure demand in the context of a regional planning strategy', in S. Glyptis (ed.) *Leisure and the Environment: Essays in Honour of Professor J. A. Patmore*, London: Belhaven.

Rodgers, H. and Patmore, J.A. (eds) (1972) *Leisure in the North-West*, Manchester: North-West Sports Council.

Rogers, G.F., Malde, H.E. and Turner, R.M. (1984)

Bibliography of Repeat Photography for Evaluating Landscape Change, Salt Lake City: University of Utah Press.

Rose, M. (ed.) (1985) *The Poor and the City: The English Poor Law in its Urban Context 1834–1914*, Leicester: Leicester University Press.

Rosemary, J. (1987) *Indigenous Enterprises in Kenya's Tourism Industry*, Geneva: UNESCO.

Rothman, R.A. (1978) 'Residents and transients: community reaction to seasonal visitors', *Journal of Travel Research*, 16(3): 8–13.

Rothman, R.A., Donnelly, P.G. and Tower, J.K. (1979) 'Police departments in resort communities: organizational adjustments to population undulation', *Leisure Sciences*, 2: 105–18.

Rottman, D. (1989) 'Crime in geographical perspective', in R.W.G. Carter and A.J. Parker (eds) *Ireland: Contemporary Perspectives on a Land and its People*, London: Routledge, pp. 87–111.

Royer, L.E., McCool, S.F. and Hunt, J.D. (1974) 'The relative importance of tourism to state economies', *Journal of Travel Research*, 11(4): 13–16.

Rudkin, B. and Hall, C.M. (1996) 'Unable to see the forest for the trees: ecotourism development in Solomon Islands', in R. Butler and T. Hinch (eds) *Tourism and Indigenous Peoples*, London: International Thomson Business Press, pp. 203–26.

Runte, A. (1972a) 'How Niagara Falls was saved: the beginning of esthetic conservation in the United States', *The Conservationist*, 26(April–May): 32–5, 43.

Runte, A. (1972b) 'Yellowstone: it's useless, so why not a park', *National Parks and Conservation Magazine: The Environment Journal*, 46(March): 4–7.

Runte, A. (1973) '"Worthless" lands – our national parks: the enigmatic past and uncertain future of America's scenic wonderlands', *American West*, 10(May): 4–11.

Runte, A. (1974a) 'Pragmatic alliance: western railroads and the national parks', *National Parks and Conservation Magazine: The Environmental Journal*, 48(April): 14–21.

Runte, A. (1974b) 'Yosemite Valley Railroad highway of history', *National Parks and Conservation Magazine: The Environmental Journal*, 48(December): 4–9.

Runte, A. (1977) 'The national park idea: origins and paradox of the American experience', *Journal of Forest History*, 21(2): 64–75.

Runte, A. (1979) *National Parks The American Experience*, Lincoln: University of Nebraska Press.

Runte, A. (1990) *Yosemite: The Embattled Wilderness*, Lincoln: University of Nebraska Press.

Runyan, D. and Wu, C. (1979) 'Assessing tourism's more complex consequences', *Annals of Tourism Research*, 6: 448–63.

Rural Development Commission (1991a) *Tourism in the Countryside: A Strategy for Rural England*, London: Rural Development Commission.

Rural Development Commission (1991b) *Meeting the Challenge of Rural Adjustment: A New Rural Development Commission Initiative*, London: Rural Development Commission.

Russell, J.A., Matthews, J.H. and Jones, R. (1979) *Wilderness in Tasmania: A Report to the Australian Heritage Commission*, Occasional Paper 10, Hobart: Centre for Environmental Studies, University of Tasmania.

Ryan, C. (1991) *Recreational Tourism: A Social Science Perspective*, London: Routledge.

Ryan, C. (1995) *Researching Tourism Satisfaction: Issues, Concepts, Problems*, London: Routledge.

Ryan, C. (ed.) (1997) *The Tourist Experience: A New Introduction*, London: Cassell.

Saeter, J.A. (1998) 'The significance of tourism and economic development in rural areas: a Norwegian case study', in R. Butler, C.M. Hall and J. Jenkins (eds) *Tourism and Recreation in Rural Areas*, Chichester: Wiley, pp. 237–47.

Sant, M. (1982) *Applied Geography*, Harlow: Longman.

Sawicki, D. (1989) 'The festival marketplace as public policy', *Journal of the American Planning Association*, Summer: 347–61.

Schaer, U. (1978) 'Traffic problems in holiday resorts', *Tourist Review*, 33: 9–15.

Scott, N.R. (1974) 'Towards a psychology of the wilderness experience', *Natural Resource Journal*, 14: 231–7.

Schwarz, C.F., Thor, E.C. and Elsner, G.H. (1976) *Wildland Planning Glossary*, Washington, DC: US Department of Agriculture, Forest Service.

Seaton, A. and Bennett, M. (eds) (1996) *Marketing Tourism Products*, London: International Thomson Business Publishing.

Seers, D. and Ostrom, K. (eds) (1982) *The Crisis of the European Regions*, New York: St Martin's Press.

Seers, D., Schaffer, B. and Kiljunen, M. (eds) (1979) *Underdeveloped Europe: Studies in Core–Periphery Relations*, Sussex: Harvester Press.

Selke, A.C. (1936) 'Geographic aspects of the German tourist trade', *Economic Geography*, 12: 206–16.

Selwood, H.J. and Hall, C. (1986) 'The America's Cup: a hallmark tourist event', in J.S. Marsh (ed.) *Canadian Studies of Parks, Recreation and Tourism in Foreign Lands*, Occasional Paper 11, Peterborough: Department of Geography, Trent University.

Sessa, A. (1993) *Elements of Tourism*, Rome: Catal.

Sewell, W.R.D. and Dearden, P. (1989) *Wilderness: Past, Present and Future*, special issue of *Natural Resources Journal*, 29: 1–222.

Shackelford, P. (1980) 'Keeping tabs on tourism: A managers guide to tourism statistics', *International Journal of Tourism Management*, 1(3): 148–57.

Share, B. (1992) *Shannon Departures: A Study in Regional Initiatives*, Dublin: Gill and Macmillan.

Sharpley, R. (1993) *Tourism and Leisure in the Countryside*, Managing Tourism Series, No. 5, Huntingdon: Elm Publications.

Sharpley, R. and Sharpley, J. (1997) *Rural Tourism*, London: International Thomson Business Publishing.

Shaw, B.J. (1985) 'Fremantle and the America's Cup. . . . the spectre of development?', *Urban Policy and Research*, 3: 38–40.

Shaw, B.J. (1986) *Fremantle W.A. and the America's Cup: The Impact of a Hallmark Event*, Working Paper No. 11, London: University of London, Australian Studies Centre, Institute for Commonwealth Studies.

Shaw, D.J. (1979) 'Recreation and the socialist city' in R. French and F. Hamilton (eds) *The Socialist City: Spatial Structure and Urban Policy*, Chichester: Wiley.

Shaw, G. and Williams, A.M. (1990) 'Tourism, economic development and the role of entrepreneurial activity', in C. Cooper (ed.) *Progress in Tourism, Recreation and Hospitality Management*, vol. 2, London: Belhaven, pp. 67–81.

Shaw, G. and Williams, A.M. (1994) *Critical Issues in Tourism: A Geographical Perspectives*, Blackwell: Oxford.

Shaw, S., Bonen, A. and McCabe, J. (1991) 'Do more constraints mean less leisure? Examining the relationship between constraints and participation', *Journal of Leisure Research* 23: 286–300.

Shelby, B. and Heberlein, T.A. (1984) 'A conceptual

framework for carrying capacity', *Leisure Sciences*, 6: 433–51.

Shelby, B. and Heberlein, T.A. (1986) *Carrying Capacity in Recreation Settings*, Corvallis: Oregon State University Press.

Shelby, B., Bregenzer, N.S. and Johnston, R. (1988) 'Displacement and product shift: empirical evidence from Oregon Rivers', *Journal of Leisure Research*, 20(4): 274–88.

Shelby, B., Vaske, J.J. and Heberlein, T.A. (1989) 'Comparative analysis of crowding in multiple locations: results from fifteen years of research', *Leisure Sciences*, 11(4): 269–91.

Shoard, M. (1976) 'Fields which planners should conquer', *Forma*, 4: 128–35.

Short, J.R. (1991) *Imagined Country: Society, Culture and Environment*, London: Routledge.

Sidaway, R. and Duffield, B. (1984) 'A new look at countryside recreation in the urban fringe', *Leisure Studies*, 3: 249–71.

Simmons, I. (1974) *The Ecology of Natural Resources*, London: Arnold.

Simmons, I. (1975) *Rural Recreation in the Industrial World*, London: Edward Arnold.

Simmons, R., Davis, B.W., Chapman, R.J. and Sager, D.D. (1974) 'Policy flow analysis: a conceptual model for comparative public policy research', *Western Political Quarterly* 27(3): 457–68.

Simpson Xavier Horwath (1990) *Irish Hotel Industry Review*, Dublin: Simpson Xavier Horwath.

Sinclair, J. (1986) 'Counting the loss of wilderness', *Habitat*, 14(3), June, 14–15.

Sinclair, M.T. (1991) 'The economics of tourism', in C. Cooper (ed.) *Progress in Tourism, Recreation and Hospitality Management*, vol. 3, London: Belhaven, 1–27.

Sinclair, M.T. and Stabler, M. (eds) (1992) *The Tourism Industry: An International Analysis*, Wallingford: CAB International.

Slee, W. (1982) *An Evaluation of Country Park Policy*, Gloucestershire Papers in Local and Rural Planning No. 16, Cheltenham: GLOSCAT.

Smith, D.M. (1977) *Human Geography: A Welfare Approach*, London: Edward Arnold.

Smith, M. and Turner, L. (1973) 'Some aspects of the sociology of tourism', *Society and Leisure*, 3: 55–71.

Smith, P.E. (1977) 'A value analysis of wilderness', *Search*, 8(9): 311–7.

Smith, R.V. and Mitchell, L.S. (1990) 'Geography and tourism: a review of selected literature', in C. Cooper (ed.) *Progress in Tourism, Recreation and Hospitality Management*, vol.2, London: Belhaven Press, pp. 50–66.

Smith, S.L.J. (1983a) *Recreational Geography*, Harlow: Longman.

Smith, S.L.J. (1983b) 'Restaurants and dining out: geography of a tourism business', *Annals of Tourism Research*, 10(4): 515–49.

Smith, S.L.J. (1987) 'Regional analysis of tourism resources', *Annals of Tourism Research*, 14: 253–73.

Smith, S.L.J. (1989) *Tourism Analysis*, Harlow: Longman.

Smith, S.L.J. (1995) *Tourism Analysis*, 2nd edn, Harlow: Longman.

Smith, S.L.J. and Brown, B.A. (1981) 'Directional bias in vacation travel', *Annals of Tourism Research*, 8: 257–70.

Smith, V. (ed.) (1977) *Hosts and Guests: The Anthropology of Tourism*, Philadelphia: University of Pennsylvania Press.

Smith, V.L. (ed.) (1992) *Hosts and Guests: An Anthropology of Tourism*, 2nd edn, Philadelphia: University of Pennsylvannia Press.

Soja, E.W. (1989) *Postmodern Geographies: The Reassertion of Space in Critical Social Theory*, London: Verso.

Squire, S.J. (1993) 'Valuing countryside: reflections on Beatrix Potter tourism', *Area* 25(1): 5–10.

Squire, S.J. (1994) 'Accounting for cultural meanings: the interface between geography and tourism studies revisited', *Progress in Human Geography*, 18: 1–16.

Stabler, M. (1990) 'The concept of opportunity sets as a methodological framework for the analysis of selling tourism places: the industry view', in Ashworth, G.I. and Goodall, B. (eds) *Marketing Tourism Places*, London: Routledge, pp. 23–41.

Stamp, D. (1948) *The Land of Britain: Its Use and Misuse*, Harlow: Longman.

Stamp, D. (1960) *Applied Geography*, London: Penguin.

Stankey, G. (1973) *Visitor Perception of Wilderness Carrying Capacity*, USDA, Forest Service Research Paper, IN THE–42, Ogden, Utah: Intermountain Forest and Range Experiment Station.

Stankey, G.H. (1989) 'Beyond the campfire's light: historical roots of the wilderness concept', *Natural Resources Journal*, 29: 9–24.

Stankey, G.H. and Schreyer, R. (1987) 'Attitudes toward wilderness and factors affecting visitor behaviour: a state of knowledge review', in *Proceedings – National Wilderness Research Conference: Issues, State of Knowledge and Future Directions*, General Technical Report INT–220, Ogden: Intermountain Research Station, 246–93.

Stansfield, C. A. and Rickert, J. E. (1970) 'The recreational business district', *Journal of Leisure Research*, 2(4): 213–25.

Stanton, J.P. and Morgan, M.G. (1977) *Project 'RAKES' – A Rapid Appraisal of Key and Endangered Sites, Report No. 1: The Queensland Case Study*, A Report to the Department of Environment, Housing and Community Development, Armidale: School of Natural Resources, University of New England.

Stea, R. and Downs, R. (1970) 'From the outside looking in at the inside looking out', *Environment and Behaviour*, 2: 3–12.

Stebbins, R.A. (1979) *Amateurs: On the Margin Between Work and Leisure*, Beverly Hills: Sage Publications.

Stebbins, R.A. (1982) 'Serious leisure: a conceptual statement', *Pacific Sociological Review*, 25: 251–72.

Stevens, T. (1987) 'Going underground', *Leisure Management*, 7: 48–50.

Stevens, T. (1991) 'Irish eyes are smiling', *Leisure Management* 11: 46–8.

Stockdale, J.E. (1985) *What is Leisure? An Empirical Analysis of the Concept of Leisure and the Role of Leisure in People's Lives*, London: Sports Council.

Stoddart, D.R. (1981) 'Ideas and interpretation in the history of geography', in D.R. Stoddart (ed.) *Geography, Ideology and Social Concern*, Oxford: Blackwell, pp. 1–7.

Stoffle, R.W., Last, C. and Evans, M. (1979) 'Reservation-based tourism: implications of tourist attitudes for Native American economic development', *Human Organization*, 38(3): 300–306.

Stone, G. and Taves, M. (1957) 'Research into the human element in wilderness use', proceedings of the 1956 meeting of the Society of American Foresters, 26–32.

Strachan, A. and Bowler, I. (1976) 'The development of public parks in the City of Leicester', *East Midland Geographer*, 6: 275–83.

Stringer, P. (1984) 'Studies in the socio-environmental psychology of tourism', *Annals of Tourism Research*, 11: 147–166.

Stringer, P. and Pearce, P.L. (1984) 'Towards a symbiosis of social psychology and tourism studies', *Annals of Tourism Research*, 11: 5–18.

Survey Research Associates. (1991) *London Docklands Visitor Survey: Summary of Findings*. London: London Docklands Development Corporation.

Talbot, M. (1979) *Women and Leisure*, London: Sports Council/Social Science Research Council Joint Panel on Leisure and Recreation Research.

Tanner, M. (1971) 'The planning and management of water recreation areas' in P. Lavery (ed.) *Recreational Geography*, Newton Abbot: David and Charles.

Tanner, M. (1973) 'The recreational use of inland waters', *Geographical Journal*, 139: 486–91.

Tanner, M. (1977) *Recreational Use of Water Supply Reservoirs in England and Wales, Research Report No. 3*, London: Waterspace Amenity Commission.

Taylor, G. (ed.) (1951) *Geography in the Twentieth Century*, London: Methuen.

Taylor, P.J. (1985) 'The value of a geographical perspective', In R.J. Johnston (ed.) *The Future of Geography*, London: Methuen, pp. 243–272.

Taylor, S.G. (1990) 'Naturalness: the concept and its application to Australian ecosystems', *Proceedings of the Ecological Society of Australia*, 16: 411–8.

Thoreau, H.D. (1854 (1968)) *Walden*, Everyman's Library, London: Dent.

Threndyle, S. (1994) 'Towns in transition: careful tourism-planning can soften the blows of changing times in resource-based economies, but there's no panacea', *Georgia Straight*, 22–9 July.

Thrift, N. (1977) *An Introduction to Time Geography*, Norwich: Catmog 13.

Thurot, J.M. and Thurot, G. (1983) 'The ideology of class and tourism confronting the discourse of advertising', *Annals of Tourism Research*, 10: 173–89.

Tillman, A. (1974) *The Program Book for Recreation Professionals*, Palo Alto, Calif.: National Press Books.

Torkildsen, G. (1983) *Leisure and Recreation Management*, London: E.&F.N. Spon.

Torkildsen, G. (1992) *Leisure and Recreation Management*, 3rd edn, London: E.&F.N. Spon.

Tourism Development International (1992) *Visitors to Tourist Attractions in Ireland in 1992*, Dublin: Tourism Development International.

Towner, J. (1985) 'The Grand Tour: a key phase in the history of tourism', *Annals of Tourism Research*, 12(3): 297–333.

Towner, J. (1996) *An Historical Geography of*

Recreation and Tourism in the Western World 1540–1940, Chichester: Wiley.

Townsend, A. (1991) 'Services and local economic development', *Area*, 23: 309–17.

Townsend, P. (1979) *Poverty in the UK: A Survey of Household Resources and Standards of Living*, Middlesex: Penguin.

Tuan, Yi-Fu (1971) *Man and Nature*, Washington, DC: Commission on College Geography, Association of American Geographers.

Tuan, Yi-Fu (1974) *Topophilia: A Study of Environmental Perception, Attitudes, and Values*, Englewood Cliffs: Prentice Hall.

Tuan, Yi-Fu (1979) *Landscapes of Fear*, New York: Pantheon.

Tubridy, M. (1987) (ed.) *Heritage Zones: the Co-existence of Agriculture, Nature Conservation and Tourism: the Clonmacnoise Example*, Environmental Science Unit, Occasional Publication, Dublin: Trinity College.

Tunbridge, J.E. and Ashworth, G.J. (1996) *Dissonant Heritage: The Management of the Past as a Resource in Conflict*, Chichester: Wiley.

Twight, B. (1983) *Organizational Values and Political Power: The Forest Service Versus the Olympic National Park*, University Park: The Pennsylvania State University Press.

United Nations (UN) (1994) *Recommendations on Tourism Statistics*, New York: United Nations.

UNESCO (1976) 'The effects of tourism on socio-cultural values', *Annals of Tourism Research*, November/December: 74–105.

Urry, J. (1988) 'Cultural change and contemporary holidaymaking', *Theory, Culture and Society*, 5: 35–55.

Urry, J. (1990) *The Tourist Gaze: Leisure and Travel in Contemporary Societies*, London: Sage.

Urry, J. (1991) 'The sociology of tourism', in C.P. Cooper (ed.) *Progress in Tourism, Recreation and Hospitality Management*, vol. 3, London: Belhaven, pp. 48–57.

Uysal, M. and Crompton, J.L. (1985) 'An overview of approaches to forecasting tourist demand', *Journal of Travel Research*, 23(4): 7–15.

Uzzell, D. (1984) 'An alternative structuralist approach to the psychology of tourism marketing', *Annals of Tourism Research*, 11: 79–100.

Valentine, P. (1980) 'Tropical rainforest and the wilderness experience', in V. Martin (ed.) *Wilderness*, Findhorn: Findhorn Press, 123–32.

Valentine, P. (1984) 'Wildlife and tourism: some ideas on potential and conflict', in B. O'Rourke (ed.) *Contemporary Issues in Australian Tourism*, 19th Institute of Australian Geographer's Conference and International Geographical Union Sub-Commission on Tourism in the South West Pacific, Sydney: Department of Geography, University of Sydney, pp. 29–54.

Valentine, P. (1992) 'Review. Nature-based tourism', in B. Weiler and C.M. Hall (eds) *Special Interest Tourism*, London: Belhaven Press.

Van Raaij, W.F. (1986) 'Consumer research on tourism: mental and behavioural constructs', *Annals of Tourism Research*, 13: 1–10.

Van Raaij, W.F. and Francken, D.A. (1984) 'Vacation decisions, activities, and satisfactions', *Annals of Tourism Research*, 11: 101–13.

Vaughan, D.R. (1977) 'Opportunity cost and the assessment and development of regional tourism', in B.S. Duffield (ed.) *Tourism: A Tool for Regional Development*, Edinburgh: Tourism and Recreation Research Unit, University of Edinburgh, pp. 8.1–8.9.

Veal, A. (1987) *Leisure and the Future*, London: Unwin and Hyman.

Veal, A.J. (1992) *Research Methods for Leisure and Tourism: A Practical Guide*, Harlow: Longman.

Veal, A. and Travis, T. (1979) 'Local authority leisure services – the state of play', *Local Government Studies*, 5: 5–16.

Vetter, F. (ed.) (1985) *Big City Tourism*, Berlin: Dietrich Verlag.

Vickerman, R. (1975) *The Economics of Leisure and Recreation*, London: Macmillan.

Vogeler, I. (1977) 'Farm and ranch vacationing', *Journal of Leisure Research*, 9: 291–300.

Waitt, G. (1997) 'Selling paradise and adventure: representations of landscape in the tourist advertising of Australia', *Australian Geographical Studies*, 35(1): 47–60.

Waitt, G. and McGuirk, P.M. (1997) 'Marking time: tourism and heritage representation at Millers Point, Sydney', *Australian Geographer*, 27(1): 11–29.

Wall, G. (1971) 'Car-owners and holiday activities', in P. Lavery (ed.) *Recreational Geography*, Newton Abbot: David and Charles.

Wall, G. (1983a) 'Atlantic City tourism and social change', *Annals of Tourism Research*, 10: 555–6.

Wall, G. (1983b) 'Cycles and capacity: a contradiction in terms?', *Annals of Tourism Research*, 10: 268–70.

Wall, G. (ed.) (1989) *Outdoor Recreation in Canada*, Toronto: Wiley.

Wall, G. and Marsh, J. (eds) (1982) *Recreational Land Use, Perspectives on its Evolution in Canada*, Ottawa: Carleton University Press.

Wall, G. and Wright, C. (1977) *The Environmental Impacts of Outdoor Recreation*, Publication Series No. 11, Waterloo: Department of Geography, University of Waterloo.

Wall, G., Dudycha, D. and Hutchinson, J. (1985) 'Point pattern analysis of accommodation in Toronto', *Annals of Tourism Research*, 12(4): 603–18.

Walmesley, D.J. and Jenkins, J. (1992) 'Tourism cognitive mapping of unfamiliar environments', *Annals of Tourism Research*, 19(3): 268–86.

Walmesley, D.J. and Lewis, G.J. (1993) *People and Environment: Behavioural Approaches in Human Geography*, 2nd edn, Harlow: Longman.

Walmesley, D.J., Boskovic, R.M. and Pigram, J.J. (1981) *Tourism and Crime*, Armidale: Department of Geography, University of New England.

Walmesley, D.J., Boskovic, R.M. and Pigram, J.J. (1983) 'Tourism and crime: an Australian perspective', *Journal of Leisure Research*, 15: 136–55.

Walsh, K., (1988) 'The consequences of competition' in J. Bennington and J. White (eds) *The Future of Leisure Services*, Harlow: Longman, pp. 37–56.

Walter, R.D. (1975) *The Impact of Tourism on the Environment*, ARRA Monograph 7, Melbourne: Australian Recreation Research Association.

Walton, J. (1983) *The English Seaside Resort: A Social History 1750–1914*, Leicester: Leicester University Press.

Ward, C. and Hardy, D. (1986) *Goodnight Campers: The History of the British Holiday Camp*, London: Mansell.

Weaver, D. (1998) *Ecotourism in the Less Developed World*, Wallingford: CAB International.

Weiler, B. (1991) *Ecotourism: Conference Proceedings*, Canberra: Bureau of Tourism Research.

Weiler, B. and Hall, C.M. (1991) 'Meeting the needs of the recreation and tourism partnership: a comparative study of tertiary education programmes in Australia and Canada', *Leisure Options: Australian Journal of Leisure and Recreation*, 1(2): 7–14.

Weiler, B. and Hall, C.M. (eds) (1992) *Special Interest Tourism*, London: Belhaven.

Welch, D. (1991) *The Management of Urban Parks*, Harlow: Longman.

White, G. (1972) 'Geography and public policy', *Professional Geographer*, 24: 101–4.

White, K. and Walker, M. (1982) 'Trouble in the travel account', *Annals of Tourism Research* 9(1): 37–56.

White L., Jr. (1967) 'The historical roots of our ecological crisis', *Science*, 155(10 March): 1203–1207.

Whitehead, J.W.R. (1993) *The Making of the Urban Landscape*, Oxford: Blackwell.

Whyte, D. (1978) 'Have second homes gone into hibernation?', *New Society*, 45: 286–8.

Wight, P.A. (1993) 'Sustainable ecotourism: balancing economic, environmental and social goals within an ethical framework', *Journal of Tourism Studies*, 4(2): 54–66.

Wight, P.A. (1995) 'Sustainable ecotourism: balancing economic, environmental and social goals within an ethical framework', *Tourism Recreation Research*, 20(1): 5–13.

Wight, P.A. (1998) 'Tools for sustainability analysis in planning and managing tourism and recreation in the destination', in C.M. Hall and A.A. Lew (eds) *Sustainable Tourism Development: A Geographical Perspective*, Harlow: Addison Wesley Longman, pp. 75–91.

Wilhelm, K. (1990) *Journeys: the dynamics of specialty tourists to Ireland*, unpublished PhD thesis, University of Maryland College Park.

Williams, A.M. and Shaw, G. (eds) (1988) *Tourism and Economic Development: Western European Experiences*, London: Belhaven Press.

Williams, A. and Shaw, G. (eds) (1991) *Tourism and Economic Development: Western European Experiences*, 2nd edn, London: Belhaven.

Williams, A.M. and Shaw, G. (1998) 'Tourism and the environment: sustainability and economic restructuring' in C.M. Hall and A.A. Lew (eds) *Sustainable Tourism Development: Geographical Perspectives*, Harlow: Addison Wesley Longman, pp. 49–59.

Williams, A., and Zelinsky, W. (1970) 'On some patterns of international tourism flows', *Economic Geography*, 46(4): 549–67.

Williams, C. H. (1985) *Language Planning, Marginality and Regional Development in the Irish Gaeltacht*, Discussion paper in Geolinguistics No. 10, Stoke-on-Trent: Department of Geography and Recreation Studies, Staffordshire Polytechnic.

Williams, G.H. (1962) *Wilderness and Paradise in Christian Thought*, New York: Harper and Brothers.

Williams, R. (1976) *Keywords*, London: Fontana.

Williams, S. (1995) *Recreation in the Urban Environment*, London: Routledge.

Williams, W.M. (1979) 'Some applications in social geography', in P. Whiteley (ed.) *Geography*, London: Sussex Books, pp. 115–26.

Winsberg, M.P. (1966) 'Overseas travel by American civilians since World War II', *Journal of Geography*, 65: 73–79.

Winter, M. (1987) 'Farm-based tourism and conservation in the uplands', *Ecos: A Review of Conservation*, 5(3): 10–15.

Withyman, W. (1985) 'The ins and outs of international travel and tourism data', *International Tourism Quarterly*, Special Report No. 55.

Witt, S., Brooke, M. and Buckley, P. (1991) *The Management of International Tourism*, London: Routledge.

Witt, S. and Martin, C. (1989) 'Demand forecasting in tourism and recreation', in C.P. Cooper (ed.) *Progress in Tourism, Recreation and Hospitality Management, Vol. 1*, London: Belhaven, 4–33.

Wolfe, R.J. (1951) 'Summer cottages in Ontario', *Economic Geography*, 27(1): 10–32.

Wolfe, R.J. (1952) 'Wasage Beach: the divorce from the geographic environment', *Canadian Geographer*, 1(2): 57–65.

Wolfe, R.J. (1964) 'Perspectives on outdoor recreation: a bibliographical survey', *The Geographical Review*, 54(2): 203–38.

Wolfe, R.J. (1967) 'Recreational travel: the new migration', *Geographical Bulletin*, 9: 73–9.

Wolfe, R.J. (1970) 'Discussion of vacation homes, environmental preferences and spatial behaviour', *Journal of Leisure Research*, 2(1): 85–7.

Woo, Kyung-Sik (1996) *Korean Tourists Urban Activity Patterns in New Zealand, Research Report*, Auckland: Master of Business Studies, Massey University at Albany.

World Tourism Organisation (WTO) (1981) *Guidelines for the Collection and Presentation of Domestic and International Tourism Statistics*, Madrid: World Tourism Organisation.

World Tourism Organisation (WTO) (1983) *Definitions Concerning Tourism Statistics*, Madrid: World Tourism Organisation.

World Tourism Organisation (WTO) (1985) *The Role of Transnational Tourism Enterprises in the Development of Tourism*, Madrid: World Tourism Organisation.

World Tourism Organisation (WTO) (1991) *Guidelines for the Collection and Presentation of Domestic and International Tourism Statistics*, Madrid: World Tourism Organisation.

World Tourism Organisation (WTO) (1991) *Resolutions of International Conference on Travel and Tourism, Ottawa, Canada*, Madrid: World Tourism Organisation.

World Tourism Organisation (WTO) (1996) *International Tourism Statistics*, Madrid: World Tourism Organisation.

World Tourism Organisation (WTO) (1998) *WTO Revises Forecasts for Asian Tourism*, Press Release 27/1/98, Madrid: World Tourism Organisation.

Worster, D. (1977) *Nature's Economy: A History of Ecological Ideas*, Cambridge: Cambridge University Press.

Wrathall, J.E. (1980) 'Farm-based holidays', *Town and Country Planning*, 49(6): 194–5.

Wright, D. (trans.) (1957) *Beowulf*, Harmondsworth: Penguin.

Wright, J. (1980) 'Wilderness, waste and history', *Habitat*, 8(1): 27–31.

Wu, C.-T. (1982) 'Issues of tourism and socioeconomic development', *Annals of Tourism Research*, 9: 317–30.

Young, G. (1973) *Tourism: Blessing or Blight*, Harmondsworth: Penguin.

Young, M. and Wilmott, P. (1973) *The Symmetrical Family*, London: Routledge and Kegan Paul.

Zetter, F. (1971) *The Evolution of Country Park Policy*, Cheltenham: Countryside Commission.

Zurick, D.N. (1992) 'Adventure travel and sustainable tourism in the peripheral economy of Nepal', *Annals of the Association of American Geographers*, 82: 608–28.

INDEX